MOUNTAIN AND ARCTIC WARFARE

MOUNTAIN AND ARCTIC WARFARE

From Alexander to Afghanistan

BARRY GREGORY

Patrick Stephens Limited

First published in 1989

British Library Cataloguing in Publication Data

Gregory, Barry
Mountain and arctic warfare.
1. Land warfare, 1900 - 1976
I. Title
355'.02'0904

ISBN 1-85260-014-4

Patrick Stephens Limited is part of the Thorsons Publishing Group, Wellingborough, Northamptonshire NN8 2RQ, England.

Printed by The Bath Press, Bath, Avon
Typeset by MJL Limited, Hitchin, Hertfordshire

10 9 8 7 6 5 4 3 2 1

CONTENTS

ACKNOWLEDGEMENTS

I wish to thank John and Diane Moore of Military Archive and Research Services (MARS) for researching and supplying the photographs for this book, and to Karyl Rey for typing the manuscript. I am also very grateful to the staff of the reading room of the library of the Imperial War Museum in London for their tireless energy and patience in supplying me with so many old books and documents to read. Recording military history has aspects of sadness, which deepened as yellow pages crumbled in my hands...

The publishers and researchers would like to thank the various archives and agencies who supplied material for this publication. For reasons of space alone, some references have been abbreviated as follows:

Bundesarchiv, Koblenz – **Bund**
Etablisement Cinematographique & Photographique des Armées, Paris – **ECPA**
Imperial War Museum, London – **IWM**
Military Archive & Research Services, Lincs – **MARS**

Pages 9-27 **MARS**; 29-36 **Bund**; 37 (t) **IWM**; 37(b)-39 **MARS**; 42 **Bund**; 43-9 **MARS**; 50 **Bund**; 51-65 **MARS**; 66-7 **Bund**; 68-97 **MARS**; 98 **IWM**; 99 **Bund**; 103-10 Institute of Military Science, Helsinki; 112-15 **Bund**; 117 **MARS**; 118-23(t) **Bund**; 123(b)-126 **MARS**; 128 **Bund**; 130-3 **ECPA**; 149-61 **Bund**; 162 Institute of Military Science, Helsinki; 164-9 **Bund**; 171 **IWM**; 172-80 **Bund**; 183 **MARS**; 184-5 **Bund**; 187 **MARS**; 189-91 **Bund**; 205 Keystone Press Agency; 206-7 **Bund**; 209-11 Keystone Press Agency; 214 US Army; 215 **Bund**; 219 Author; 222 **IWM**; 223-4 **Bund**; 225 US Army; 226-32 C. Casewit; 235-6 **Bund**; 236-7 **IWM**; 237 **Bund**; 239 Swedish Defence Ministry; 242-3 US Marine Corps; 250 MOD/**MARS**; 259 Eugene Kolesnik; 261-4 US Army; 267 **MARS**; 269-72 DoD, Washington DC; 274-7 **MARS**; 286-7(t) Norwegian Defence Ministry; 287(b)-288(t) US Navy; 288(b) NATO; 289(t) Swedish Defence Ministry; 289(b) Austrian Defence Ministry; 290 Finnish Defence Ministry; 291-3 West German Defence Ministry.

ACHILLES
I do believe it; for they passed by me
As misers do by beggars, neither gave to me
Good word nor look. What, are my deeds
forgot?

ULYSSES
Time hath, my lord, a wallet at his back,
Wherein he puts alms for oblivion,
A great-sized monster of ingratitudes.
Those scraps are good deeds past, which are
devoured
As fast as they are made, forgot as soon
As done. Perseverance, dear my lord,
Keeps honour bright; to have done, is to hang
Quite out of fashion, like a rusty mail
In monumental mock'ry.

William Shakespeare, *The History of Troilus
and Cressida,* Act III, Scene iii

THE FIRST WORLD WAR

CHAPTER 1
IN SNOW AND ICE

When, during the early part of the twentieth century, the study of political geography—or geopolitics—became fashionable, the control of the 'heartland' (or plains) was seen as the key to military strategy. The leading proponent of this theory was Sir Halford Mackinder who, after graduating from Oxford in Modern History, developed strong, political aspirations, which had been nurtured at the Oxford Union. Mackinder's new, clear-cut concept of geography as a bridge between the natural sciences and the humanities soon won attention. At that time a group of men at the Royal Geographical Society were making strenuous efforts to raise the status of geography as an academic discipline in Britain and to secure for it an adequate place in the educational system. Mackinder's success on delivering his paper on 'The Scope and Methods of Geography' resulted in his appointment as Reader in Geography at Oxford, the first such appointment in a British University.

Although Mackinder's theories appeared startlingly 'new' to the thinkers of the day, men had, after all, over the centuries built castles and, later, fortresses in the flatlands for defence against approaching armies. Even in the twentieth century massive concrete fortifications were to be built to defend frontiers—the 'castle concept', persisting even in the fire-bases of the Vietnam War. All these years the great mountain ranges of Eurasia remained strangely aloof and irrelevant to the landpower struggle for the 'heartlands'. Since the days of Alexander the Great and Hannibal of Carthage, armies have occasionally had to fight their way through mountain passes. In later years, gun emplacements built into mountain slopes have dominated the valleys below, but it was not until the First World War that mountain fastnesses were to become actual battlefields. The Arctic regions figured even less prominently in military thinking: the climate was inhospitable in the extreme and the terrain was equally uninhabitable. These ice-bound wastelands were scarcely worth fighting over.

In Scandinavia, the practice of fighting in Arctic conditions can be traced to the Stone Age. Impressions of skis dating from that time—and those of the Bronze Age—have been found in the marshes of Swedish Lapland. The Stone Age carvings on the rock at Rødøy in Tjøtta, northern Norway, are the most ancient images of skiers in existence. The oldest Swedish image of a skier is on a runic stone from near Uppsala dating from the middle of the eleventh century. This does not mean, however, that skis were not known in southern Sweden before that date. Frequent reference is made to skiing in the old sagas, and the mythical founder of Norway, Nor, is said 'to have waited until there was good snow' to go south to found his kingdom. Ull, the stepson of Thor, was the pagan ski-war god, and to keep him company there also existed a ski goddess—Skade, mentioned in an old song that dates from about AD 800.

In fact skiing has been known for an

approximately equally-impressive array of centuries in northern and central Asia, which has led one authority to place the ski's country of the origin in the region of Baikal Lake in Siberia. Skiing is described sufficiently clearly in the annals of the Chinese dynasty T'ang (AD 618-907), where it is said about the Kirghizes that 'whenever snow has fallen they will hunt their game on wooden horses'. Another tribe, which lived east of the Kirghizes, was even called by the Chinese the 'wood-horse Turks'. A Chinese source from AD 980 describes hunting on skis among the inhabitants of the desert region, southeast of Kirghizes.

To sum up, it is quite certain that skis were known in great antiquity throughout the north of Europe and Asia, while North American Indians were also acquainted with the use of similar equipment—the snow-racket, though its age remains uncertain. Since, however, contact must have existed between the North American Indians and the North Asiatic peoples across the Bering Straits, it may be assumed that Canadian snow-rackets are not dissimilar in shape to Arctic skis.

Skis came in different shapes and sizes depending on the region of origin. The southern type was used initially by the races inhabiting the Ural Mountains, Central Russia, the Baltic provinces, southern Sweden, and probably the southern parts of Norway. The Arctic type is still used by the Siberian peoples. The central Nordic type is exclusively used in Finland. Reference is made to military skiing in a Norwegian Army manual compiled in 1762. The skis used were of the Osterdal type, which were made of best silver-fir wood, were of unequal length, and often—though not necessarily—of unequal breadth. What was to be universally known as the Telemark ski, in familiar use in the twentieth century, has certain characteristics of Finnish origin. Rigid bindings for the feet, with toe-irons, did not come in until the turn of the century. The first ski sticks could be used as clubs and spears. Other early versions were used as maces and

shovels. The introduction of two sticks had two advantages: the skier's equipment was lightened and the two sticks enabled the skier to move faster on flat, or gently-sloping, ground, and in climbing uphill.

The Swedes used ski troops with great success against Norway in the Northern Seven Years War (1563-70). In 1590 a Finnish force of 600 skiers defeated a Muscovite invasion. The Swedes also used ski troops outside Scandinavia, notably in their wars with Poland. These troops used short, broad boards, about 5 ft (1.5 m) long and 1 ft (30 cm) wide, or the so-called 'forest ski', which must be classified as belonging to the southern type. The Norwegian army did not take to skiing seriously until the late seventeenth century. A special Ski Corps was established in 1747. It consisted of three *Nordenfjelds* (northern mountain) and three *Søndenfjelds* (southern mountain) companies. The uniform of a Norwegian ski soldier displayed a blatant disregard for the necessity of camouflage. The trousers were yellow—as was the coat, with red reverses. A red hat completed the picture. Officers wore top-hats as became gentlemen. But already in 1788, during the reorganization of the Norwegian army, modest 'field-grey' replaced the old ski uniform.

Before the present century, leading a large army across mountains was usually a means to an end. Alexander the Great (356-323 BC) pursued the Persian king, Darius, over the mountains to the sacred city of Persepolis and went on into the mountains of eastern Persia. In so doing he ventured beyond Greek geographical knowledge. Alexander's army, as if lost in limbo, met bitter resistance from the mountain peoples of what is now Afghanistan. It took more than two years to subdue these eastern ranges, which were terrible in winter. Hannibal of Carthage left Spain for Italy in the spring of 218 BC with about 35,000 seasoned troops. Since Rome controlled the seas he went overland across the Pyrenees and the Alps. His force included elephants. It is thought that Hannibal's army crossed the Alps somewhere

In May 1800 Napoleon, leaving the political turmoil behind him in Paris, led an army over the Alps into Italy, took the Austrians in the rear and decisively defeated them at Marengo. Crossing the Alps in such wintry conditions required determination and ingenuity. In this illustration the French army approaches the hospice at St Bernard. Note the cannon barrels hauled on sledges made from hollowed tree trunks.

between the Little St Bernard and Montgenèvre Passes. He did not begin to cross until early autumn, which meant he encountered winter-like conditions in the Alpine region. His force suffered greatly from the elements, and by the time he reached northern Italy his army was reduced to about 26,000 men.

In May 1800, Napoleon, leaving the polit-ical turmoil behind him in Paris, led an army over the Alps into Italy, took the Austrians in the rear, and decisively defeated them at Marengo. Bonaparte himself led 37,000 men through the Great St Bernard Pass whilst General Moreau brought 15,000 men to join him in Lombardy via the Simplon and St Gotthard Passes. As a diversion, he further moved 5,000 Frenchmen through the Mt Cenis Pass. The French intrusion in Spain and Portugal (the Peninsular War, 1809-14) forced many Spanish-resistance fighters to take to the mountains, coining the term *guerrilla* for the first time. The Duke of Wellington's army became well used to the rugged mountains of Spain and in 1813 the Iron Duke, now in supreme command of all allied forces in Spain, pursued the retreating French army across the Pyrenees, thus invading France.

Élite mountain troops do not appear in our history books until the latter part of the nineteenth century, when the development of climbing techniques ran closely in parallel with the rising interest in mountaineering as a sport. Earlier attempts to ascend peaks were inspired by other than sporting motives: to build altars or to see if spirits or dragons actually haunted once-forbidden heights; or to get an overview of one's own or a neighbouring country. Mountains presented barriers to progress, but over many centuries the passes among them were gradually opened as routes for military expansion, exploration, communications, and trade. It is a far reach in time, however, from Moses's ascent of Mt Sinai and the breaching of the Alps with a herd of elephants in the third century BC, to the first recorded climbing of Mexico's Mt Popocatépetl in 1595 by Cortes' soldiers.

As a sport, mountaineering emerged less than 150 years ago, when English, French, and German climbers, together with their Swiss guides, began in the mid-nineteenth century to penetrate and to ascend seriously the mid-European Alps. By 1870 all of the principal Alpine summits had been scaled and climbers began to seek new and more difficult routes on peaks that had already been ascended. As the few remaining minor peaks of the Alps were overcome by the end of the nineteenth century, climbers turned their attention to the Andes of South America, the North American Rockies, the Caucasus, Africa's peaks, and finally the Himalayan vastness. As the twentieth century developed, the truly international character of mountaineering began to reveal itself. Increasingly, Austrians, Chinese, English, French, Germans, Indians, Italians, Japanese, and Russians turned their attention to opportunities inherent in that greatest of goals, the Himalayas, the largest mountaineering landmass of the planet.

Although Switzerland's neutral stance has guaranteed that nation's absence from the annals of modern war, it is not surprising in view of its geography that it was quick to develop a model Alpine army. Skiing was introduced to Switzerland in 1868 by a Norwegian sportsman, Konrad Wild. The first ski club (Ski Club, Glarus) was founded in 1893, and also in that year the Gotthard Command of the Swiss army made the first Swiss attempts at soldiering on skis. Soon after one mountain battalion was equipped with skis and a *'Schneeschuh-Ausrüstungreserve'* was set up. Ski classes were organized for officers and other ranks, as well as winter exercises on skis in patrolling, sharpshooting, and solving tactical problems.

The First World War gave a powerful impulse to military skiing in Switzerland and it was in 1917 that mountain training—and skiing in particular—received a fully-recognized status in the Swiss forces. After that, instruction in mountain warfare underwent a rapid development. Climbing and skiing skills were soon seen by the Swiss High Command not only as military necessities but also as vital recreations. During the Second World War years, ski classes for all officers and men as well as specially-devised competitions were started, while the reserves were regularly called up for ski refresher courses. These activities formed part of a physical-fitness campaign, which included ski courses for Swiss Air Force personnel. At least half the officers and men of the Swiss army became specialist Alpine troops.

The great importance attached to skiing by the Swiss High Command at that time fol-

The development of Alpine military skills ran closely in parallel with the growth of the pastime as a civilian sport. The Swiss Alps in the nineteenth century became the Mecca for adventure-seekers from many parts of the world. In 1827 John Auldjo became the tenth Englishman to make the assault of Mont Blanc. In his book The Ascent of Mont Blanc, *he depicted in a series of his own watercolours the harsh reality of mountain climbing. In the two reproduced here, the artist illustrates 'A dangerous part of the glacier' and 'Sliding down a snow wall'.*

lowed clearly from the fact that in the staff of every brigade or division there was a special ski officer who was responsible for ski training, the maintenance of ski equipment, its replacement, and generally all matters connected with skiing. Ski training in the Swiss army, after a brief refresher course, consisted mainly of 'toughening exercises' in the form of long Alpine tours in full kit, fighting on skis (which did not substantially differ from Scandinavian training), and other tactical exercises. The Swiss Alpine soldier was not only required to ski but was also expected to climb (either with or without skis), to know how to deal with glaciers, the use of an ice-axe and crampons, rope and pitons, to negotiate the skill of roped skiing, and to acquire sufficient practice in step-cutting—in fact, he had to become an all-round mountaineer. The difficulties of the Alpine terrain and the dispersion of troops demanded high qualities of leadership from officers and NCOs, and considerable resourcefulness from the lower ranks. This necessitated strenuous and persistent training, and constant refresher courses to keep the cadres in good trim.

As far as skiing pure and simple was concerned, one most important thing the Alpine soldier had to learn was to keep formation in downhill running. (This often proved more difficult for good racers than with indifferent skiers, as the former were apt to show a tendency to run too far ahead.) The speed of ascent had to be adjusted to the weakest skiers of the group, so that the soldiers kept together and never ceased to form a single unit within earshot of their commander. Naturally, the distance from soldier to soldier varied depending on the natural conditions and the dangers of avalanche, which would almost certainly dictate longer intervals. Whenever possible, however, the whole section or platoon moved in parallel tracks, a few yards from one another, each man a little behind the other, so as to form a 'step-ladder' (or a half-V) that contracted or expanded as conditions required but always moved as a single whole at a constant speed.

The next section followed some distance behind. When the nature of the terrain did not allow such an arrangement or it was thought best to conceal the number of men in the patrol, the men ran as nearly as possible in the track made by the commander. This had the disadvantage that the skiers out front raised snow dust in the faces of the men following. For training in downhill running, strongly-undulating slopes were chosen. Also, ski running in formation through intricate forest passages demanded considerable experience and discipline, being a favourite exercise of military ski instructors.

Apart from exercises in formation skiing and Alpine manoeuvres, numerous ski competitions were regularly organized for army personnel. These consisted of the already-familiar patrol races, downhill (straight) and slalom contests, whose description here would hardly be justified as they did not differ in substance from similar civilian events. The Swiss, however, introduced a special kind of military relay race that provided an interesting test of Alpine ski proficiency and deserves a detailed description. As an example of such a race, we shall take the military ski meet of I Corps held in Château d'Oex on 8-9 February 1941.

The programme of the meet consisted of the relay race and the patrol race, 77 teams of six men each competing in the first of these. The relay race's course formed a loop so that both the start and the finish were in the same place, and it was divided into six sectors with distinct terrain characteristics. One man in each team had to negotiate his sector in full army kit as best he could and pass the 'message' to his comrade who ran the next relay. The total length of the course was 20 miles (32 km), and the difference in altitude between its highest and lowest point amounted to 544 ft (166 m).

The race at Château d'Oex was run under difficult conditions. A thaw set in on the eve of the meet (the usual malice of Alpine weather), and a heavy rain was followed by frost, which converted the lower portions of the course into a glass track. Higher up, the conditions were better and some fresh snow had fallen. Despite this, downhill running was very difficult and involved considerable breakage of matériel, especially sticks. The race was won by the team of the 68th Gebirgs Grenzwacht Regiment (Mountain Frontier Guards) in a little over four hours. Other first-line Alpine teams came in close behind, and the results of the Landwehr (second-line militia contingents comprising age classes of 32 to 40) ranged between five and six hours. There was no marksmanship test, and a shooting competition was held separately—but the meet did not otherwise differ from the ordinary Scandinavian type.

Going back in time to the years immediately preceding the First World War, the general staffs of the main European powers had shown interest in mountain training. The French and the Austrians were the most advanced thinkers in this respect. The French army, in close collaboration with the Club Alpin Français, commenced military skiing lessons in the winter of 1901-2. In general, the Norwegians were extremely helpful in developing the mountain skills of the French. Every infantry company and every battery of artillery in XIV Corps of the French army (Western Alps and Jura) sent men for regular instruction to the École Normale de Ski, founded in 1903 at Briançon for military personnel. Soon after, similar schools were also set up in Pau-Cauterets in the Pyrenees and in Gérardmer in the Vosges. It was at Briançon that the Italian Alpini received, in 1904, their first initiation into military skiing. Austria-Hungary, with its mountainous frontiers, took enthusiastically to mountain warfare training. Skiing became a permanent feature of the winter training of the Austrian Kaiserjäger. Every Jäger battalion had a detachment of sixteen men under an officer, and artillery also had its own ski patrols. When the First World War broke out, the Austro-Hungarian army and the Italian army were soon to be locked in a mountain war, the gigantic scale of which was to be unique in the history of warfare.

CHAPTER 2
ITALIA IRREDENTA!

Italy's land frontiers form part of one of the great mountain systems of Europe, stretching from the Gulf of Genoa in the west to Vienna, and rising between the plains of northern Italy and of southern Germany. The Alps do not present so continuous a barrier as the Himalayas, the Andes, or even the Pyrenees. They are less extensive than the Urals or the Scandinavian highlands. They are formed of numerous ranges, divided by comparatively deep valleys. The mountain mass forms a broad band, convex towards the north, while most of the valleys lie between the directions west to east and southwest to northeast. Many deep, transverse valleys intersect the prevailing direction of the ridges, which facilitate the passage of

One of the Austrian heavy guns placed on a snow-capped peak in the Trentino. Before the First World War the Austrians held all the geographical advantages in a mountain campaign but the Italians, at great cost in lives, were nevertheless to seize the advantage in the bitter war to be fought on their northern frontiers.

An Austro-Hungarian night patrol makes its way cautiously along a ledge in the Dolomites.

An Italian 305-mm gun bombards an Austrian fort on a remote mountain peak.

man, animals, and plants, as well as of currents of air that mitigate the contrast that would otherwise be found between the climates of the opposite slopes. The term *alp* (or *elm* in the Eastern Alps) is strictly applied to the high-mountain pastures and not to the peaks and ridges of the chain.

In the Alps, three main divisions are generally distinguished: the Western Alps, extending from the Colle di Tenda to the Simplon Pass; the Central Alps, extending from the Simplon Pass to the Passo di Resia (Reschen Scheideck); and the Eastern Alps, extending from the latter to the Radstädter Tauern route, with a band outward toward the southeast in order to include the higher summits of the southeastern Alps. Assuming these divisions, it is convenient to subdivide the whole mountain system into eighteen smaller groups—five in the Western Alps, seven in the Central Alps, and six in the Eastern Alps.

The Italo-Austrian theatre of war, which was determined by the international frontier formed between Italy and Austria in 1866, was located in the Eastern Alps. It was concentrated

on its western sector in the Dolomites of south Tirol (from the Brenner Pass to the Passo di Monte Croce Carnico, and south of the Pustertal). This was the Trentino front, which includes two cities, Trent and Bolzano, the latter being the third largest Alpine city. Further east the so-called Alpine front was located in the Carnic Alps, which is part of the southeastern Alps (east of the Monte Croce Carnico). The Carnic Alps are part of a division that includes the Julian and the Karawanken Alps, both of which extend into present-day Yugoslavia.

The Italian national problem of the unredeemed provinces (*Italia Irrendenta!*) weighed heavily on the minds of every Italian. It was necessary once and for all to resolve the question of the 'iniquitous frontier', that is to say the Trentino frontier, which having been traced to the Italians disadvantage in 1886, represented a real Austrian menace. The Trentino, or South Tirol region, spanning a line running north of Lake Garda to the present Austrian border at the Brenner Pass formed a giant spur or salient into Italian territory. The Austro-Hungarian army had in spite of the Triple Alliance built strong fortifications in the Trentino mountains over a period of a decade or more. The Trentino front thus formed a salient from which the Imperial armies could assault southwards into the Lombardy plain from commanding positions. The initial battle front, stretching some 400 miles (645 km), in fact formed a great letter 'S' in shape and contained two salients. The Trentino salient in the west was extremely dangerous to the Italians and was for them a front line committed to defence. In the Trentino the Austrians were in possession of an impregnable fortress.

The battlefront from Switzerland to the Adriatic Sea, which was almost as extensive as the whole of the Western Front in Belgium and France, divided itself naturally into three sectors: The Trent, the Alpine, and the Isonzo fronts. The line was wholly mountainous throughout its length except for some 30 miles (50 km) on the Isonzo front on the extreme right wing, and here the coastal lowlands were hilly and rough enough to create barriers. The Udine salient, another name for the Isonzo front, favoured the Italians, who were committed to the offensive in this region. The provinces of Lombardy and Venetia bear numerous rivers on their plains, which flow southeastward into the Adriatic Sea. Near the sea the Venetian plain is low and marshy with extensive lagoons along the shore line. The marshy belt varies in width from 10 to 30 miles (15 to 50 km) and creates a serious military obstacle. Between the mountains on the one hand and the marshes on the other, only the rivers oppose the movement of troops over the level surface of the plains.

At the beginning of the war there was a

A heavily armoured Austrian fort at Malberghetto in the Carnic Alps.

The same fort after a prolonged bombardment by Italian guns.

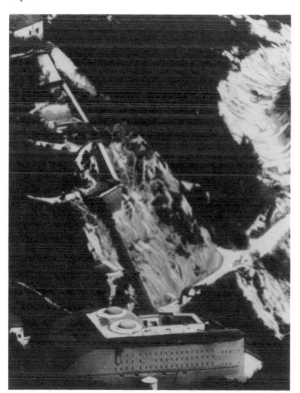

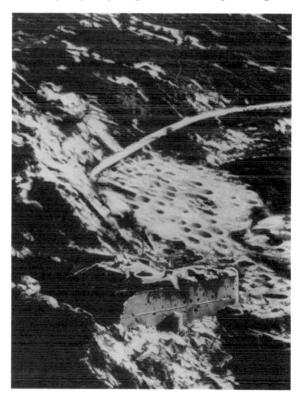

unique situation on the Italo-Austrian front, for on all the other fronts the first phase of the operations was a war of movement. Not so here, where the Austrians used their pre-war enterprise to impose on the Italians the methods of warfare most suited to themselves, and from the very first day of the war the Italian army had to face a deadly war of attrition. The Austrians had armed along the entire length of the front. Strategic railways and roads were built in the border areas. The Trentino and Alpine fronts had been turned into one of the most strongly-fortified areas in Europe. Every mountain and every hill bristled with artillery. Here was a formal fortress protected by elaborate fortifications with the steel-plated domes that were such a familiar sight in Belgium. Hundreds of dug-outs were constructed in the rocky masses and deep-cut canyons; miles of trenches were dug and protected by barbed wire; blockhouses were built; new roads were constantly made to improve communications; and the railways were extended.

The work of modernizing the Isonzo front's defences was left to the last because the Austrian staff had not decided just where the line of resistance was to be established. On 21 April 1915, orders were given to the effect that 'the passage across the Isonzo, south of Tolmino, be closed and the defences along the western edge of the Carso be organized'—the Carso being an extremely bleak plateau situated east of Gorizia and noted for its abundance of sharp stones. The Austrians were thus well prepared

Great ingenuity and hard labour were required by the Italians to haul their heavy guns into mountain positions to combat the strongly entrenched Austrian fortifications and other positions.

The Italian Alpini were the élite of the Italian army. Recruited mostly of hardy stock from the Alpine regions, these highly trained soldiers with their distinctive feathered headgear undertook routine patrols and engaged in combat action at the highest mountain altitudes. Here an Alpini patrol edges its way down a slope with the aid of a rope.

for any breakthrough by Italian forces. On this front, gargantuan battles were fought for the Piave and Isonzo River lines, twelve battles taking place along the Isonzo alone. The Isonzo lay as a barrier to Trieste but although the key city of Gorizia, which lies on the river's right bank, was captured by the Italians in August 1916, the Italian, Austrian, and eventually German armies were to be deadlocked in battle for many months in the treacherous terrain of the Carso.

From the beginning of the war, Italy's real problem lay with the Austrian salient in the west. Whatever initial success the Italians might have in attacking the mountain strongholds of the Trentino, they were faced with more mountains to cross and valleys and gorges to penetrate. Italy had to act on the defensive on this front, maintaining large forces to prevent the Austro-Hungarian army advancing south to the plain. This did not create passive defence lines for the Italians. They had to make their own

strongholds and outposts in the mountains, which provided the bases from which to attack the Austrians even in the harshest winter conditions. Those readers familiar with Ernest Hemingway's *A Farewell to Arms* will have gained the impression that the war on the Italian front was a seasonal affair with hostilities closing down for the winter months. Not so in the mountains, where troops were known to live in camps blasted out of the rock for six months at a time supplied by human porters, donkey and sleigh, or the trolleys of the *telerifica* or aerial railway, which played a prominent part in the operations in the Alps as a means of transportation and communications.

Whilst the Trentino contained no strategic objectives for the Italians, a massive effort was mounted to keep the Austrians under control. The Austrians, lodged in their mountain positions, were well aware that successful offensives mounted from the Trentino front penetrating the Lombardy and Venetian plains might cut

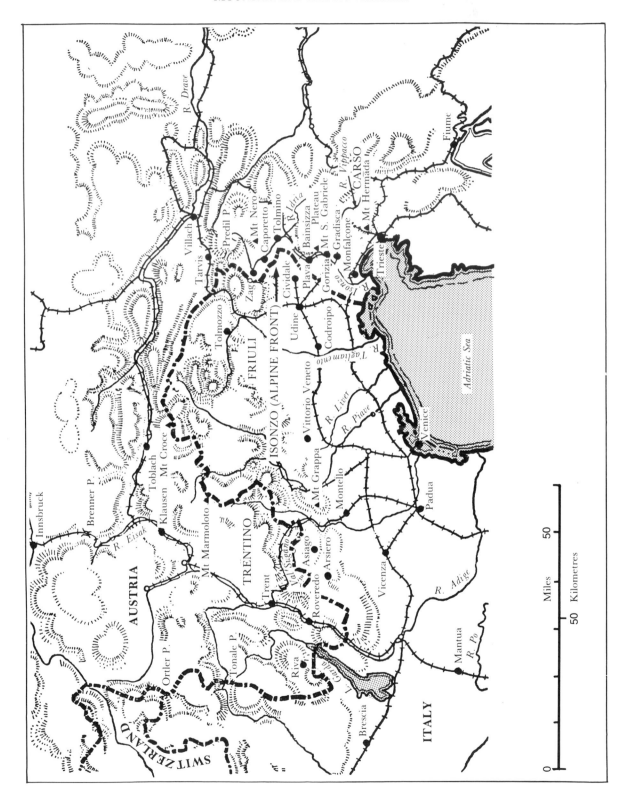

the Italian army off on the Alpine and Isonzo fronts. As we have seen, the Trentino came down like a giant wedge into vital Italian areas, opening a wide gate through the mountains into the rich plains to the south. This salient in Italy's natural line of defence was in itself serious enough, but its importance was increased by the fact that it lay so far to the west of the Isonzo front. The threat posed by the Austrian forces of splitting the Italian army (and the Allied forces that went to its aid) was a very real one.

During the first 29 months of the war in Italy, the fighting was almost wholly among the mountains. As will be seen from the profile, altitudes in the Alps average about 3,000 ft (915 m) above sea-level, a large part above 6,000 ft (1,850 m), and, in some cases, over 9,000 ft (2,750 m). Accounts of the mountain war appear somewhat fragmentary, disjointed, and even confused. This is due to the extremely broken nature of the ground on which this remarkable warfare was pursued. Operations were split up into a great number of small actions in separate sectors of the front. This holds true for all but the major operations such as Gorizia, Caporetto, the Piave, and Vittoria Veneto. On no other front did the soldiers of any nation lead so arduous an existence as here.

The Italian's battle order on 24 May 1915, under its supreme commander Victor Emmanuel III, consisted of four armies—four independent army corps numbering altogether some 40 divisions, not counting two Alpini groups of the Second Army and 16 battalions of Alpini of the Fourth Army. As the war developed there were at least 78 Alpini battalions in the Italian army. On the other hand, the Austro-Hungarian army, mobilized in 1914, possessed

six armies, consisting of 16 army corps of which two were assigned to mountain operations. The total strength was of 60 infantry and cavalry divisions, plus independent and Landsturm brigades. The mountain corps each comprised two divisions.

The Italian *corps d'élite* numbered the Alpini, the Bersaglieri, Arditi, and Granatieri. The Alpini, who in the First World War overtook the Bersaglieri as the favourite corps of the Italian people, originated from earliest times as mountain warriors. The Roman Empire could not subdue these mountain tribes, and they held out against the kingdoms of Europe, both medieval and modern. A handful of 'highlanders' were capable of repelling an army corps. One might say they were the fathers of modern trench warfare, 370 of them in 1690 successfully holding trenches and keeping at bay the armies of the King of France and the Duke of Savoy. The Waldensians, whose origins are lost in antiquity, were the best known of the 'mountain men'. They did not adhere to the Catholic faith and, for the most part, led exemplary lives. However, on occasions they committed hideous massacres in keeping with the spirit of the age. Crusades were organized against them whenever Christendom was not otherwise engaged. The Waldensians and other Alpine denizens have fought, almost without intermission, from the darkest ages to the expulsion of Austria from Lombardy and Venice.

The Alpini of the First World War dated from the period immediately following the *Risorgimento*, when the new Kingdom of Italy had acquired a mountain frontier marching with Austria. Raised mostly from among the Alpine populations—and some from among the Abruzzi—they were a splendid body of men when the war broke out. The Alpini were actually founded by Victor Emmanuel II in 1872 when he formed them into a corps. His new kingdom was, however, so poor that his army remained a mere skeleton for some years, and the Alpini were slow to reach the perfection they attained in the First World War. It was the

The Italian Front 1915-18: The Alpine heights dominated the bitter conflict that raged between Italy on the one side and Austria and Germany on the other for three long years.

Alpini who, in the years 1915-18, guarded the hundreds of miles of higher Alps, quartered in snow-bound arêtes and gullies for three winters of actual warfare, under conditions that would have killed troops less skilled in snowcraft, less hardy, and less patient by inherited instinct.

Had the First World War gone on for much longer, the Italian army might have consisted entirely of Alpini. More solemn, more earnest than the proud Bersaglieri (the sharpshooters), the veteran Alpini, by their example, encouraged even the lowlanders and city dwellers to fight in the mountains. Instead of the Bersaglieri's soft, low, rather flamboyant, lady-like hat with its cascade of cock's feathers, the Alpini wore a kind of felt, Winston billycock or brimmed policeman's helmet, with one short, sharp feather pointing upwards. The

The Alpini, like the crack mountain troops of other nations, were expert skiers. Here an Alpini column moves up a mountain slope, each man carrying his skis, rucksack and personal arms. After making the ascent, the column dons its skis and prepares to make a swift return to its base in the valley below.

feather holder was a woollen tuft in the battalion colour (yellow for depot), while the regimental number appeared in the centre of the cap badge, the company number appearing on the shoulder wings. The badge itself was an Alpini horn superimposed on crossed rifles surmounted by a flying eagle. Apart from the headgear (the Alpini and Bersaglieri eschewed the steel helmet), the mountain troops wore standard infantry uniform, but in winter were clad in a variety of warm, improvised clothing. One special outfit consisted of a fur hat, duffle coat with fur collar and cuffs, fur mitts, and the most magnificent fur boots rising to the knees.

It is said that the Alpini of the First World War had inherited their ancestors' simple faiths. They believed in the lore of the mountains: vampires, hobgoblins, witches, fairies. They also believed that Christ died for them, and that the saints protected them in all their daring deeds. They would think nothing of exposing themselves to the danger of walking a dozen miles to replenish the oil-lamp before some miraculous image of Our Lady. And when a highland shepherd or soldier came to a way-

side cross or chapel, he knelt down, with his forehead on the stones or snow, and prayed for the glorious dead, for a glorious victory. Among the Alpini companies were found many men who, from sheer devilry or frustration in life, had dedicated themselves to death. They were known as the 'lost souls', and were always ready to volunteer as had their medieval forebears for 'forlorn-hope' raiding parties.

The Alpini were experts on skis and with climbing tackle—skills developed by the veteran 'mountain men' since infancy. They were all perfectly suited by training and tradition for any acrobatic feat in the Alpine ranges. The snow was their native element. The Alpini were as much at home on the side of a precipice as any Chamonix guide. From their earliest days they had scaled perpendicular cliffs for pleasure, chased chamois, and swung themselves from peak to peak like human apes. No rock was too sheer nor too slippery for their ascent, though

An Alpini patrol supported by a machine-gunner waits expectantly for any sign of enemy movement.

This Alpini look-out has a commanding view of the valley below. They would ascend or descend the rock face like the expert climbers they were to and from their lonely posts, returning to their base on the low ground.

they may be weighed down with all the equipment of war. They were especially expert in the use of ropes, with which they would lasso the crags above in order to assist their climb. Few sentries or observers in modern armies have been faced with the physical challenge, as did the Alpini, of climbing several thousand feet to take up their posts on a mountain ledge, and buglers as a rule do not sound the reveille greeting the Alpine dawn on the roof of the world.

However, the Austrian defenders, equally at home on the mountain peaks, were ever on the alert, and often cut a rope, dashing its human burden to the abyss below. To circumvent this, canny Alpini threw up decoy ropes. The Austrians rushed forward and cut them while the assault party was creeping up another

way. Once at the top, the Alpini would rush the enemy's stronghold, carrying it by storm. The Austrians, on the other hand, preferred more cautious tactics. When they wanted to attack a mountain they waited for dense clouds to fill the valleys so that they could wriggle up unseen. At the summit, they paused to recover their breath, then opened up with a heavy barrage of fire to test the strength of the defensive position, only fighting at close quarters if there was absolutely no alternative. An enemy patrol might be dislodged from a mountain path and sent to its death engulfed in an avalanche triggered off by the guns of a mountain battery. Alternatively, an enemy contingent lodged on a glacier could be eliminated by sapping into the base of the glacier to bury explosives. The fate of the mountain élite in this case was to be preserved for the years to come in a monolithic tomb of ice!

The cries of '*Italia Irredenta!*' and '*Trieste o morte*' had inspired a fine fighting spirit in the Italian army and the terrain over which the Italian campaign was fought bred success. Of the other élite regiments, the Bersaglieri were founded by General La Marmora in the 1840s, and soon became the crack regiment of the little Piedmontese army that played so great a part in the making of Italy. They won their reputation in the Crimea in 1855 by the side of their English, French, Turkish, and Sardinian allies, and in the wars that freed their country from the Austrians and Papalists in 1848-9, 1859-60, 1866, and 1870. Their nodding plumes and springing step, and the blare of trumpets behind which they ran into battle, became a symbol of the Italian army to all Europe. The Bersaglieri, who were essentially crack riflemen, took great pride in their trumpets, whose musical salute frequently greeted the Alpine dawn. The famous Bersaglieri trot was discarded as a method of marching—partly on medical grounds—and many Bersaglieri *ciclisti* (bicycle) battalions were assigned to the Isonzo front.

The Arditi were the storm troopers of the Italian army. They were specially trained, kept in the rear away from the trenches until the day of the battle, and then hurried up in Fiat lorries to carry the enemy positions. The Arditi; in their open-necked jackets and with the crest of the dagger and palms on the sleeve, became a familiar sight to all in the last year of the war. Some of the Arditi battalions were given special physical and athletic training, and to see the *flamme nere*, as they were called on account of their black nightcaps, march past singing, stripped to the waist, was to display the martial spirit at its most advanced level. Skill in flame-throwing, bomb-throwing, and the dagger at close quarters, were the favourite Arditi arts. Holding the trenches by rifle fire after their capture was left to the ordinary line infantry.

The Arditi lived in an atmosphere of

In summer, the lower slopes of some areas of the Alpine region, especially the eastern sector such as the Carso, consists of barren rock piles. Here an Italian soldier is seen stationed in an ideally situated look-out post that would be hard to detect from any direction or level.

bombs and flames. In order to enlist into the favoured corps from a line regiment, the aspirant had to satisfy the instructors by way of an examination that consisted of running through a machine-gun barrage—a certain percentage of volunteers were inevitably wounded. The Arditi also had the reputation of throwing bombs at each other and at passers-by—some would say out of sheer high spirits. They were in constant trouble with the Carabinieri, the police, who in the war carried out the disagreeable duties of military police. The Arditi called the Carabinieri 'aeroplanes', on account of their wide-winged hats. A Carabinieri was once found bound in a mountain road with a label attached to him: '*nemico abbatuto dagli arditi*' ('enemy aeroplane brought down by the Arditi'). The Arditi were to appear again in the Second World War where, in North Africa, they performed sabotage duties such as wrecking railway lines—a role not dissimilar to that of the British Special Air Service (SAS), which was raised in Egypt in 1941.

The Granatieri were selected for their height. They were involved in the winter of 1915, in the fighting on Sabotino and Oslavia, where they lost very heavily. Transferred subsequently to the Duke of Aosta's Third Army,

they went again and again into the desperate fighting on Carso and Hermada, and after the retreat took a leading part in the successful defence of the lower Piave. Their reputation stood very high, and was dearly bought. The reputation of the Italian army is generally summed up today in an overview of the half-hearted performance of Mussolini's army in the Second World War (1941-3). It must be remembered that the rank and file of the army of the Fascist state had become politically disaffected early in the war. Who is to say they had not inherited the fighting qualities of their fathers in the First World War?

CHAPTER 3
AUSTRIA'S MOUNTAIN SALIENTS

Austro-Hungary, with her mountainous frontier, had for some time presented a training ground for ski troops. A certain Colonel Bilgeri, who has been called the Father of Austrian Military Skiing, introduced the skill to the Tiroler Corps as early as 1894—seven years before the French army, in association with the Club Alpine Français, held its first military ski classes under French and Norwegian instructors, and ten years before the Italian Alpini received its first initiation at Briançon in moving on skis as a military exercise. An Austrian, H. Czant (a zealous and patriotic military skier) published in 1907 a mountain warfare manual, *Militärgebirgsdient in Winter*, in which he reflected his pioneer experiences in the Bihar Mountains (Transylvanian Alps). He discussed, furthermore, the relative advantages and disadvantages of skis and snow-shoes and gave a few hints on the transportation of machine-guns on snow in the mountains. The book received great appreciation among students of mountain warfare in Germany and even saw a French translation. A number of other works on the subject also appeared in Austria more or less simultaneously.

Austrian troops assembled at an Alpine outpost in the Trentino in the early weeks of the war.

By the time the world war began, skiing was a permanent feature of the training of the Austrian Kaiserjäger, adopting the practice of Mathias Zdarsky's so-called Lilienfeld technique. According to Bilgeri, shortly before the war every Jäger battalion had a ski detachment of 16 men under an officer, and artillery also had its own ski patrols. Regular military ski classes were organized every year for trained troops. In 1915, the Austrian Alpenjäger had ski detachments as well as general staff officers, and some special units in the Austro-Hungarian army had received ski training. Likewise, other troops of the Hapsburg Empire, stationed in the mountainous regions (Carpathians, Sudeten), were not unacquainted with skiing, particularly with regard to patrolling and liaison duties.

German military skiing was mainly confined to Bavaria. In 1914 Bavarian skiers raised a volunteer force, known as the Bayrische Ski Battalion, which was incorporated in 1916 together with the similar Prussian Ski Battalion of the 3rd Jäger Regiment and sent to the Alpine front. The Command of the 6th German Division (Bavaria) foresaw the use of skis for patrolling, for small, mobile, machine-gun detachments (two machine-guns in each) and for machine-guns mounted on ski-sledges, for members of the staff, and for medical service. During the winter operations of 1914-15 (it was an exceptionally severe winter) German and French skiers met in the Vosges. Apart from minor skirmishes, there were two major engagements. The French Chasseurs Alpins, operating on skis, distinguished themselves in the battle of St Dié on 31 December 1914 and were mentioned in dispatches. On the days of 13 and 14 February 1915, an all-out ski engagement took place between a French battalion and the Bayrische Ski Battalion. Accounts of the confrontation in the snow are scarce, but it must be assumed from what little information is available that the French came out of the battle on top.

Ski patrols used by both sides clashed head on on the Italo-Austrian front, where the Tirolian skiers rendered a brilliant account of themselves in the operations at Arresa and Asiago. In the Carpathians, Austrian and German skiers (using white camouflage covers) severely harassed the ski-less Russians. Russian

This Austrian photograph of an Italian mountainside position reveals an ingeniously constructed wooden stairway designed for easier access to the summit.

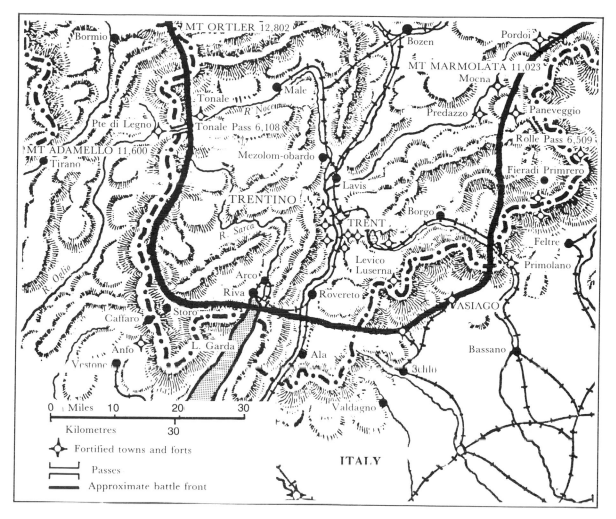

The Austrian salient in the Trentino: This hotly contested Alpine Zone, which was strongly fortified by Austria in the pre-war years, was regarded by Italy as an intolerable intrusion on their territory.

ski troops did not take an active part in the fighting, for two reasons: the best skiers in the Russian Imperial army were Finns and they had been exempted from front-line duties; and Russian hunter commands had not been trained for mountain work and could not be advantageously employed in the Carpathians, where most of the fighting was taking place on the southern sector of the Russian front. Skiers were, however, certainly used occasionally by the Russians for special duties, medical service in particular. There are also records of Austrian skiers operating on the Balkan front and even in Turkey, where they carried out patrol work.

The most advanced positions in the Carnia (Alpine front), as in the Trentino, were amid the eternal snows. Here the guns were emplaced in ice caverns that could only be reached by tunnels cut through the drifts. Here the Alpini spent their days wrapped in shaggy furs, their faces smeared with grease as protection from the stinging blasts, their nights in holes burrowed in the snow, like the igloos of the Eskimo. They ran the risk of being cut off from supplies for months on end. On the Alpine sector operations had to be conducted in very high altitudes, often amid deep snow and ice and blizzards, on the edges of dizzy precipices and deep gullies, where a false step meant being hurled down hundreds of feet. Sheer peaks and other lofty positions could be held by a handful of men with a few machine-guns against whole brigades, where stones dropped from great heights were as deadly as shell or shrapnel. The Carso sector on the other hand—an extension of the Isonzo front east of the Trieste—was a howling wilderness of stones as sharp as knives, which tore the strongest boots to pieces and mangled the feet of the most hardened mountaineers. Every shell that exploded here had its deadliness multiplied tenfold by the fragments of rock added to the jagged edges of broken steel. There was no water except for that carried up in barrels on mule-back.

From the first winter, the Italian army in the mountains had to teach itself to live, and to fight, in a region where conditions were all but incredible. A well-organized system of logistics was not sufficient: a special plan was required to enable the troops to live a normal life under absolutely abnormal conditions. In other words, solutions to numberless problems were sought, whereby transport could be maintained to serve the men unfailingly, whereby natural body heat could be sustained, water, food and housing could be supplied, and the frozen trenches made habitable. Above all, it was imperative that the first line of the offensive should be made safe and comfortable along the extended front, where snowstorms were ever falling and covering up defence works, and where it was necessary that the troops, detailed for sentry work, should have sufficient shelter. Trenches were covered in matting, and the soil was walled and paved with wood. In the hewn rocks and in the armoured shelters, troops who were not needed for the immediate firing line

were housed. Further reserves and those off duty lived in thousands of specially-erected sheds built of brick, cement, and wood, and in the Alpine cottages they found.

The Italian nation helped generously. Countless women toiled daily from dawn to dusk, making and sewing the needed winter garments, such as flannel shirts, underclothes, stockings, woollen scarves, gloves, caps, cloaks, chest-protectors, sleeping-bags lined with skin, and boots and clogs protected against dampness. Foot-and-hand warmers were distributed freely to those on trench duty. The forward guards in their mountain refuges were later well looked after with bricks that, when heated and wrapped in a cover, helped to keep the soldiers warm in their sleeping-bags. Ration-heaters were made of paper compressed into cubes and coated in wax or of solidified spirit. Small stoves were also used that consumed animal fat. Thermos flasks were used to provide hot soup, even for those engaged on outpost duty. All rations were increased to allow each soldier a minimum of 3,900 calories a day, and for those operating in the bleaker mountain zones, at least 4,700 calories a day. The water question had to be considered, especially in those parts where the streams were likely to freeze or where there was no water supply, as on the highlands of the Asiago plateau and the wilderness of the Carso. This was solved by manpower and mule-drawn sleighs.

Thus it was that hundreds of thousands of men—the majority of whom, as the war progressed, were drawn from southern Italy and Sicily where snow is unknown—could winter in such polar conditions, ready for military operations, while remaining in excellent health. Many of them lived at a height of over 10,000

Above right *Austrian troops man a forward entrenchment ready to repel any probing attack by the Italian infantry.*

Right *Motor trucks parked alongside an Austrian roadside encampment near the front line.*

ft (3,050 m). In order to gauge the amount of labour required for such undertakings, it may be noted that one single army corps, dwelling in the mountain zone, needed 300,000 wooden planks, of which two-thirds were borne on human shoulders or dragged up by hand; 280,000 blankets (as many vests, pants, and pairs of stockings); 80,000 winter coats; and 60,000 fur chest-protectors. The Austrians—with their advantage of having solid, fortified positions constructed before the outbreak of the European war, and their experience of mountain warfare in the Carpathians in the winter of 1914-15—proposed a series of short, sharp engagements resulting in territorial gain. However, they were constantly harassed by Alpini ski-raids. The skiers, clad from head to foot in white, were always busy reconnoitring and starting firefights.

The Austro-Italian battle fronts were served from both sides by efficient railway systems. It must be remembered that little more than forty years had elapsed since the iron horses and their carriages had first made their mark on the logistics of the American Civil War (1861-5). Austria possessed a most carefully-planned railway network. Its main-line railway ran around the whole half-moon of the frontier, but in places it had few feeders as the terrain made it almost impossible to construct them. The lack of branch lines meant that any major Austrian offensive had to concentrate in certain strategic areas, such as Gorizia, to the north of Gorizia, and in the Trentino. The Italian railway system was not as complete as the Austrian. It consisted of a double line, paralleling the frontier, with six cross-lines connecting the two main systems. Spurs ran up the

Above far left *An Austrian signaller operates a field telephone sited in a dug-out built into the side of Mount Lambu. Laying the line was often a hazardous task, especially in the Alpine winter conditions.*

Above left *In the First World War on the Alpine mountain frontiers, the Italians particularly made use of the* telerifica, *the 'ski lift' principle, which became common to ski resorts throughout the world. The overhead wires and pulleys were not, however, to lift troops to the top of a mountain or across a ravine for recreational purposes. Fighting men including the wounded,* matériel, *rations — anything too heavy to be man-packed or carried on mules — were carried to and from otherwise inaccessible positions. In this photograph, a group of Austrians are stationed at the base of their supply-lift apparatus with a view of the Austrian Tyrol in the background.*

Above *An Austrian patrol scales a rock face. Like the Alpini, the Austrian Jäger were 'mountain people', raised as youngsters to be climbers and skiers, and in the First World War the Austrians were to establish a reputation as mountain troops which has continued to be second to none until the present day.*

valleys in front of the Alps. All the railways were single track except for the Verona-Venice and Venice-Udine lines as far as Casarsa—a city on the Tagliamento River some 20 miles (30 km) south west of Udine.

In order to serve their mountain positions, the Italians built their *telerifica* (a system of overhead steel wires supported by towers), which had the appearance of passenger lifts at ski resorts. Instead of cable cars, however, the wires carried cradles containing men, artillery components, cases of ammunition, sacks of food, and medical supplies. The *telerifica* traversed valleys and abysses and was much more to the troops than simply a conveyor of supplies—it was a means of maintaining morale for the 'mountain men', who may have had to live on the peaks for several months at a time. Even the higher slopes of the Alps had been 'urbanized'. Miles and miles of Italian trenches had to be blasted out of solid rock. Barbed-wire entanglements formed barriers in the snow. Galleries were excavated in the icefields. Mountain paths and stepways were constructed, and tunnels built through the snow. Observation posts were erected in positions at over 7,000 ft (2,100 m). Artillery and mortar fire were a constant danger in causing avalanches.

The Italian army maintained an immense effort in logistics, which served them well in two winters of war. Almost 2,000 miles (3,000 km) of trenches were built, from the simple to the most complicated, from that consisting of a single parapet to that of ferro-concrete. Some 10,000 spacious huts were also erected in the winter of 1916-17, which were capable of housing more than half-a-million troops. During the same winter, 11,320 cu. ft (320 m^3) of timber were sawn up in the mountain workshops and used with 20,000t of metal in the construction work. These mammoth efforts enabled one million soldiers, each in turn, to sleep in proper bedsteads, either of iron or wood, with mats or mattresses. About 5,000,000 sq. yd (4,030,500 m^2) of living space was heated by 20,000 stoves. Millions of sacks and countless lengths

Above *The successful conduct of the Alpine war depended on establishing gun emplacements and observation posts in commanding positions on the high ground. The communication trench leading from this Italian look-out post suggests that other similar vantage points have been built along the ridge, probably acting as 'nerve centres' for heavy artillery placed along the lower slopes.*

Below *Although the machine-gun had been used with telling effect as early as the American Civil War (1861-65) and the Franco-Prussian War (1870-71), this still comparatively new weapon of war was used with devastating effect against advancing infantry in the war of attrition that was waged on most fronts in the First World War. This Italian machine-gunner would have been capable of routing an infantry company with a hail of plunging fire sprayed on the lower ground.*

of barbed wire were needed. For the assault upon the rocks, if not for their conquest, explosives were used that were capable of flinging nearly 3,000,000 cu. ft (85,000 m³) of hard rock into the air.

As the inclemency of the season grew, so the troops exposed to it were given better and more nourishing food. Rice, macaroni, meat, wine, and coffee were not enough. The authorities also issued tea, rum, and Marsala. Each meal had to prove substantial and it had to be served hot. Canteens were erected as near the front lines as possible, and the food was conveyed thence by motor vehicles, carts, sleighs, animals, and men. Where such arrangements were impossible, hoards of provisions were stored in the natural refrigeration of the icefields, as in polar expeditions. The beef required for the Italian army in one year of war equalled that consumed in one year throughout the whole peninsula prior to the war. Demand for corn was heavy. Early in the campaign some 3,000 head of cattle were slaughtered daily; later, with other food supplies at hand, this was reduced to one third. At least 1,000 large bakeries were busy every working day and night turning out bread; macaroni, rice, cheese, and potatoes were also a daily necessity. Tobacco (considered practically a complement to the rations) was ever generously supplied. At the end of 1916, over two-and-a-quarter million pounds (1,021,500 kg) of cigars, cigarettes, and pipe tobacco were supplied to the army that, along with the pipes distributed, totalled 160 million lira in value.

Roadways were the most important means of supplying the mountains. The Italian forces had overcome enormous difficulties in the construction of the necessary roads, from the lowlands to the most rugged and loneliest peaks. Roads had to be made, as far as it was possible to make them, as well as paths that could encompass the most precipitous rocks, and bridges that could span precipices. The 3,000 miles (4,800 km) of roadways built by the Italians and that which already existed in the

war zone were rapidly extended, enlarged, strengthened, levelled, improved, and modified to enable the endless train of motor trucks and heavy traction-engines haul immense loads. Yet this was not enough where roads ended and the terrain seemed to bar further progress. Paths had to be hewn, winding higher and higher to the dizzy heights above. Paths had to be strengthened with posts and protected against avalanches and landslides.

Soldiers with gun, pick, and shovel were hardly enough to cope with all the road construction work. Another army of labourers was enlisted and was daily employed in bringing up to the assigned areas carts filled with gravel and special equipment. The snow—the bitter enemy of the soldier and labourer—was a constant hazard and challenge. When clearance of the snow was not possible, sleighs were used. When this was impossible, covered galleries were adopted,

Left *Although his calm demeanour suggests that this photograph is a posed shot, this Italian 'bomber' is about to throw a flighted hand-grenade from a front-line trench.*

Below *A party of Italian artillerymen haul their guns on to the high ground.*

Above *Italian infantry advance swiftly in a dangerously exposed situation on rough, stony ground.*

Below *An Alpini infantry company clad in snow apparel advances into action on the slopes of the Adamello mountain against an Austrian position.*

prepared first with strong beams and roofing, or new galleries were pierced into the snow itself, several feet in height and extending to the front—in all, possibly some hundreds of miles long. The Italians throughout the winter also concealed their road positions from the watchfulness of the enemy by erecting screens of matting. Screens were also erected in open spaces so that work and movement could continue unhindered by fire from the Austrian lines. Hundreds of bridges were erected, including wooden constructions, folding bridges, and pontoons and other temporary means of crossing rivers. Communications by water were also improved by the construction of canals connecting important rivers such as the Po, Adige, Tagliamento, and Isonzo.

The most effective method of destruction open to both sides lay with the deployment of artillery of every calibre, and with howitzers and mortars. Austrian artillery (placed in their fortified positions in the mountains) dominated all the possible Italian lines of advance into the highlands. The only area where the Italians might conduct a successful offensive lay to the east on the Isonzo front, but since Napoleon had overthrown Austria by clambering over the Carnic and Julian Alps, Austrian engineers had turned this corner of the Alpine chain into a Gibraltar. The first important system of earthwork fortresses was built after the Napoleonic wars. The system was strengthened after Napoleon III overthrew the Austrians in 1859, in the battles that freed Lombardy. And when the Italian kingdom was fully established by the war of 1866, the mountain roads to Trieste and Vienna were again fortified in a more formidable manner. Another great reconstruction followed the siege of Port Arthur, which was the first important test of the power fortresses had of resisting high-explosive shell. Then in 1910, when the German and Austrian staffs made the great discovery that their new 11- and 12-in howitzers rendered all armoured and concrete works practically useless, the Alpine fortresses were remodelled, and positions were selected on

An Alpini patrol guided by its leader makes its way along a slippery ledge on the descent to its valley base.

the plateaux for earthwork systems of defence, in which mobile siege-guns could be used.

Without the benefit of pre-war mountain fortifications, the Italians in 1915 had to catch up hastily with the Austrians, by making their own and hauling up their guns (field artillery, anti-aircraft guns, long-range 'heavies', howitzers, and infantry mortars) by various methods. Fiat trucks, traction motors, tractors, and horses conveyed even 10- and 11-in naval guns up tortuous mountain roads. However, the beast of burden of the Alpine mountain battery was inevitably the mule, the inherent hazard being that to lose a mule over the edge of a precipice might well mean the loss of part of a gun. The Italians gained some added firepower from the newly introduced armoured cars, and some support was received from the Adriatic fleet.

The Italians placed their anti-aerial artillery in the highest mountain positions, but the Austrian air force tended to ignore the battle fronts, preferring to bomb historic cities in the plains to the south of the Alpine ranges.

Far above the snow-line, the heaviest artillery was mechanically hauled up the sheer sides of perpendicular heights to emplacements where often, until then, human foot had never trodden. Men and guns cradled in open cars attached to the overhead wires of the *telerifica* flashed from peak to peak, through the clouds, and at dizzy altitudes above the ice-bound valleys beneath. Here and there small parties of men struggled with ropes to push and pull the guns up pathless slopes of snow, rocks, and ice.

Finally, superior heights secured, aerial railways established, opposing armies entrenched in snowy plains among the clouds, and guns emplaced on the loftiest crags, a great duel would commence between them. Guns fired from summit to summit, down into entrenchments in the plains and up against lofty ramparts of rock. They boomed across immense white valleys, as often glittering in the winter sun as shrouded in fog or capped in cloud. And the *mitraglieri*—the quick-firing cannon—machine-gun and the rifle were also there, thumping shells and spitting bullets into the snow. Trenches were rushed, lost, and taken, even as in the mud-filling plains of Flanders and northern France.

CHAPTER 4
THE MOUNTAIN WAR 1915

Italy's declaration of war on Austria-Hungary on 23 May 1915 was followed by a similar declaration against Turkey on 20 August. Bulgaria joined the Central Powers to fight Serbia on 19 October. Italy's quarrel with Turkey was partly due to the latter's refusal to allow Italian subjects to leave Asia Minor freely. But as the year passed, and though the Kaiser recalled his ambassador immediately after the declaration against Austria, there were no declarations of war between Italy and Germany. The reason for this remarkable and apparently inconsistent attitude was no doubt to be found in the fact that Italy was nowhere in territorial contact with Germany and, moreover, there was a mutual desire shared between the two countries to maintain and to pursue commercial interests for as long as it was feasible to do so. The attitude of the average Italian towards his near German neighbour was ambivalent, but the other *Entente* Powers were naturally persistent in their attempts to persuade Italy to make a formal declaration of war against Kaiser Wilhelm II.

Once in the field, Italy became the most vigorous and adventurous of the Allied Powers. The day after the declaration of war, while Austrian aircraft were bombing Venice, General Cadorna flung large bodies of his troops into Austrian territory, to establish what the Italians considered to be the real frontier between the two countries. Italian strategy was, at first, to ring the southern Tirol and occupy all the passes. The main concentration of these offensive manoeuvres was directed on the eastern

side and in the centre, from which the Austrians might descend upon Italy with a view to preventing an Italian advance upon Trieste. Engaging Austrian forces along the entire front of the mountains, peaks, and glaciers of the titanic serrated chain of the Alps was vital to Italian interests. In order to prevent the Italian forces passing across the Isonzo, the Austrians might well have attacked their rear, forcing the passes of the Trente, of the Cadoria, and the Carnia. The Italian attempt on the Isonzo, which meant fending off the Austrians on to their left wing and their rear, required the employment of the major part of General Cadorna's forces.

Count Conrad von Hotzendorf (often referred to simply as Conrad), in command of the Austro-Hungarian forces, had indeed planned to launch an all-out attack once war was declared, but the Italian offensive, which commenced on the night of 23 May, met with early successes. General Cadorna's instant move along the whole extent of the front succeeded in checking the Austrian advance. The main drive of the Italian Second and Third Armies, although successful in numerous operations, found the Isonzo front positions immensely strong. By 16 June, the first offensive efforts of the Italians were over and a pause of a few days was made to complete the mobilization, to bring up fresh troops, and to prepare for a new drive. The Italians had, however, crossed the Isonzo in the neighbourhood of Caporetto and captured Nero, about 7 miles (11 km) from Tolmino. The experience gained in these first few days of the war was to determine the type and method of attacks employed for the remainder of 1915.

The first Battle of the Isonzo began on 23 June 1915 and lasted until 7 July. It consisted of thrusts along the Gorizia bridgehead and the Carso. On 23 June the Austrian Fifth Army occupied a line from Mt Nero to the sea, divided in five sectors, with ten divisions—a total of 113 battalions and 132 batteries that, during the battle, were reinforced by three divisions from VII Army Corps. The Italian attack on the entrenched positions of Tolmino and Gorizia was carried out by the Italian Second Army (ten divisions, 136 batteries, of which nine only were of medium calibre). This attack resulted in modest gains in the Tolmino sector and enemy trenches were taken on the slopes of Sieme, Mrzli, and in front of St Maria and St Lucia.

This is how an Austrian observer described the Italian attacks: 'The first line troops advanced under the protection of their artillery fire, the sappers carrying gelatine tubes to blow up the barbed wire. The defenders allowed the attacking troops to approach the entanglements, and then opened on them such a withering fire that the few survivors were obliged to seek safety in a rapid retreat.' The offensive carried out by the Italian Third Army on the Carso (five, then ten divisions with 76 batteries, of which four were of medium calibre) had better results. There the Isonzo was crossed north of Sagrado on the Dotton Canal, and the first step on the Carso—Polazzo—was captured, as well as the slopes of Mt San Busi and a hill facing Mt San Michele. The battle cost the Italians 14,950 men; the Austrian losses were 10,400. On the Western Front, trench conflict had become known as a war of attrition; the Italians soon coined a name for their war—'*logoramento*' ('war of exhaustion').

The second Battle of the Isonzo began on 18 July, after about ten days preparation, and lasted until 3 August 1915. The objectives were the same: the heights of the upper Isonzo, the Gorizia area, and the Carso. In spite of plans

This Austrian photograph was taken in 1915 during one of the early, tentative offensives against the Italian lines.

to co-ordinate the Italian attack with a Franco-British onslaught on the Western Front and a Serbian offensive, the Italians attacked on their own. The principal thrust by the Third Army was directed to the San Martino-San Michele tract, which was Gorizia's pillar of defence. The Second Army was to attack at Tolmino and Plava, but only with a view to tying down Austrian forces. The Third Army consisted of three army corps, plus one independent infantry division, three cavalry divisions, and eight aeroplane squadrons. Some 34 batteries of medium guns were in action on this front. The Second Army, spread out on a broader front, operated with III Corps and two reserve divisions.

After the first Isonzo battle, the Austrians had been reinforced by about five divisions, and the Fifth Army—from Tolmino to the sea—had a total of 103,000 rifles, 286 machine-guns, and 431 artillery pieces. About half of these forces were concentrated on the Carso. The battle, commencing on 18 July, saw heavy artillery bombardments by both sides and hand-to-hand fighting in the trenches. On 20 July, the Italians occupied the trenches of Castelnuovo, and six battalions reached the top of San Michele, which dominated the whole of the Isonzo plain and the low valley of Gorizia. On 21 July, Austrian General Boog led 18 battalions in a successful attempt at dislodging the Italians from San Michele, but the Austrians were not so successful in completely driving the Italians off the mountain. On 26 July, the Italians retook the summit, only to be hurled off it by the Austrians later the same day.

By 3 August, the battle on the Third Army front was coming to an end. The Austrians had suffered nearly 42,000 losses, the Italians 31,500. The Second Army now took the brunt of the action in the Gorizia area. In front of the city, 12 Italian divisions succeeded in breaking through three consecutive enemy lines on the Podgorna and in occupying the summit. The Austrian 58th Division reacted violently. Attacks and counter-attacks succeeded each other but the Italians were able to hold a posi-

An Italian machine-gun position ideally sited overlooking road-ways suited to military traffic down in the valley, but on the other hand very vulnerable to air attack. Military aviation, although in its infancy and often hampered by poor visibility in the mountains, was an effective means of reconnoitring enemy strongholds and outposts.

tion half way up the strongly-contested high ground. In the Tolmino zone, three Alpini battalions with elements of the Italian 8th Infantry Division, succeeded in occupying the great platcau called Mt Rosso, a little south of Mt Nero, chasing out—after a bitter fight—four Austrian Jäger battalions that were in occupation. Three times the Austrians counter-attacked, but the position remained in the possession of the Italians. Small gains in territory were also obtained at Plava. The Italians lost

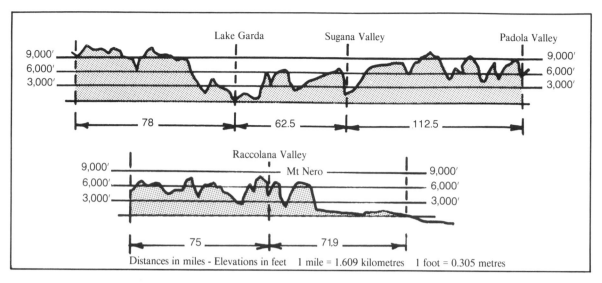

Profile of the Alpine Front until 1917: This cross-section of the snow-covered mountain ranges graphically illustrates the natural barriers that existed between the adversaries.

10,762 men on this sector against 5,402 Austrians.

The second Battle of the Isonzo having ended, the Italian Command began to mass troops and equipment in order to launch an offensive in the upper Isonzo, and it was considered necessary to attack the Plazzo and Tolmino sectors on the right, lower down the river. The attack commenced on 12 August and carried on until the end of September in the difficult mountain zone of the higher Isonzo: Rombon, Cuckla, Javorek, Lipnik, Mt Nero, Vodil, and up to the heights of San Maria and San Lucia—steep slopes guarding Tolmino. Nearly six Italian divisions took part in the action, supported in all by heavy and medium guns. Four Austrian divisions faced them with strong, well-sited artillery. The fighting was as violent in this sector as in the most-contested parts of the Carso.

In the north, the low valley of Plezzo was occupied, and an attempt was made to conquer its own supports: Mts Rombon and Javorcek. Of the first, the Italians succeeded in taking the important position of Cuckla and the slopes, but not the top. Very little was gained against the steep, rocky walls of Javorcek. By means

of brisk fighting, the Italian occupation was extended from the Ursic towards Lipnik. For a brief period Mrzli was conquered, but this position was later lost with severe losses to the Italian regiment that made the assault. At Sleme, very costly attacks were broken up by thick-wire entanglements. The heights of San Maria and San Lucia were attacked several times. After having broken through several defensive lines with heavy losses, the summit was reached, but had to be abandoned because of the devastating concentration of Austrian artillery fire. Operations were suspended at the end of September. They had only partially achieved the desired objectives, as only slight progress had been made against Tolmino. The low valley of Plezzo, however, was barred against the Austrians, and this represented a minor success for the Italian army.

The fighting had not let up in the difficult mountains of the Trentino, nor did the Italian First Army remain primarily on the defensive, as General Cadorna had intended. On the other side, the Austrians had not only been reinforced by the arrival of new units but had also strengthened their fortifications and heavy armaments in the sector. From the beginning of the advance up to the middle of August, various Austrian attacks had been repulsed, and in the Giudicarie, Mts Lavaneck and Cima Pizzola had been captured and many other positions of minor importance. In the second half of August heavy fighting took place in the Valsugana area. Mt Civaron was occupied, and the line of the River Maso was reached. The occupation of Cima Rava and Cima d'Asta was followed by the occupation of the Forcella Magna. To the west, the hotly-contested position of Mt Maronia, in the Posina sector, was also taken by the Italians. In September, the Italian army continued its attacks, some with negative results, others more successful, such as the capture of Malga Pioverna and the steady progress made towards Rovereto, in the Val d'Ampola, and in the Val di Ledro.

Meanwhile, the Italian Fourth Army was endeavouring to force the Austrian fortifications in the Cadore region. On three occasions, between 5 July and 4 August 1915, an offensive was carried out, resulting in the breaking of the Austrian line and the gaining of the spurs

The only effective way in which the Italians could even attempt to neutralize the Austrian fortifications, which had been constructed as part of Austria's defence policy in salient mountain positions long before the outbreak of war, was by constant artillery bombardment by heavy guns. Even broad-barrelled guns were adapted for use by the army. This impressive artillery piece, mounted on tracks and which might be described as an early example of a self-propelled gun, is elevated for high-angle fire which would have made a heavy impact on even the strongest concrete emplacements.

under the Col di Lana (but not the height), the Forcella di Fontana Negra, part of the Tofane and of the head of the Travenanzess valley, the Col di Bois and the Bois height, the Cima di Falzarego. However, the advance on Toblach was not possible either then or later, and the fighting for this most difficult of all mountain regions was reduced to a struggle by the Italian and Austrian soldiers to stay alive in the harsh conditions.

The Italian forces in the Carnia zone were assembled in strength by mid-July, and faced the Austrians on two sectors—that of But-Degano to the west and that of Fella to the east. The Italian occupation of Pal Grande-Freikopen-Pizzo Avostanis was a very serious threat to the Austrians. After a series of short, sharp raids, the Austrians returned to the attack in full force from Pizzo Avostanis, between 5 and 8 July, but it was destined to failure. The Italians, attacking in the Paralba zone (7-8 August), met with no better success. At last, on 14 September, the enemy attempted to gain ground, attacking from Pal Piccolo, Pal Grande, and Freikopel, with a flanking attack from Mt Crestalta and Col di Cretta. But in spite of some initial success against the Italian first-line positions, the action did not meet with success. Meanwhile, on the eastern sector of the Carnia, Italian artillery was battering the Austrian forts of Predil and Raibl, and the infantry occupied the important positions of Forcella Cianalot and Pizzo in the Val Dogna. During early autumn four more Austrian divisions arrived in the Carnia zone.

While the Italian operations in the Trentino, Carnia, and Carso continued to register some success, the Italian Supreme Command made every effort to muster superior forces to continue the offensive on the Isonzo. It might be said that Italy was alone among the Allies in being in the war for deliberate gain (*Italia Irredenta!*); Serbia, Russia, Belgium, France, and England had been obliged to take up arms either because they were attacked or had gone to the aid of friendly powers. The Italian

Supreme Command felt under some pressure to keep up the attack once started. This was partly to justify the call-to-arms of Italian manhood, and partly to encourage Italian industry to produce the weapons, ammunition, and equipment, especially artillery and aeroplanes, that were needed to drive the Austrians out of the mountains and valleys forming the frontier of the two nations. As it happened, Italy was in no way capable of raising the men and *matériel* that were available to France and England on the Western Front.

The third and fourth Battles of the Isonzo started on 18 October and lasted until the beginning of December. (It was the Austrians who divided the battle into two parts for historical purposes, the third battle ending on 4 November.) The Italian scheme was to attack the wings (Plava and Carso salients), then the centre (Oslavia, Podgora, and San Michele), simultaneously attacking Tolmino. The main thrusts were to be assisted by diversionary and mock assaults on other parts of the front. After a three-day bombardment, the Italian infantry commenced to attack from Plezzo to the sea. The pattern of the fighting was very similar to that of the previous offensives: much blood was shed at Plava, Sabotino, Podgora, and then on the Carso at San Michele, Sei Busi, and Cosich. Attacks were repeated four or five times, positions taken and lost and then retaken. The Command of the Austrian 58th Division wrote: 'Today [29 October] the battle has certainly been the fiercest up to now in the Italian campaign.'

A pause ensued after 4 November, while the Italians regrouped and the Austrians took the opportunity to mend their defences. The offensive (the fourth Battle of Isonzo was continued on 10 November, again from Plezzo to the sea). The Italians admitted that 'The advance was checked everywhere by means of wire entanglements and various obstacles which the unceasing work of the defenders had brought to such a depth, that it was practically impossible to destroy them by ordinary means'.

The Italians' main deficiency was in artillery. Their official report stated that 'the quantity and calibre of our artillery was still far from what was required to have even a minimum effect; let us remember the artillery used by our allies and the results obtained by them'. The fourth Battle of the Isonzo ended in early December, a period of adjustment following with only local actions—both sides attempting to consolidate their positions.

The Italian autumn offensive had resulted in the extension of their occupation of the low valley of Plezzo, at Mt Nero, at St Maria and St Lucia di Tolmino. At Plaza the Italians captured the strong positions of Globna and Zabora. To the west of Gorizia they occupied Oslavia and gained the summit of the hills, going even further at certain points. On the Carso they extended their occupation to the approaches of the heights of San Michele and Sei Busi. The Italian gains were not vast, but they drew some comfort from the belief that they had relieved pressure on the Russians and Serbians on other fronts. The fighting on the Italian-Austrian front had indeed been bitter. One Austrian historian assessed that 'In 47 days, the Italians attacked Sabotino 15 times, Podgora 40 times, and Oslavia 30 times'. During the period of the third and fourth Battles of the Isonzo, a time when heavy rain turned the trenches into a sea of mud, Italian losses—on the Isonzo alone—amounted to 116,000 men. (On the Carso certain regiments lost 50 per cent of their men.) The Austrian losses were not so high, but still heavy: 72,000 men, of which 12,000 were taken prisoner.

While the autumn fighting was in progress on the Isonzo, important operations were being carried out in the mountain salient to the west. In the Trentino, the Italians took complete possession of Val di Ledro, with the low valley of Bezzecca and the positions between Garda and Adige, right up to the advanced defences of Rovereto, and the spur of the Zugna Torta, as well as important positions in Val Sugana. In Cadore, the Italians held on to Rauhkofl, the Cristallo group, Sasso di Mezzodi, Sasso di Stria, and many other difficult positions. Frostbite figured highly among the combatants' 'wounds'. The Italians also made progress in the Falzarego-Lagazuoi regions, towards the top of the Col di Lang (taken on 7 November and then lost again), and to the slopes that lie between Sarso di Mezzodi and Cordevole. In Carnia, during October, the Austrians attacked Mt Crestalta and Mittagskofel, but both attacks were completely repulsed, although the Austrians outnumbered the Italians in men, machine guns, and artillery.

CHAPTER 5
THE MOUNTAIN WAR 1916

With the coming of the first winter, the Italian Supreme Command made every effort to lessen the discomfort of its army operating in the mountains and valleys. Troop positions were drawn up in deeper echelons, leaving fewer in the front lines; trenches were covered with sheets of metal, wood, and sand bags; the dug-outs were lined with wood; and the soldiers were supplied with woollen clothes and more stoves to keep food—and their bodies—warm. However, these measures alleviated but did not eliminate the suffering of hundreds of thousands of men exposed to the Arctic weather. In Carnia, as early as September/October, temperatures of −18°F (−28°C) had been experienced and in the Cadore sometimes even −28°F (−34°C). This resulted in many cases of frostbite and, later, of avalanche cases. Summing up, General Cadorna stated that 'The provision of means for thousands of men to pass the winter in a perfect war condition and in perfect health, even in mountainous zones very often surpassing heights of 2,000 metres and even 3,000 . . . was a really great task and can justly be considered with pride'.

Whilst the Italian army was busy with preparations for a spring offensive, France—attacked at Verdun—asked Italy to launch a major drive to tie down as many Austrian troops as possible on the Italo-Austrian front. On 11 March 1916, the Italians yet again commenced operations from the Plezzo line. The Italian Second Army, manning the front from Plezzo to Gorizia, met with strong resistance. The fifth

Battle of the Isonzo was thus set in motion. In front of Gorizia, Italian troops succeeded in occupying important positions over familiar ground on the Podgora, in the Oslavia sector, and towards the Sabotino, but the Italians were not able to take full advantage of their success. On one sector near San Martino, the Austrians repulsed seven attacks—the Italians penetrating the positions with their eighth attack. A counter-attack succeeded in driving out the Italians, with the exception of small units. Italian losses were estimated at about 1,200 men. From 11 to 19 March, the Austrians lost 3,500 men, and the losses continued because the attacks did not cease even when operations on a grand scale were at an end. A strong Austrian counter-offensive followed the Italian attacks. This was launched with a view to lessening the pressure in front of Tolmino and Gorizia, but the Austrians, after having gained territory, were everywhere driven back to the trenches from where they had started. On 29 March, the main operations of the latest battle on the Isonzo ended, and the usual local attacks recommenced.

Minor operations were especially swift in the mountain zone. On 30 March, the Rauhkafl was conquered after a swift action, and was held for several days by the Italians against counter-attacks until it was finally lost through a concentrated attack by Austrian artillery fire. In the Marmolada sector, Pizzo and Punta Serauta (nearly 10,000 ft—3,000 m high) were captured; in the Padola-Visdende sector, the Cima

Undici and the Sentinella Pass were taken on 10 April. At the Col di Lana, a colossal mine (which had taken several months of excavation by Italian sappers) was packed with explosives that literally blew the top off the mountain (17 April), to be occupied quickly by Italian troops. The Italians also made progress towards Mt Sief. Strongly-contested successes were also obtained in Val Brenta and more importantly in Val di Ledro.

The operations carried out on the Adamello, at a height of over 10,000 ft (3,000 m), were particularly striking, especially in view of the difficulties of the terrain that had to be overcome, and the continuing, very cold weather. On 12 April, the slopes of the Lobbia Alta Dosson of Genova—Mt Fumo (11,214 ft— 3420 m) were scaled and occupied by the Italians. On 20 April after a long battle, the Italian army, taking advantage of the success obtained, attacked and captured the second enemy line on the frozen crests of Crozzon di Lares, and the Lares and Cavento passes. Later, overcoming fresh resistance, the Italians captured the crest of the Crozzon di Fagorida and the pass of the same name until, at the beginning of June, part of the Genova valley was occupied. This series of operations, carried out

The fight for Gorizia: an Italian field gun in action in the Carso.

This Italian encampment has been virtually concealed in a rocky cliff face in the inhospitable Carso region, a major scene of conflict in the war.

This Alpini trooper suspended with a seemingly casual grip from the telerifica *must surely qualify as one of the world's first airborne troops.*

An Austrian heavy mortar sited to lob bombs into the Italian trenches.

over so long a period and at such altitudes (10,200-11,500 ft—3,100-3,500 m) in glacial regions—where it seemed impossible for any military action to take place—were probably unique in the annals of mountain warfare.

The time had come for the Austro-Hungarian army to assert itself on the Italian front. General Conrad, whose pet scheme the offensive was, chose the Trentino for his 'Strafe-Expedition' to 'punish' the presumptuous Italians and, moreover, to cut off their armies on the Alpine and Isonzo sectors. In previous years Conrad had commanded a division at Innsbruck (just north of the city of Trent) and had made a careful study of the terrain. The Trentino was a vast gateway to the plains. Here in the area of the Asiago plateau, which lies to the southeast of Trent and south of Val Sugana, was a comparatively short distance through the mountainous belt. The only reason Conrad had not put his plan into operation before was that the battles of the Isonzo had kept him rather busy. The Germans, who at that time were still

not actually at war with Italy, were against the proposed offensive, stating a preference for Austrian heavy artillery to be sent to Verdun. Instead, Conrad reinforced the Trentino front with nine Austrian divisions from Galicia (on the Russian front), persuading the Germans to send nine of their own divisions to Galicia. He was also to obtain more reinforcements from the Balkan front.

Reports of the Austrian concentration throughout the winter of 1915-16 periodically reached Italian headquarters. General Cadorna was criticized for not taking adequate steps to counteract the impending offensive. The facts, however, show that he did attempt to act in a sound manner. He reinforced, very materially, the Italian First Army, which was to act on the defensive in this operation. Cadorna's foresight was, though, substantially undermined by General Brusati, who commanded the First Army and who failed to prepare a defensive zone with a main line of resistance backed up by two, three, four, or more lines in the rear,

An Alpini machine-gunner lies in wait in the snow.

to fall back on if necessary. General Brusati's disposition of troops and *matériel* was not satisfactory to General Cadorna when the latter went over the plans of the First Army and its positions just before the Austrian attack. It was too late then to make extensive changes. General Brusati was superseded on 8 May 1916.

General Cadorna stopped all preparations for another push on the Isonzo front and hurried all available reinforcements to the Trentino front. Not only was the First Army reinforced but the Fifth Army was also brought up to strength by transferring troops from the Second and Third Armies (on the Isonzo front), troops from Libya, and newly-formed troop units from the interior of Italy. The First Army, at this time commanded by General Percori-Giraldi, had its boundaries extended from Lake Garda to just north of Val Sugana. The Fifth Army was concentrated to the right in the Vicenza-Treviso area as a strategic reserve. Another Italian army, the Fourth, was located to the north of the Fifth Army's positions in the western Carnia. The Austrian forces, which were effectively directed by Conrad, were under

the supreme command of Archduke Karl Franz Joseph. The main Austrian offensive force in the Trentino was concentrated in two armies: the Third, commanded by General Kovess von Kovesshaza (who had been victorious in the second Austrian invasion of Serbia), and the Eleventh, commanded by General Dankl (who had commanded in Galicia in the early part of the war). In opposing forces, the numerical strength of the Austrians far outnumbered the Italians in battalions of infantry; in artillery the disparity was even more marked—the Austrians even possessed three 16-in guns of the very latest design.

General Conrad's two armies massed one behind the other so as to gain greater penetrating force. He chose the highlands of Folgaria-Lavarone as the direction of his attack, with the long, pre-determined intention of taking, in the rear, the mass of the Italian troops on the Isonzo. On 15 May, the Austrians started the offensive on the wings—between Val Lagarina and Val d'Astice in the west, and Val Sugana in the east. In the western sector, the Austrians attacked the front lines of defence, which were bitterly contested by the Italian troops. The Austrians were held up at the principal line of resistance—Conizugna and Passo di Boole. Here the attacks ferociously succeeded one another, but were always repulsed by strong Italian resistance. Between the Pasubio and the Astico, firing from heavy-calibre guns got the better of the defenders, who were also held under artillery fire from the Austrian forts. The Italians were forced back. The last bound, carried out in an orderly manner under the protection of an Alpine group, brought the line to Mt Cogolo-Novegno, an extreme height in view of the plain, and here every Austrian attempt to advance was thwarted by the Italians.

In Val Sugana, the Austrians (having overcome the advanced posts) were at first not only held up but were also driven back by Italian counter-attacks. However, the Italian Supreme Command, not wishing their troops to be scattered on too many defence lines, ordered the troops to be pulled back on the line of the Maso (Cima Caldiera-Civaron-Cima d'Asta). The enemy endeavoured to advance on 25 and 26 May, and in fact succeeded in taking Mt Civaron, but was heavily defeated at Mts Cima and Ravetta, until the attacks were abandoned. On the Asiago plateau, the action also started on 15 May with a strong concentration of Austrian artillery fire. General Cadorna gave orders to fall back on the main line of resistance. After four days of hard fighting, when certain sections of this line were lost, further orders were given to fall back to the marginal line that stretched from Mt Cengio to Mts Pau-Lanerle-Kaberlaba-Sisemol-Tondarecar-Marcesine. The first phase of the offensive may be considered to have ended towards the end of May. The resistance on the wings had hemmed in the attack and had helped break its impetus.

It may be difficult for readers, who have not seen this terrain, to envisage the style of warfare that took place in the Trentino at this time. On no other front had the armies encountered such appalling obstacles. The most inaccessible regions of the Vosges mountains in France, the most difficult, irregular valleys and ranges of the Carpathians, and the labyrinth of the Balkan mountains were less of a barrier compared to these great, rocky mountains, steep valleys, precipices, and chasms. This overwhelming, almost impassable mass of rock was indeed a difficult place in which to fight. The lines went over the mountains at heights of up to—and over—7,000 ft (2,100 m) in elevation, with the intervening valleys making combat quite spectacular.

Although the Italians appeared, at the end of May, to have the situation under control in the Trentino, the Austrian High Command felt so confident of final victory that on 1 June Conrad informed his troops that only one mountain remained between them and the plain (and thus the defeat of the Italians). On 4 June the Austrian forces were within 18 miles (29 km) of Vicenza and the mainline railway, but their strength had been exhausted. Conrad von Hotzendorf's gamble was doomed to failure. Cadorna could have mobilized over a million men to fight the Austrians on the plain. Violent Austrian attacks persisted (on the Pasubio, the Novegno, the Cengio, the Le Merle at Mt Fiore, and Zovetto) and went on until the middle of June but—as happens in most offensives—the first phase, the phase that offered the greatest gains, was over. On 2 June the Italian Supreme Command was able to announce that the Austrian efforts no longer caused anxiety, and orders for a counteroffensive were given. Cadorna had a trump card in the Fifth Army, which could be sent in to the counter-attack at the appropriate time.

The Italians launched their counteroffensive on 14 June, three days before the Austrians announced their effort was over. By 16 June, the Italian Fifth Army was hammering the Austrian lines with no less than four corps. The Austrians, menaced on the wings and pressed in the centre, were obliged to fall back on a rear line (prepared beforehand) that passed by Zugna Torta-Pasubio-Mt Cimone, the northern side of the Val d'Assa-Mt Mosciagh-

Mt Zebio-Mt Ortigara-Mt Civaron Valle del Maso. The fighting broke out violently again on this line. However, the Italian Supreme Command was faced with the dilemma: should they concentrate their major effort in destroying the Austrian 'punitive' forces in the mountains of the Trentino, or should they return to their Isonzo battleground?

While the Italians were making up their minds, the fighting in the mountains continued apace: on 2 July an Austrian attack on the Pasubio was repulsed; on 6 July the Italians attacked the Corno di Vallarsa, which was taken and lost again; on 23 July the Italians attacked Mt Cimone with surprise, which brought about brilliant results; and on 22 to 25 July the Italians attacked Cima di Portule but were unsuccessful. Thus the 'Strafe-Expedition' ended without the Austrians gaining their objectives. In the words of Germany's Field Marshal Hindenburg, 'The disillusion experienced through the failure of the offensive against Italy, which had been heralded with such exaggerated promises, was profound.' But the Italian losses were heavy—148,000 men—the Austrians less heavy but by no means light—between 90,000 and 100,000 men.

The results of the Austrian attack in the Trentino, and its initial success, caused great consternation amongst Italian politicians and brought about the fall of the Italian Cabinet. Upon the resignation of Salandra, the 'grand old man' Paolo Bosselli formed a new government. Bosselli was undoubtedly too old for the job of Italy's senior ruling politician, and when the battle of Caporetto came a little over a year later, he in turn gave way. However, even though the Trentino offensive—or Battle of Asiago— had caused momentary dismay in Italy, the result of the campaign was to benefit the Allies' general situation in a very remarkable and far-reaching manner. The Austrian attack had, after all, failed in its main purpose and, still more importantly, it had (by draining the Central Powers' resources of manpower and artillery on the Eastern Front) given the Rus-

sian General Brusilov his chance for a successful offensive. As a consequence of that success, the Central Powers—which had been very much in the ascendancy during the first half of 1916— now found the situation reversed, and the Allies looked to the future with more confidence than had hitherto been the case.

The fifth Battle of the Isonzo had been broken off when units from the Second and Third Armies had been hurried to the west to stem the tide of the Austrian attack in the Trentino. The success of the Italian Fifth Army in the region had greatly raised Italian morale. The Italian plan for the next Isonzo offensive was to assign to the units of the Third Army objectives in three general sectors (the Italian army's mission was to be a complete breakthrough):

1. VI Corps was to attack the key position of Gorizia, which meant taking the hills just northwest of the city.

A gun barrel is lifted across a ravine by telerifica.

2. VII Corps—three days before the main attack—was to make a holding attack in its sector, to attract enemy reserves.
3. The right of XI Corps and XIII Corps were to attack the high Austrian positions in their front, in conjunction with the attack of VI Corps.

Whilst General Cadorna was preparing the Gorizia manoeuvre, other operations were taking place in the mountains that had an important bearing on the sixth Battle of the Isonzo. In May, the Fourth Army captured the contested position of Mt Slef, and in June engaged the Austrians in the Ampezzana region, with some advantage. On 11 July the imposing mine of Castelletto, on the Tofane, was exploded, and the position occupied by the Italians. From 21 July to the end of the month, important operations in the mountains were carried out. These operations surprised the Austrians and permitted the Italians to occupy the Colbricon and Rolle Passes, the height of the Cavallazza, the heads of the Travignolo and San Pellegrino valleys, and the intermediate zone as far as Cima Bocche. Other operations were carried out on nearly the whole front, on the Ortler, the Adamello at the head of the Genova valley, the Plezzo zone, the Carso, Monfalcone, and in front of Mt San Michele. The Austrians, attacking in the area of San Michele on 29 July, used poison gas for the first time: the Italians were taken by surprise and suffered great loss.

The Italian plan of attack on the Isonzo envisaged the Third Army—commanded by the Duke of Aosta—launching its drive from Sabotina to the sea, a manoeuvre that had been carried out in each of the previous Isonzo offensives. The Second Army was assigned to keeping the Austrians engaged in the northern sector. The Third Army, therefore, had the greater part of the men and *matériel*: 16 divisions (203 battalions) and 1,904 guns (of which 344 were of medium and heavy calibre, besides mortars that were largely new from the factory lines). The Austrian Fifth Army faced them, occupying a line from Mt Nero to the sea comprising 124 battalions and 688 artillery pieces, of which 257 were of medium and heavy calibre. The Austrians everywhere dominated the Italian positions. Line upon line of defence positions were preceded by row upon row of entanglements, supplied by caves and dug-outs. The result was a real model of fortification.

On 4 August the Italian operation at Monfalcone commenced and bitter fighting ensued, but the action in this area did not succeed in attracting Austrian forces from the Gorizia sector. In the Isonzo offensive of early August the fighting was to take place essentially on the wings, at the Sabotino and at the Podgora, with a connecting action in the centre. At 07.00 on the morning of 6 August, the preparatory artillery barrage started. At 16.00 the Italian infantry attacked. The attack on the Sabotino, which had been carried out before on numerous occasions, was an instant success, the infantry assault overcoming the Austrians. The rampart that had cost the Italians so much blood finally fell, and the entire garrison was taken prisoner. The attack on Podgora was also successful. Having gained the crest on the flanks, the Italian units arrived at Grafenberg, where they fought all night against continuous Austrian counter-attacks. Only one position at Mt Calvario resisted, although it was practically surrounded.

In the centre, the Italian attack encountered strong obstacles, but it succeeded in overcoming the well-defended trenches of Oslavia, reaching Peuma. Some Italian patrols had already reached the Isonzo River line. During the night and the following day (7 August), the Austrians attacked strongly in the Sabotino zone and further south towards Podgora, in order to extricate themselves from a difficult position. The fighting continued with the lines being moved many times. The ground was fought over step by step. However, on 8 August the Italian success became apparent. With Peuma and Mt Calvario and Podgora captured, and with Grafenberg retaken, the Italians threw

themselves towards the Isonzo and beyond. Gorizia was entered and the Italians were triumphant in success. The Italians hastily formed a mobile group (cavalry and Bersaglieri cyclists) and sent it in pursuit, hoping to catch the Austrians on their second line of defence. This hope was not realized.

By 7 and 8 August, the Austrians had reinforced their second line of defence. This line from Mt Santo-San Gabriele-San Caterina was joined with the Carso and Volkovniak. The action of the Italian cavalry, and later the infantry, was not sufficient to extend the victory tide to this zone. At this time on the Carso, the bridgehead of Gorizia was attacked, as well as the other stronghold of the bridgehead, Mt San Michele. The latter was captured by the Italian 2nd Division, and held against continuous and repeated Austrian counter-attacks, which went on during the night of 6 to 7 August, and during the following two days, the fighting being very violent. Gorizia finally fell to the Italians, and the attack on the Carso was extended. The Italians succeeded in consolidating and enlarging their positions from Mt San Michele to the Vippacco. On 10 August the Austrians—who later affirmed that on the Carso alone they lost (between 4 and 8 August) about 23,000 men—retired beyond Vallone, on a front that, from Nad Logem via Oppacchiasella-Nova Vas-Lago di Doberdò, reached Debeli and the hills to the east of Monfalcone.

The Italian push did not cease. On 12 August the Austrian line was attacked: Nad Logem, San Grado di Merna, and Oppacchiasella were occupied by means of lightning attacks. Further south the heights of Mt Debeli were taken. The battle continued. On 14 August the attack was restarted along the whole front from Plava to the sea and continued on the following two days but now with scant results. Preparation of a new line of artillery, which was

This relaxed Italian sentry studies his own shadow at the entrance to a cave on a slope of Mount Nero.

Above *An Italian gunner, who has been installed in a mountainside snow cave, studies his simple instrumentation to observe his target and gauge the elevation of his gun.*

Below *This Italian light artillery piece has been sited in a valley to fire into the lower slope of a mountain.*

now too far away from the newly-occupied positions, was necessary to attack the new enemy lines. Therefore a new battle was started for the capture of Austrian positions at Plava, at San Caterina (near Gorizia), at San Marco, and at Castagnevizza until General Cadorna, realizing that more methodical preparations were necessary for this phase of the operation, suspended the offensive (17 August). The sixth Battle of the Isonzo cost the Italians about 51,000 men and the Austrians about 40,000. The Italians captured 19,758 Austrian prisoners, 30 field guns, 100 machine-guns, as well as various other items of equipment.

The capture of Gorizia was the biggest uplift to Italian morale in 1916. The Italians were also thrilled by the capture of those bastions, which had figured so largely in the Isonzo battles to date: Sabotino, Podgora, San Michele, and they had finally climbed the heights of the Carso. The Italian success was widely felt. Austrian Field Marshal Borovic wrote that 'The zone which protects Trieste is becoming ever thinner, every step back makes the front longer and an even greater number of troops becomes necessary' During the period July-September 1916, the battles of the Somme were in progress, in which the British were attempting to relieve pressure on the French at Verdun; Italian troops joined the Allies in Salonika; Italy and Romania declared war on Germany (27 August); Hindenburg succeeded Falkenhayn as Chief of the German General Staff; and German and Bulgarian forces invaded the Dobrudja (Romania). The Russians had registered a major success against Austro-Hungary on a front extending from the Pripet marshes south to the Romanian border, and the Russians were preparing to follow up their earlier successes in Galicia.

The Trentino and Gorizia operations had been a great drain on Italian resources but Cadorna was determined to exploit his successes and attack along the whole Gorizia-Carso front. So, included in the same order that, on 17 August had stopped the fifth Isonzo offensive,

were new orders for the next attack to take place as soon as the troops had been reorganized, and the artillery lined up ready for a new move. Three more battles (the seventh, eighth and ninth offensives) took place between 14 September and 14 November 1916. For the seventh battle the Italian plan was as follows. Whilst the Second Army was to hold Gorizia firmly, the Third Army was to attack on the Carso, concentrating their efforts to the left, where the highest part of the Carso lies—that is to say, on the slope that almost forms a stairway from Mt Faiti to Mt Trstelj, and then descends steeply on the Vippacco. The Italian forces on the Carso consisted of ten divisions, with 960 guns besides the mortars. The Austrians, on this occasion, were outnumbered by at least 20,000 men.

The attack took place on 14 September, and the Austrian line was broken, on a narrow sector, on the Carso. The important position of San Grado di Merna was captured. On the evening of 17 September action was suspended, partly due to the adverse weather conditions in the mountains. The Italians captured 4,100 Austrian prisoners; Italian losses amounted to 18,000 men. Having fortified their captured positions, preparations were made for a further Italian push, which took place on 9 October (eighth Battle of the Isonzo) and this time it was extended to the heights east of Gorizia, besides the Carso. Here, in spite of ferocious resistance, the Italian infantry succeeded in breaking through the Austrian positions at Vippacco, advancing to the second line, capturing Nova Vas—a strongly-fortified base—and the western slopes of Pecinka and the outskirts of two villages, Loquizza and Boscomalo (Hudi Log). On the right Jamiano was reached, but a violent counter-attack caused the Italian troops to fall back. The Suter slope and the heights near St Pietro were taken by the Italians and held against strong counter-attacks. Strongly pressed by the Italians, the Austrians were obliged to fall back on a rear line that went from Veliki-Krib, Pecinka, to Loquizza and Boscomalo. On

12 October the offensive ceased. The Italians had made considerable territorial gains for the loss of 23,000 men; Austrian casualties were not made known but it was thought they are about the same as the Italian losses.

The ninth Battle of the Isonzo took time to get underway, the Arctic weather halting the advance on several occasions. It was 31 October before the Italian infantry began to move forward. They conquered the Veliki-Krib, the Pecinka, and later the whole of the front from Mt Faiti to 765 yds (698 m) west of Castagnevizza. In a third effort the heights of Volkovniak were stormed and the nearby heights at Castagnevizza were captured. Furious Austrian counter-attacks were repulsed and all the captured positions held. In the region to the east of Gorizia, Italian progress was not so apparent—a major difficulty was caused by the rain and mud in the marshy Vertoibizza, where the troops fought up to their waists in mud. On 4 November the offensive ceased. It had cost the Italians about 29,000 men but they had advanced beyond the Vallore, and had gained good positions from which to make further attacks, having inflicted heavy casualties on the Austrians. From August to November, the Italians had taken about 40,000 Austrian prisoners.

Whilst the autumn offensives were taking place on the Isonzo, some spectacular fighting was taking place elsewhere in the mountains. The operations in the Val Travignolo, which had achieved brilliant results for the Italians, were continued in August. During these attacks, which made great demands on the climbers, the Cima del Cauriol (7,800 ft—2,300 m) and later Mt Cardinal—of roughly the same height as Cauriol—were conquered and held against strong counter-attacks. In October, by the fantastic means of scaling the rocky walls, the second height of the Colbricon was taken, and then the Costabella, a rocky height systematically organized with defensive caverns, and finally Basa Alta (7,900 ft—2,400 m) north of Mt Cardinal. Thus the Italians had gained possession of the mountain heights that look out on the Avisio, menacing the entrenched camp of Trento. At the same time fighting continued on the Pasubio where, after a long struggle, the Italians succeeded not only in extending their lines but also in capturing the Cosmagnon and the ground up to the slopes of the Roite, thus ensuring the safety of their Vallarsa lines. Later, the Austrians—imitating the feats of the Italian engineers—exploded a mine under the top of Mt Cimone (23 September).

The year 1916 did not end with very satisfactory results for the Allies. Victory, which in August had seemed so near, was again far away in December. The crushing of Romania, the first signs of French exhaustion, and the clear symptoms of the weakness in the Russian war machine, had been given much thought by the Allied commanders. Perhaps only England, although licking its wounds from the Somme, somehow escaped the gloom. The programme of action for 1917 was agreed upon in November 1916 at Chantilly. There it was agreed that the Allies should attack simultaneously in order to demonstrate the superiority of their forces over those of the Central Powers. In fact the Allies possessed 450 divisions against 350 enemy divisions: 11 million soldiers with 24,000 guns, against 7 million with 20,000 guns. The prudent use of such forces by the Allies should have gone a long way towards victory. Unfortunately, the Allies never fully developed the 1917 plan, and the year verged on disaster for them.

The winter of 1916-17 on the Italian front was very severe and tested the organizational abilities of the commanders on both sides. Snow as much as 13 ft (4 m) high was recorded, and violent avalanches exceeded any in living memory. The pause in the fighting caused by the severe weather was used both at the firing line and on the home front in Italy to strengthen the structure of and supplies to the army. One significant factor was the organization of 52 new field batteries, 44 mountain batteries, and 166 heavy batteries, and 1,000 guns of medium calibre were manufactured besides more than

An Italian sand-bagged headquarters dug-out is placed 'somewhere' in an Alpine battle area; the seated troopers are no doubt reading letters from home.

4,000 machine-guns. The numerical strength of the Italian army was also increased: eight new divisions were formed, with 96 battalions.

During the winter the Italian Supreme Command had studied all possible means whereby the projected spring offensive might be crowned with success. They counted particularly on reducing their forces on the Trentino front, especially the artillery, so as to concentrate them on the Isonzo. However, the rumours of an Austro-German attack through Italy, which greatly pre-occupied the Allies, gave the Italians urgent food for thought so that, whilst preparing for yet another offensive on the Isonzo, they had also to give due consideration to defending the other two sectors of the line, the Trentino and the Alpine fronts.

In April the Italians gave orders for an offensive to be carried out on the following lines. First, there was to be strong artillery action along the whole front line from Tolmino to the sea, so that the Austrians remained uncertain as to the direction of the attack. Second, an attack would be mounted to the north of Gorizia, on a front from Mt Cucco via Mt Vodice-Mt Santo to the mountains to the east of Gorizia. Last, the Third Army would push forward on the Carso, towards two barriers—the last before reaching Trieste—of Mts Trselji and Hermada.

CHAPTER 6
THE MOUNTAIN WAR 1917

The tenth Battle of the Isonzo (12 May to 18 June 1917) was carried out according to plan. On 12 May a violent bombardment took place against the Austrian lines. On 14 May the troops of the Gorizia zone occupied the nearby heights facing Plava, Zagora, the forts of Zagomila, the top of Mt Santo, and the heights in front of Gorizia, whilst a crossing of the Isonzo succeeded brilliantly. The Austrians fought with their customary tenacity but the Italians continued to advance, finally occupying the heights of Cucco e Vodice, but not those of Mt Santo (which were taken and lost many times), nor most of San Gabriele. From 22 to 26 May, the action in this sector slowed down, mainly because ammunition was becoming scarce. Here the Austrians left 7,115 prisoners, 18 guns, and piles of equipment.

On 23 May a new phase commenced, the attack of the Third Army on the Carso. Here the Italian left wing made little progress, while the right and centre broke the enemy lines from Castagnevizza to the sea, penetrated them and surrounded the two halves, passed Lukatic, captured Hudi Log and Flondar, and certain units pressed as far as San Giovanni and Medeazza. Some Austrian prisoners captured in one day vouched for the success of the advance, which continued until the first week in June. The total of Austrian losses had been 23,680 prisoners and 38 guns. However, the Austrians were in no mood for surrender. They launched counter-attacks, particularly on the Vodice, Mt Santo, and at San Marco, where as many as ten took place.

A very strong Austrian counter-offensive broke out on 4 June in the sector from Faiti to the sea, which lasted with terrific fighting for three days. To the left and the centre, after various setbacks and followed by a firm stand, the Italian line could not be moved and remained between Versic and Jamiano. To the right, however, Italian troops were obliged to give way. The fighting had been very bitter. Austrian General Pitreich wrote:

> Day and night, particularly on the Carso front, furious hand to hand fights took place. If the obstinacy with which the enemy tried, with repeated efforts, to obtain its objectives both at point 652 of Mount Santo (that is to say Vodice) and in the Vippacco zone caused stupefaction, on the other hand the massed attacks against the solid defence of the Comen Plateau, appeared to be of a daring madness.

The ferocity of the Italian attacks explains the heavy losses: 157,000 against 80,000 Austrians. It must not be forgotten that during the tenth Battle of the Isonzo, the Austrians (to distract attention) had also attacked in the Val Sugana, on the Asiago plateau, on the Pasubio, and on Civaron, but had everywhere been repulsed.

Whilst General Cadorna prepared new efforts on the Isonzo, the Italians made a move to improve their positions on the Asiago plateau, as they had done in October 1916 on the Pasubio. Cadorna ordered an action to break the enemy front on the Ortigora and so carry their occupation to the back of Cima

A First World War military artist has recorded a splendid impression of an Alpini company forcing a frontier pass in the Carnic Alps.

Portale-Mt Meatta and to the heights of Mt Mosciagh-Mt Rasta. The attack, carried out by four divisions of infantry and Alpini and supported by a heavy mass of artillery, commenced on 10 June and was successful on the right during the first few days. Having taken the Angella Pass and, after bitter fighting, various heights of the Ortigora, the Italians finally captured the summit of that mountain. The left wing did not succeed in gaining its objectives.

However, on 25 June the Austrians, having hurriedly called up reinforcements that were put under the command of one of Austria's best commanders—General Goiginger—started a strong counter-offensive. Pitreich wrote that

'The Italians had suffered such heavy losses along the entire front that they were unable to profit by the break in the line'. After an epic battle nearly all the positions, won by the Italians with so much loss of blood, were retaken by the Austrians or evacuated by the Italians (29 June). Thus, after nineteen days, painful failure came to an end—important operations that had cost the Italians 26,000 men and about half that amount to the Austrians.

In July 1917 the Allies met in Paris to consider a situation that was far from satisfactory. The French army, after its horrendous losses (especially at Verdun) was reluctant to take the offensive. Marshal Pétain continued to say, 'I

Above *An Italian soldier excavates a snow gallery which will provide shelter with some warmth and comfort amongst the snow-clad Alpine peaks.*

Below *Italian troops man-handle an artillery gun which has been shrouded in protective tarpaulin.*

am waiting for the Americans'. Imperial Russia was virtually out of the fight, although Kerensky did his best to infuse new energy into the Russian soldiers. The Allied Command once again put pressure on the Italians to keep up the attack, a policy that suited at least one Italian— General Cadorna—who was reluctant to give up the fight until Italy's goals, for which the young nation had entered the war, had been achieved. Thus commenced the eleventh Battle of the Isonzo, otherwise known as the Battle of Bainsizza, which lasted from 18 August to 15 September 1917.

The Italian Supreme Command intended to carry out this offensive with the maximum forces available, by reducing the strength of their units on the Trentino front to the indispensable minimum, and by gathering on the Isonzo front 53 divisions and 3,600 guns (2,400 of which were of medium calibre), besides the mortars—the strongest force to be assembled by the Italians up to that time in the war. The Second Army (General Capello) comprised 26 divisions and a half, a cavalry division, and 2,366 guns. The Third Army (the Duke of Aosta) comprised 18 divisions and 1,200 guns. Supreme Command held in reserve six divisions and a half, besides a division and half of cavalry. The two Italian armies numbered 304 battalions against the Austrian Fifth Army's 258. The Austrians succeeded in obtaining at least three divisions from the Eastern Front, the Fifth Army being composed of 23 divisions in all. The Isonzo defences were increased: a triple line of trenches went from Telmino to Gorizia, one at the bottom, one half way up, and one on the heights of Kuk (not to be confused with the Kuk captured by the Italians in May), of the Jelenik, and of Kobilek. The greatest concentration of Austrian forces was on the Carso, on Mt Hermada— Austria's last great stonghold in front of Trieste.

On 17 August a strong bombardment, assisted by monitors of the Italian navy and about 90 guns on loan from the Allies, preceded the attack. The XIII Infantry Corps (General Diaz) and XII Infantry Corps (General Sailer) of the Third Army succeeded in advancing towards Selo and San Giovanni. The first corps, fighting fiercely, were able on the following days to advance beyond Versic Korite and Selo to reach the valley of Brestoviza. The second corps reached San Giovanni, capturing a great number of Austrian prisoners. The left wing of the army, however, had difficulty in advancing beyond Faiti, and the enemy positions were gained and lost several times. Any progress made was strongly opposed. The Austrians made repeated and effective counter-attacks from 4 September onwards: in the end the right of the Third Army had lost the greater part of the advantages gained during the first few days. Operations on the Third Army front on the Carso were suspended, the main effort now being absorbed by the Second Army, which was to capture the Bainsizza plateau, operating from the Gorizia area.

Here on 17 August a really formidable bombardment commenced, but it was not always sufficient to silence the Austrian machine-guns, many of which were placed in caves. It so happened that only six among fourteen of the bridges thrown against the Isonzo during the night—between Antrovo and Doblar—were completed and able to be used. This held up and complicated the movement of the left wing towards Lom, but not that of the other divisions that, having broken through the first enemy line, advanced decisively towards their objectives. The XXIV Corps (General Caviglia), having occupied the Crest Fratta-Semmer, advanced especially vigorously on the third enemy line. On 20 August the manoeuvre succeeded. The strongholds of Kuk 711 and Jelenic were occupied by means of frontal and flank attacks, and on 23 August so were the last centres of enemy resistance. Oscedric and Kobilek also fell, whilst on the right wing, on the 24 August, the long-contested Mt Santo was captured.

However, progress on this plateau— without roads, without resources—exhausted the Italian troops, who lacked provisions and sometimes even water. It prevented the artillery from advancing and the transport of munitions from following on. So after having penetrated a few miles, the push was held up against the new Austrian positions that had been hastily reinforced. From 25 August onwards, the Isonzo offensive became a battle of minor actions. The Italian Supreme Command ordered the offensive of the Second Army to cease, with the exception of concentrating an attack in the Gorizia area, and with great precision on San Gabriele. Here an even stronger mass of artillery than before was concentrated, and the battle lasted from 4 to 10 September. An Austrian officer wrote of the San Gabriele that it was 'a kind of Moloch which swallows a regiment every three of four days and—even if we do not confess it—changes ownership daily'.

G.M. Trevelyan, in his *Scenes from Italy's War,* wrote:

> During the first half of September 1917 San Gabriele was a terrifying shambles, continually changing hands under the concentrated fire of two masses of artillery, both in full efficiency. Division after division were thrown into the fray on both sides to fight for the capture of that natural fortress. The losses were terrifying, as both attackers and defenders were implacable. In the end the summit remained divided between two heroic armies.

On 15 September a short, sharp fight on the Bainsizza ended the great offensive. The Italian losses numbered 166,000, including 18,000 missing or prisoners of war. The Austrian losses were not given although the Italians claimed 30,000 Austrian prisoners.

The German General, von Ludendorff, summed up the Bainsizza battle:

> At the end of August, the Eleventh Battle of the Isonzo had begun on a front of 70 kilometres and proved successful for the Italians. Early in September the fighting was continued with determination. The Italians were again successful. The Austro-Hungarian armies had indeed held their ground, but

their losses on the Carso Plateau had been so heavy and they were so shaken that the responsible military and political authorities of the Dual Monarchy were convinced that they would not be able to stand a continuation of the battle and a twelfth attack on the Isonzo. The Austrian Army on the Italian front needed a stiffening by German troops.

As early as 26 August 1917, the Austrian Emperor-King Charles had written to the German Kaiser, asking for help. The idea of facing or conducting another Isonzo offensive with Austro-Hungarian troops alone no longer seemed feasible to the Central Powers. The 23 divisions on the Julian front with 1,800 guns were reinforced by 14 more—7 German and 7 Austrian, with 1,000 guns (800 of them German), and the Plezzo-Tolmino sector was selected as the line to attack. The spearhead force consisted of eight Austrian and seven German divisions, with a total strength of 168 battalions corresponding to 24 Italian battalions. The force assigned to the offensive constituted the Fourteenth Army, commanded by the German General von Below, and was divided into four groups, namely the Krauss group (three Austrian divisions deployed from Mt Rombon to Mt Nero), the Stein group (one Austrian and three German divisions, from Tolmino to the Idria), the Scotti group (one Austrian and one German division, on the Lom plateau), and four divisions in reserve. The Tenth Austrian Army (General Krobatin) in the Carnia, and the Second Isonzo Army (General Henriquez) —forming part of the Borovich Army group opposite the northern edge of the Bainsizza plateau—were to support the action of von Below's force.

The objective of the offensive, as set forth in the operations order of the Fourteenth Army Command, was 'to drive the enemy from the Carso area, unfavourable for defence, and beyond the Tagliamento, and to attain the Gemona-Cividale line'. To secure this objective it was necessary to gain absolute possession of the Plezzo-Tolmino and Caporetto areas. The Mt Maggiore-Mt Matajur-Mt San Martino-Mt

Kuk-Mt Globocak line had therefore to be conquered as the first objective by means of an advance, and the pressure continued in a southwesterly direction as far as the Gemona-Tarcento-Cividale line, and if possible the Tagliamento. At the same time, the Tenth Army was to descend from the Carnia on Gemona by the Fella valley, and the Second Isonzo Army was to attack the heights between the Isonzo and the Judrio, surmount Mt Kolovrat, and try to capture Mt Korado. General Krafft von Delmensinger was not satisfied with these objectives, suggesting that at least the Adige line should be attained.

The date of the operation, known as the twelfth Battle of the Isonzo or the Battle of Caporetto, was adjourned several times on account of the inclement weather. It was to commence not with the usual prolonged bombardment that would reveal to the Italians where the real attack was to take place, but with a short and extremely intense fire, followed immediately by the infantry attack between Plezzo and Selo at 08:00. The operation was to be carried out according to a method successfully practised on the Eastern Front at Riga (and later in France, in March 1918), entrusted to specially-trained assault units amply supplied with

An Italian machine-gun team fires from a well-protected position on Mount San Michele.

machine-guns, hand grenades, bomb-throwers, and flame-throwers. As soon as the break-through had been effected by the storm troopers, the infantry was to rush forward, penetrating the enemy positions in small detachments, escorted by light artillery and machine-guns mounted on motor lorries. In the mountain zones, the advance was to be prefer-

Opposite *Both the young and the old serving with an Austrian militia unit pose for a photographer by the wayside in the Alpine frontier region.*

Below *An Italian infantry column wends its way across a snow-carpeted valley prior to another foray on to the high ground.*

ably conducted along the high roads, valleys, and gaps in the terrain, without at first troubling to gain control of the heights as this would involve delays and heavy losses, whereas the enemy positions on the mountain tops could be subsequently outflanked and turned. The main object was to gain possession of the chief bulwarks of the defence and the vital points of the lines of communication so as to shatter the enemy's nervous system. The method was quite new on the Italian front, and the defenders were wholly unprepared for it. This explains at least in part the Austro-Germans' swift and almost incredible success.

The Italians were not unaware of these preparations. By 6 October, 43 enemy divisions had been identified including the Bavarian Alpenkorps. Any idea of an Italian offensive was abandoned, and preparations were made to meet a hostile onslaught. The threatened area was held by General Capello's Second Army, deployed thus: IV Corps (General Cavaciocchi) from Plezzo to Costa Raunza opposite Tolmino, with three divisions in the front line, plus several battalions of Alpini and Bersaglieri, and one division, in reserve; XXVII Corps (General Badoglio) from Costa Raunza to Kal on the Bainsizza plateau, with four divisions, one of which, the 19th, was about equal to an army corps. The southern sector of the Second Army zone, as far as the Vippacco, was entrusted to XXIV Corps (General Caviglia), II Corps (General Caviglia), II Corps (General Albricci), VI Corps (General Lombardi)—11 divisions all told. General Capello thus disposed of 9 corps (25 divisions), actually 351 battalions of which 224 were in the front line.

At 08:00 on 24 October, after the explosion of two huge mines on Mts Rosso and Mrzli, the infantry of the Fourteenth Austro-German army made their assault. General Krauss, commanding the forces in the Plezzo sector, drove ahead with the Saga defile as his first objective, but he also meant to capture the Stol as well, as he believed that if that position were captured, the Italians would be forced to

Above *An Italian blockhouse which appears to have been subjected to severe bombardment.*

Left *These Italian observers perched precariously on an Alpine mountain peak are exposed to the full fury of the elements.*

evacuate the whole front. By 09:30 the Italian IV Corps' front was broken through in its central sector at Fornace, and the attackers advanced along the bottom of the valley but were at first held up at Saga. The lateral sector of the Rombon and Cezsoca resisted on the first lines for a while, but on being threatened by the advance along the valley, fell back. Before early afternoon, the Austro-German forces had also broken through the 43rd Division's front and spread into the Za Kraju basin. On the right of the division, the attackers took Peak 2133 north of Mt Nero, and appeared in the Kazliak area. The 46th Division was attacked by the 50th Austrian and the 12th German Divisions.

General Stein succeeded in breaking through between the two Italian corps positions, overwhelming a battalion of the 19th (Napoli) Division. The Italian line was thus punctured between Mrzli and the river. Von Lequis's 12th German Division, exploiting this success, opened a passage to the right bank of the river, thus breaking through before noon the first line of defence on the left of the Isonzo near Gabrije. Soon after it overcame the second line near Seliscc. By mid-afternoon, the German division captured Caporetto (in German, Karfreit), a village whose name was given to the whole battle and that has found its way into the annals of military history. The same day the Germans swept over the Starjiskin-Staroselo-Matajur line, and by evening IV Corps' front extended from Valle Uccea to Robic by Mt Stol, Potoki, and San Volario.

In the meantime, the Alpenkorps (von Berrer's group) attacked the Italian positions directly opposite Tolmino. By a skilfully-conducted advance it overcame the first lines, and through the gap thus created the 12th German Division was able to push forward up both banks of the river. The valley being full of mist, some of the Italian units on the heights to the right of it did not even see the enemy below, and consequently took no action to stop them. The Alpenkorps, advancing from Volzana (west of Tolmino), now attacked the Kolovrat, held by part of the Italian 19th Division. The Berrer and the Scotti groups pushed on to the left between S. Maria and S. Lucia, and between S. Lucia and Doblar towards Monte Jeza and the ridge separating the Isonzo from the Judrio Valley and dominating both—with the intention of descending the Isonzo while the Stein group was marching upstream.

On 25 October the Second Army Command informed Cadorna that the breakthrough on the IV Corps' front had caused the loss of all its positions east of the Isonzo, that the enemy were advancing on the Creda and attacking the Stol with success, and pressing on Luico. The Stol was held by the Alpini, who had evaded capture at Plezzo and on Mt Nero and who, when their ammunition ran out, defended themselves with stones. Now, however, they found themselves surrounded and overwhelmed. Some of them managed to break through the Austro-German forces and reach Bergogna on the Natisone. But the loss of the position was a serious blow for the Italians. The Potenza Brigade put up a gallant fight in the defile between Mts Matajar and Mia, but Italian infantry sent up to defend a part of the Matajur arrived late in the day, not knowing what to do, and was unable to hold out.

On 26 October Mts Maggiore and Juanez—both bulwarks of a defended line—fell, and General Cadorna ordered the whole of the Second Army to fall back on the Tagliamento. The withdrawal was to commence from the northwest, the Carnia force was to resist at Chiusaforte at the confluence of the Val Raccolana and Val Fella, and the Fourth Army was to retreat from the Cadore on to other lines of resistance, eventually taking over Mt Grappa from the First Army. For the first time since the beginning of the war on the Isonzo front, the enemy was on Italian soil. Early on 27 October, the Italian Commander-in-Chief ordered the withdrawal of the Third Army. It was a painful decision as the Duke of Aosta's army was still undefeated, but it had to be taken as the Third Army's lines of communication were threatened, and the whole force was in danger of being lost. Before it evacuated the Isonzo area, the plain had to be flooded in order to delay the Austro-German advance.

Vast masses of men, horses, guns, and transport of all kinds now began to pour across the Friuli plain towards the Tagliamento. Many units marched in good order, maintaining discipline and holding on to their arms and equipment. Others were dispirited and became stragglers. With these troops were hordes of civilians—men, women, and children—fleeing before an enemy who committed widespread

atrocities. On 29 October the Third Army succeeded in getting across the Isonzo but the
Austro-German forces overwhelmed units of the
Italian VII Corps on the Torre line between Solt
and Beivara, and that same day entered Udine
early in the afternoon, from whence the Italian
Commando Supremo and the Second Army
Command had withdrawn only a few hours
previously. During the occupation of Udine,
General von Berrer was killed by an Italian
carabinier as he was driving into the town in
his car.

Concerned by the plight of the Italian
army, the British and French governments
offered military assistance to Italy. The very day
of the breakthrough at Caporetto, General
Delmé-Radcliffe, head of the British Military
Mission at the Commando Supremo, had
announced British help. The offer was con-
firmed by the two Allied authorities (Britain and
France) who, a month earlier—not believing in
the coming Austro-German offensive—had
withdrawn most of the heavy guns they had sent
out as soon as General Cadorna decided not
to launch a new offensive on his front. On the
morning of 30 October, General Foch arrived
from the Western Front at Treviso, where the
Commando Supremo had been transferred, to
discuss the situation with General Cadorna.
The French commander made many useful
suggestions but it was Cadorna's and not Foch's
decision that the Italian army would fall back
over the River Tagliamento and establish a
defence line on the Piave River. In all, five British and six French divisions arrived in Italy
before the end of the year, but made no impact
on the immediate situation.

Above right *The mule as a beast of burden was a familiar
sight in the mountain war in Italy, 1915-18. This party with
a mule making its way slowly along a mountain roadway
includes a member of the American Expeditionary Force.*

Right *These Italian infantrymen defending a base area are
obviously under heavy attack by an enemy force.*

On 30 October, while masses of Italian troops were slowly crossing the Tagliamento, the Austro-German forces entered San Daniele, north west of Udine, constituting a menace to the Pinzano and Codropo bridges to the north of the line of retreat. The Bologna Brigade and other infantry units tried to hold up the advance and succeeded for a time, but at 14:00 General Agliardi, who was in command, ordered the three Codroipo bridges to be blown up. It was a premature measure, and a considerable number of men and batteries remaining on the left bank fell into the hands of the advancing troops, including a large number of heavy and medium guns that had been withdrawn in the face of incredible transport difficulties from the Bainsizza. Large Italian forces were now deployed along the right bank of the Tagliamento opposite the Austrians and Germans on the left. But Cadorna knew that that river offered no real security and that the final battle for Italy must be fought on the Piave.

There were now signs that the Austro-German advance was beginning to slow down. Field Marshal Borovic had let the Italian Third Army slip through his fingers. In truth, the terrible fighting on the Carso had broken the spirit of his forces, as well as that of the Italians. In his attempt to advance in a north-westerly direction with his Austrian army group, he had become entangled with the Fourteenth Army, much to the annoyance of von Below. Italian rearguard actions involving the cavalry proved effective in causing delays in the advance, the invaders also being hampered by bridges that had been demolished. By 30 October, the Third Army was reaching the Tagliamento, after heroic acts of seamanship by the Italian navy had helped many units to cross the flooding waters of the Isonzo.

The retreat towards the Piave was now proceeding in an orderly manner. Rearguard actions on the Tagliamento and the Livenza were well fought by units of all arms. Columns of men and transport, which before the Tagliamento had marched in confusion, spread

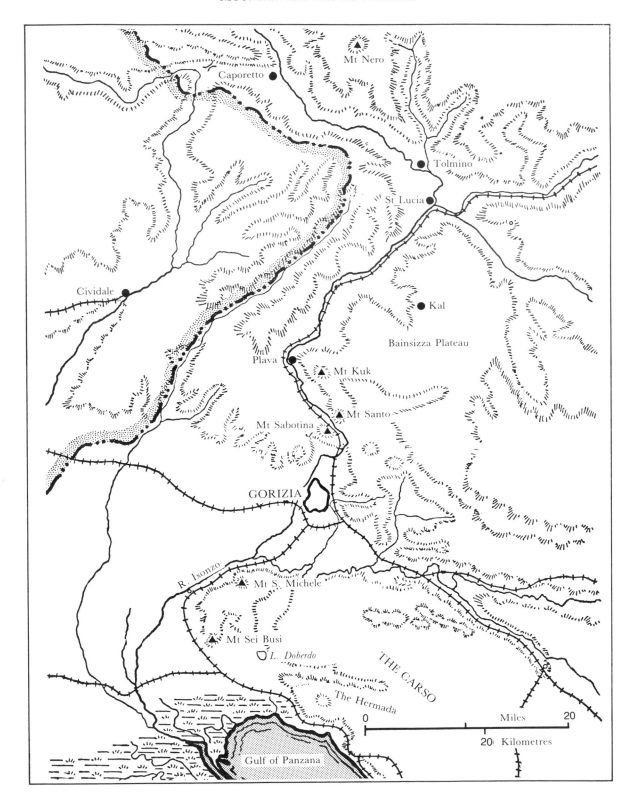

Mt Nero

Caporetto

Tolmino

St Lucia

Cividale

Kal

Bainsizza Plateau

Plava

Mt Kuk

Mt Santo

Mt Sabotina

GORIZIA

R. Isonzo

Mt S. Michele

Mt Sei Busi

L. Doberdo

THE CARSO

The Hermada

0   Miles   20

20   Kilometres

Gulf of Panzana

out to the right and left of the main body, after crossing the river, proceeding to rejoin it. Many disbanded brigades were rapidly reformed. A notice board would be put up by the roadside with the name of this or that unit, and soon the scattered men belonging to it would stop to wait for their comrades. Even in the broken Second Army, many units retained their formation and spirit. Some of its detachments held up an enemy force for twelve hours on the Mauria Pass between the upper Tagliamento and the upper Piave valleys. At the beginning of November, the Belluno Alpine Battalion, which had suffered dreadful losses on the Stol, reached its depot headquarters at Belluno. The fighting in this mountain area held back the Austro-German forces, hampering the liaison between Krobatin's forces and Conrad's, and thus helped the orderly retreat of the Italian Fourth Army from the Cadore.

By 7 November the greater part of the Third Army, after crossing the Monticano and the Livenza, reached and crossed the Piave. The withdrawal of the Fourth Army was also going ahead—it had been ordered at first to defend the pass at Serravalle, near Vittorio, but this was now no longer necessary as that area was to be evacuated. At Longarone to the north of Belluno on 9 November, however, the Austrians

Left The Isonzo Front: The River Isonzo was the scene of no fewer than 12 major battles, which gained little ground for either side in the three-year campaign.

and Germans did get across from the Carnia, by the Vajont valley, and intercepted the retreat of a large column of Fourth Army troops. The Italians fought hard to cut their way through on 10 November, but only a small portion succeeded in getting away over the mountains; the rest, some 10,000 in all, were captured. General Di Giorgio's Special Corps, which had been formed to absorb straggler units, had fought a fierce rearguard action on 6 November, and now—having fulfilled its mission—followed the other forces and crossed the Piave.

The Piave line was now held by fairly numerous Italian forces, and on the Grappa massif between the Piave and Brenta, positions were being hurriedly completed so as to bar the access to the plain between the two rivers. On 7 November, General Cadorna had issued his impassioned appeal to his armies to resist to the last man. 'We are inflexibly determined,' he concluded, 'on the new positions from the Piave to the Stelvio: the honour and the life of Italy are being defended; let every fighter know what is the cry, the command issuing from the conscience of every Italian—to die, not to retreat!' These were the General's last words as Commander-in-Chief. On 8 November he was informed that he had been superseded, and on the following day he handed over his command to General Armando Diaz, who had been appointed to succeed him. The end of the twelfth Battle of the Isonzo-Caporetto is officially given as 9 November.

CHAPTER 7
THE MOUNTAIN WAR 1918

The situation in which the Allies found themselves at the beginning of 1918 was one of great anxiety. Both the French and British forces had suffered appalling losses during the course of 1917 and were in no mood to plan a major offensive. The Russian, Serbian, and Romanian armies were out of action, and the few divisions that had arrived from America were still only partly trained. The greater part of them were not to arrive until the summer. On 21 February the Germans launched a violent attack in Picardy. The British army, experiencing for the first time the German tactics already applied on the Italian front, were dangerously driven back. Fortunately, the arrival on the scene of forty French divisions prevented a more decisive defeat. On 27 May the same tactics swept the French back from the Chemin des Dames and brought the Germans within 37 miles (59 km) of Paris. Six of the eleven British and French divisions were recalled from the Italian zone of war, and Italy sent to France two divisions of the Second Army and about 60,000 labourers.

The overwhelming shock of the Caporetto disaster did not produce the effect on the Italians the Austro-German forces had calculated. Instead of a complete breakdown of the Italian army and an internal revolution, the whole nation pulled itself together, and the army settled down grimly to the task of holding the new line and saving the country. General Diaz, who was impervious to political pressures, calmly surveyed the military situation. The

reorganization of Italian forces proceeded, in spite of enemy pressure, and the new line was gradually strengthened. From the Stelvio to the Asiago plateau it was practically unchanged; thence it cut across the Grappa massif, descended on to the Piave at Pederobba, and followed the course of this river to the sea. But on the Asiago plateau and on the Grappa it was not yet stabilized. At the turn of the year the Italian III Corps and the First Army were ranged from the Stelvio to the Brenta—a mass of 400,000 men—and were ready to fight. The Third and Fourth Armies, about 300,000 men utterly exhausted by the fighting retreat, were stationed from the Brenta to the sea.

In the remaining winter months, the Italians fought a 'battle of recovery'. The advanced positions at Gallio and on Mt Ferragh were lost to the Austrians. The Pisa and Toscana Brigades were forced back somewhat, but they counter-attacked and regained the lost ground. In the Grappa area the Austrians were more successful and, attacking in greatly-superior numbers between 15 and 17 March, they captured the northern peaks of the massif, Mts Tomatico and Roncone, and later Mts Prassolan and Cornella, and occupied the Quero gorge, forcing the Como Brigade, after a desperate resistance, back to Mt Tomba and Monfenera, and the village of Fener. On the Piave, the Silesian Division was repulsed at Vidor. Another Austrian force succeeded in getting across the river at the loop near Zenson but failed to exploit their success. But at Fagaré the Novara and 3rd Bersaglieri Brigades decisively defeated the Austrians, and the Italians gradually regained control of the situation.

Having failed on the Piave, the Austrians delivered further blows on the Grappa and Asiago sectors. Di Giorgio's Italian XXVII Corps fought desperately on the blood-stained heights of the Grappa. The struggle was with rifle and bayonet, hand grenades and stones, anything that might serve to hold up the oncoming enemy tide, and the Italians used corpses as barricades. Mt Fontenasecca was lost. On Monfenera the 9th Mountain Artillery Group, placed in a very advanced position, had all its guns destroyed or buried in landslides produced by enemy shells, nearly all its men killed or wounded, until its commander, Captain Di Rocco, led a bayonet charge of the few survivors

An artist's impression of an Alpini regiment as it approaches the foothills of Mount Nero. The officers standing by the small, tented encampment observe the work of Italian artillery bombarding the mountainside.

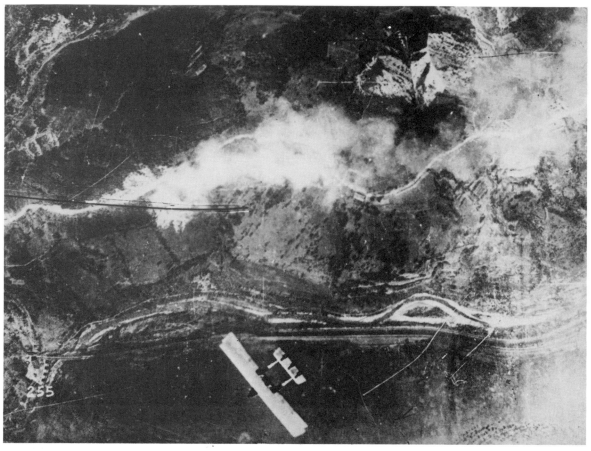

An Italian Caproni Ca 3 biplane aircraft carries out a bombing mission on an Austrian supply route.

right on to the Austrian machine-guns. Mt Tomba was the most vulnerable point in the Grappa area, with its slow eminences and its valleys' ease of access. Desperate engagements were fought on its slopes, and the best Austrian and German units were hurled into the deadly mêlée. Part of Tomba was lost. The summit of Pertica was taken, retaken and lost again, in spite of the magnificent efforts of the Monte Baldo Alpini Battalion. When the Basilicata Brigade was relieved on Mt Tomba one of its regiments had only 400 survivors.

As the winter progressed, the main focus of Austro-German attacks was on Grappa and the surrounding mountains. Strong Austrian and German forces assaulted one mountain stronghold after the other. At the defence of Mt Valbella by the Italian Feltre Battalion, officers' servants, cooks, and telephone operators all threw themselves into the battle and suffered heavy casualties. In spite of many setbacks, the Italians resisted enemy attacks with great determination along the entire front. British units experienced their first taste of mountain warfare on the Montello sector. The winter 'battle of recovery' for the Italians came to an end. Even Marshal von Hindenburg realized that the Austro-German forces would be unable to secure enough Alpine positions to present a serious threat to the Piave line. The Grappa-Piave line was, as one Italian general wrote, 'a definite accomplished fact, decisive for our war and for

76

the general war'.

With the advent of better weather the opposing armies sized each other up on the Piave. The Allied forces comprised the Italian Third Army, the Eighth Army (the reconstituted Second Army), and the Fourth Army, as well as the Sixth Army (which included the British XIV Corps and the French XII Corps), the First Army and the Seventh Army. The Ninth Army (formerly the Fifth) was in reserve. The Austro-Hungarian armies were the Fifth (or the Isonzo) Army and the Sixth under Borovic, the Tenth and Eleventh under Conrad. The Archduke Eugene was the Commander-in-Chief and General Arz his Chief of Staff. The Austrians still believed that the Italian troops were morally inferior to their own, and regarded the Italian positions between the Astico and the Brenta as extremely precarious. Field-Marshal Conrad, who was a specialist on that sector, said that the situation of the Italian army was that of a shipwrecked mariner clinging to his hands with a spar, and that by cutting off his fingers with a hatchet he would be forced to sink into the depths.

The Austro-Hungarian forces (the Germans had by this time been withdrawn from the Italian front) launched their assault on 15 June 1918. Three operations were given high-sounding names: that on the Altipiani was called the 'Radetzky Offensive', the one on the Piave the 'Albrecht Operation', and the attack on the Tonale Pass the 'Avalanche Action'. The Austrians, whose offensive spirit was very high, were promised much loot in the form of 'good food and abundant booty'. General Diaz, on the other hand, had his own plans for a large-scale offensive. He wanted to attack from the Altipiani towards the Val Sugana, and had communicated his scheme to the Allies. But on 28 May he informed the French and British Commands in France that in view of the coming enemy operations he would not launch his own attack, and would concentrate on defensive preparations instead.

The objective of the main attack in the

These mountainside huts provided the Alpini with great comfort compared with the snow holes and galleries excavated at the higher levels.

mountain area was to break through the Italian lines on the right between the Val d'Assa and the Val Franzele, and descend on the Thiene by the Val Canaglia and on to Bassano by the Val Frenzela. On the left it was to overcome the southern edge of Mt Grappa and turn the Italian position on the Piave. In the first onslaught, the troops of the Austrian Eleventh Army succeeded in the Altipiani area in penetrating into the sectors held by the British forces near Perghele and south of Roncalto, but they were repulsed by a counter-attack in which the French also took part. Further south the enemy gained some ground near Cesuna, but lost it in a counter-attack, in which the artillery of X Corps helped, and fell back leaving 1,000 prisoners and seven guns behind. In the centre the enemy forced the French to evacuate the Capitello Pennar salient and occupied it, but were unable to emerge from it in spite of repeated attempts, and in the afternoon the 78th French Regiment drove them out again, taking 500 prisoners.

The fighting on the right was even more violent. The Austro-Hungarians, after having demolished by gunfire the defences of Valbella, Col del Rosso, and Col d'Echele, held by the Italian XIII Corps, penetrated into the lines as far as Cima Echer and Busa del Termine, closing the Val Chiama. But under the vigorous counter-attacks of the Pinerolo and Lecce Brigades they were slowly driven back, retaining only Col del Rosso and Col d'Echele. On Grappa, held by De Bono's IX Corps, Conrad's forces at first registered some successes. The plan, as in the previous autumn, was to turn the flanks of the main massif by capturing the positions east and west of it—Val Brenta on one side, the Solaroli, Mt Tomba and Monfenera on the other—so as to debouch on to the Piave near Pederobba. If Grappa fell the whole defensive system between the Piave and the Brenta would collapse, and with it that of the Altipiani—and the Piave armies themselves, if threatened in the rear, would be forced to fall back, even if undefeated, as had happened to

the Third Army after Caporetto.

At the first onslaught the enemy captured the Col del Miglio, Col Feniglio, and Col Moschin, the key positions, and threatened Col Raniero, the wing support of the line of chief resistance. Only on the Asolone did the 18th Division and the Bari Brigade hold their own. Further east the enemy (helped by the mist) had also advanced wresting Mts Pertica and Coston from the VI Corps. But the latter, in spite of its inferior strength, prevented them from advancing further. Infantry and gunners fought together. The field guns had to be abandoned but the breaches and sights were first removed. The mountain batteries continued to fire until the Austrians were actually among the guns and even then the gunners managed to withdraw their guns on to another line on the slope of the Osteria della Cibera, whence they opened fire again.

On the Solaroli, Valderoa, Coston Valderoa, Val Calcino, and Col dell'Orso, the most violent attacks were delivered, and in spite of the gallant defence put up by the Como and Ravenna Brigades (XVIII Corps), the northern part of the salient was lost. However, the central sector held out, and at the Porte di Salton a battalion of the 120th Regiment, although surrounded, defended desperately. The Austrians tried to complete their conquest of the Solaroli by calling up the 20th and 48th Divisions, but even with these reinforcements they failed to achieve any definite success. The left wing of the Grappa Army had been broken through to a depth of about a mile, on the right there was danger of a turning movement, and in the centre the XVIII Corps was forced to attempt a counter-attack, whatever the conditions on its right and left, as a retreat would have been extremely difficult on account of the precipitous nature of the ground to its rear.

The reserves promised to the Grappa army were not forthcoming, as they had been diverted to the Piave sector where the situation at that moment looked even more alarming. But its own units counter-attacked, and soon the action of VI Corps proved successful. An Italian infantry battalion reconquered Peak 1503 east of the Asolone, while part of the assault battalion ascended Val Damon and swept up the enemy infiltrations. The gunners took part in the action and recaptured their lost guns. The Austrians thus lost ground they had gained—except the important Peak 1490. The Ravenna Brigade, which had recaptured Peak 1671, failed on Peak 1676 of the Solaroli. A battalion of the 119th Regiment (XVIII Corps) and units of the 120th counter-attacked towards the Porte di Salton and took 200 prisoners, recaptured Peaks 1292 and 1240, and attacked Mt Spinoncia. Here they were held up and eventually forced back. On the Altipiani and the Grappa generally, the Austrians gained the upper hand.

As General Giardino, Commander of the

Two scenes from the three-year war fought over the possession of desolate mountain fastnesses. The Italian troops were constantly on the move to search out the enemy. The Alpini with the shrouded snow apparel were known as 'sky companies' and their ski tracks were to be found in the remotest Alpine areas.

Grappa army, wrote:

> at 3 a.m. on the 15th the whirlwind burst on the Grappa, at 10 all was smashed up, three of the last key positions were lost, the Austrians looked down on Bassano; the soldiers of the Grappa, without assistance, worn out, decimated, dashed forward again and again to the attack; the giant shook his leonine mane and hurled his assailants far away and broke them up. In twenty-four hours all was over and we could think of the Piave as inviolate.

A gigantic reversal in fortune had in fact taken place. The Austro-Hungarian offensive had met with such a check on this sector that no single division was capable of renewing the attack. The attackers had lost 347 officers and 7,095 men had been killed, 1,262 officers and 12,484 men were wounded, and 171 officers and 13,667 men were either prisoners or missing.

On the Piave, Borovic aimed at securing possession of the whole of the Montello hill, which dominates that tract of the river from the right bank, and then deploying in the plain beyond in an area covered with a network of roads. Other forces were to cross near Salettuol in the northern part of the Grave di Papadopoli island. Thus a broad and powerful bridgehead would be created enabling the reserves to cross over and gain possession of the Montebelluna-Treviso railway. The Austrians attempted to effect a junction between the 17th Division (XXIV Corps) on the Montello and the 33rd (XVI Corps) advancing from the Grave di Papadopoli. But the southward movement of the 17th was held up by the Italian 50th near Giavera and the Abbazia di Nervesa, the 48th southeast of the Montello and the 79th Engineer Battalion, while the 31st Division

The snow and ice lingers in this bleak scene from the mountain war.

attacked the troops of the Austrian XVI Corps. Thus a junction was not achieved.

Meanwhile, Austrian troops had succeeded in crossing the Piave further downstream and secured a footing on the opposite bank between Candelà and Capo Sile. But they were unable to consolidate their gain and fan outwards. The Caserta Brigade contained a part of the enemy forces between Candelà and San Bartolomeo, while the Casenza and Potenza Brigades and units of the Italian Third Army held up the Austrian VII and XIII Corps thus preventing the link-up of the two bridgeheads. The Italian 25th Division firmly held the ground between the two Austrian corps (between Zenson and Croce). Thus, in both the Montello area and on the lower Piave, the two attempts at pincer-like operations failed and all efforts to estab lish a connection between the two main areas occupied by the Austrians across the river failed. Borovic was ordered to hold the Montello area at all costs to facilitate the passage of the rest of the Isonzo army across the river. He could expect no help from the Austrian forces on the Altipiani-Grappe sector.

In the afternoon of 16 June, Italian counter-attacks were delivered on the Montello. The Palermo and Barletta Brigades and the 48th and 50th Divisions reconquered some of the lost ground, as well as many of the guns previously lost. On the lower Piave, the Italian Third Army also counter-attacked and recaptured Fagarè, Bocca di Collalto, and La Fossa, while the Sassari Brigade and four Bersaglieri cyclist battalions regained the Croce position. The Austrian High Command sent up further reinforcements, and later the Fagorè and Musile bridgeheads were extended slightly. On 17 June they were linked up by means of counter-attacks from Zenson and Gorfo. On the same day the Austrians also counter-attacked on the Montello and extended their occupation as far as the railway between San Mauro and San Andree, but failed to reach the Ponti della Priula owing to counter-attacks of units of the Aquila Brigade.

On 17 June the Piave began to flood and this added greatly to the difficulty of supplying the two Austrian forces across the river, which were shortly cut off from each other. On 18 June, when the waters were at their height, the Austrians began to admit failure. On the next day the Italians counter-attacked on the Montello, and Borovic, realizing that a disaster was imminent, reported accordingly to the Emperor-King, who had already taken the precaution of shifting his quarters back to Spilimbergo on the Tagliamento. The Austrians realized that their great Piave offensive had little chance of succeeding but the battle in the bridgeheads continued to rage throughout 20 June without decisive results. On the lower Piave the Austrians threw further reserves across the river, and drove the Italians from the Fossalta-Caseria-Capo d'Argine line but failed to advance any further. Gradually, the Austrian pressure was felt to be relaxing and the Italians concentrated on using their artillery to pound the opposing forces. In eight days of epic fighting the Italians at last proved that they were in control of their campaign against the Austro-Hungarian Empire. From 24 to 25 June, the Italian Third Army cleared the Austrian bridge-heads across the Piave.

General Diaz began preparing for a general offensive once the Battle of the Piave was over, but in spite of pressure from the Allies he was in no hurry to launch the attack. The Italian plan consisted of two parts. In the first phase an attack was to be launched in the Mt Grappa area between the rivers Brenta and Piave with the object of cutting the Austrian army in two and separating the forces in the Trentino from those on the left bank of the Piave. In the second phase the Austro-Hungarian forces along the Piave from the Montello to the sea were to be attacked, concentrating on the junction between the Austrian Sixth Army and the Isonzo army. It was to be the classic manoeuvre of driving a wedge through so as to split the enemy and then crush the two limbs separately.

On 25 September General Caviglia, Commander of the Italian Eighth Army that was to assault the Piave line, was summoned to the Commando Supremo and the plan was communicated to him. A day or two later General Giardino, Commander of the Fourth Army on the Grappa, was also informed of it. In the meantime, the transport of troops and *matériel* was put rapidly in motion—no light task as 21 divisions, 1,600 guns, 500 trench mortars, and 2,400,000 shells had to be moved into the battle zone. By 10 October the movement was complete. The Italian forces were distributed in the following order of battle: Seventh Army (Tassoni) from the Stelvio to Lake Garda; First Army (Giraldi) from Garda to the Melette di Gallio in the Asiago area; Sixth Army (Montuori) on the Altipiani; Fourth Army (Giardino) on the Grappa; Eighth Army (Caviglia) on the Montello; and the Third Army (the Duke of Aosta) on the lower Piave. Between the Fourth and Eighth Armies, the newly-created Twelfth Army—commanded by the French General Graziani—was inserted, and the sector between the Eighth and the Third was entrusted to the new Twelfth Army, commanded by the British General, the Earl of Cavan. The Twelfth Army comprised one French and three Italian divisions, the Tenth two British and two Italian divisions. There was another French and another British division included in armies under Italian command.

The Austro-Hungarian army was somewhat stronger in manpower, comprising 58 divisions with 724 battalions (its battalions usually consisted of four companies, instead of three, as in the Italian case) but weaker in artillery, having only 6,030 guns, and it suffered from the disadvantage of being spread out along exterior lines with a weak link between the Tirol and Piave areas. It was divided into two army groups, one in the Tirol-Trentino-Asiago areas, commanded at first by Field-Marshal Conrad, and the other along the lower Piave under Field-Marshal Borovic. Since 15 July, Conrad had been superseded by the Archduke Joseph who,

on the eve of the battle, was appointed Commander-in-Chief of the whole Italian front, General Krobatin taking over the Tirolese command.

The Battle of Vittoria Veneto, which was the name of the last great battle on the Italian front, was divided into two major operations, one in the mountainous Grappa area and the other on the Piave. The left of the area from the Roccie Anzini to Peak 1490 was held by De Bono's IX Corps, comprising the 17th and 18th Divisions, with the 21st in the army reserve; the centre was held by General Lombardi's VI Corps (15th and 30th Divisions, with the 22nd in the army reserve), extending to the slopes of the Asolone to the Croce di Valpose; and the right was held by General Montanari's XXX Corps (47th and 50th Divisions, with the 80th in the army reserve), extending to Mt Tomba. The sector between Mt Tomba and the Piave was entrusted to I Corps (General Etna), which formed part of the Twelfth Army under the French General Graziani. Most of the Italian troops on the Grappa had been on the mountain for many months and were well seasoned in combat on the precipitous heights.

The Italians launched the offensive at 03:00 on 24 October 1918, just one year after Caporetto. The infantry crept forward under devastating artillery cover across the difficult ground leading to the steep Austrian positions in Val Calcina and on the Solaroli and Valderoa slopes, which were its objectives. The gunfire increased in momentum, and when the heavies began to die down the lighter guns shrieked out their message, followed by the angry snarl of the machine-guns and the patter of rifles. Thus the infantry began their advance.

The Austro-Hungarian resistance was extremely obstinate, and while in the first impact of the assault the Bari Brigade (IX Corps) captured the Asolone, and the Basilicata Brigade the advanced positions of the Col Caprile, Austrian counter-attacks forced the Bari back from the Asolone and held up the advance of the Basilicata. In the central sector the Pesaro Brigade (VI Corps) gained possession of Mt Pertica and, on the Cremona, of the ridge between that peak and Mt Prassolan, but these gains were soon lost as a consequence of the hurricane of artillery and machine-gun fire and infantry counter-attacks. Further to the right the Lombardia and Aosta Brigades of the XXX Corps captured some positions on the Solaroli and Mt Valderoa, the Aosta securing 400 prisoners.

In the Altipiani area Italian and Allied troops engaged the Austrians in order to prevent them from sending reinforcements to the Grappa zone. A French regiment captured Mt Sisemol and took 800 prisoners; it held the captured position until evening so as to disguise the real intentions of the Italian Command. A British battalion also took 200 prisoners near Asiago. Meanwhile, another operation on an even larger scale was being attempted on the Piave. The plan was to cross the river on 24 October at the Grave di Papadopoli, where a shingly island divides the stream into two main branches. Units of Lord Cavan's Tenth Army succeeded on the night of 24 October in securing a foot-hold on the Grave, but because the waters had again risen after the heavy rains, bridges could not be thrown across until the morning of the next day. The heaviest burden of the fighting thus continued to be borne in those first days of the battle by the forces in the Grappa, and the Austrians sent four more divisions and an extra regiment to reinforce their own troops in that area, instead of to the Piave where the main Italian attack was to be launched.

Early on 25 October the Italians attacked the principal enemy strongholds in the Grappa sector—Asolone, Pertica, and the Solaroli. The attack was preceded by a terrific artillery bombardment and a vigorous infantry attack took Asolone, which was followed by an advance on to the trenches of Col della Berretta. Mt Pertica fell to the Pesaro Brigade and the 18th Assault Detachment (VI Corps) after a desperate, four-hour engagement. The 13th Moun-

tain Artillery Group smelt out the Austrian machine-guns and enabled the Italian infantry to hold the newly-captured peak. To the right of the Pertica, the Bologna Brigade and the eighth Alpini Group repeatedly attacked the Col del Cue, Col dell'Orso, and the Solaroli, but failed to make headway.

The Austrian resistance still held firm and on 25-26 October ten more battalions and the Edelweiss Alpine Division were thrown into the furious fighting on the Grappa. The 34th Division had also been ordered to the same area, but it was held up by a new Italian offensive opposite the Montello on the night of 25 October. The Forli Brigade, which had relieved the Bari, tackled the terrible Asolone once more and actually attained the summit, but was forced back by the Austrians with heavy losses. Nor did the attack by the Pesaro and the 18th Assault Detachment at the strongly-fortified Osteria del Forcelletto position fare better. The Abruzzi Brigade's attempt on the Col Caprile in 26 October was likewise fruitless, the Roma and Cremona's attack on the Prassolan resulted in heavy losses and no substantial advance, but the 239th Regiment of the Pesaro and the 18th Assault Detachment did make some progress on the northern slopes of Pertica.

Further east, the Austrians counter-attacked the Istrice position held by remnants of the Aosta Battalion. The Austrians hurled themselves onto the position from all sides but the Alpini charged the attackers with the bayonet and succeeded in driving them off. The attack on Mt Forcelletto by two Austrian regiments was likewise repulsed by the Italian 40th Regiment, and afterwards some companies of the latter, of the 39th, and of the Pelmo Alpini Battalion captured Peak 1186 of Mt Forcelletto. The first two attacks on Col del Cuc were repulsed, but the third was successful. The Lombardia and two Alpini battalions had less luck in their attempt on the Col dell'Orso-Solaroli positions, and the Austrians from the latter and from the Valderoa resumed the offensive and tried to overwhelm the two companies of the Aosta Alpini on the Istrice. However, the mountain men held on grimly and forced the assailants to fall back.

On the Grappa, the furious fighting continued unabated and the Austrians sent reinforcements in the form of the 60th Division and the 20th Schützen Division. October 27 passed off quietly on the Asolone, but the Pertica, Solaroli, and Valderoa sectors were heavily engaged. On the Solaroli-Valderoa sector, the mist enabled the Austrians to approach the Valderoa saddle and the Istrice unseen, and to capture both positions, which made Valderoa itself untenable and forced its defenders to evacuate it. On 28 October the Austrians heavily bombarded the Italian lines and approaches in order to hold up further counter-attacks, and on the morning of the next day the Calabria Brigade and three assault detachments captured Asolone, while the 9th Assault Detachment and two infantry battalions got within a mile of Col della Berretta. The Austrians could, however, still sting, and by what proved to be their last offensive effort recaptured the lost positions.

While this gigantic diversionary action was in progress in the Grappa area, preparations were being made by the Italians for what was intended to be the main attack across the Piave. The river flows to the sea in a southeasterly direction except along the base of the Montello, where its course is due east. Between Quero and the sea its average width is about 275 to 378 yards (250 to 300 m); at the Grave di Ciano between Vidor and Falzè it is just over a mile (2 km) wide, and at the Grave di Papadopoli twice that distance. The banks are steep and difficult, and between the Ponti della Priula and the sea there are artificial embankments as a protection against floods. The floods are sudden and frequent but never last more than five days.

The plan was to cross on the Eighth Army front, for which eight bridges and thirteen foot-bridges were to be built; one bridge and one foot-bridge were for the Twelfth Army, one bridge and several foot-bridges for the Tenth.

Before the bridges were built some detachments of Arditi and infantry were ferried across in boats. However, the heavy rains rendered the transportation of the materials difficult and also caused the river to rise considerably, thereby inducing the Comando Supremo to suspend the crossings on the Eighth and Twelfth Army fronts. Lower down where the channel was divided into many branches by the islands of the Grave di Papadopoli, on the Tenth Army front, the Italian pontoon companies were able to transport two British units, the 2nd Battalion of the Honourable Artillery Company and the 1st Battalion, Royal Welch Fusiliers over to the island on the evening of 27 October. The Austrian garrison was taken by surprise and 350 prisoners were captured.

By 27 October, Italian, French, and British contingents on the Tenth Army front had established three small bridgeheads on the left bank of the Piave thanks to the efforts of the bridge-builders. They attacked at once, relying heavily on information from their rear lines from the plucky swimmers—the 'caimeri del Piave'. The situation appeared uncertain for the Allies until, on 28 October the Eighth Army was ordered down the river and broke over the bridges opened by the Tenth Army and advanced toward Monticano. At that moment the Austrian Sixth Army facing the Italian Eighth and Tenth Armies received the order to retire to its second line of defence. The following day proved to be the final turning point, as Austrian resistance began to falter before the determined advance of the three central armies. In some places the Austro-Hungarians stood their ground stubbornly, in others they made a half-hearted stand, and in still other sectors they crumbled. The real dissolution occurred among the Austrian reserves; some refused to counter-attack, while others mutinied.

Whilst the Allies edged forward beyond the Piave, the fighting in the mountain wilderness of the Grappa was resumed. An important Austrian position near Valdobbiadene was the Montagnola hill bristling with machine-gun

One of the heavy calibre artillery guns assembled by the Italians to bombard the Austrian mountain strongholds. A gun such as this would have been capable of sending its shell in excess of 15 miles (24 km).

nests, and this the Alpini group, reinforced by the Stelvio Battalion, was now determined to tackle. The attack, conducted by the Verona Battalion and a company of the Stelvio, was at first held up by the Austrians' devastating fire; but Captain Tonolini, an Alpini officer, dashed across the dangerously exposed ground at the head of two platoons of his company, and struck the enemy in the flank with such impetus that a number of the defenders were captured and the rest put to flight. Tonolini himself was killed, but the Verona Battalion were enabled by his heroic action to gain possession of the Montagnola. That same day the French 107th and 108th Regiments captured Mts Pianar and Perlo, the Bassano Alpini got on to Col di Roc, and the whole Alpini force was soon within a short distance of the Valdobbiadene itself.

Beyond the Piave the Eighth Army was marching on Vittorio Veneto, the Campania Brigade on the left towards Miane, the 66th Division in the centre towards Folina and Soligo, XXII Corps on Valmarino and Vittorio itself, and VIII Corps on the right reaching Colle della Tombola and Mt Cucco, capturing the remaining enemy batteries in that area, and occupying Susegana. Further to the east, south of Conegliano, the Austrian 43rd and the 26th Schützen Division held until then in reserve, attempted a counter-attack on the Tenth Army front but were easily repulsed by units of the Italian XVIII and the British XIV Corps, and the Sassari and Bisagno Brigades occupied Conegliano in spite of hostile resistance. Some British cavalry then seized a bridge across the Monticano between Vazzola and Cilmetta, which the Italians had tried in vain to blow up. The Twelfth Army crossed the Piave at Settola Alto and, while the French 78th Regiment occupied Segusina (capturing 1,000 prisoners and 18 guns), the Alpini advanced in the Cesen area, dashing forward from height to height, overcoming all resistance until they had pinned down the Austrian forces in the folds of the hills. The I Corps, advancing up the right bank of the Piave, captured Quero.

On the Grappa the battle continued to rage throughout 29 October, for here the Austrians still held firm. Units of the Italian IX Corps and various assault detachments bore the brunt of the fighting, some of them managing to reach the summit of Asolone where they were attacked by the Austrians who were superior in number and so were forced back. The IX Assault Detachment on the Col della Berretta, now reduced to a mere handful, was also attacked furiously by far more numerous Austrians, but it held its own until, finding itself completely isolated, it too had to fall back. The Italian Grappa army was, however, fulfilling its task by pinning down the best units of the Austro-Hungarian army, preventing reinforcements from being sent to the Piave, and even attracting the last available reserves. The conquest of the Cesen Hills by the Alpini, the cutting in two of the Austro-Hungarian Sixth Army, the advance of the Italian Twelfth Army along the natural line of retreat of the Austrian forces on the Grappa, and the delay of 24 four hours in commencing that retreat, were to prove fatal to the whole of the Austro-Hungarian forces.

The last Austrian resistance south of Col Caprile and northeast of Pertica gave way, and the line was now broken through at many points. Col Caprile, Col della Berretta, Asalone, Prassolan, Spinoncia, the Solaroli, and Mt Zoc were soon occupied, the enemy resisting sporadically and even attempting occasionally to counter-attack, as on Prassolan. Nothing, however, could now withstand the advancing avalanche, and by late afternoon on 31 October the Exilles and Pieve di Cadore Alpini Battalions were in Feltre, where the civil population helped the Italian soldiers to rout out the last Austrians. The 57th Division (Eighth Army) came in for some heavy fighting on the San Baldo Pass, but it soon broke the Austrian resistance and pushed forward so rapidly that its vanguard captured a whole enemy battalion, which it found resting on the way. It reached the Piave between Lentiai and Trichiana. The 48th Division of the same army also had to overcome some obstinate resistance

on the Faldalto Pass and the Canaiglio Forest, while the 2nd Division advanced on Ponte vella Alpi on the Piave.

The retreat of the Austrian Sixth Army was blocked by the Italians, at Vittorio Veneto, which had been captured on the morning of 30 October. All the Italian armies were now advancing and the Austro-Hungarian forces were degenerating into an undisciplined rabble. However, several of their units still had some fight in them. The XIII Corps, comprising the 14th Italian and the 24th French Divisions—preceded by two assault detachments and the Lecce Brigade—were spreading over the Asiago plateau on 1 November. The Murge Brigade, overcoming the last hostile resistance in that area, gained possession of the long-disputed Melette salient, capturing 3,000 prisoners and all the artillery defending it. On the previous night the 70th Infantry clambered on the steep Mt Spitz and the Col Chiar from the Brenta valley by means of ropes, capturing 35 guns, which they immediately turned on the retreating enemy. Further to the left of the Sixth Army, the XII Corps encountered more vigorous resistance. The right wing of the 48th (British) Division managed to get on to Mt Catz, but the left of that unit and the Italian 20th were held up for a while and unable to emerge from the Val d'Arsa.

The Commander of the 48th decided to try to outflank the position by attacking Mt Mosciagh, while the 20th was to continue its attempt to ascend from Val d'Assa. By dawn on 2 November, the 48th was on Mts Mosciagh and Interotto, and the 20th had also effected considerable progress. With the collapse of the Camporovere defences, the XX Corps (also of the Sixth Army) was able to push ahead rapidly. The Fourth Army, after descending from the Grappa and occupying the Feltre basin, ascended the Val Sugana to Primolano and Tezze, and one of its divisions at Grigno cut off the Austrian retreat from the Altipiani. The Padova Light Cavalry had scrambled down from the Grappa by footpaths and one of its squadrons, covering 60 miles (96 km) in 24 hours, reached the Piave above Feltre. Units of the Eighth Army, which had reached the Piave still higher up, were at Belluno by 23:00 on 1 November, and the 2nd Assault Division, after cutting its way through enemy forces concentrated near Ponte velle Alpi, dashed on to Longarone and Pieve di Cadore. These movements cut the line of retreat up the Piave for large numbers of Austrian forces, who consequently doubled back and tried to find a way of escape up the Cordevole (a tributary of the Piave), but there they found awaiting them the Reggio Brigade, which made a big haul of prisoners and guns.

The final collapse had commenced on the night of 30-31 October, when the struggle turned into a series of isolated encounters with Austrian units who were no longer in concert with the Hungarians, who had defected from the empire. They were pursued, cut-off, captured, and overtaken by Allied troops. On the night of 31 October-1 November, two Italian naval officers, Raffaele Rossetti and Raffaele Paolucci, penetrated into the port of Trieste in a tiny torpedo boat and sank the Austrian battleship *Viribus Unitis*; on 3 November an Italian naval expedition landed Bersaglieri at the port. On the same day Trento was occupied by the Italians. The Italian war aims (*Italia Irredenta!*) had thus been achieved after over three years of bitter fighting, the capture of Trieste being hotly contested by the Serbians under the auspices of the newly-established Yugoslav National Council in Zagreb. The war had cost the Italians 650,000 dead and almost 1,000,000 wounded. The estimated Austro-Hungarian casualties numbered over 800,000 killed and wounded, but many of these were to be accounted for on other fronts. Vittorio Veneto, a small town in the Treviso province, Veneto region, 22 miles (35 km) north of Treviso at the edge of the Venetian plain, like Caporetto, played only a small part in the great battles that took their names. Both rank as two of the most decisive battles in military history.

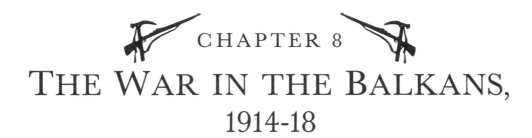

CHAPTER 8
THE WAR IN THE BALKANS,
1914-18

The setting for the campaign in Macedonia was one of mountain grandeur combined with malaria-infested lowland, its focus for the Allied forces being on the ancient port of Salonika. Ancient Macedonia was at first a kingdom, then a Roman province for a thousand years. However, that region of northern Greece to which we today infrequently refer and seldom visit as tourists has well-defined natural boundaries. Macedonia may be said to consist of the valleys of four great rivers, the Mesta, the Struma, the Vardar, and the Vistritsa. Its eastern boundary is, first, the lower Mesta, then the Dospad range; its northern boundary follows the lofty Rila Dagh, the heights—lesser but still almost impassable from north to south, between the Struma at Kyustendil and the Morava, and between the Morava and the Vardar; its western boundary is the great chain of mountains beginning with the Sar Planina,

Serbian gunners defend their northern frontier against the Austro-German invaders.

which separates it from Albania and cuts it off from the Adriatic. To the south there is no barrier comparable to these, and the boundary here may be described as running along latitude 40 to the sea.

The mountains on three sides are of savage grandeur and as inaccessible as any in Europe—impassible over the centuries for purposes of trade or war except along the corridors cut by certain rivers. Those to the west form the strongest barrier of all, the peaks being 7,000 ft (2,150 m) high, and the steep-faced ridges all along from 4,000 to 5,000 ft (1,200-1,500 m). Hardly anywhere has nature shut off one land from the other more completely than here. It is true that the Romans, who were daunted by no such gradients, made a military road from Dyrrhachium (Durazzo) through Salonika and Xanthi to Constantinople. But west of Monastir (now Bitolj) their *Via Egnatia* can no longer be traced. Although twentieth-century engineering could find its way through such barriers, the key to military manoeuvre lay in the possession of the river valleys, which were everywhere dominated by precipitous heights. It is the Vardar corridor that gives Salonika its strategic significance, and would have perhaps made it the first port of the Near East but for national rivalries and their artificial barriers. The history of the country is as tangled as its mountains. Philip of Macedon's victory at Chaeroneain (338 BC) imposed the conqueror's will upon Greece and allowed his son, Alexander, to claim to be representative of Greek culture. The untimely death of Alexander in 323 BC cut short the dominance of a civilization that, even if it had not changed the course of history, would have relieved Macedonia of the obscurity into which it was destined to dissolve.

After the Turks captured Salonika in 1430, the whole of Macedonia remained in their possession for nearly five centuries. Revolt against the Ottoman Empire simmered in the Balkans throughout the nineteenth century. At the turn of the century, the Christian Balkan states—Bulgaria, Serbia, and Greece—were possessed by the 'Macedonian Problem', and in the First Balkan War of 1912 these nations, which had all known the Ottoman yoke, formed an alliance that swept Turkey out of Macedonia. But Bulgaria, which had borne the brunt of the fighting, could not agree with Greece and Serbia on the division of the spoils, which resulted in the Second Balkan War of 1913, in which Greece and Serbia defeated Bulgaria, largely thanks to Romania invading her Bulgarian neighbours from the north. As a result of the Treaty of Bucharest of 9 August 1913, Serbia extended her territories to include northern Macedonia to just south of Monastir. Greece got all of southern Macedonia to Kavalla, including that port. Bulgaria, supported by Austria, was comparatively fortunate in being allowed to annex the valleys of the upper Struma and Mesta and also in obtaining egress to the Aegean between Kavalla and Dede Agach, although the latter was merely a roadway. However, Bulgaria had to hand over to Romania a large strip of the southern Dobruja on the shore of the Black Sea.

Greek leaders at the outbreak of the First World War were divided in their potential loyalties. King Constantine I was unquestionably pro-German but Premier Venizelos favoured the Allies, and on 3 October 1915 an Allied expeditionary force, consisting of French and British troops commanded by the French General Maurice Sarrail, landed at Salonika. The contingent of 150,000 men had been increased by July 1916 to 250,000 men under the banner of the Armée d'Orient, which included the regrouped Serbian army, which by this time had arrived from Corfu. At their peak the Allied armies numbered 350,000 men, which included the Greek army. The Allied gesture of support was aimed at solving the 'Serbian Question' by supporting the Serbian-Greek alliance and Bulgarian mobilization greatly accelerated the dispatch of French and British troops to the Macedonian front. The Central Powers were well informed of Allied plans and made their dispositions accordingly. One of Falkenhayn's last acts as Chief of the German General Staff was to send two German divisions, one of which had seen some action on the Western Front in the Vosges mountains, to reinforce the Bulgarian army in the Macedonian theatre. (The main German-Austrian forces in the Balkans at that time would be engaged on the Romanian front.)

The Allied forces were ill-equipped to fight on high ground whether it was steep hills or mountain slopes. The British Salonika army was well provided for with mountain artillery and pack mules, but there was nothing in the infantrymen's scale of equipment to enhance their proficiency as mountain goats. The British 10th Division, which took over the Kosturino sector in the Salonikan hinterland on 10 November 1915, found savage, almost trackless country, broken up by steep hills and ridges, whereon scent scrub and a few dwarf oaks miraculously grew amid huge outcrops of rock. A sudden change in the weather proved far more deadly than the Bulgarians, who had wisely gone to ground. On 26 November rain began to fall, soon turning to snow and rendering the tracks impassable. An intense frost accompanied by a high wind followed, which developed into a severe storm, and in the course of a few days played havoc with the troops, especially those on the hill-tops. The men were soaked to the skin by the rain and snow, and the bitter frost then froze their clothing on them. Greatcoats were frozen so stiff that when taken off they stood unsupported, splitting like boards if an attempt was made to beat the frost out of them. Sentries resorted to wearing horse-blankets. The officers had to prevent their men from lying down during the coldest nights, keeping them on the move to stave off the coma that appeared to be creeping over them.

By mid-July 1916 the Russian Imperial army, after defeating the Austrians on the Dniester, stood at the foot of the Carpathians and there was excitement, not only in the *Entente* capitals but also in Bucharest. The Romanian

army by popular demand was about to march into Transylvania to 'liberate' the three million Romanians living within the Dual Monarchy. Bratianu, the Romanian prime minister, informed the French minister in Bucharest that he was prepared to enter the war on the side of the Allies provided the Russians continued their offensive and co-operated with the Romanian army, and that Bulgarian forces were engaged by a full-scale offensive from Salonika. Negotiations thereupon began for the signing of a formal military alliance.

General Sarrail quickly completed his plan of operations. There was a flurry of activity around Salonika and on the main roads leading from the port. The Serbs, whom Sarrail planned would form the spearhead of his initial assault, began to march westward on 17 July in order to take over 60 miles (95 km) of the front from the French, well beyond the Vardar and facing the mountain peaks that marked the old frontier of their land. A chain of enemy agents, recruited from the peasantry of the Struma valley and the high land east of Salonika, spread the news up to the Bulgarian lines, and Sofia knew that the Serbs were on their way long before they reached their positions. Bulgarian intelligence circles might well also have been informed of British units training along the Struma, the French guarding the route of the Vardar, machine-gun companies arriving for the British divisions, and a squadron of the Royal Flying Corps disembarking from Alexandria. An Italian division was on its way and 800 Albanian partisans, who had been training with the Italians. But, most intriguingly of all, a brigade of Russians, 5,000 strong, stepped proudly ashore at Salonika at the end of July. Physically these men seemed giants, a magnificent sight as they marched eight abreast through the city, bayonets gleaming on their long rifles. There was, as yet, no sign of the defeatism that was to sap the Tsar's army before many months were out. It was clear to all Salonika that an offensive was imminent.

The Serbian units fared badly on their first

Bulgarian troops march through a typical mountain pass near Bielogradchik. According to a Bulgarian account, Serbian soldiers, 'without any cause', crossed the frontier on 12 October 1915, in an attempt to occupy the heights west of Bielogradchik. In response, the Bulgarians captured, after a sharp battle, the heights of Kitkä, in Serbian territory.

clash with the Bulgarians, who boasted that they would be in Salonika in a week. Sarrail did not panic but abandoned his plan for a major assault along the Vardar; the main attack was still to come in the west, as he had always intended. The newly-arrived Italians were to relieve a French division in the extreme northeast of the front, 4,000 ft (1,200 m) up in the Belasica Mountains on the old Greco-Bulgarian frontier, while the French—with the Russian brigade—would be hurried across to Lake Ostrovo. As the Italians had been in the Salonika area for little more than a week, there was some risk attached to this manoeuvre but the Italian troops had a fine record from skirmishes in the Alps and it was assumed, rightly, that they would have little difficulty in establishing themselves among the mountain peaks.

In spite of Bulgarian onslaughts on a ridge west of Ostrovo, which were repulsed five times by the Serbians, Sarrail pinned all his hopes on this western sector. The governing considera-

tion behind his strategic assessment was the strength of the enemy positions to his north, along the mountain chain that ran from the Vardar, through Doiran, to the Rupel Pass. British and French reconnaissance raids early in August had met heavy resistance in this sector (which was manned, in part, by a German division). Not only did this formidable obstacle exclude an advance along the Vardar valley into Serbia, but it also reduced the value of an offensive from the line of the Struma into eastern Macedonia. In this area the Allies were under threat from the Bulgarians, who were well placed to advance from their northern wall down the Rupel Pass.

The Serbians themselves wished to liberate a corner of their land and capture Monastir, a town of some 60,000 inhabitants. However, other considerations lay behind Sarrail's choice of this area as the main field of battle. From Monastir, two valleys ran northeastwards to the upper Vardar: one, a difficult route, followed a mountain stream known as the Crna and rejoined the Vardar slightly north of the furthest point reached by the French in an abortive advance the previous year; the other led over the Babuna Pass to the town of Veles. Reach either of these objectives and the Vardar defences would be turned—and, looking further ahead, the way would be open to Skopje and old Serbia, in the north west or, continuing north eastwards up further valleys, to the mountains around Sofia itself, only a 100 miles (160 km) away. There was much to commend Serrail's grand design—provided that the enemy defences in front of Monastir could be broken before the onset of the autumnal rainstorms.

At 06:00 on the morning of 12 September, the French and Serbian artillery opened up around Lake Ostrovo, the mountain wall behind the Bulgarian positions. The mountains echoed the sound of the guns, so that the infantry awaiting the assault had the distinct impression that they were under bombardment themselves! The Serbians faced the twin summits of the Kajmakcalan, a mountain crowned by a ridge 1,500 yd (1,400 m) long, which separated an eastern peak 7,700 ft (2,350 m) above sea-level from a western peak 500 ft (150 m) higher still. The Bulgarians made mountain artillery positions well above the lower slopes and observation posts on each summit, looking out over the lesser hills beyond Ostrovo and down to the plain. Behind the Kajmakcalan lay the defiles through which the Crna had cut its winding route, and westward was Monastir. So long as the mountain was in Bulgarian hands there could be no advance. There had been no major assault of this character at such an altitude on any other front, not even in the Italian Alps.

The Serbian First Army, led by General Mišić, took the lower slopes of the Kajmakcalan without difficulty following a precipitous road as far as the village of Batachin, and for three more days the Serbians pushed relentlessly ahead under successive artillery barrages. But beyond Batachin the guns were of little use: a belt of beech forest shielded the tracks up to the summit. Once the forest was cleared with the bayonets, there was nothing above but the bare face of the mountain, with each natural gully and cleft manned by the defenders. In the early hours of 19 September, men of the Drina Division reached the top and once more the Serbian flag flew on home soil. This extraordinary battle on the roof-top of the Balkans was renewed after a week. The Bulgarians, despite pressure from the British on the central sector of the front, moved five regiments west of the Vardar. The Serbians hauled up mountain guns to the old Bulgarian observation posts on the ridge between the twin peaks. The counterattack came on 26 September when the Bulgarians threw the Serbians from their mountain-top positions; four days later the latter had regained them and the Bulgarians abandoned the Kajmakcalan for good.

Meanwhile, two French divisions and the Russian brigade were attempting to turn the Bulgarian right flank. The first objective was the town of Florina, which stood on a ridge commanding the valley from Ostrovo to Monastir. Today, tourists seeking to enter Greece from Yugoslavia by the alternative route to the Vardar valley drive from Monastir to Florina station in little more than half an hour. Apart from the customs-posts on the frontier at Kenali there is little to be seen except isolated farmhouses. On both sides of the valley the mountains rise in magnificent splendour—although less steep in the west than in the east—but between them the grassy plain has no natural obstacles. Yet in 1916 it took the Allied troops six weeks to make their way along this corridor to Monastir, for around Kenali the Bulgarians had dug trench fortifications as formidable as any on the Western Front. Before the valley was cleared, the position cost the Allies over 2,000 lives—and French General Cordonnier his command.

Cordonnier's reluctance to cross these trenches infuriated Sarrail, who removed his subordinate from his post on 16 October (a few days after the French and Russians had been slaughtered after a frontal assault on Kenali). All this while the Serbians were keeping up their pressure on enemy forces, which included Germans in the bend of the Crna. Sarrail saw the importance of supporting this sector and he sent reinforcements to Mišić for operations beyond the Crna. At the same time he moved more French units westwards, where they linked up with irregular bands of Albanians who were harrying the Bulgarian positions south of Lake Prespa. An Italian brigade was moved into the area. It was along the Crna, despite the irregular terrain and the appalling weather, that the offensive was first resumed after a lengthy spell of heavy rain. On 10 and 11 November two Serbian divisions and a regiment of French Zouaves captured more than a thousand prisoners, the majority of them Germans who claimed they had been deserted by their Bulgarian ally.

The French pushed forward on 14 November capturing Kenali, and Sarrail could see that Monastir was within his grasp. On 17 November the dawn was bright and clear, the white contours of the mountains and the roofs of Monastir standing out sharply in the freezing air. The Serbians stormed two hills east of the town while the French, Italians, and Russians edged forward from one small village to the next. By noon on 19 November the Allies—headed by a young French cavalry officer—entered the silent and shuttered town. After nine weeks of hard campaigning, Monastir had fallen. The capture of this town was celebrated as a major triumph. The Bulgarian front had been broken, but the enemy was only a few miles north of the town, which remained within range of its artillery throughout the winter of 1916-17. The Allies' important task now was to safeguard what had been gained until the snows melted and new divisions reached the battle line. Hence on 11 December offensive operations on the Macedonian front were suspended 'for the time being'. For the exhausted divisions resting above the snow-line, the order came not a day too soon.

By the second week of February 1917, General Sarrail had devised his next offensive. The Army of the Orient would attack at five different points along its front. The main assault by the Serbians, in the Moglena Mountains to the east of the Crna loop, would aim at taking the Bulgarian defences along the Vardar in the rear. To the west, French units would advance between Lakes Prespa and Ochrid, also moving eastwards so as to link up with a Franco-Italian group advancing along the upper Crna between Monastir and Prilep. At the same time, the British 28th Division would lead a fourth attack against the Belasica Mountains across the valley between Doiran and the Rupel Pass. Beyond the Struma, the British 10th and 27th Divisions would occupy the town of Seres. If all went well, French, Serbian, and Italian units would advance on the Bulgarian capital, Sofia,

This natural stronghold, further consolidated with baskets of sand, was established by the Allies on the Salonika front and christened Fort de la Macedoine. The entrance to the fort is seen in the centre of the photograph.

through Kumanovo or Stip and the British would wheel northwards and seize the Rupel Pass, from which there was a direct route up the Struma to Sofia, 120 miles (190 km) away.

The Allied spring offensive of 1917 was launched on 24 April. On the British sector the 26th Division was to attack over a front 2,650 yds (2,425 m) westward, and the 22nd Division was to support its left flank for another 2,000 yds (1830 m). The 60th Division was to relieve pressure on the main attackers by raiding Bulgarian positions in the Machukovo salient, a few miles east of the Vardar. During the evening of 24 April the Hampshires, Devons, and Wiltshires of the 79th Brigade (26th Division) assembled in the gullies to the south of a lake. Before them was the hillock known as the Petit Couronné that, with its western offshoot, was the first line of the Bulgarian defences and therefore formed the immediate objective. Half a mile back lay another ridge, no less heavily fortified. And above this line, some 2 miles (3 km) from the British positions, was the greatest obstacle of all—the bare-topped hump the French had named the Grand Couronné, a feature similar to the natural fortress in Lorraine. Even this was not the end of the defensive positions, for the Grand Couronné was itself overlooked by 'Pip Ridge'—long and steep and tapering to a razor's edge crest.

The Grand Couronné dominated the whole area. With its summit at less than 2,000 ft (600 m), it was not strictly speaking a mountain (the Kajmakcalan was four times its height), but it loomed dangerously over the British force. A Bulgarian observation post at the summit of the Grand Couronné was likened to the 'Devil's Eye'. Sooner or later the eye must be pierced and that could only be achieved by scaling the high ground by frontal assault. The British troops attacked at night, plunging into the Jumeaux ravine and across a swiftly flowing stream. When they emerged from the hell of the ravine, two powerful searchlights threw their beams across the open ground exposing the attackers to a withering cross-fire. The British infantry did little more than penetrate the inner line of trenches on the Petit Couronné that night. Not a single Allied soldier climbed higher than the foothills of the Grand Couronné in the coming weeks. The weeks turned into months, and the Devil remained aloof in his citadel until the war was over.

The main thrust of Sarrail's spring offensive was launched at dawn on 9 May. The French 16th Colonial Division moved forward in the centre of the Crna loop supported by the Russian 2nd Brigade on the right and the Italian 35th Division to the left. At the same time further east in the Moglena Mountains, the Serbian Second Army—under General Stepanović—assaulted hill positions south of the Dobropolje: a limestone wall little more than half as high as the Kajmakcalan but far steeper. Around Monastir each side threw hundreds of rounds of high explosive across the valleys but, apart from patrol activity, the infantry remained in their trenches—and all remained quiet in the outposts between Lakes Prespa and Ochrid. In the Crna loop all went well for a while. The Russians captured the village of Orle, on a mountain spur more than a mile behind the enemy line. But the momentum of their assault had carried them too far and no one followed them up. The French 16th Colonials and the Italians made, if anything, less progress than the Russians. In spite of Allied pressure the Monastir-Moglena sector of the enemy line was firmly under the control of the German-Bulgarian forces. On 10 May there was a disastrous breakdown in the Allied system of command and confusion reigned.

The situation was little better up on the Moglena. There too, on 9 May, all had at first gone well but by noon the attackers had been halted. Throughout the next few days, the Serbians clung desperately to a hill they had taken, although the initiative had passed to the Germans and Bulgarians who remained firmly entrenched above them. The whole action became a formless artillery duel. The infantry tried again a few days later: Stepanović sent the

Sumadija Division up the steep approaches to the Dobropolje. The Serbians broke off the action on Sunday, 13 May, when fog swirled over the valley, but on the Monday evening (14 May) they took two spurs within a mile of the summit. It was the limit of their achievement. Thereafter they awaited orders to advance that never came.

That May, the only real success of the Allied armies came on the banks of the Struma—the sector of the front to which least attention had been given in the previous weeks. These operations of the British XVI Corps, which was commanded by Lieutenant-General C.J. Briggs, were primarily intended as a subsidiary feint. After four days of artillery bombardment, the 10th (Irish) Division was to advance a few miles while the 85th Brigade of the 28th Division was to seize two vital Bulgarian outposts on the left bank of the Struma at a point where it turns northeastwards towards Rupel. This was very different country from the Doiran or the Moglena—here the mountains lay several miles back and all the action took place in the open, sometimes on marshy ground but often in fields in which the only cover came from the high crops of corn or maize.

By this time, however, it seemed most improbable that any progress at all would be made up in the mountains. There was still, though, the Serbian First Army, which comprised three infantry divisions, a cavalry division, and the 4th Russian Brigade. After a week of action on both its flanks in the Moglena, the First Army was still in its trenches between the Crna loop and the Dobropolje. At first General Bojović, the Serbian Chief of Staff, had informed Sarrail that he was keeping the First Army in reserve to exploit any breach in the enemy line. The idea made sense. The First Army now comprised hardy veterans accustomed to mountain warfare and long marches in difficult country, and they were still commanded by General Mišić, who had led them in the assault on the Kajmakcalan eight months previously. But as the enemy line failed

to break, Sarrails's demands on the Serbians became more and more insistent. Still Mišić would not move. He did not have the force to scale the mountain facing him; he would not go forward until the Dobrolje was in the hands of the Serbian Second Army. Yet the Second Army, too, had reluctantly come to a halt. On 21 May, Bojović, convinced that Sarrail's policy would only expose the Serbs to useless losses without compensatory gains, formally requested him to call off the whole offensive. That evening Sarrail notified his commanders that operations would cease. The spring offensive of 1917 had lasted only twelve days.

A full year elapsed before the Allies launched another offensive on the Macedonian front. By this time General Sarrail's head had rolled and he was succeeded in command of the Army of the Orient by General Marie Louis Adolphe Guillaumat, who had commanded the French Second Army at Verdun. The Serbian army was greatly reinforced from the Eastern Front and, with Croats now in its ranks, was assuming the constitution of a genuinely Yugoslav army. The Greek army was now also in strength in Macedonia. Guillaumat's plan in May 1918 was to launch joint operations (Franco-Italian) in Albania, southwest of Lake Ochrid, primarily to engage the Austrians and prevent their units moving to other battle areas. The British XVI Corps, with Greek support, would occupy a number of villages beyond the Struma, and there would be a Franco-Greek assault on a Bulgarian salient west of the Vardar.

And so it was that a classic mountain battle took place—the attack by the Greeks, with French support, on the Bulgarian salient at Skra di Legan on 30 May. The Skra di Legan is an irregular-shaped rocky summit some 10 miles (15 km) west of the Vardar, just on the Greek side of the frontier with Yugoslavia (or, as it was then, Serbia). Inaccessible even today, 70 years ago it was far more remote than the Kajmakcalan or the Dobropolje. The Allied positions were served by a winding track that twisted over

Romanian soldiers recross the boundary river after their incursion into Transylvania.

two mountain ridges down to a railhead beside the Vardar at Gumendye, more than 12 miles (20 km) to the southeast. Until the French engineers gave this track the appearance of a road, it was impossible to bring up supplies let alone heavy guns. And even when the road had been constructed, there was no certainty that it would stand up to sufficient traffic for even a limited offensive.

The Skra di Legen was far more than a geographical obstacle. Heavily fortified, with shelters under protective slabs of rock and a cluster of machine-gun emplacements rising like steps on the face of a cliff, it was in many ways a complementary position to the Grand Couronné, which lay a similar distance from the Vardar on the opposite bank. Just as Pip Ridge and the 'Devil's Eye' dominated the Doiran sector, so the defences of the Skra di Legen, which ran for nearly 2 miles (3 km) along a spur projecting from the main Bulgarian line, determined the fate of any attack launched along

8 miles (13 km) of bleak rock-face on the right bank of the Vardar. If ever a general assault were to be made on the Bulgarian front, the Skra di Legen (and its support lines) had to be captured. And Guillaumat entrusted this mission to the 'mountain men' of the Greek Cretan Division and the Archipelago Division of Zymbrakakis's 'National Defence Army'.

Throughout the last fortnight of May, French and British guns were smuggled up through the valleys and sited around the village of Ljumnica, whence they commanded the flank of the Skra and the Bulgarian support lines. The Bulgarian observers noted the increased artillery activity, which included the arrival of an 8-in howitzer battery. However, they were puzzled about Allied intentions. The whole front, on both sides of the Vardar, erupted into activity on 28 May. Patrols were out around Doiran and in the French positions beside the Vardar. The shells crunched down alike on Pip Ridge and on the Skra. But still the Bulgarians could not make up their minds: where would the attack come? Which was the feint? Surely the British did not intend to go forward again up Jumeaux ravine and Pip Ridge?

In the early hours of 30 May, with the sun coming up behind them, the Greek troops scaled the Skra. The Bulgarians were taken by surprise. Half the machine-gun emplacements seemed unmanned, and the Greeks reached the Bulgarian lines almost as soon as the creeping barrage. Within a little more than an hour the Greeks had captured not only the Skra but also the Bulgarian positions to the west. Only in the east was there a fight and even that was settled by the end of the morning. The Bulgarians counter-attacked in the afternoon and in the following night, but nothing could dislodge the Greeks. If the Skra were to be regained it would be necessary to bring up reinforcements and mount a carefully-planned operation. Guillaumat withdrew the Greeks and replaced them with more experienced French troops, but the Bulgarian attack never materialized. The Greeks had achieved a famous victory, a resumption of the cavalcade of success in the Second Balkan War. All Greece was agog with delight.

Interest in the Macedonian front began to wane—Guillaumat was replaced by Franchet d'Espérey, who had previously declined the Salonika command. On the evening of 13 September Mišić explained his formula for final victory to d'Espérey from a mountain vantage point over the enemy lines, and the old Serbian general was allowed the privilege of choosing the date for the attack. A huge artillery bombardment opened up on 14 September, 36,000 French, Serbian, and Italian infantrymen waiting with their rifles ready. The Kajmakcalan and Floka were to be used as observation points for an attack on the Vetrenik-Dobropolje-Sokol sector. The Serbian Sumadija stormed up the southwestern slope of the Vetrenik by tracks that twisted around the steep slopes like paths on the face of a cliff. The eastern Vetrenik was an even tougher obstacle, with a heavy fire coming down on the attackers as they hauled themselves forward, scrambling for footholds in the rock. The Vetrenik was not in Serbian hands until the early afternoon.

Between the Vetrenik and the Dobropolje, the 17th French Colonial Division (which included four battalions of Senegalese) spent two gruelling hours holding off five Bulgarian counter-attacks on the heights known as the Kravički Kamen. There the enemy held positions on a plateau pocketed with ridges that, in the course of the morning, were stormed and lost and stormed again by both sides in confused fighting so that, by noon, French and Bulgarians alike were exhausted. Not until 16:00 did the Sumadija Division (advancing from the Vetrenik) go forward with the bayonet alongside the French and Senegalese and carry the defences. The Dobropolje pyramid was known to be well fortified and it proved a difficult obstacle. The French had to use flame-throwers for the first time in Macedonia to overcome the fierce resistance by Bulgarian machine-gun units. However, in less than two hours the

Dobropolje was seized, and the Allies were thus provided with a forward observation post from which artillery bombardments could be directed on the second and third lines of defence. The Sokol, on the other hand, held out all day—only after dusk were the Serbians and the French together able to carry the summit in a frenzied rush forward.

On their flank, the Yugoslav Division crossed the old frontier between Greece and Serbia early in the evening. Their objective—the Kozyak—lay a few miles to the north. Mišić ordered his men on, gripped with patriotic fervour. By dawn on 16 September, the Yugoslavs were ready to assault the Kozyak mountain,

French soldiers dig trenches in the Monastir region on the Salonika front. The Allies engaged in a long struggle, gradually tightening their grip on this mountain stronghold.

while the Timok Division faced a ridge to the northeast of the main Bulgarian defences. The fighting on 16 September was no less grim than on the previous day. On the Kozyak the defenders threw back attack after attack, but later in the day the Bulgarian defence cracked. Even so the Kozyak was not completely in Serbian hands, for a German reserve battalion was rushed up from the neighbourhood of Prilep and dug in on a ridge north of the mountain. However, the end was at hand. Mišić continued to exploit his successes throughout 17 September, although the German battalion, the 13th Saxon Jägers, fought stubbornly on the ridge.

While the Serbians and French pressed forward over new ground, the British and Greeks struggled across ravines and up hills that were all too familiar to them—the Petit Couronné, Grand Couronné, and Pip Ridge with the 'Devil's Eye', observing day after day every movement for miles around. The ghost town of Doiran remained near and inaccessible. The Allies gained little on this sector but their losses were staggering—as great as the Serbians and French whose efforts had, however, resulted in success. But two De Havilland 9s of 47 Squadron, RAF, reconnoitring the Vardar and Strumica valleys on the morning of 21 September, reported that the roads were choked with Bulgarian and German horse and motor transport heading into Bulgaria. The British patrols found outposts facing them empty and deserted. A few hours later the Seres Division moved up the Grand Couronné. The dead still lay unburied on the slopes where they had fallen in the previous days. The 'Devil's Eye' and all other concrete emplacements had been abandoned.

The general assault delivered on 14 September by the Serbians, French, British, Greeks, and Italians had overall been an amazing success from the start. By 17 September the Allies had advanced 20 miles (32 km), the Serbians distinguishing themselves especially in furious charges with the bayonet, singing patriotic songs. By 27 September the road to Sofia lay open as the remnants of Bulgarian units, split and demoralized, struggled homeward. The German Eleventh Army was cut off and forced to surrender. It was useless for the Germans to attempt to urge the Bulgarians to rally. Yet there was no serious threat to Sofia or any other town of importance in Bulgaria. The capital was 130 miles (209 km) from Kosturino at the border, over five ranges of mountains forming a natural line of defence. The Allies might still have been held by the Bulgarians at the mercy of a grim winter, but time was running out for the Central Powers. Bulgaria was declared a republic at Radomir on 27 September and an armistice was signed at Salonika on 30 September. It was 16 days since Mišić had ordered the guns to open up. Bulgaria had surrendered, but the Allies had failed in at least one war objective on this front—they had failed to sever German-Turkish lines of communication.

An Austrian heavy mortar sited on the Red Tower Pass on the Romanian front in 1916. This mortar was positioned to lob its bombs on to targets on the far side of a mountain over 6,000 feet (1,830 m) high.

THE SECOND WORLD WAR

CHAPTER 9
THE WINTER WAR

The first violent action on land in the Second World War took place during the 'Winter War' between Finland and Russia, which commenced on 30 November 1939 and ended on 1 March 1940. Few more stirring tales of heroic endeavour were to turn sour on the Allies than those of the Finns. Britain, especially, was swift to pledge its support of Finland and the western world was shocked by the Russian victory as winter turned to spring in 1940. Paradoxically, Britain was soon to form an alliance with Soviet Russia and the defeated Finland with Nazi Germany. In Britain and France the winter months of 1939-40 were known as the 'phoney war'—nothing seemed to happen, but press reports from Finland gave (for some in the west) a foreboding of impending conflict. The sound of distant thunder echoed no more strongly than at the Admiralty in London where the First Lord, Winston Churchill, advocated sending an Allied relief force to assist the Finns—a northern plan of campaign that was to take more tangible shape in the Norwegian campaign of April-June 1940.

In 1939 Finnish independence was scarcely 21 years old. From 1809 to 1917 Finland had been part of the Russian Empire, in which it had the status of an autonomous grand duchy. Finland's internal autonomy was respected for many years but in the 1890s the Russians sought to increase their control of the province, which led to a campaign of patriotic resistance to Russian imperialism. The consequences of the 1917 Russian revolution were superimposed on this militant background. The Bolshevik Government had recognized Finland's independence at the end of December 1917, at a time when there were still large numbers of revolutionary-minded Russian soldiers and sailors in the country. When, in January 1918, the Finnish socialists (the Reds) proclaimed a workers' government in Finland and tried to overthrow the new bourgeois republic (the Whites), a bitter civil war broke out. In this war the Russian Government and its troops in Finland gave arms and assistance to the Reds, while the Finnish Whites received aid from Sweden and Germany. The Reds were defeated and savagely repressed, while their leaders fled to Russia where they founded the Finnish Communist Party.

After the German defeat of Poland in 1939, when the country was divided between Germany and Russia, the latter—fearful of Hitler's motives—began consolidating a Balkan sphere of influence. Mutual-defence pacts with Latvia, Estonia, and Lithuania were followed by the immediate inrush of Russian troops for their 'defence'. From Finland, Russia demanded a similar agreement, including occupation of the southern portion of the Karelian isthmus and other island and mainland base areas. Finland, rejecting these demands, mobilized forces along its frontier, under the command of their rather old but much-respected Marshal Baron Carl Mannerheim, veteran of three wars. The Russians demanded the immediate withdrawal of Finnish troops.

Finland, which is bordered in the northwest by Sweden and Norway, forms a vast eastern frontier with Russia stretching from the Arctic Ocean in the north to the Gulf of Finland in the south. There were two factors that compensated to some extent for Finland's deficiencies in manpower and *matériel*. The first was the existence of a prepared line of defence on the Karelian isthmus, the main and most vulnerable sector of the front. This defensive belt is invariably referred to as the Mannerheim Line—a First World War system of field fortifications, all cleverly knitted into the rugged terrain and heavily-wooded areas—but the implied comparison, which the name suggests, with the French Maginot Line is quite misleading. The defensive front across the isthmus was about 43 miles (70 km), long with its two flanks anchored on the heavy coastal batteries of Koivisto in the west and Kaarnajoki and Yllapaa at the Lake Ladoga end—the only fortress artillery the line possessed. The River Vuoksi, a formidable natural barrier, covered the eastern third of the position. Between the Vuoksi and the Gulf of Finland there were broad stretches of lake and swamp, which were natural obstacles in summer but rather the contrary when frozen in winter and, between the swamps and lakes, there were stretches of open country through which the roads and railway passed.

The second asset held by the Finns was the quality, if not the quantity, of their troops. The Finnish army had long since broken with continental military tradition: Finnish troops were trained as individualists to perform tactics based on local conditions. Most of the frontier was once a wilderness of lake and forest crossed by infrequent, poor-quality roads. If an approaching armoured enemy column could be halted, Finnish troops moving swiftly across the wilderness could strike at the flanks and rear of such a road-bound force. The Finnish army was trained to move fast across any kind of terrain, to avoid head-on clashes, to strike always at the flank and rear of an enemy, and to make flexibility and movement compensate for their inferior numbers. In winter conditions this meant, above all, that the Finnish soldiers, warmly-clad, moved on skis—and all Finns are accustomed from childhood to skiing in forest conditions.

If the possibility of skiing came as a surprise to most countries of the world, skis in Scandinavia were no military revelation. A heavy snowfall makes open countryside all but impassable for mechanized transport. The cavalry of the period also encountered great difficulties in snow-bound terrain, which also reduces the mobility of troops on foot. A snow layer of only a few inches reduces marching speed by half, and the resulting fatigue rises even higher in ratio to the distance of ground to be covered. In really deep snow, wading in full kit becomes purgatorial and infantry can hardly venture more than a few paces from the beaten track. The ski conquers these difficulties with ease. Though wet or very deep fresh snow can be dangerous for a skier, these inconveniences can never be compared with those with which the foot-slogger has to cope. Groups of highly-trained skiers can cover short stretches of undulating ground at a rate of some 8 mph (13 km/h). It was calculated at the time that Norwegian, Swedish, or Finnish ski troops could cover at least 30 miles (50 km) a day in full kit.

Scandinavian units, dressed in white camouflage overalls or capes of balloon silk or simply of canvas, employed a wide variety of equipment to assist movement over snow. The two fundamental types of ski used in the Scandinavian armies were the general-service Telemark ski (with a ridge) of the broader, touring type (*terrangskida*), about 2.75 in (7 cm) in the waist, and the narrower, racing ski with parallel sides, 2.4 in (6 cm) broad. A hybrid type was sometimes found in the Swedish army: a light ski shaped like a racing ski on the inner side and like a Telemark ski on the outer. Birch or ash wood was normally used.

In the Swedish army tow-irons with

Above *Government (White) troops are photographed with a sledge-mounted gun on their way to Tampere during the Finnish Civil War of 1918. In this brief but bitter conflict fought in the aftermath of the Bolshevik Revolution in Russia, the Finnish Communists failed to take control of this former province of Imperial Russia.*

Below *Fully armed and equipped White troops assembled at a wayside halt ready to entrain for the battle front.*

adjustable jaws, screwed onto the board, (of the so-called Ericksson type), a toe and a heel strap (the latter with a usual clamp), were used with general-service skis. With racing skis, special racing bindings of the Bergendahl or similar models without heel-strap were mostly—though not exclusively—used. The Finns were of the opinion that heel-straps proved cumbersome when skis had to be quickly removed in action. This, however, could be of advantage only in flat or undulating terrain, and in mountains a firmer grip on the foot was necessary than a normal Langlauf binding (without heel-strap) could give. Also, the old, unadjustable Huit-feldt bindings were in use in Scandinavian armies, and they formed the standard equipment of the Norwegian forces before the invasion of the country in 1940. In the 1939-40 campaign the Finns even fought on Lapp toe-strap-and-loop bindings, and Finnish soldiers also used simple, primitive toe-straps without either loop or toe-irons. The use of the latter two types of bindings implied Lapp moccasin boots (*lappskor, finnskor*) with upturned toes, but since such bindings contained no metal parts it had a definite advantage in low temperatures. Snow-shoes were used only by drivers and stretcher-bearers. Horses on soft-snow tracks also had special snow-shoes (*truger*) fitted to them but this often resulted in broken ankles for the horses.

There were three basic types of ski-sledges. The ski-sledge proper (*skidkalke*) was used for the transport of ammunition, supplies, and the wounded. It was a light, low sledge, about 1 yd (1 m) across and 2 yd (2 m) long, mounted on two skis. It had a dragpole in front, but this served not so much for pulling the sledge as for stemming it when running downhill. The sledge was hauled on two ropes of unequal length by two men (one man may have sufficed for a lightly-loaded or empty sledge). The haulers normally moved on skis, except in difficult terrain or on hard crust. The different lengths of the two ropes were so adjusted that both men could move freely on skis without interfering

with each other. The drag-sledge (*dragkalke*) was a somewhat heavier and larger type. It was used for special purposes and often required more than two men to pull it. Sometimes teams of two or more specially-trained dogs or reindeer were used as draught animals. A horse could pull a whole train of ski-sledges, one behind another.

The machine-gun sledge was a variety of ski-sledge of special construction. It was used for the transport of heavy machine-guns and was so arranged that the weapon could be fired without being removed from the sledge. Also, trench mortars could be transported on such

Opposite *When, in November 1939, Soviet territorial demands on Finland were refused by the Finns, a state of war was declared between Finland and Russia. The Red Army greatly out-numbered the Finnish army but the Finns were in their element fighting in the severe winter conditions. The famed Mannerheim Line, as a national system of defence works, was no replica of France's Maginot Line, however, which was thought to be impregnable at the time. The Mannerheim Line consisted largely of simple trenches dug in the pattern of the example shown here. The Finnish infantry confidently expected nonetheless to repel all advances by the Red Army.*

Below *Lack of specialized equipment led the Finns to improvize during the Russo-Finnish War. On the left is a stacked charge while on the right the soldier carries a 'Molotov Cocktail', a bottled petrol concoction, which when ignited was widely used to destroy Soviet tanks.*

Finnish troops of the 9th Division return from their destruction of two Russian divisions at the Battle of Suomussalmi during late December 1939. The early Finnish victories such as Suomussalmi attracted enthusiastic coverage in the world press.

sledges. When the machine-gun had been taken off, the sledge could be used as an ordinary ski-sledge. A cavalry ski-sledge was somewhat heavier than the previously-described models, having two dragpoles on the sides instead of one in the middle. The dragpoles were attached to the sides of the saddle and the sledge was thus towed by a cavalryman. Usually there were two platforms on the sledge: a higher and longer one in the forepart where the machine-gun together with its ordnance-sledge (*pjaskalke*) were accommodated; and a low, short platform with a hand-bar in front where two crewmen could ride in a standing posture. Sledges of this kind were used by Finnish and Swedish cavalry, particularly for the transport of machine-guns, trench mortars, and ammunition.

Ski-sledges could be assembled in an emergency at a moment's notice using one or two pairs of skis, ski sticks or wooden bars, wire and cord. For special purposes, particularly in the Arctic areas, a one-man Lapp sledge, called a *pulka* was often used. The *pulka* was a boat-like construction, consisting of a light wooden frame that rested on two or three runners and was attached to the skier's waist by two osier or bamboo 'tentacles'. Cross-bars and a piece of tent-cloth formed the bottom of the *pulka* and gave it the necessary span. The load was wrapped into the side-flaps of the cover and tied or strapped to the sledge. A medium machine-gun could be carried on a *pulka*. *Pulkas* were particularly useful for small patrols operating in mountainous or thickly-wooded terrain.

The Russians, whose prowess in the snow—as is later described—was undistinguished as compared with the Finns, introduced motor sledges, but opinions were divided as to their usefulness. The Russians were even reported to use a sort of 'tank-sledge'—iron-clad motor sledges—in their initial assault on the Karelian isthmus. It seems, however, that the device did not prove very successful. A motor bicycle with a short, broad ski before the front wheel to trample down the snow-ploughed roads, but was quite jerky and demanded skilful riding. It acquired greater stability when provided with a side-car mounted on a sleigh-runner. Aircraft in winter were often fitted with skis instead of wheels, which made landing and taking off possible in moderately-deep snow even on uncleared level ground, such as frozen lakes or fjords. In 1939, for example, the obsolete British Bristol Bulldog biplane fitted with skis gave a good account of itself flying with the Finnish Air force.

Although in principle ski troops could go anywhere on snow-bound terrain, it was usual for a large column to be preceded by a 'tracking detachment' whose job it was to mark a track through deep, fresh snow. The movement of ski troops took place in two, three, or more single-file columns (the soldiers goose-stepping one after another), not less than 2 yd (2 m) apart, though in the operational zone or in difficult terrain further dispersal was often advisable. Men belonging to the same lower unit generally followed the same track. The 'marching' speed was adjusted to that of the weakest skiers, but side patrols of proficient racers were sent out to keep watch on the approaches. Ski-sledges with ammunition, reserve skis, supplies, etc., followed in the rear. When heavy transport was included in the column, it followed in the wake of a snow-plough detachment. When a snow-covered road was negotiable, Scandinavian and Russian cavalrymen—who carried a rope on the right side of the saddle—were used to tow bunches of ski-troopers and this was an effective way of bringing up reinforcements. Star performers amongst the Finnish skiers were even reported, on reaching the edge of a frozen river after a cross-country trek, to shoulder their skis and proceed along the icy surface on skates!

Scandinavian bivouacs were sited in places that had ease of access to firewood (spruce twigs or straw) and drinkable water. The forest suggested itself as a site most likely to meet these requirements. Unfortunately, however, in most cases the snow in the forests is both loose and deep. Therefore ravines, flat terraces at a mountain foot, etc., were in general far better choices for an encampment. Tents were transportable in parts, and when erected could each accommodate 4, 8, or 16 men. Tents were connected by footpaths and ski tracks and trucks were also laid down for patrolling the area. The outside walls of the tent near the ground were covered with spruce or pine twigs (any conifer or evergreen would do equally well, but those with flat branches were best suited) pointing downwards and then buried in the snow to a depth of 1 or 2 ft (30 or 60 cm), which served to give additional protection against the wind. The floors inside the tents (they did not have canvas floors) were made to slope towards the centre, and the beds were made on the slopes under the walls on a layer of spruce twigs—first larger and coarser, then smaller and finer, if possible—then covered with straw or hay, which imitated

A Finnish sniper uses a captured Moissin Nagent 7.62 mm M1918 rifle fitted with a telescopic sight.

a mattress.

The Scandinavians borrowed the Eskimo's art to make snow-caves and igloos. Construction of a snow-cave is only possible in hard, wind-packed snow at least 5 ft (1.5 m) in depth. Suitable locations are found on the lee and sometimes windward sides of big stones or rock buttresses where a drift wall has built up. The entrance to a snow-cave is made as small as possible, just big enough to let a person through. The inside walls are beaten up with the flat side of the spade to give them greater strength. When the shelter is complete and its inhabitants lodged inside, the entrance is filled with snow blocks prepared in advance for this purpose or closed by means of a tent cloth. An opening is made in the snow roof with a ski stick to allow smoke from the oven to drift away.

Several types of igloo were employed. The most common—the round igloo for two people—is made by first describing a circle in the snow with two skis used like a pair of com-

Finnish troops encamped on the ice prior to an attack on a Russian troop concentration.

passes. The upper layer of snow is then removed from inside the circle and the remaining snow trampled into a hard floor. The igloo dome is made from snow bricks, which are laid spirally all around the cleared circular space, building a snow wall of gradually lessening radius. Thus, in the end, a complete snow dome emerges that should not be too high but should allow a measure of freedom of movement to the two people who will inhabit it. When this is ready, an entrance is cut out in the wall on the lee side so as to admit a person in a creeping position. A small opening is made in the roof for ventilation, and only a few finishing touches remain to complete the construction. Larger igloos, either round or square, can be built on similar lines. Snow walls were also built for use as stables, a piece of tent cloth being used for a roof.

Whereas the Finns were in their element in the 'Winter War' of 1939-40, the Russians made no disguise of their lack of experience as ski troops. The Russian record reveals some interesting statements. One military commentator expressed the opinion at the beginning of the Finnish campaign that 'We have not remembered the earlier traditions of the use of skis for the heroic struggle with the Whitefinns'.

A member of the Soviet 70th Infantry Division, which was largely recruited from city-dwellers in Leningrad and which occupied the extreme left of the Karelian front throughout January, February, and March of 1940, recalled that after the division had been in the line for a month.

> skis were issued. We put them on. I could see that my friends were reluctant and puzzled; they did not seem to understand the nature of skis.
>
> 'I will tell you a secret, boys,' said Punin, 'I have never been on skis.'
>
> 'Why do you suppose that the Finns are so good on skis?' said the company commander. 'It is because they are raised up under winter conditions, and we, who are city people, if we take part in winter sports, do it on ice skates, and we have forgotten about skis. However, we must now concentrate on them.'

In another account the difficulties encountered in training the Red Army man to handle his skis properly were underscored:

> In between the fighting the men improved their skill on skis. Comrade Mirovonski insisted that he could do better in the snow without them.
>
> 'Skies are difficult, we can get the Whitefinns without them. Why must we practise?'

One evening I was despatched with Mirovonski on a patrol. An hour had not yet passed when, breathing hard, the red, robust soldier was asking for mercy.

'But how can you fire, comrade commander? It is difficult to hit the enemy while standing, but lying down with skis is impossible.'

I then taught him how to handle them. Skis are very necessary on patrol, in action and on roads.

The lack of ski training in the Red Army units engaged in Finland was not surprising for some fifteen divisions deployed in the campaign were from the Leningrad area, and of these five were raised from true 'city slickers', from inside the city limits itself. The Russians admitted that Finnish ski-troopers managed to attack rear wagon trains, artillery positions, and staff headquarters but there was evidence that during the battles on the Karelian isthmus, Russian scouting and patrolling techniques began to show an improvement. However, once the line was penetrated by these small parties of men they more often than not met with disaster at the hands of the Finnish soldiers in the lakeland, swamp, and forest areas of eastern Finland.

On the other hand, if Ivan cut a seemingly absurd figure in the snow, the odds in the 'Winter War' were weighted heavily in his favour. As a pro-Finnish writer observed, 'Skiing in the Soviet Army, after the 1939-40 war in Finland became the subject for international ridicule: which, however, was only partly justified and has certainly been greatly overdone'.

On 30 November 1939, the Red Air Force attacked Helsinki and Viipuri and the war was set in motion with a declaration of hostilities. Between 30 November and 15 December, Red armies totalling nearly a million men smashed at Finland, striking from the east and southeast. They were opposed by Finnish forces totalling 300,000 men, of which about 80 per cent were mobilized reservists. Soviet amphibious attacks on the southern coast were repulsed but in the far north a Russian column seized Petsamo, pressed a short distance south, and

then was stopped. The main Russian attacking force, driving into the Karelian isthmus, was hurled back with heavy loss at the Mannerheim Line. Other Russian columns passing into the vast lake and forest region of eastern and central Finland were quickly bogged down in the heavy snows and freezing temperatures.

In eastern Finland, the Russian 163rd Division moved in two columns over narrow roads and through densely-wooded areas converging at the village of Suomussalmi. Deep snow impeded its advantage and temperatures dropped to $-40°F$ ($-40°C$) biting deeply into the invaders, who were without Arctic clothing. On the Russian flanks, Finnish Civil Guard units in white smocks swooped silently on skis, sniping at supply vehicles and field kitchens. On 11 December the Finnish 9th Division attacked without waiting for their artillery. The

Horse and sledge was frequently used to carry supplies in the 'winter war'. The Finns clearly used the forests as guerrilla hideouts from which to strike swiftly at the more conventionally trained Soviet troops.

Russians were soon joined by their 4th (Motorized) Division but by Christmas Eve the two Russian divisions were fighting desperately to extricate themselves from a trap formed by the Finns. Suomussalmi proved to be a defeat for the Russians, who suffered losses of about 27,500 killed or frozen to death. Following this and similar repulses, the Russians regrouped but the Finns, who were promised a strong expeditionary force from Britain and France and were over-confident with success, calmly awaited the next assaults.

Between 1 and 13 February, the Russian Seventh and Thirteenth Armies launched massive attacks—supported by tremendous artillery bombardments—against the Mannerheim Line. Finally a breakthrough was effected near Summa (13 February). The Finnish right wing and centre were rolled back to Viipuri. On 12 March 1940, Finland capitulated.

The Finnish defence was conducted by well-led, disciplined soldiers, familiar with the terrain and weather conditions and utilizing tactics geared to those conditions. The Russian offensive was amateurishly planned, without regard to terrain, weather, or the logistical problems involved, but it was finally successful because the Russians were prepared to sacrifice so many of their lives. Some claim that 200,000 Red Army men were killed in action. This may be grossly exaggerated, but the Russian dead in the 'Winter War'—an almost forgotten episode of the Second World War—made an important contribution to the outcome of the vaster conflict. Adolf Hitler and his generals assumed that Soviet Russia, inferior in leadership, tactics, and weapons, would be a pushover for the forces of the Third Reich. This view of Soviet military prowess was unfortunately shared by many foreign observers, including Britain, France, and the USA.

Finnish skiers use reindeer for transport in the Arctic region near Petsamo in the latter stages of the war. When moving over frozen lakes and rivers, skiers swapped their skis, which were then carried on their shoulders, for ice-skates, which they used with equal skill for cross-country manoeuvres.

CHAPTER 10
THE CAMPAIGN IN NORWAY 1940

As the brief Polish campaign of 1939 drew to an end, and the 'phoney war' developed in which both sides seemed to make no positive moves on the French Western Front, thoughts in London, Paris, and Berlin turned almost simultaneously to Scandinavia. The 1,000-mile (1,600-km) long western coastline of Norway, with its ports and fjords connected by the Inner Leads, was undoubtedly an important factor in a war between Britain and Germany. The Leads—a coastal waterway from the North Cape to Stavanger, passing for much of its distance between islands and the mainland and for all of its distance well within territorial waters—were open, without interference, to ships of both combatants for passage. The British viewpoint, as expressed by Winston Churchill, then First Lord of the Admiralty, was that the Royal Navy should lay mines in the Leads and that the army and RAF should be landed along the Norwegian coastline to prevent the Germans deploying surface raiders and submarines from its ports.

In addition, there was the matter of Swedish iron ore. In peace-time, Germany imported some 20 million tons of ore annually, about half from the French fields in Lorraine and half from Sweden. With the French supplies closed to Germany, those from Sweden became vital to its industry and war effort. These, except for a small supply from central Sweden, came from the Gällivare deposits in the north and were shipped from Luleå in the Baltic and Narvik in northern Norway. In winter, when the Bal-

tic froze, the whole of this supply came through Narvik, kept open by the Gulf Stream. Luleå, Gällivare, and Narvik were connected by rail, but there was and is no direct road from Narvik to Gällivare. From Narvik ships followed the Leads south to Stavanger, the Skagerrak, and the German ports. For Sweden to stop the ore traffic would probably lead to a German invasion and in any case the Swedes were not averse to the new Nazi regime. Churchill even entertained the idea of sending a naval squadron into the Baltic, equipped to combat German air power, mines, and torpedoes, not to mention neutral ice.

During February 1940 an ambitious plan was formulated to send two Allied brigades (Anglo-French) to secure Narvik and the line to Luleå for the passage of another two or three British and French brigades to join the winter campaign in Finland. To protect Sweden against German reaction, a territorial division, the 49th Infantry Division, would capture Trondheim, Bergen, and Stavanger for the passage of one British regular division, the 5th Infantry Division, and two territorial divisions via Trondheim to Sweden. Six-and-a-half squadrons of the RAF, two of them Gladiator biplanes, would accompany the expedition, and four home-based heavy-bomber squadrons would support it.

The 5th Battalion, the Scots Guards, raised from Alpine enthusiasts, was sent to Chamonix, the home of the Chasseurs-Alpins, to train for operations at Narvik. In London,

When the Germans invaded Norway on 9 April 1940, the main force was landed under the strong cover of naval warships from the sea combined with air-landing operations by key assault troops. The German 3rd Mountain Division, which was in part deployed in the Narvik area, had been well trained to operate in Arctic conditions but the Gebirgsjäger were nonetheless severely tested in the brief campaign. Here German skiers are about to move across country on an offensive patrol.

the end of the Finnish war left these plans in suspense. Both Churchill and Sir Edmund Ironside, Chief of the Imperial General Staff, still pressed for the execution of the plan but Neville Chamberlain's War Cabinet ordered that the military operation be cancelled. Even the Guards ski battalion was disbanded, a move the British army had every reason to regret in the coming campaign. The minelaying force did set sail on 5 April, to lay their mines on the morning of 8 April. Meanwhile, five infantry and one Guards battalions were embarked in cruisers at Rosyth and in transports in the Clyde in readiness to set sail for Norway.

In Berlin, the formal directive for Operation 'Weserübung' was issued on 1 March. Denmark ('Weserübung Sud') and Norway ('Weserübung Nord') were to be invaded simultaneously. Denmark was, in the main, to be occupied by motorized troops. In Norway attacks would be made on the five coastal cities,

Oslo, Kristiansand, Stavanger, Bergen, and Trondheim, and on Narvik. Thereafter, follow-up forces would move in through Oslo to link up and reinforce the outlying forces. For this, Group XXI was allotted six divisions, of which three would provide units for the initial assaults: the 3rd Mountain Division for Trondheim and Narvik, the 69th Infantry Division for Bergen and Stavanger, and the 163rd Infantry Division for Kristiansand and Oslo. The three follow-up divisions, to enter Norway by sea through Oslo, were provisionally allocated areas for deployment: the 196th, Trondheim and Andalsnes, enabling the 3rd Mountain Division to concentrate in the Narvik area; the 214th to Stavanger and Kristiansand, freeing the 69th and 163rd for Bergen and Oslo respectively; and the 181st east of Oslo to the Swedish border. In addition, Group XXI was allocated light tanks, artillery, railway troops, a signals battalion, and three companies of parachutists.

A light German mountain gun mounted on a sledge-like carrier for easier movement over the snow.

The German invasion of Norway, which was launched on 9 April in the initial phase, comprised six groups. Group 1 for Narvik consisted of ten destroyers carrying 2,000 men of the 3rd Mountain Division, escorted by the pocket-battleship *Gneisenau* and battleship *Scharnhorst*. Group 2 for Trondheim comprised the heavy cruiser *Hipper* and four destroyers carrying 1,700 men also of the 3rd Mountain Division. Group 3 for Bergen numbered the light cruisers *Köln* and *Königsberg,* the auxiliaries *Bremse* and *Karl Peters,* two torpedo boats and five fast patrol boats, with 1,900 troops of the 69th Division. Group 4 for Kristiansand and Arendal was formed by the light cruiser *Karlsruhe,* the auxiliary *Tsingtao,* three torpedo boats and seven fast patrol boats, with 1,100 troops of the 163rd Division. Group 5 for Oslo was made up from the heavy cruiser *Blücher,* the pocket-battleship *Lützow,* the light cruiser *Emden,* three torpedo boats, two armed whalers and eight mine-sweepers, with 2,000 troops of the 163rd Division. Group 6 for Egersand cable station consisted of four mine-sweepers with 150 troops of the 69th Division. Simultaneously with the sea assaults, air assaults were made at Sola airfield near Stavanger and Fornebu airfield near Oslo—at Sola by one parachute company followed by two battalions of the 69th Division air-landed, and at Fornebu by two parachute companies followed by two battalions of the 163rd Division also air-landed.

The German invasion to 'prevent English plans to expand the war theatre' resulted in the occupation of the most important points on the Norwegian coastline. The task that was to be accomplished now was the establishment of land communications between these points, especially to Bergen and Trondheim—imperative for the securing of the coastal bases to threaten Britain's sea lanes. To do this it was necessary to negotiate 310 miles (500 km) in a far-flung, snow-covered mountain region that gave all the advantages to the defenders who were equipped with skis. Most of the route was through narrow valleys or desolate table lands. In the thickly-wooded chains of hills of central Norway, the 62-mile (100-km) long Lake Mjös separated the march routes to the Gudbrand valley in which a highway and railway line lead to Trondheim and Andalsnes. The other, narrow gauge, railway line to Trondheim ran in the Österdal, which starts at Kongsvinger. On the railway line to Bergen the narrowing of the valleys begins as soon as Hönefoss. West of the Grol, wild mountain chains separate the highway from the railway. Roads that were ice-covered or bottomless in thawing weather hindered the movement of the troops; deep snow in the meadowlands and insufficient mountain equipment impeded the fighting. It was also necessary to take into account the blocking of roads and the destruction of bridges and tunnels, etc.

In southern Norway, 'Weserübung Nord' had, by the evening of 9 April, seized the main cities and communications centres—Oslo, Kristiansand, Stavanger, Bergen, and Trondheim. Only a small portion of each of the five Norwegian divisions in the south got a chance to fight. The Norwegian army comprised a small regular cadre and a national army to be called

The skills of the Eskimo were used by the Scandinavian armies of northern Europe. The Germans also learned the art of building homes in snow and ice, as is demonstrated by this Gebirgsjäger resting in his sleeping bag during the Norwegian campaign.

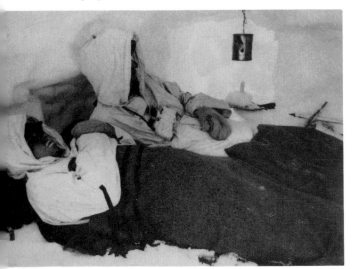

out on mobilization. The system provided for six infantry divisions, each allocated to a command district. The militiamen, after initial training, served each year for 24 to 30 days in their field units, where exercises with skis and snow-shoes maintained a high priority. Northern Norway (consisting of the provinces of Nordland, Troms, and Finnmark), forming the command district of the 6th Division, Narvik, and the military training camp, Elvegaardsmoen, had also fallen late on 9 April. But the capture of these places was not sufficient to dominate or paralyze all the Norwegian military forces in northern Norway. The mobilizations, which Major-General Carl Fleischer, Commander of the 6th Division, ordered on the night of 8 April for the provinces of Troms and Finnmark, went forward unaltered.

In southern Norway, early April is known as the so-called '*forefallstid*'—'fore-spring'—when winter begins to relax its grip on the land and snow disappears from the coast and southern slopes of the valleys, when a thaw sets in on the roads damaging their hard surfaces of beaten snow and ice, and when ice on the lakes and rivers begins to thin out and break. Thus, when serious land fighting began, the sea coast was already free of snow cover, as was also most of the lower country in the neighbourhood of Oslo and the southeast. Even higher up in the valleys during the later encounters, the southern slopes were already clear of snow. However, it continued to lie deep on the less-exposed mountain-sides and in the forest, and full-winter conditions prevailed in the high mountainous districts. In these circumstances the use of the ski was somewhat circumscribed. Nevertheless, a considerable number of the Gebirgsjäger (German mountain troops) made use of them both in the actual fighting and as a means of transport in their rear lines. The Norwegian army was put on skis as a matter of course. Young Norwegians escaping from Oslo after the German occupation of the capital took to their skis as the most certain and elusive way to join Norwegian units resisting the enemy onslaught in the mountain valleys.

In the eastern part of Norway, north of Oslo, only one infantry battalion, the Gudbrandsdel Battalion of the 4th Infantry Regiment, had been mobilized before the outbreak of war. This battalion stationed at Trandum Gardermoen, on the so-called 'neutrality guard' (*nøjtralitetsvakt*), was equipped with skis, snowshoes for men and horses, and special sledges that could be put on cartwheels to negotiate snow-covered ground, as well as with white camouflage overalls. Another battalion was raised in the south during the first days of the war and also equipped with skis, but only incompletely. Many pairs of skis had previously been sent to Finland so that there were insufficient skis in the depots for all the soldiers, and these had to be collected from the civilian population. Thus in Hamar and Lillehammer soldiers were sent from house to house to acquire all available ski equipment, which was willingly surrendered by the owners. In the southern part of the country, in Valdres, Gudbrandsdal, and Osterdel, Norwegian units operating on the northerly sides of the valleys, where snow lay deep, used skis. Ski detachments were also sent out to attack the Germans' flanks and rear. Most of the Norwegian units, however, operated without skis, and skiers were used only for special purposes. Only in the Trøndelag, northern Osterdal, and in the Narvik district was it a 'full-dress' winter campaign.

The simultaneous arrival of General Eduard Dietl's 3rd Mountain Division and a heavy snowfall in the Narvik area on the night of 9 April was too much for the 1st Battalion of the 13th Norwegian Infantry Regiment, which had been hastily moved from Elvegaardsmoen to Narvik to defend the city and the railway from Narvik across the border to Sweden. This battalion was effectively knocked out and the 2nd Battalion, the 15th Infantry Regiment, whose home base was at Elvegaardsmoen, got stuck in the snow marching across the mountains between Salangsdalen valley and Gratangsdalen while returning to base. Consequently, the

German mountain troops captured the Elvegaardsmoen camp and with it a huge haul of weapons, ammunition, clothes, equipment, provisions, etc., and at the same time gaining a firm footing on the north side of the fjord where, in the Bjerkvik area, they created a base from which the attack could be pressed further north against the Bardu region—strategically the most important part of northern Norway.

In England, Admiral of the Fleet the Earl of Cork and Orrery was, on the afternoon of 10 April, summoned to a meeting with the First Sea Lord at the Admiralty in London. The former was informed that he was to take command of a naval force that was to sail immediately to Narvik. Major-General P.J. Mackesy was similarly instructed to take charge of a force consisting of two companies of the 1st Battalion, the Scots Guards, 1st Battalion, the Irish Guards, and the 2nd Battalion, the South Wales Borderers, already bound in a troop convoy for the same destination. The naval-military force formed a base on Harstad Island, where the British troops made contact with the 6th Norwegian Division, whose headquarters was in the

A German observation post at Hönefoss in the early weeks of the campaign.

Bardu area. On 20 April, the Earl of Cork and Orrery was placed in sole command of the operations. On 24 April a naval bombardment of the Narvik defences was carried out with the object of making the Germans surrender. The 1st Battalion, the Irish Guards, was held on board ship to land and occupy the city, but the bombardment was not sufficiently successful to warrant the assault.

Major-General Mackesy was apprehensive — to say the least—about the involvement of British troops in Norway. In the *Supplement to the London Gazette* of 10 July 1947, Mackesy wrote retrospectively his assessment of his troops' prospects in the snowbound theatre of war:

> Although nobody without personal experience of Arctic winter conditions can possibly picture the climatic difficulties we experienced in the early days a word or two of description may not be out of place. The country was covered by snow up to 4 feet and more in depth. Even at sea level there were several feet of snow. Blizzards, heavy snow storms, bitter winds and very low night temperatures were normal. Indeed until the middle of May even those magnificent mountain soldiers, the French Chasseurs Alpins, suffered severely from frost bite and snow blindness. Troops who were not equipped with and skilled in the use of skis or snow shoes were absolutely incapable of operating tactically at all. I had no such troops at my disposal when I first landed. Shelter from the weather was of vital importance.
>
> It soon became certain that the enemy held Narvik in considerable strength. All the existing defences had been handed over intact by the Norwegian garrison. A personal reconnaissance convinced me that topography favoured the defence and that an opposed landing was quite out of the question so long as the deep snow and existing weather conditions persisted and so long as my force lacked landing craft, tanks, adequate artillery support, adequate anti-aircraft defence and air co-operation. The problem was, not one merely of landing, but one of carrying out a subsequent advance of several miles; yet owing to the configuration of the ground, not even during the first mile could support be given by ships' guns.

The immediate British objective was to secure the peninsulas, north and south of Narvik, from which observed artillery fire could in due course be brought to bear on the German defences on these peninsulas. The 1st Battalion, the Irish Guards, was assigned to the Bogen area and (at a later date) the 2nd Battalion, the South Wales Borderers, to Ballangen. A detachment of the 1st Battalion, the Scots Guards, was landed in the Sag Fjord on 14 April, moving forward to co-operate with the 6th Norwegian Division in the Forsbakken area. The state of the roads, well covered with snow and ice, and the impossibility of moving across country without skis, for the time being prevented further progress by these forces.

The British troops operating in the Narvik area, and on other sectors of the Norwegian front, were—according to press reports in Britain—also equipped with skis. But it appears that such snow equipment as they possessed was totally inadequate and came under scathing criticism from the Norwegian experts. No general winter plan had in any case been worked out in advance, and most of the British soldiers lacked sufficient training for serious operations on skis. Only the main roads were more or less free of snow, which lay several feet deep on both sides. Thus the columns were forced to keep to the beaten track and the dispersal of troops was made difficult, which served to increase their vulnerability to attack from the air. It was also impossible to throw out effective patrol screens to the flanks, which enabled the Germans to spring unpleasant surprises on the British units groping their way in strange surroundings. Another handicap was the lack of elementary knowledge of winter hygiene and bivouacking. (Tents were too heavy and more suited to erection by fatigue parties on Salisbury Plain. They were difficult to transport and no arrangements were made for their heating.) This caused great hardship to soldiers unaccustomed to the rigours of the northern climate. In the light of these experiences, the British Government's decision to disband the experi-

mental ski battalion after the ceasefire in Finland would appear rash in the extreme.

General Mackesy's hopes of prosecuting more vigorously the land operations in the Narvik area were raised by the arrival of French General Béthouart with a demi-brigade of the Chasseurs-Alpins. Two battalions of these élite troops were directed to advance, in co-operation with Norwegian forces, from the Gratangen area to Bjervik at the head of Herjangen Fjord. One battalion co-operated with the South Wales Borderers on the Ankenes peninsula, where the latter had been landed without opposition although counter-attacked later. The Brigade de Haute-Montagne consisted in fact of two demi-brigades of six BCA battalions: the 5th Demi-Brigade with its three battalions was assigned to the Narvik highlands, and the 27th Demi-Brigade with its three BCA battalions to the Namsos sector. Each battalion included a company of 'éclaireurs skieurs', used for reconnaissance, patrol, and special tactical work.

Of the Chasseurs-Alpins, General Mackesy wrote:

> Even those first class troops, the Chasseurs-Alpins, trained as they are, to snow conditions, found themselves very seriously hampered, indeed almost immobilized, by the soft deep snow. There was a small proportion of

German paratroops land in the Dombas area of northern Norway.

ski troops in each battalion, and a lack of snow shoes for the remainder proved a serious handicap. They suffered severely from frost bite and snow blindness. The troops in the front line were subjected to continual low-flying air attacks against which, owing to the state of the ground, they could not adequately protect themselves either by digging or by dispersion. (Later when I was enabled to allocate a small number of light anti-aircraft guns to the French troops, the effect was excellent.) Nevertheless they made some progress and took no little toll of the enemy.

The Frenchmen, fresh out of the Haute-Montagne School at Chamonix with their special clothing and equipment, were appalled at the state of affairs in the ranks of the South Wales Borderers, who were 'sans mitrailleuses, sans skis, sans DCA' but the Chasseurs were swift to lend a comradely hand in assisting the Welshmen to master the art of combat in the snow. As one Frenchman commented on the Norwegian campaign, 'La neige était épaisse (80 centimetres, à 1 metre et fondante) . . . la terrain difficile . . . la marche extremement pénible'.

The arrival of a demi-brigade of the French Foreign Legion and of a Polish brigade, coupled with rapidly-improving weather conditions and an accession of much-needed equipment (notably anti-aircraft artillery), and a very limited number of landing craft and a French company of tanks, facilitated the undertaking of more active operations on the Narvik front. The Foreign Legion undoubtedly stole the limelight from the Chasseurs-Alpins but the legionnaires made use of the Alpine skiers for scouting. The Polish Highland Brigade (Carpathian Chasseurs), operating on the Narvik front, were equipped with skis but apparently made little or no use of them. None of the Polish troops could ski well enough to negotiate the difficult mountain terrain. In the pre-war Polish army, troops were sent for training to the mountainous southern regions. In the Carpathians the Poles had six regiments of Mountain Chasseurs, who were equipped with skis and ski-sledges. Machine-guns were transported on these sledges and dog teams were used as draft power. The 'Carpathian Chasseurs' operating in Norway in 1940, however, were hastily raised and trained in Scotland from the Free Polish Army, and were less well equipped than their pre-war counterparts with their jerseys, windjackets with hoods, special ski boots and light touring skis made of ash with adjustable toe-irons, and short, cavalry rifle and bayonet.

In general Allied troops were not, or only partly, equipped for winter warfare, and Norwegian detachments were placed at the disposal of both British and French commanders for patrolling duties. White camouflage was relatively little used by the Norwegians, largely for two reasons: the advanced season of the year and the lack of sufficient stocks. Accordingly, Norwegian Lottas (women conscripts) were set to work on sewing camouflage capes and wind-blouses (jackets), so that ski units and detachments operating in the snow-covered localities could be equipped with these items. Both British and French units dispatched to Narvik had white camouflage covers, white-painted helmets, and white screens for artillery.

In the first month of the war in southern

Two views of the powered snow vehicle which was used by the Germans for medical evacuation and other purposes. The vehicle skimmed the surface of the snow when moving at speed like a motor-boat over water.

Norway, Norwegian ski detachments were very active on the left flank of the German forces advancing from Oslo. They continually harassed the German rear and interfered with German lines of communication. Several bold sallies were made by Norwegian skiers against the forward German positions near Roa and Hønefoss where German detachments were caught by surprise and completely annihilated at the cost of a very small loss of life on the Norwegian side. German thrusts across Nordmark against Solør and Hadeland were repelled by small detachments of Norwegian skiers, in whose opinion the Germans in the forest did not prove very formidable opponents. One part of the Gudbrandsdal Battalion engaged in the fighting at Minnesund was able to accomplish a successful withdrawal in the face of far-superior enemy forces—thanks to the use of skis. Later on these units operated on skis in Trysil, where snow was abundant, and made several raids on the Germans at Elverum. Also in Telemark and Rogaland, ski guerrilla raids were in progress and a heavy toll was levied on the enemy attempting to advance into the mountains.

Although the subject of German and Austrian mountain troops is covered separately in this book, it is appropriate to note here that both Germany and Austria—united in the Second World War in the cause of the Third Reich—had a strong mountain-warfare tradition. The two Germanic nations were equipped with some of Europe's most majestic mountain ranges and the Gebirgsjäger, as we have seen, experienced classic mountain combat in The First World War on the Italian and Balkan fronts. The Treaty of Versailles restricted Germany to a small army of 100,000 men, but the Reichswehr paid special attention to mountain training and civilian sports' organizations were encouraged to take up skiing. It was said that, in the Germany of the Third Reich that succeeded the Weimar Republic with Adolf Hitler's rise to power in 1933, over a million people were skilled in the use of skis.

In 1940, German skiers were used in Norway as follows:

1. Infantry patrols not exceeding one company in force for patrolling, scouting, occupation of strategic points, and direct offensive operations.
2. Medical service, signals, and telecommunication units.
3. Detachments of machine-guns up to two machine-guns in each, particularly for work in the mountains.
4. Artillery staff, officer patrols for scouting and observation, fire direction, etc., particularly with high-angle-fire guns (howitzers).
5. Organs of command: staff officers, staff personnel, and telecommunications service.

When the occasion demanded, larger German units were put on skis. However, the German troops who fought in the Norwegian Campaign of May-June 1940 contained only a small proportion of skiers, except in the Tirolian Alpine regiments, and their use was very much in the above pattern—the rules for which dated back to 1917. White camouflage covers were used by the Germans, as in the First World War, but now they were equipped with quick-firing automatics. The Tirolian contingent played a conspicuous part in the fighting in Norway, but the German infantry of the line also possessed small groups of skiers who co-operated with the soldiers on foot or, equipped only with snowshoes, acted as screens for the main columns.

On 12 April the Germans commenced broadening their hold on the Oslo area by advancing northwards and fanning out in every direction. On 13 April German troops occupied, in the southeast, the fortress of Fredrickstad that had been evacuated voluntarily by the Norwegians. On the same day and after a brief battle they took the small mountain fortress of Greaker and despite a big bridge obstruction they reached Halden. Other fighting groups forced a crossing of the turbulent Glommen near Spydeberg. By evening the Norwegians were pushed back to Mysen with the aid of three bomber aircraft, and the fortress surrendered early on 14 April. On the night of 15 April the last strong-point in the sector, the fortress of Trogstad, fell into the hands of a German detachment advancing from Lilleström to Mysen.

On 13 April the Germans also made some progress to the north of Oslo. Motorized troops and an Alpine battalion that had been brought up by rail advanced via Eidsvoll to the southern end of Lake Mjøsa. In addition one combat group split, its main forces driving via Sandvika, constantly engaging the Norwegians and pushing to Hønefoss despite destroyed bridges, roads, and snow-covered mountain terrain. One battalion drove to Tyristrand via Drammen. Now the German Command could order the units on the right to advance on Kongsvinger and Hamar and the units on the left to advance along the road to Bergen. After British troops landed on 14 April at Andalsnes and Namsos, the establishment of the line of communication to Trondheim and the securing of the rail line and highway near Dombas became imperative for the Germans. On the same day German parachute troops jumped in small numbers at Dombas, and dive-bombers attacked the railway to Andalsnes.

In order to establish land communication with Trondheim and to destroy the Norwegian forces barring the way, the German units on the right flank gave pursuit through Elverum into Österdal, and via Hamar into the Gubrandsdal. The units on the left flank, whose Oslo forces were engaged at Hønefoss and Kongsberg, were ordered at first only to make strong motor reconnaissance via Raufoss to Lillehammer and on to Dombas. In addition, the reinforcement of the troops at Trondheim was begun by means of air transport. On 14 April, with reinforced reconnaissance, a German column located the Norwegians on the east shore of Lake Mjøsa at Strandlökka. The Norwegians, resting their flank on the lake, were determined to resist stubbornly. The German column, which had been brought up from the Lillestrom region during the night, remained facing the Norwegian positions on 15 and 16 April. Mountain chains under deep snow made an encirclement of the Norwegians' east wing impossible.

The most conspicuous German victory gained by a combined manoeuvre of ski and armoured forces was the battle of Mjøsa. The Norwegians were in fact entrenched on both sides of Lake Mjøsa and along the River Vorma, and for several days all German attempts at a breakthrough were unsuccessful. But on 17 April Tirolian ski troops succeeded in crossing the frozen Vorma and the half-unfrozen Mjøsa, where artificial rifts had been blown up in the ice. Many were drowned on the way, but a considerable force reached the opposite shore and outflanked the Norwegian positions on the western side of the lake. Simultaneously a tank attack was launched from Hønefoss along the Randsfjord, and other mechanized columns reached Flisa in Solor. The Norwegian forces holding positions on both sides of the Mjøsa had to beat a hasty retreat to escape envelopment by the German pincers. Gjøvik and Hamar were surrendered, which constituted a fatal blow to the defence of southern Norway.

Skiers operated on both sides during the fighting in the Gudbrandsdal, which followed on the defeat of the British and Norwegian forces at Lillehammer. On 24 April the Norwegian General Headquarters sent two expeditions on skis into the mountains. Their task was to harass the German flank and to interfere with enemy communications in the rear. Both ski detachments carried out successful raids. During the battle of Kvam, where British troops had been holding positions for three days against the 196th German Division, a detachment of 50 Norwegian skiers was dispatched from the headquarters of the 2nd Division in Otta into the mountains east of the valley. The Norwegians, after some skirmishes with German patrols, reached the Hillingen *seter* (summer cheese-farm) on the right German flank, where they discovered a German field battery in position at the foot of the hillside. The battery was immediately attacked with machine-gun fire and annihilated.

In the subsequent retreat up the valley from Kvam, this Norwegian ski detachment acted as cover for the left flank of the British forces and after a rough mountain march of six days safely reached the Romsdal. In their final attack on Kvam, German ski troops played a prominent part. The attack was launched at night and flares were used to increase visibility—an interesting new development in this type of operations. The Germans made frequent use of parachutists in their push through the Gudbrand valley. Soon after the first parachute attack on the important road junctions of Dombas and Dovra, special anti-parachute squads on skis were set up. Groups of twenty expert skiers were posted for this purpose at Tretten, Otta, and Dombas, which commanded most of the roads in the district. They had lorries at their disposal and as soon as German parachutists were reported, they rushed up to the farthest point accessible by road and then raced on skis to surround and intercept the Germans before they had time to do any

The legs supporting the front portion of the barrel of this German machine-gun have been fitted with a special 'Shoe' for firm placement in the snow.

damage or establish positions. This arrangement proved very effective and the parachute menace had soon been completely mastered. The German parachute experiment in Norway was not entirely successful. Many parachutists were dropped in outlying mountain districts where the opportunities for sabotage were very restricted.

In the fighting in the northern reaches of Österdal, notably in the district of Røros that was uniformly covered in snow, Norwegian guerrilla operations continued for some time after the fall of Tynset and the Norwegians, moving on skis after nightfall, succeeded several times in recapturing their positions lost in daytime in the face of German superiority in arms and aircraft—though they were seldom able to maintain their lines unbroken for long. In western Norway nearly the whole of the Norwegian 4th Division had succeeded in carrying through their war mobilization, despite the loss of their main depot at Bergen and, unlike the other Norwegian divisions, they were well-equipped with artillery. The infantry battalions of the 4th Division operated without skis, but three special companies of crack skiers were attached with full winter kit.

Some men from these ski units were sent south across the mountains from the railway station of Geilo in order to stem the German push against Kongsberg and Numedal, in which manoeuvre they had some success. Others harassed the left flank of the German advance from Bergen towards Voss and Myrdal, where some sharp encounters were fought. There were also some ski detachments among the troops hastily mobilized at Hønefoss and Brandbu who rendered a good account of themselves in attacks against the German rear and lines of communication. Later on these troops were forced back into Valdres, where they were joined by some units of the 4th Infantry Division. A defence line was established and the German advance stemmed. In their attacks the Germans used ski troops combined with infantry moving on snow-shoes.

Back in London—where the winter snows had long since subsided, although a chill wind blew up Whitehall from the continent of Europe—Lieutenant General C.J.E. Auchinleck, CB, CSI, DSO, OBE, was summoned on 28 April to meet the Chief of the Imperial Staff (General Sir Edmund Ironside—no stranger to Arctic conditions after his sojourn in northern Russia with the Allied Expeditionary Forces after the First World War). The upshot of the meeting was that on 6 May, Auchinleck—an officer of the Indian army who had been uprooted from his Indian 'homeland' to take over Southern Command to prepare Britain's defences against invasion—was appointed General Officer Commanding-in-Chief designate of the Anglo-French land forces and of the RAF in Norway. The following day he was dispatched with impatient gestures by Winston Churchill, First Lord of the Admiralty (three days later Churchill was Prime Minister) to Norway aboard a Polish liner, where he landed after an uneventful voyage at Harstad on 11 May.

As evidence that the British Government was still optimistic about the outcome of the Norwegian campaign, the 'Auk' (as he was to be affectionately known by thousands who served under him in later campaigns in the Second World War) received the following basic instructions:

> That the object of His Majesty's Government was to secure and maintain a base in Northern Norway from which it would be possible:-
> i. To deny iron ore supplies to Germany via Narvik.
> ii. To interfere with iron ore supplies to Germany from Luleå in Sweden.
> iii. To preserve a part of Norway as a seat of Government for the Norwegian King and Government.

Whether or not Auchinleck, on sighting the snow-clad mountain backcloth to the port of Narvik, was reminded of his beloved Himalayas and the North-West Frontier of India and thus inspired by the challenge of mountain warfare is not recorded, but there is no evidence that he was assisted by any reliable information on campaign conditions in Norway from Whitehall. On 13 May, when Auchinleck was fully in command of the Anglo-French forces in northern Norway, the battle dispositions were as follows.

In the Narvik area the Germans were firmly in possession of the port and city and the whole peninsula on which Narvik stands. One battalion of the Chasseurs-Alpins and the 2nd Battalion, the South Wales Borderers, had a foothold on the Ankenes peninsula but were not yet in possession of Ankenes itself. Two battalions of the Foreign Legion and one battalion of the Polish contingent were holding the Bjerkvik-Oijord area and in contact with the Germans to the east. One battalion of Chasseurs-Alpins was posted to the north of the Foreign Legion, having advanced from the direction of Gratangen, and was in contact with German elements about Hartvigvand. Fleischer's 6th Norwegian Division (five battalions of infantry and a few mountain guns) was stationed to the north and east of the Chasseurs-Alpins and in touch with the Germans in the Graesdalen valley and to the east of it. Another battalion of the Chasseurs-Alpins was located near Gratangen. A Polish battalion occupied a position near Harstad on the south shore of the Ofot Fjord and another at Salangen.

South of Narvik on the Mo-Bodo sector, the 1st Battalion, the Scots Guards, less one company and one independent company at Mo, faced German units that had landed on the Hemnes peninsula 20 miles (32 km) south of Mo. The Guards were reinforced by field guns and a Bofors light anti-aircraft regiment. In the Bodo area, there was one company of Scots Guards and three 'independent companies'. The 1st Battalion, the Irish Guards, was scheduled shortly to arrive to fight alongside the Scots Guards. On 16 May Auchinleck reported to the Chiefs of Staff that 'it should be possible to

Above *General Eduard Dietl, the dynamic German Gebirgs-jäger commander (on the right facing the camera) talks to one of his mountain troopers after the conclusion of the Norwegian campaign in 1940.*

Right *German troops take cover in the Norwegian snow.*

maintain the integrity of Northern Norway' with adequate forces that he outlined in detail, but on 17 May a telegram was sent in reply to the effect that for Auchinleck's assault on the Narvik and Mo-Bodo sectors, his force would be limited to twelve French and three British battalions, with ten independent companies with 'proportionate' artillery, engineers, and 'services', 48 heavy and 60 light anti-aircraft guns, one Hurricane squadron, one Gladiator squadron, and, possibly, one army co-operation flight.

Narvik lies at the tip of a peninsula bounded on its northern and southern sides by two fjords: Rombaken to the north and Bjef-fjord to the south. Along the southern shore of the peninsula ran the iron-ore railway into Sweden. North and north east of Rombaken Fjord are the high mountains that dominate the peninsula on which Narvik and the railway stood. The men of the German 3rd Mountain Division (some 1,750 of them), who occupied Narvik, were in fact in a precarious position. The Narvik garrison was formed by the 139th Gebirgsjäger Regiment, whose three battalions

(the 1st, 2nd, and 3rd) had landed in the area on 9 April. The German mountain battalions had barely taken up their first positions when Royal Navy destroyers penetrated the fjord, destroyed the German ships at anchor, and established a formidable blockade outside Narvik Fjord. The Gebirgsjäger were now isolated from their homeland by the sea route, from the rest of their division, and the German army as a whole in Norway.

General Dietl, the Gebirgsjäger commander, was well aware of his numerical inferiority—Dietl reinforced his garrison with

a naval battalion formed from men from the ships destroyed by British destroyers. The sailors were placed on the northern shore of the peninsula to guard the railway while his Jäger battalions began to probe northwards and north eastwards into the mountains that rise sheer from the edge of the fjords. Dietl organized salvage detachments that dismantled the naval guns and radio sets from the sunken German destroyers. Ammunition was also brought up out of the wrecks so that the Jäger would have some degree of support in the fighting that was about to develop on the Narvik sector. One day a flight of Ju 52 transport aircraft landed a battery of 75-cm mountain guns. The Narvik element of the 3rd Mountain Division was without transport and desperately short of equipment. Dietl, aware that adequate food and clothing were needed by men fighting in the mountains in the bitter climate of winter, even sent divers down into the waters of the fjord to bring up supplies from a sunken whaling ship.

The Norwegian 6th 'Polar' Division (thus named after its experiences in the snow, mounting 'neutrality guard' on the Finnish border during the Russo-Finnish war) became a constant threat to the Gebirgsjäger in the mountains behind Narvik. The Norwegians, operating on skis, occupied the high mountain ground north of the Rombaken Fjord and near Bjønefjell in the German rear. Later in May, when the snow began to melt, skis were only retained for the troops holding the highest positions in the mountains. The objective of the 6th Division was to cut off lines of retreat by the Gebirgsjäger into Sweden. From 13 April the Norwegians and Germans were locked into battle for positions in the mountains in conditions of intense cold and deep snow. Fighting patrols from both sides struggled to seize dominant mountain peaks. The Germans at that time possessed no proper camouflage clothing—there were no quilted suits and none of the winter warfare equipment that subsequently became standard issue for German mountain troops.

Visibility in the mountains was frequently reduced to a few yards by the thick mists. Snow fell almost continuously, causing deep drifts through which the Gebirgsjäger waded slowly towards their objectives. Food that had been rationed since the opening of fighting was reduced, and the small portions were then further reduced. Their normal daily ration consisted of five slices of bread washed down with melted snow water. They lived in small tents, covered by a single blanket, and they were without fires or heating of any sort, for there was little combustible material in the bare mountains or on the open stony heights. Over the weeks the Germans—hungry, cold, tired, and outnumbered—were gradually driven from the mountains in blinding snowstorms. Step by step they were forced back along the railway line where the mountain men fought for the cover of the tunnels and where patrols met and clashed. By the third week in May, 15,000 Allied troops had been put into action against the Gebirgsjäger and the sailors. The offensive on 10 May, however—when German forces struck across the borders of Holland, Belgium, and France—overshadowed the plight of the German garrison in the Narvik area.

On 23 and 25 May Dietl received his first considerable reinforcements since mid-April: two parachute companies dropped to him. By early June the rest of a parachute battalion had reached him. He considered that he was still short of 1,500-2,000 men for the strength he needed to hold out. Even Dietl's dynamic personality seemed unable to keep the German mountain troops on their feet. Men could be persuaded only with difficulty to move from one position to another, and fell asleep even under machine-gun fire. Nor were the Norwegians much better off. In the high plateau the men received no warm food and had no shelter other than snow holes. Norwegian battalions, on narrow fronts, had difficulty in communications and supply. Signal cable sank during the day into the snow, where they froze hard and could not be moved. Ammunition and rations, carried by pack horse to supply points in the Graesdal and Randal, had then to be manpacked up slopes too steep for the horses. In the valley floors, the spring thaw turned communications into a trackless mire.

Whilst General Auchinleck's forces were poised with extreme hesitancy to assault Narvik and drive General Dietl's Gebirgsjäger into Sweden, German forces to the south had set their course to drive northwards to relieve the Narvik garrison. The fighting in central Norway had come to an end by early May. The British 15th Infantry Brigade had arrived at Andalsnes from France via Scotland on 17 April, where the tommies found the snow difficult to negotiate in their hob-nailed boots. On 22 April Lieutenant-General Massy was appointed commander of all British and French troops in central Norway, with orders to co-operate with Norwegian General Ruge in the defence of the area and to capture Trondheim. As it happened Massy never had the opportunity to leave London, and General Paget assumed command of Allied forces in the region. Some famous British regiments—the York and Lancasters, the King's Own Yorkshire Light Infantry, and the Green Howards—saw some sharp action along the roads in the mountainous area in the vicinity of Andalsnes. However, any hope of capturing Trondheim soon became a forlorn hope. Although Allied naval forces held the upper hand, the Luftwaffe enjoyed air superiority and on 28 April General Paget had the distressing task of informing General Ruge that the Allies had decided to abandon central Norway.

The British and French withdrawal from Namsos on the night of 2 May, and Norwegian capitulations in the region on 3 May, opened the way for the German 181st Infantry Division to advance to Namsos and Grong, which it did on 4 May. The Germans now set themselves the task of advancing northwards overland to the relief of Narvik. Major-General Feuerstein, commanding the 2nd Mountain Division, was placed in charge of the operation, for which he had available his own division of two mountain

regiments plus the elements of the 3rd Mountain Division, which were not defending Narvik. Both the 2nd and 3rd Gerbirgsjäger were truly Austrian divisions, the 2nd having been formed on 1 April 1938 at Innsbruck, and the 3rd at Graz on 1 April 1939. Both divisions had served in Poland in 1939 and were to form Gerbirgs Corps 'Norway', under General Dietl, on 14 June 1940—General Julius Ringel assuming command of the 3rd Mountain Division at that time.

Starting from Grong on 5 May in commandeered transport, the leading German units repeatedly found themselves held up by Norwegians holding road obstacles but, in spite of them and of the bad roads and thaw, they had advanced 125 miles (193 km) from Grong when, on 10 May, they made contact with Norwegian and British troops holding a position south of Mosjøen. The probability that the Germans would advance north to the relief of Narvik had been realized by the Allied Command when the evacuation from Namsos was decided upon. It had been hoped to use two battalions of the 5th Demi-Brigade Chasseurs-Alpins to delay the German advance between Grong and Mosjøen, but their commander, General Audet, considered that the road was impassable in the thaw, at least to his troops who would be under German air attack. The French Alpine troops were evacuated with the British troops at Namsos. The Norwegians fought tenaciously and were joined at Mosjøen by the British 4th and 5th Independent Companies on 8 May. The independent companies—the forerunners of the commandos—had been raised only in April, shortly after the German invasion of Norway, from 3,000 volunteers from the Territorial Army and formed into ten independent companies for irregular warfare.

Altogether a force of five independent companies and a small headquarters known as Scissorforce was, in fact, sent to Norway under the command of Colonel C. McV. Gubbins. Each company comprised 20 officers and 270 men, organized in three platoons of three sections and fire support, engineer, and head-quarter sub-units. The men were equipped with rucksacks, snow-shoes, Arctic boots, leather jerkins, and sheepskin coats, and each company was given 30 days' normal ration, five days' pemmican, 100,000 rounds of small-arms ammunition, and a generous allowance of £4,000 in British and Norwegian currency for local purchases. Thus equipped, the companies were expected to live off the local population, delay the German advance, and raise the help of the Norwegian population, some of whom were displaying increasingly pro-Nazi tendencies. The independent companies were a brave experiment by the War Office but the early commandos were no match for the former guides, ski instructors, and peasant farmers raised and trained in the mountains of Austria and Bavaria.

The Arctic Highway northward from Trondheim passed, for long stretches, beside fjords with frequently-placed operational ferry

German troops clear a barricaded mountain roadway in the final stages of the Norwegian campaign, April 1940. By this time there was no sign of snow at the lower altitudes in the mountains.

stages. The advancing Gebirgsjäger stuck to the mountains avoiding the water-crossings. Had the commandos developed the amphibious skills they were to perform so successfully later in the war, the German advance northward to Narvik might have been another story. At Mosjøen on 8 May, Gubbins found that a Norwegian battalion was holding a position 25 miles (40 km) south of the town. That position was lost on 9 May, but a near one, covering the road and the blown railway bridge, was taken up immediately south of Mosjøen. The town was itself unsuitable for defence, but the road north from it would offer many further opportunities for delaying action.

The German advance continued and Gubbins abandoned the 35 miles (56 km) of difficult mountain road between Mosjøen and Elsfjord, and re-embarked Nos. 4 and 5 Companies in Norwegian steamers near Mosjøen. From these they were transferred to destroyers and landed at Bodo. The Norwegians withdrew overland to Elsfjord, from whence they were ferried to Finneid, abandoning a great deal of their equipment at Elsfjord. By now an Allied decision was made to reinforce the southern front at Narvik. A battalion of Scots Guards, less one company, was landed at Mo early on 12 May. The Germans were shortly advancing on Mo and the Norwegians were alarmed at the speed with which their country was falling to the enemy. Even so, the Germans' rear lines of communication were becoming rapidly extended, and they were also facing the problem of supply in the wet snow and mud of the thaw.

The Narvik peninsula was now a salient, 6 miles (10 km) and 3 miles (5 km) across, flanked by Allied forces across a water obstacle that was, nevertheless, dominated by their own ships. The main difficulty in attacking it was a shortage of landing craft: those available for the Bjervik landing had now been reduced to two motor-landing craft and three assault craft. A small beach was found opposite Oijord, which could be seized and held until the landing craft could return with more troops. After some delays and postponements, the attack was set for 28 May. Bombardment opened at 23:45 on the night of 27 May, the cruisers *Cairo, Coventry, Southampton,* and five destroyers firing from the fjord, French and Norwegian artillery firing across it. By early morning the French Foreign Legion and a Norwegian infantry battalion were ashore and advancing to take high ground behind the beach. In conjunction with the landing, the Poles attacked at Ankenes and Beisfjord, meeting stubborn resistance. A German counter-attack from Ankenes drove them back, but they returned to the attack, capturing the village.

Narvik was entered on 28 May, the Germans withdrawing to a new line on high ground, 4½ miles (7.25 km) east of the city, covering the upper part of Rombaksfjord above the Straumen Narrows. On 1 June an attack along the southern shore of Rombaksfjord forced the Germans to make a further withdrawal. Meanwhile in the mountains to the east, the Norwegian 6th Brigade, having trouble with the thaw and the flooded river between the two massifs, pressed its attacks on the higher ground, threatening to take Rundfjell and so reach the German base at Bjørnfjell, which could cut Dietl off from his last supplies. By 7 June they were ready to attack Rundfjell, and they made some preliminary advances preparatory to a main attack on 8 June.

The Norwegian attack was never made. The Anglo-French force was ordered to evacuate northern Norway. Since mid-May the victorious Germans had been pouring into France after breaching the Allied line in the Ardennes. France was on the point of collapse and the British troops were urgently needed to defend their homeland. The last British troops left Bodo on the night of 31 May. There remained the problem of evacuating 24,500 men, and as much of their weapons and equipment as possible from the area of Harstad and Narvik. Fifteen troopships left with the British and French troops on board in two convoys on 7 and 9 June. The last party to embark, a rearguard of Chasseurs-Alpins and British engineers and control personnel, went aboard the *Southampton*, which formed part of the second troop convoy. The King and Government of Norway embarked in the British cruiser, *Devonshire*, on the evening of 7 June at Tromsø. A preliminary armistice between the Norwegians and Germans came into force on the night of 9 June. Dietl, acclaimed a hero in Germany, treated Ruge with courtesy and generosity, and Norwegian troops were allowed to return from the mountains, disband, and return to their homes.

The campaign in Norway was a typical example of mountain warfare, in which German air supremacy proved the decisive factor. In many cases skis were indispensable as a means of transport, while the practical impor-

tance of ski troops for patrolling and protecting main columns on the move, for harassing enemy communications, and for inflicting sudden thrusts at vital points, was more than once amply demonstrated. The campaign also showed the advantages enjoyed by troops using skis in retreat. Units that had not been so equipped were often lost without trace, while skiers managed to escape even when surrounded. The most interesting military development was the use of skiers for a diversion in conjunction with a mechanized drive. Much medical work was done with the use of skis and ski-sledges. Norwegian winter equipment— tents, tent-stoves, sledges, and snow-shoes (for horses and drivers)—proved excellent and indispensable in operations on the Narvik front.

British prisoners in Norway. The British Expeditionary Force, which had been despatched in such haste to Norway in April 1940, was ill-equipped to fight in the rugged mountain conditions.

CHAPTER 11
THE ALPES MARITIMES 1940

When, on 10 June 1940, Benito Mussolini declared war on France, the Germans had virtually conquered the French nation. However, French troops still manned their mountain fortifications and valley strong-points in the Alpine region of southeastern France, awaiting the Italian onslaught and unmoved by the momentous events taking place in the north. French troops effectively defended a 250-mile (400-km) line that curled westwards from a point east of Mont Blanc before spiralling southwards through the Alpine massif to the Mediterranean east of Nice. The Alpine front was studded with concrete fortifications on the mountain sides that housed heavy artillery and commanded the valley routes. Blockhouses and command posts were sited alongside the roads. The French defensive zones comprised the Rhône sector held by the 'Armée des Alpes', commanded by General Olry (who exercised responsibility for all the French forces in the region) with its headquarters at Annecy in the Haute-Savoie; the Savoie and Dauphiné areas assigned to XIV Corps commanded from bases at Saint-Paul-sur-Isère and La Roche-de-Laîne (Hautes-Alpes) respectively; and the Alpes Maritimes defended by XV Corps with its command centre at Vence.

Eleven French divisions, of which seven were mountain-élite, and a brigade of Spahis, were stationed on the frontier. The front-line Alpine and colonial troops were backed up by a huge force of infantry, marines, and artillery units with air cover charged with staving off a possible advance on Grenoble and Chambéry. A much larger force had manned the French Alpine fortifications before the war, but the massive German offensives of 10 May into France and the Low Countries had called for heavy reinforcements—the Chasseurs-Alpins, the Alpine infantry, and the 'ski scouts' remaining in the Alps being amongst the best troops the French army had to offer at the time. The Italian force, comprising two armies (the First and the Fourth) under the Prince of Piedmont and outnumbering the Frenchmen by three to one, launched an all-out assault on 22 June spearheaded by their own Alpine élite. Only 22 years had elapsed since the end of the First World War and the great battles of the Trentino, the Carnic and Julian Alps, the Isonzo, the Piave, and the Carso. The fifteen-day Battle of the Alps proved to be a strenuous but less-deadly affair. As the winter snows in the valleys and passes turned to yellow slush, the French army claimed a major victory in a little-known episode of the Second World War.

The French XIV Corps, whose insignia was a mountain butterfly, was commanded by General Étienne Beynet. The corps zone was divided into five sectors (Beaufortin and Tarentaise, Mauriénne, Briançonnais, Queyras, and Ubaye), advancing from the Col de la Seigne into the Tarentaise valley, which is dominated by a series of peaks and glaciers rising to over 10,800 ft (3,000 m)—the Glaciers des Glaciers, Mont Tondu, Col d'Enclave, and Tête d'Enclave. The Italians first made contact with the

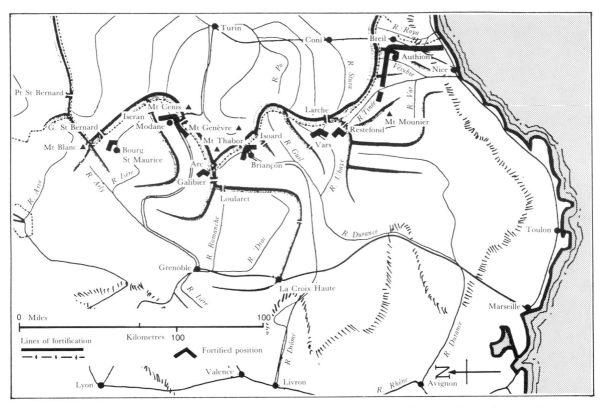

Above *The French system of fortifications in the Alpes-Maritime: This corner of south-eastern France, in peace-time a tourist wonderland, was the scene in June 1940 of France's ten-day war with Italy.*

Below *French Chasseurs-Alpins take part in ski training in the Briançon area. The French* Armée des Alpes *took part in a 16 day war, 10-25 June 1940; and while the main French forces in the north were on the point of complete collapse, the Chasseurs might justifiably claim they had won their war against the Italian invader.*

French outposts with their skiers. However, the invaders' main effort was made by motorcycle units roaring along from the Petit-Saint-Bérnard Pass. The French gunners on the mountainsides, though, played havoc with the motorcyclists, who in any case found the road conditions difficult to negotiate. At one location in the mountains, the French succeeded in surrounding two Italian Alpini battalions, whose troopers found their automatic rifles would not function satisfactorily in the cold conditions. All the skills of mountaineering were used, ascending and descending precipitous heights, when small parties of and even solitary Frenchmen would emerge from their fortifications to track their Italian opponents in the mountain wilderness.

The rugged mountains abutting the Mauriénne valley also bristled with French fortifications. Here the French army's main concern was to defend the approach to the town of Modane. On 10 June the French destroyed several bridges and a railway tunnel in the Haute Mauriénne, but the Italians attacked with twelve infantry battalions covered by heavy artillery fire. On Mont-Cenis, a group of about 100 Chasseurs, supported by artillery and manning a garrison at a lofty altitude, successfully defended their strong-point against Alpini— the Italians collecting their dead from the mountain slopes after a four-day battle. The Italian climbers had only rocks to protect them from plunging machine-gun fire. The Italians, advancing on the lower slopes, were unhampered by snow, and a column of armoured cars moved into the valley.

The Briançonnais area, covering the approach to the old town of Briançon, was also impressively defended by concrete fortifications, which the Italians ineffectively attempted to mortar. The key fortified positions, which the French call *ouvrages*, were, in the north, at Janus and Montgénèvre, blocking the right wing of the Italian advance and, in the south, at Gondran and Aittes, which faced the left wing of the advance. Observing the approaching

Italians from turreted ramparts, heavy artillery and machine-gun bursts took their toll of the attackers. In turn the Italians mounted artillery barrages at the *ouvrages* with the heaviest concentrations on Gondrans and Aittes—but poor visibility set in, adding to the confusion and chaos.

Le Queyras sector formed a salient with Briançonnais and Ubaye at its base points. Operations commenced in the vicinity on 18 June with the Italians sending forward reconnaissance parties. The main focus of attack was on the village of Abries, which lies a few miles east of the Château-Queyras. The French evacuated the village of Valpreveyre, after a severe Italian bombardment, but although the Alpini assault lost its momentum, the Italians continued to infiltrate. At one spot south of Abries, a French officer cadet, the local chief of gendarmerie, and four Chasseurs, who were scouting near a wood, surprised a group of 12 Alpini who voluntarily laid down their arms only to be joined by another bunch of 35 Italians, who were equally anxious to avoid any confrontation and to surrender.

A Chasseur calmly prepares to make a traverse of a ravine in the Alpine battlefield in southern France.

Above *A Chasseur machine-gunner mans a mountain-top position.*

Below *Chasseurs occupying a vantage point on high ground. The Italians deployed their own Alpini skiers to combat the French mountain men, but the Italian army made every effort to force passage through the valleys with their motorized columns.*

The Ubaye valley was one of the most important invasion routes in the Alps. A highway passed through the valley, which was bordered in the north by the de Sautron and de Monges high ground, and to the south by the des Fourches massif, which rises to 11,000 ft (3,350 m). Italian patrols started combing the area on 20 June. The Italians were not slow to send their units into the high altitudes, but the network of French fortifications on the mountain slopes and in the valley was hard to penetrate. The Italians concentrated their attacks on the village of Larche situated in the centre of the valley, behind which lay the village of Saint-Ours, which was protected by strongly-fortified positions at Roche La Croix Supérieur, Roche Croix, Bas Saint-Ours, and Haut Saint-Ours. Deep snow on the des Fourches massif

made mountain operations difficult and the battle for the Ubaye became an artillery duel of not insignificant proportions.

The French XV Corps' role in the Alpes-Maritimes was to defend the valley approaches to the fashionable, Mediterranean resort of Nice. The French force, largely Chasseurs-Alpins and infantry with artillery support, included a demi-brigade of Chasseurs drawn from the Pyrenees. The insignia of XV Corps was a head-and-shoulders silhouette of an Alpine Chasseur with his distinctive beret shown against a background of mountains. The Corps' commander, appropriately enough, was named General Montagne. The Italians attacked in a familiar pattern with Alpini battalions preceded by skiers along the frontier line, extending in the north from Saint-Dalmas-

A Chasseur patrol tests its equipment in an Alpine wilderness.

Salvage some 37 miles (60 km) to the sea. The Italian mountain troops were mainly grouped in the centre—the Livorno Infantry Division manning the extreme right flank and the Modena and Gemona Infantry Divisions the extreme left flank on the coastal littoral.

The Livorno Division made good progress in the '*haute montagne*', deploying mountain artillery most effectively, but in the Vésubie area an Alpini battalion, the Val Arroscia, was badly mauled by French machine-gun fire and those Italians not killed were taken prisoner. The Italians, on 20 June, attempted a breakthrough in the centre of the line in the direction of Breil, but registered no great success. In the coastal area the Italians sent no less than 42 battalions towards Nice. Armoured trains were used, the French making frantic efforts to block tunnels along the rail routes. The Italian Regia Aeronautica became increasingly active causing more damage to hotels and *pensions* at Menton and Cap Martin than they did to French fortified positions.

The Battle of the Alps (10-25 June 1940) came to an end with the signing of the armistice. On 17 June, the ageing First World War hero, Marshal Philippe Pétain, heading a new French Government, asked Hitler for the conditions of surrender. In the early minutes of 25 June, the six-week battle for France was over. The nation had suffered a disaster-at-arms—but not so the French mountain men.

CHAPTER 12
OUTPOSTS IN THE ARCTIC

On 5 August 1940, twelve Norwegians—whom fate had thrown together in a Salvation Army hostel in Iceland—decided to form their own 'private army' in order to continue the fight against the Germans. They called themselves 'Norwegian Company, Iceland', and began collecting equipment suitable for ski troops. Six weeks later, still officially unrecognized by either the British or Norwegian authorities, the force (which had now increased to eighteen) hoisted the Norwegian flag for the first time in Iceland in the name of the Norwegian army. So began the first phase of the Free Norwegians' participation in the war in the Arctic. It took them all over the Northern Hemisphere—Iceland, Greenland, Spitsbergen, Jan Mayen, and Arctic Norway itself being amongst the coldest spots.

The story of the Norwegian participants in the Arctic War began soon after the fall of Norway, when some of the large numbers of men who escaped across the North Sea to continue the fight against the Germans landed in Iceland. Others came to Iceland by various other means: some in a small boat that had been returning to Norway from a polar expedition in Greenland and that had put in at Iceland; one man on a Finnish ship, on which he had escaped and which had been intercepted by the British; and another who had come from Spitsbergen. Among them was one Norwegian army lieutenant and a Dane, who had volunteered and had served in Norway as a captain. These were the men—without money and,

except for the two officers, in civilian clothes—who were staying at the Salvation Army hostel in Reykjavik. They all wanted to fight, but they wanted to fight as Norwegians and not as part of the British forces, which at that time were occupying Iceland.

With the exception of the Dane (who sailed to Britain at the first opportunity), all the Norwegians decided to stay in Iceland where they thought they could render the best service. For one thing they knew that the British wanted to form a ski battalion and needed instructors in the use of skis. On 20 August the 'Norwegian Company, Iceland' rented a small villa on the outskirts of Reykjavik, which they used as living quarters. Credit for food and materials was obtained from Icelandic firms in the name of the Norwegian army, and the British provided uniforms and rifles. The Norwegians took their battle-dress blouses to a shop in Reykjavik where the title 'NORWAY' was embroidered on the shoulders, with two Norwegian flags, the staffs crossed, just below. This insignia, incidentally, remained the emblem of the Norwegian army in Iceland for two years.

After a brief period of training with the Duke of Wellington's Regiment, the Norwegians began their own ski training and the Icelandic authorities placed a mountain hut at their disposal. With dog teams and additional equipment that had come from a German meteorological expedition (which had been captured when on its way to Greenland), the troops moved into their new centre. There they hoisted the Norwegian flag, and each morning thereafter continued to salute their colours in true military fashion. The unit consisted of scientists, hunters, seamen, fishermen, and schoolboys. Not all were good skiers at first, but they soon became proficient, and at the same time they perfected themselves in all the techniques of polar life—dog-team driving, bivouacking in the snow, hygiene, and so on. The Norwegian military headquarters in London was slow to recognize the unit in Iceland but agreed that the twelve best skiers should be unofficially attached in pairs to British units, in order to teach these troops to ski and to live with a minimum of discomfort in the snow and ice.

In November, the 'Norwegian Company, Iceland' was established as an official unit of the Royal Norwegian Army. The British offered to the Norwegians a half-constructed camp at Akureyri on the north coast, to be used as a ski-training camp. It was in fact an ideal place, with first-class mountain runs nearby and good firm snow. In the New Year of 1941 the Norwegians moved in, and even while the camp was being completed each Norwegian instructor took 15 or 20 British troops under his charge and began training them in the mountains.

Each group of trainees remained in the mountains during the whole of the course, learning everything possible about the techniques of life in the Arctic. Meanwhile the British obtained considerable quantities of equipment such as tents, sleeping bags, stoves, ski-boots, and proper winter clothing, with Icelandic ponies to transport it to the snow-covered training grounds up in the mountains. Then, on 19 January, 'reinforcements' arrived in the form of 27 Norwegian soldiers who had done their recruit training in Scotland. Most of them were good skiers and they soon learned the best methods by which to train the British soldiers. It was then that the Norwegian unit received a surprise: twelve of the best men in the small company of instructors were needed for a 'secret mission'.

At this time the Allied military authorities were busy with plans to establish a more efficient and comprehensive meteorological service in the Arctic. One of the first places named in these plans was Jan Mayen, hundreds of miles to the north of Iceland. Before the war the Norwegian state maintained a meteorological station at Jan Mayen as it did at Spitsbergen and in northern Norway. Four men were at the observation post on Jan Mayen when Norway was attacked in April 1940. Cut off entirely, except for radio, they continued their work transmitting their reports to Britain instead of to Norway. Their relief was planned as soon as possible, but it was the late summer of 1940 before a little ship, which had been a fishery inspection boat in Norway but which had succeeded in escaping to Britain, left Britain for Jan Mayen. She was the *Fridtjof Nansen* and she had on board ample supplies of first-class polar and radio equipment and a small force of men. These men—Norwegians—were to occupy Jan Mayen and keep the Germans at bay.

The northern seas at this time were almost clear of ice, and *Fridtjof Nansen* made good progress. Soon the high, snowy mountain of Beerenberg came into view, its peaks shrouded as usual in clouds. Jan Mayen is of volcanic origin, the mountain itself being an extinct volcano. When it erupted aeons ago, the lava had streamed into the sea and patterned the ocean bed with tremendous reefs. The ship cruised around the underwater reefs of lava rock, searching for a passage to a suitable landing point on the island. On one of these treacherous reefs the *Fridtjof Nansen* foundered. There was just time for all on board to scramble into the lifeboats before the ship sank. All equipment and supplies were lost. The men went ashore and joined the four 'weather men' who for so many months had lived alone. A radio message for help was sent out and a few days later a rescue ship arrived to take the men off. The island was to be evacuated until such time as another expedition could be organized. Before they departed, the radio station was destroyed. Nothing that might help the Germans was left on Jan Mayen.

It was now known almost for certain that a German expedition would be sent to occupy Jan Mayen before the Arctic winter set in, and so a watch was kept. Before long, patience was rewarded. A small ex-Norwegian hunting vessel, which had been seized by the Germans in Norway, came steaming up to Jan Mayen from the south. She cruised along the jagged coast looking for a suitable landing place. Then a British naval destroyer came into sight. The skipper of the German ship did not wait—he knew he had no chance. He simply drove the ship ashore and while he and his men floundered in the icy water—their lifeboats had been swamped immediately they were launched—the ship, complete with all its equipment and supplies, went to the bottom. The Germans scrambled ashore and stood on the rocks shivering in the cold, waiting for the British to take them off to transport them to the inevitable prisoner-of-war camp.

Allied forces were strained to the utmost at this time, but it was still essential that Jan Mayen should be in Allied hands. This time a British expedition was sent. The ship reached Jan Mayen, but the weather was so bad that it could not possibly approach the shore. For fourteen days the ship lay tossing in heavy seas while everything froze. The venture was then abandoned and the ship sailed instead to Greenland. As Jan Mayen was now in the grip of the Arctic winter, the Allies had the satisfaction of at least knowing that the Germans could not now seize the island. Steps were taken immediately, however, to prepare a third expedition that was to be ready by the early spring. The Norwegians, this time from the ski-training camp at Akureyri, were to form the party.

The British had requested the Norwegians to undertake the task because of their better knowledge of Arctic conditions—and, of course, Jan Mayen was also Norwegian territory. Indeed, British officers who had been to the island on an earlier occasion had declared that

Jan Mayen was quite uninhabitable. This view is understandable, as no plants grow on Jan Mayen's 140 sq. miles (225 km^2) of lava rock—except a hardy Arctic moss that is found in thin layers in the more sheltered parts, and the only animal life there comprises blue fox, Arctic birds, seals in the winter, and occasionally polar bears that arrive on the drift ice. The twelve men were told nothing other than that they were needed for a 'secret polar expedition', and that they must be tough, prepared to live in Arctic conditions, and devote themselves to the task in hand to the very end if necessary. Eventually the expedition was ready—dogs, sledges, food supplies, tools, arms, and ammunition.

Two little Norwegian ships arrived at Reykjavik. The first was *Vesle Kari*, a stout ship that was specially reinforced to stand the strain of pushing through the pack ice of the northern seas. The other ship was *Honningsvaag*, a Norwegian navy patrol boat. On 19 February 1941, the two ships set sail. The only man on board who knew their destination was the Norwegian officer in charge. Up the east coast of Iceland they steamed, but soon they were enveloped in one of those sudden Arctic storms. The ships took a merciless battering and were so damaged that they could not continue the voyage. They put into Akureyri for repairs, covered in ice from bow to stern. *Vesle Kari* was the worst hit, with its bows smashed and considerable damage to its superstructure. The commander was impatient in case the Germans forestalled him at Jan Mayen, but he realized that it would be foolhardy to proceed before the repairs were properly carried out.

On 7 March another start was made. This time the men were more fortunate, for the weather remained calm. For three days they cruised, the men thinking their destination to be Spitsbergen. Then the mountain of Beerenberg was seen beyond the horizon, wearing, as usual, a halo of cloud. Only then were the men called together and told where they were going as well as the nature of the expedition—namely, to occupy Jan Mayen, to build up its defences from scratch, to keep the Germans out, to build and maintain a meteorological station, and to build their own huts and cook their own food. None of the twelve men constituting the occupying force had any illusions about the task ahead. Above all considerations, they would be living in isolation. But the Norwegians knew something of the vagaries of Arctic weather and the monotonous routine of polar life. And to them Jan Mayen was something more than an inhospitable rock: it was part of Norway.

Soon the whole island came into view, the brown cliffs and rocky beaches, the dazzling white snow and the high mountains. Surrounding the island was a dense pack that stretched for miles. Through this the *Vesle Kari* would have to force a passage, which would probably entail days of hard work. But on cruising along the edge of the belt a channel was discovered— the ice had cracked through almost to the shores of the island. The month of March, however, is reputedly the worst month of the year on Jan Mayen and, although it was calm as the two ships approached the island, a sudden storm might break. If that happened when the boats were in the middle of the pack-ice the ships could be crushed to matchwood in a few minutes. However, the risk had to be taken and the ships steamed up the narrow sea lane without mishap. As they did so a German plane appeared, but at that moment *Honningsvaag* was hidden by fog and the Germans made no attempt to attack the little *Vesle Kari* and soon disappeared. The channel ended a little distance from the shore in a solid block of frozen water. This became the quay for the two boats.

When the order was given to unload the ships, the Norwegians' difficulties really began. Although it was easy enough to get the equipment overboard it was not so easy to take it ashore. The frozen sea was covered with deep snow—too deep for the dogs to be used. The men, therefore, had to don skis and haul the materials themselves. And when they reached the landing stage—a steep gradient of loose rock—they had to manhandle everything. While the work of unloading the most important equipment proceeded, a scouting party went into the interior to find a suitable camp base. As luck would have it the men found a hut that was still standing. It was a tiny hunting-lodge capable of sleeping four, and under the circumstances it was a valuable find. It was also situated in an ideal site, protected on three sides by high land. It was decided that this should be the camp base. Once again equipment and supplies had to be manhandled, this time across rough, rocky country. And always a rifle or Bren gun was kept handy—just in case.

For several days the men were kept busy carrying fuel, food, ammunition, etc. They broke off only to snatch a few hours' sleep either on board ship or in the tiny cabin. From time to time violent storms broke out but disappeared just as quickly as they came. Their first task was to erect a small radio station from which they could transmit the weather readings that were taken right from the outset. However, the biggest job of all was to transport the prefabricated house, which had been shipped from England, to the inland site. While some of the men were carrying the sections, others were dynamiting the rock in the hillside to make a level foundation. No sooner would they clear the site when a sudden freezing storm would obliterate it once again, and the frozen snow had to be blasted away. Then, when the time came to erect the hut, it was discovered that the assembly instructions that had been packed with the sections had been destroyed by the water shipped during the storm off Iceland and by the frost. Thus in a climate so cold that the building tools could not be held for more than a few minutes at a time, the Norwegians had a problem on their hands—and a painful one in the bitter cold!

Among the supplies unloaded were two, rather old, artillery pieces—a two-pounder and a six-pounder. Not one of the men knew how to operate them so they had only the small arms to rely on if the Germans came to Jan Mayen.

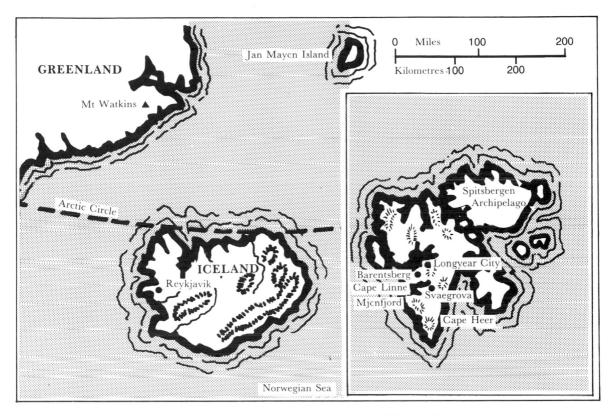

Outposts in the Arctic: These maps demonstrate the remoteness of Jan Mayen Island, which was a symbol of Free Norway throughout the Second World War, and of the Spitsbergen Archipelago, situated deep inside the Arctic Circle, and far removed from the European battlefields.

Within a month the bulk of the equipment and supplies were safely ashore, but on 7 April a third ship arrived with more supplies—the Norwegian ex-hunter *Bull*. An extra effort was made to unload her because the spring thaw was setting in rapidly, and unless the ships got away almost immediately they would be held up by the breaking ice. Within a short time the ships were on their way. Twelve men wrapped in polar clothing stood on the frozen shore watching their last tangible link with the outside world disappear, not knowing what the future held for them.

With supplies safely ashore, with a house to live in, and a radio station built, the garrison was more or less settled. As the weather improved German planes flew over, machine-gun and bomb attacks doing no damage. Although twelve men were obviously too few to deal with a determined German attack, they had great faith in themselves and they also knew that they had allies in the storms and fog, in the reefs and the jagged coast. The twelve Norwegians made plans, however—just in case. Food supplies were cached at various points on the island so that in the event of the Germans landing and pressing them back they would have food at hand. And on one of the mountains they built a second, reserve, radio station, accessible only by rope. The Norwegians reckoned they could defend this position for just as long as it took their Iceland base to send supplies.

More men and supplies arrived over the

139

months. Although there was not a single tree on Jan Mayen there was never any shortage of wood to build huts. Plenty of wood drifted across the Arctic from Siberia, and many useful items were found cast on the foreshore from wrecks at sea. A new radio station was built, and additional defence and observation posts were erected at various strategic points on the island. Defence sectors were allocated to the men and a full guard was mounted. By July the defence of the island was fairly complete and so far no Germans—other than airmen—had come near. Then on 22 July the new contingent included gunners equipped with a number of modern anti-aircraft guns. Jan Mayen was now a formidable fortress.

The 'weather men' were posted at a number of different points on the island—as the climatic conditions on Jan Mayen are so variable there can be a storm on one side of the island whilst the sun shines on the other. In mid-year on the island there may be three days of unbroken sunshine at a time, and when the weather is good in the brief summer the Arctic is beautiful. The sparse moss blossoms with a tiny pinkish-red flower and seems to grow right up the Beerenberg until it is lost in the cloud. And daylight reigns the whole time. At midnight the sun shines behind the mountain peak and glitters brilliantly on the highland snow. Each of the 'weather huts' were given colourful names such as Foxhole, Home of the Fog, Walrus Alley. Miles and miles of telephone cable connecting the huts were laid in the summer, always a foot or two above the ground where it was least exposed to the storms.

At the main base camp, meteorological reports were transmitted eight times a day. The community was now completely self-contained and prepared for the winter. The last supply ship left at the end of July, and the garrison would now be on its own until the next ship came six or seven months later. The last signs of summer rapidly disappeared, and the 'fog season' came. Thick, clammy fog blotted everything out for miles, and it was always accompanied by a biting cold. Then came the darkness of the polar winter, unbroken except for the lights of the aurora borealis. And the storms began to descend in their full fury. Bags filled with powdered lava-rock were piled around the huts to prevent them from being blown away, and some were given added strength by propping drift-logs against the walls. Air pockets were built in the hut entrances to prevent the cold entering when the doors were opened, and the combustion stoves were kept going day and night.

Although only two or three hundred yards separated the telegraphists' hut from the meteorological headquarters, it was discovered that at times it was impossible for a man to cross from one to the other without facing the danger of being swept away by the wind. Because of this a wire hawser was stretched between the two buildings so that if it was essential for a man to reach the other hut when a storm was at its height, he would be able to crawl over the snow holding on to the wire guide. During one of these storms a husky, which had left its hole in the snow, was carried away together with the stake to which it was fastened, and was never seen again. That gives some idea of the ferocity of the Arctic winter on Jan Mayen island. Hunting in the winter time was very popular, for it not only helped to vary the diet but it kept the minds occupied. The first polar bear to set foot on the island after the Norwegian occupation was soon shot and its skin, after being cured, was sent the following summer to King Haakon as 'a present from free Norwegians on free-Norwegian soil'.

This first winter for the men of Jan Mayen went without serious trouble. The regular daily quota of weather reports continued to be received in Britain. The island's coast was patrolled regularly and the guards were constantly on duty. They had to make their own life and, used as they were to polar conditions, they succeeded where many might have failed. With the turn of the year, however, it was found that great inroads had been made into the food supplies and, as it was not known when a relief ship might be able to get through, rationing had to be introduced. In March 1942, however, the first ship of the year arrived—the first outside contact for over seven months. It was a happy band of shaggy, bearded men who watched that relief ship grind its way through the ice.

During the summer months of 1942 there was once again feverish activity, including the erection of new huts and defences. The German air raids were resumed, but once more they were without effect. Icelandic ponies were brought to the island—they had to swim from ship to shore—and the animals eased the transport situation considerably. An electric power-plant driven by a windmill was installed and electric lighting took the place of tallow candles. New supplies were distributed throughout the island, repairs were carried out, and in general everything was once more organized for the long winter ahead. The Jan Mayen community was no longer based on improvisation. Those days were over by the end of the summer of 1942. Now the garrison even had fresh meat to look forward to in the winter, for a number of pigs had been imported and were fattened on camp swill ready for slaughter. The importation of hens was less successful (the birds died) and most of the sheep brought from Iceland suffered the same fate—the moss and the very sparse patches of coarse grass were insufficient to maintain them.

The Germans never once attempted to set foot on Jan Mayen during the entire course of the war. With the exception of air attacks, they took no offensive action at all. U-boats were frequently seen off the island re-charging batteries, but they always took care not to come within range of the Norwegian coastal guns. Life in the Arctic in the summer months could be exhilarating. For recreation, climbing expeditions were mounted on the towering Beerenberg with its great snow drifts, its crevasses, and sheer cliff sides. The mountaineers climbed through the clouds and stood on the summit gazing across a sea of swirling mist. The soldiers sometimes swam in the freak lagoon of fresh water at the southern end of the island. Here a great bar of lava rock closes the mouth of a section of indented coast to form a lagoon that is filled with water from the melting snows. The water is bitterly cold even in high summer, but the islanders were tough. Ski-jumping for fun was also popular, championships being arranged on frequent occasions. Stores of birds' eggs—mainly gull and auk—were also collected during the summer months to provide a valuable addition to the island diet. Expert climbers were equipped with ropes and lowered over the sheer cliff edges of the coast to reach the nests on the ledges—a dangerous job with lava rock as sharp as a razor, and one that was entrusted only to the most skilled.

During the winter there were often times when movement out of the huts was absolutely impossible for days—sometimes weeks—on end. Apart from the usual sedentary pursuits (reading, playing chess or cards, or other games) the men found suitable materials for creative work. With driftwood collected from the shore some beautifully hand-carved furniture was made on Jan Mayen. Magnificent metal work was produced, too, with metal salvaged from crashed German aircraft. The first machine crashed somewhere on Beerenberg and the Norwegians never succeeded in locating it. The second one met its doom when it struck the mountain side behind the camp. The crew of six were dead when they were found by the Norwegians. The German airmen were buried on the mountain, and their graves were marked with simple crosses made from driftwood. Practically every man on the island made himself an ornate dagger with the salvaged material: knives with fine steel blades, handles and sheathes of polished perspex. One was specially made and engraved for King Haakon; another for the heir-presumptive, Prince Harald.

In winter time too, when the seas around Jan Mayen are frozen, thousands of seals appear. Armed with cudgels, the Norwegians would scramble across the ice floes to catch the baby seals whose skins were quite valuable, and whose carcases provided meat for the dogs. The annual catch on Jan Mayen averaged 200 to 300 baby seals. Hunting in one form or another helped to stave off the dreaded 'polar sickness'—when a person becomes depressed and lethargic with the monotony of the life and the surrounding desolation. The principal prize was the skin of the blue fox, of which there are considerable numbers on the island. Every man on Jan Mayen was allowed to catch two foxes a year, which went into a common pool to be shared out at the end of the year.

Next in importance came the shooting of birds, principally the auk. These birds added considerably to the variety of the diet, but to shoot a bird on the wing with a .303 rifle bullet was no easy task. Those who were not marksmen on Jan Mayen quickly became so. Despite the climate, the health of the men on the island remained good. In fact the only occasions when they contracted common colds was when they boarded the supply vessels during the summer. In winter time colds were avoided by taking regular steam baths. This consisted of pouring melted snow on to heated stones placed in the huts and standing in the steam. The men would then run outside and roll in the snow. Such was life on the Arctic island of Jan Mayen in the Second World War, 1941-5.

Although the twelve best skiers had been ordered on their 'secret mission' to Jan Mayen in January 1940, the balance of 'Norwegian Company, Iceland'—numbering about thirty men—continued with the task of organizing the ski-training school at Akureyri. Everything required in the way of equipment (most of which was made to Norwegian design and by Norwegians in Britain and America) was shipped to Iceland, and the full training programme was put underway. The British troops received instruction both in theory and practice on the mountain slopes of northern Iceland. When they had mastered the art of skiing they learned to drive dog teams, to live in tents to build snow huts, and to dig comforta-

ble quarters in the snow itself. They had to learn all the arts of combating Arctic weather and snowstorms, and to make the best of limited Arctic rations. In short, they learned how to make their homes with nature at its worst.

All through the winter of 1940-1 this training was carried out by the handful of instructors at the highest possible pitch, but when in 1941 American troops arrived on Iceland to help guard the trans-Atlantic strategic link between North America and Britain, the Norwegian authorities were requested to provide more ski troops to act as instructors to the Americans. In September of 1941 a further force of some thirty Norwegian ski troops arrived in Iceland from Scotland and, operating as a separate unit, they began instruction. They set up a school at Reykjavik, which also included a section for winter-warfare training and the equipment provided was of the very finest quality. Indeed, this school became the biggest and the best organized of its kind in the world. The British wanted at least one company in every battalion stationed on Iceland to be trained as ski-soldiers, but the training went so rapidly and so well that not only was this object soon achieved but also several companies in every battalion—and in some cases every man in a battalion—learned to ski.

During the second winter one group of Norwegian instructors taught the theory at Reykjavik, where the course lasted for three weeks, followed by a similar or longer period of training in the mountains nearby. The second group comprised a practical school at Vinhei-majokulen (meaning the 'home of the wind'), which consisted of a tented camp. The wind in these mountains is the most powerful anywhere recorded, and consequently proved an ideal conditioning site for the trainees. Tents were often blown away and the men had to dig deep into the snow for shelter. To avoid losses in men and equipment, however, the company (which normally numbered about 200) generally moved into the valley upon the approach of fierce storms. The organization of transport to this tented camp 3,000 ft (900 m) up in the mountains, was of course, a difficult problem, but with the aid of Icelandic ponies or, if the snow was very deep and the terrain particularly bad, huskies, the difficulties were overcome. The Norwegians who arranged this transport soon learned to know the vagaries of the mountain weather in this locality, and always succeeded in getting through without losses, although they were often obliged to dig in until storms passed over.

During the first two winters in Iceland, the Norwegians trained no fewer than 10,000 British and Americans as ski and mountain troops. Not one man was lost during all the rigours of training for which the Norwegians were responsible. By the end of 1943 the Norwegians' task was completed. British and American units had by then sufficient skilled instructors of their own—if required—but as it was by then there was hardly an Allied soldier stationed on Iceland who was not able to ski. Some Norwegian instructors, nevertheless, remained in Iceland where they maintained a small training school for Americans and where they also acted as instructors at a special recreation hostel for Allied troops. Here, on almost the same lines as a peace-time Norwegian tourist hotel, they taught the servicemen all the skills of a ski resort.

For more than a year after the German occupation of Norway there was little news about the Arctic archipelago of Spitsbergen. Those Arctic isles covering thousands of square miles, whose coal mines had a combined Norwegian and Russian output of three quarters of a million metric tonnes a year, seemed to have been forgotten. The Germans had not bothered to occupy them—but they took great care to obtain the Norwegian-produced coal, which was sent to Norway by steamship. When Norway was invaded there were about 1,000 Norwegian men, women, and children living at Spitsbergen. They were mostly engaged in the mining industry centred round the Ice Fjord and resided in Longyear City, but a number of trappers and hunters lived in the interior. The coal season was just about to start on Spitsbergen (which is sealed off by ice during the winter) when the Germans attacked Norway in April 1940, and in the two critical months that followed the inhabitants waited anxiously. The governor called up all the men who had military experience and they were armed with all available weapons—mainly rifles normally used for polar bear and seal hunting, and a number of shot-guns.

However, no attack was made on Spitsbergen, and there was nothing much the population could do but carry on with its way of life. The output of coal fell considerably, though, as the miners had no wish to help the Germans. The winter came with its polar darkness and the severing of communications (except for radio) with the rest of the world. Then came the summer of 1941. In June, Russia was attacked by Nazi Germany; there was a considerable Russian mining community at Spitsbergen, mainly centred at Barentsburg that is also situated in Ice Fjord. German military operations were expected daily. Nothing happened, however, until the middle of August. Then warships steamed up Ice Fjord. But they were British warships commanded by Admiral Vian. The Norwegians hoped that the British had come to occupy the islands, but that was not the case. They had just come to have a look round. Three coaling ships, which were loaded and ready to sail for Norway, were seized and diverted to Britain.

Anxious days followed but the tension was at last broken on 25 August by the arrival of a British, Canadian, and Norwegian commando force. This force had come not to occupy the islands but to evacuate the population and to destroy the coal mines and other installations that might be of use to the Germans. Twenty-four hours later the Russian community of about 2,000 was on its way on British ships to Murmansk. Meanwhile the Allied troops began their demolitions. Norwegian trappers—about thirty of them—were called in from the interior.

With the remainder of the Norwegians they packed their personal belongings and prepared to leave the Arctic land that was their home. They were all to leave for Britain where the men would join the Norwegian armed forces.

Mining machinery, overhead conveyors, landing stages, everything in fact that might help the Germans in the event of their taking over the islands was destroyed. Hundreds of thousands of tons of coal were set on fire. Six days later, the Norwegians—standing on the decks of the British ships—watched the barren, snowy islands disappear over the horizon. All except one man. He was a miner who had lived there for years and he flatly refused to leave. He was the only man left in the vast archipelago of Spitsbergen. Three weeks later, however, a German force that landed on Spitsbergen found him. He was taken prisoner and sent to Norway.

In the spring of 1942 the Allies decided to re-occupy the islands to establish a new meteorological station there. The job was given to the Norwegians. It was not known whether the Germans were still there or how many there might be, but in May 1942 two small ships, *Isbjorn* (an icebreaker) and *Selis* (a sealer), left an Allied port for Spitsbergen. There were about a hundred men on board all told, including the ships' crews, and sufficient equipment, supplies, and arms to maintain the force for a long time. When the ships reached the southern approaches of the islands it was daylight throughout the 24 hours. The weather was good and it looked as though the last stages of the journey would be free of ice. But when the ships turned into Ice Fjord the broken ice had frozen again. Thus instead of being able to reach the shore immediately, many hours would be needed to break the ice. The work was begun at once.

One-third of the force was sent across the ice carrying only their bare equipment, in order to reconnoitre and prepare the way for unloading. The remainder of the men were divided equally between the two ships. Suddenly, out of the sun, roared a big four-engined Condor.

It sprayed the two little ships with bullets whilst the Norwegians answered with Lewis guns and rifles. A second, third, and fourth Condor came into the attack, raking both ships that were lying line ahead. All but the ships' gunners were ordered overboard on to the ice. They scattered whilst bullets sprayed around them. The planes came in again, this time dropping bombs. *Isbjorn* was hit and sunk immediately. *Selis* was then set on fire and blazed furiously. For an hour the planes attacked the men who lay flat on the ice. When it was all over the Norwegians gathered on the shore and took stock of the situation. Fourteen men, including one of three British officers who had accompanied the expedition, had been killed, and eight were seriously wounded. The force was practically devoid of equipment.

The force now moved up to the former Russian settlement of Barentsberg where one of the larger huts was converted into a hospital. While the wounded were being tended, others returned to the still-blazing *Selis* to see what they could salvage. They went aboard with ammunition bursting all around them and rescued as much equipment as possible, including three rucksacks, a damaged radio receiver, and a number of rifles. Another party, meanwhile, made a tour of Barentsberg, and to their delight found large quantities of tinned and other foodstuffs and plenty of blankets that had been left behind by the Russians the previous year. Clothing was the principal shortage. In subsequent days the Germans made regular air attacks, but caused no further damage or casualties.

Barentsberg was not very well suited for defence against land attack, but as the wounded could not be moved the camp had to be maintained there. A force of nineteen men, however, was equipped as well as possible with the object of making the 50-60 mile (80-95 km) trek across deep snow and rough, mountainous country to the former Norwegian settlement at Svaegruva, at the extreme end of Van Mijenfjord south of Ice Fjord. This force made a non-stop march over terrain often reaching 3,000 ft (900 m). It took them 32 hours. One man was lost in a snow-covered crevasse. At Svaegruva a defensive position was set up. On 16 May another patrol was equipped at Barentsberg with the object of making a 50-mile (80-km) journey farther up Ice Fjord to reconnoitre Longyear City where it was believed a German force might be established.

As the journey was a difficult one and probably fraught with many dangers, a second party followed a day later. Four days afterwards both patrols returned to report that there were between twenty and forty Germans at Longyear City where an air-landing ground had been constructed on the ice. One patrol had reached the settlement by going through a labyrinth of coal pits in which some of the men had previously worked, one exit of which faced directly on the Germans' positions. They hid there and watched the Germans' every move. As the condition of the wounded at Barentsberg improved, more and more men could be released, and gradually the force at Svaegruva was reinforced. Meanwhile, radio operators had managed to repair the damaged radio receiver and among the stores in the settlement they found bulbs, batteries, and other articles that enabled them to make an improvised Aldis lamp.

On 26 May—twelve days after the first German attack—an RAF Catalina aircraft flew over Barentsberg. It kept its distance, not knowing whether it was friend or foe below. It was then that the home-made Aldis lamp saved the situation. An SOS and a request for supplies was flashed and seen by the aircraft's crew. The plane then flew off. The Germans kept up their air attacks and one bomb that found its target crashed right through one wall of the makeshift hospital—but fortunately it failed to explode. On 29 May another Catalina aircraft arrived and dropped supplies and automatic weapons. By this time all the Norwegian forces except for the seamen and the wounded had been transferred to Svaegruva.

With plenty of blankets and tinned food the Norwegians were fairly comfortable. The only food shortage was fresh meat and this was soon remedied. One of the officers, who had lived in Spitsbergen at the time of the evacuation, remembered that the Russians used to keep considerable numbers of pigs at Barentsberg and he knew that they had been shot when the Russians were evacuated. A search was made and the snow was shovelled away from the pigsties. Sure enough they found the carcases—frozen and fresh. Some of them had been chewed by Arctic fox, but the meat was in perfectly good condition. Seals were also found and shot, whilst birds' eggs taken from the cliffs similarly added to the variety of the diet. A shortage of sufficient clothing caused some privation and boots that had become badly worn on the rough ground were almost useless. No German land attack ensued and the Norwegians refrained from any offensive action because of the lack of equipment and arms.

Meanwhile an RAF plane had tried to get through to take off the seriously wounded, but it was forced back by bad weather. It was not until early in June that a Catalina finally succeeded in landing on the ice-free sea in the fjord. Seven of the most-seriously wounded were taken on board and flown to Britain. On 14 June a second plane arrived for the remainder of the wounded, and for a British and a Norwegian officer who were required to report on the situation. It was only after they had given their reports that it was decided not to evacuate Spitsbergen again as had been intended, but to send reinforcements to help destroy the German force. This next expedition landed at Barentsberg on 2 July. In the meantime, extensive patrolling and reconnoitring had been carried out by the Norwegians and every German defensive position had been pinpointed. With this information the now newly-equipped force together with the reinforcements planned the attack. By 15 July all was ready and the troops moved off to cross the 50 miles (80 km) or so of rough country that separated them from Longyear City. It was only then when it was discovered that the Germans had taken the opportunity to flee whilst preparations for the attack were being made. They had evidently been evacuated by air.

The Norwegians were now in sole possession of the Spitsbergen archipelago. Most of the original force remained stationed there, while the balance of the troops who were no longer required were returned to Britain. All that remained was to establish defences to deal with any German assault and to establish a normal garrison routine. German planes occasionally appeared but failed to cause any excitement. The meteorological station was re-established, and a three-hourly weather service was beamed to Britain. During the winter, guards and patrols were maintained and for amusement the men engaged in outdoor pursuits such as trapping, hunting, and skiing. Life on Spitsbergen was by no means easy. Sudden storms would often envelop the routine patrols when crossing the sea-ice or the mountain ranges with their treacherous snow-covered crevasses.

Two incidents in 1943 demonstrated the rigours of survival within the Arctic Circle. On 2 January a patrol discovered the few remaining survivors of a British merchant ship that had been wrecked off the most southern point of the Spitsbergen archipelago. On the shore at the entrance to Ice Fjord the patrol found nine British seamen huddled together in a hut for warmth, suffering from hunger, frost-bite, and exhaustion. In the same hut were the bodies of fifteen other seamen who had perished. The survivors were taken to Barentsberg where they recovered. They told a tragic story.

Their ship was wrecked on 6 October 1942. The crew managed to get into two lifeboats but the two boats had become separated. One was never seen again. The other, containing 24 men, reached the entrance to Ice Fjord. They managed to get ashore, and sheltered in a hut they found there, where they lived for nearly three months. Fortunately they found just sufficient food in nearby huts. The fifteen men died from frost-bite and from the exposure they had

suffered in the open boat. But the most tragic part of the story was that if the seamen had only walked for a few hours up to the high ground behind the huts they would have been able to see Barentsberg camp a few miles away and signal for help.

Later in the year—March 1943—two Norwegian soldiers had a very narrow escape from death. They were on patrol along the Ice Fjord coast south of Longyear City when suddenly a great storm descended. With equal suddenness the sea-ice began to break up. They were unable to get back to the shore. There was only one course open to them and that was filled with perils. It was to attempt the crossing of the 10-mile (16-km) wide fjord in order to reach the opposite shore. The storm was still raging as the two men began the journey across the broken ice, jumping from floe to floe. It was so cold that they could not rest for more than a few minutes at a time—they had to keep moving. It was not until two days later that they finally scrambled ashore on the other side of the fjord where they found a hut in which to rest. To reach camp again now meant making a long detour around the Ice Fjord, and the route they mapped was shaped like a horseshoe. They had to cross arms of the fjord that were still frozen, climb over high, rocky country, and through deep snow. It took three weary days on short rations to complete the 50-mile (80-km) journey. 'Just part of our job', was their comment afterwards.

It was in September 1943 that the German battle fleet supporting troop ships put to sea in order to carry out its first full-scale offensive action since the attack on Norway in April 1940. The objectives of this powerful fleet (which had so long remained inactive and had shirked an open clash with the Allied navies) was to destroy the Norwegian garrison on Spitsbergen and everything there of value to the Allies. So, on the early morning of 8 September, the battleship *Tirpitz* and battle-cruiser *Scharnhorst*, together with seven or eight destroyers, were seen near the entrance to Ice Fjord by the Norwegian look-outs stationed at Cape Heer. Their appearance explained why the Luftwaffe had been so active during the past few hours.

Gun positions at both Cape Heer and Barentsberg were manned as the German fleet steamed right up to the mouth of the fjord. Three destroyers turned into Green Fjord, on which Barentsberg stands. One of the battleships and two destroyers took up position in the middle of Ice Fjord and the other battleship and two or three destroyers lay a little further out to sea, proceeding towards Advent Fjord. While the German ships put into Green Fjord, Cape Linne—on the extreme tip of the entrance to Ice Fjord—was bombarded. There was no Norwegian garrison here, however. The Norwegian lieutenant in charge of the battery at Cape Heer had only nine men in his force, but he made ready to defend the position. One of the destroyers steaming up Green Fjord broke off and pulled in towards the shore about midway between Cape Heer and Barentsberg. At the same time a smaller enemy ship broke off and sailed towards land just below Cape Heer. German troops stood on the deck, but the larger ships were still out of range of the ten men manning the gun. The position looked hopeless, and the Norwegian officer in charge ordered seven of his men to retire while he and the other two men prepared to meet the Germans.

As soon as one of the destroyers came within range the three Norwegians opened fire. Suddenly, however, German soldiers appeared behind them. The gun was turned on the German troops, but before the magazine could be replaced a shell from the battleship lying well out to sea near the island of Festning landed near the gun position and made it impossible for the Norwegians to carry on the fight. One of the men, a corporal, was wounded in the leg, but all three of them managed to escape.

Meanwhile, the German attack against Berentsberg had begun. The Norwegians had only three guns—two of them small calibre anti-aircraft guns. Apart from the gun crews all the Norwegians were sent to the rear as reserves.

Thus only a handful of men opposed the attack, which began with a heavy bombardment. The two German destroyers that steamed up Green Fjord were subjected to the full fire of the small Norwegian guns, and one of the 40-mm anti-aircraft guns, manned by a lieutenant and seven men, fired 150 shells, most of which hit the destroyers. One of the German ships steamed up the fjord until it was right outside the town, and the Norwegians could see the landing troops on her decks when they opened fire. The cries of the German wounded on this destroyer could be plainly heard, and when smoke began to pour from it she withdrew to the other side of the fjord out of range. From this safer distance, however, she continued to bombard the tiny Norwegian garrison.

For half an hour the fight went on. By this time the town and the Norwegian gun positions were saturated with shell fire. In addition, enemy troops had landed east of Barentsberg, near Finness, and several hundreds more had landed to the west of the town. Both forces were advancing. The heavy fire from the destroyers was also threatening the Norwegian reserves who were lying at the rear end of the town. There was no other alternative but to retire. The guns were therefore destroyed and a way of escape was sought. This was difficult because heavy fire was raking the best escape route. Many of the German shells, however, fell on the coal and slag heaps just outside the town, and as a result a 'smoke screen' of coal dust was put up, enabling the Norwegians to escape unseen and without drawing any enemy fire. Thus the greater part of the Barentsberg force managed to reach higher land, but the German infantry troops that followed caused them to retreat even further into the mountains where they hid concealed even from the Luftwaffe planes sent out to hunt them. At about 06:30, just over four and a half hours after the attack began, the sirens on the German ships howled and the German forces evacuated the smoking ruins of Barentsberg, returning to their ships and taking their dead and wounded and prisoners with them.

Meanwhile the other battleship and its destroyer had proceeded up Ice Fjord towards Longyear City, which lies in Advent Fjord, a branch of the Ice Fjord. The Norwegian garrison here was even smaller than the one at Barentsberg. The guns at Hotelness, at the entrance to Advent Fjord, were about to be brought into action when the officer in charge of this outpost saw that one destroyer sailing alongside the coast was flying the White Ensign. This destroyer then opened fire leaving the Norwegian force in no doubt that it was a German and not a British vessel. The Norwegians' position became hopeless when a German landing party was put ashore, and the eleven men took to their heels. Five of them were taken prisoner. The other destroyer continued towards Longyear City, and when she was first observed by the Norwegian garrison she, too, appeared to be flying a flag other than the German flag. Because of this the Norwegians delayed their fire. Soon, however, this destroyer was joined by another and the two began to bombard the settlement. German troops poured ashore and the Norwegians retreated. The German advance was delayed, however, by a Norwegian corporal who fought a lone rearguard action armed only with a Bren gun, and who fired magazine after magazine until he was wounded.

The Norwegian troops retired in small groups, slowly working their way inland towards Sverdrup City followed by German soldiers armed with machine-guns and hand grenades. At 08:00 the Germans sounded the withdrawal and once again took their dead and wounded and prisoners on board their ships, but continued to bombard Sverdrup City. Meanwhile the battleship that had come up the fjord with the destroyers fired at every possible target—huts, houses, and various installations. An hour later the bombardment ceased, and the German battle fleet sailed back to the safety of the Norwegian fjords, leaving the Norwegian garrison to re-occupy the wrecked towns and gun positions, and struggle with the inevitable task of improvising shelter against the coming Arctic winter. The German onslaught on Spitsbergen had cost six Norwegian lives and a small number of prisoners.

CHAPTER 13
THE WAR IN THE ARCTIC

The fighting on land in Arctic Europe between 1941 and 1945 was usually confined to the few highways that existed in these inhospitable northern territories. Northern Finland, which was the base for German land operations against Murmansk and the supply routes from Archangel, has been described as a land of 70,000 'blue seas', wild rivers, and forests 'without end'. Even in summer the landscape has a starkness that is likely to appeal to only the most ardent adventurers. In winter, which lasts from October to May, the lakes and rivers are frozen over and the snow lies 3 ft (1 m) deep. The dense forests, lakes, swamps, and rock-strewn fells and tundra confined methods of transport to pack animals—horses and reindeer—and the soldiers used skis for cross-country movement. In view of the immense difficulties involved in mounting an offensive in these conditions, it is not surprising that the German and Finnish advance into the USSR in 1941 made little progress, and that the Russians were unable to regain lost ground until nearly three years had elapsed.

A Gebirgsjäger mountain team moves to occupy a defensive position in Lapland with a horse-drawn field gun mounted on skis.

The Arctic conflict between the Germans and the Russians defending the land approaches to Murmansk was largely stalemate for over three years. Here German mountain troops make a routine inspection of the trenches.

The main line of communication in northern Finland is the road that runs from Kemi at the head of the Gulf of Bothnia, through Rovaniemi and Ivalo to Pechenga and Kirkenes. Although before the war the road was said to be in good condition and adequately equipped with petrol filling-stations and tourist inns, the road ran through a wilderness. Swamps, fells, and forests dominated the scene and there were few human settlements. Further west another road leads from Tornio along the Finnish side of the Swedish frontier through Muonio to Skibotn at the head of Lyngenfjorden. Between Muonio and Skibotn the road was, however, at this time little more than a cart track. Rovaniemi is the most important road and river junction in northern Finland. Apart from the main road between Kemi and Pechenga, four other roads that meet there are noteworthy. One, which runs northwest, connects the main road with Muonio and the Tornio-Skibotn road. A second leads east to Kemijärvi, Salla, Kairala, and Alakurtti, and eventually to Kuusamo and the south of Finland, with branches forking eastwards from it to Kesten and to Ukhta. A fourth, roughly parallel to and some distance to the west of the third, connects Rovaniemi with Pudasjärvi and the south.

The only main railway in northern Finland also passes through Rovaniemi: it runs parallel to the road from Kemi through Rovaniemi to Kandalaksha. Salla, Kuusamo, and Pudasjärvi are connected by a cross-country road. There is another important junction north of Rovaniemi at Ivalo, where a road branches northwest to Lakselv at the head of Porsangen and there meets the important coastal road from Pechenga and Kirkenes to Skibotn, Narvik, and the south of Norway. The last-named road winds close along the Arctic coast, leaving the shores of the fjords only to traverse the mountains lying between them. Generally very narrow, the road is characterized by an endless succession of S-bends and also by numerous steep inclines. For troops moving along it during winter, depending upon horse-drawn transport when the surface is covered with snow or ice, it is only just passable. Inside the Soviet frontier the main line of communication is the Murmansk railway—roads are practically non-existent in this part of the USSR.

After the operations round Narvik in 1940, General der Gebirgstruppe Eduard Dietl had been given command of Mountain Corps 'Norwegen' (later known as Mountain Corps XIX), consisting of the 2nd and 3rd Mountain Divisions. At the time of Germany's attack upon the USSR in June 1941 this corps was concentrated round Kirkenes. On 22 June Dietl moved into northern Finland, ostensibly to protect the mine at Nikel', where he occupied Pechenga in accordance with a previous agreement with the Finnish authorities. Four days later Finland formally entered the war on the German side, and Dietl prepared to advance upon Murmansk (Operation 'Platinfuchs'). The German staff officers were hampered by a lack of adequate maps of the area. As one of them sarcastically observed, the 1912 edition of Baedeker was more up to date than some of the 'top secret' information provided by the High Command.

Meanwhile Mountain Corps XXXVI, consisting of the 169th Infantry Division and SS Mountain Division 'Nord' (later known as the 6th SS Mountain Division), was sent partly from Germany and partly from southern Norway (through neutral Sweden) to the area around Rovaniemi. The commanding officer, General der Kavallerie Feige, received orders to capture Salla and advance on Kandalaksha (Operation 'Silberfuchs'). At the same time a Finnish corps, consisting of two divisions, concentrated at Suomussalmi and Kuusamo. The Finnish Major-General Siilasvuo was ordered to advance on Loukhi and Kemi, and to assist the Germans at Salla. The three corps were placed under the command of Generaloberst Nikolaus von Falkenhorst, who established his headquarters at Rovaniemi. All these movements (known collectively as Plan 'Blaufuchs')

had been planned by the Germans in 1941.

On 29 June 1941 Mountain Corps XIX advanced into Russia driving towards Murmansk, but after advancing only 20 miles (32 km) came to a standstill early in July on the tundra west of the Litsa River. A German attempt to cross the river between 13 and 17 July met with fierce Soviet resistance and Dietl was forced to withdraw. The Russians now took the initiative and made a sea-borne landing behind the left flank of the corps but were beaten back. Dietl did not attack again until 7 September—eight days after the first Allied convoy arrived at Murmansk.

The Germans again failed to drive the Russian defenders from the commanding heights on the east bank of the Litsa, but this time succeeded in establishing themselves securely upon the left bank. The German advance in this sector now came to a halt some 30 miles (50 km) west of Murmansk. All Dietl's efforts to seize Poluostrov Ribachy, the peninsula that juts out into the Barents Sea northeast of Pechenga, proved unsuccessful, and the Soviet garrison maintained itself there on the German flank until the Germans finally retreated westwards in 1944.

Meanwhile, on 1 July 1941, Mountain Corps XXXVI had begun an advance on the extensively-fortified town of Salla, which was stormed on 8 July. On 19 August the German offensive was renewed and Kairala fell after nine days of bitter fighting. Alakurtti was captured a few days later and a battle was fought for the possession of two commanding heights some distance further east. Despite desperate Soviet resistance these two fell into German hands in September, but Feige's advance was finally held by the Russians 24 miles (38 km) west of the Murmansk railway. The Russian troops had frequently set fire to the forests to trap the Germans and they had also made use of tanks. For their part the Germans had made use of their infantry and artillery. The latter arm was entirely dependent upon horses for transport—often as many as ten horses to one gun.

The third and southernmost attacking force, the Finnish Corps, likewise failed to reach the Murmansk railway and came to a halt at Kesten and Ukhta. Nevertheless, the Finns succeeded in reaching the Murmansk railway between Kemi and Leningrad in September 1941. The branch line to Archangel remained in Russian hands, however, and the flow of Allied supplies was uninterrupted. Thus, by the end of 1941, the Germans had failed to seize Murmansk and to cut the supply route into the interior of Russia, a fact that was henceforth to be of supreme importance to the Allies. All that they had achieved of the original objectives was control over the mine at Nikel'. The Germans blamed the Finns for their combined failure on this front. Apparently the Finns had insisted that the logistics of supporting more than two divisions in the wild terrain at once were unsound. Dietl would have favoured a combined blow by the three corps on one sector but the 'hero of Narvik' had to admit that the immense difficulties of the terrain had caused even him to doubt whether it would ever be possible to capture Murmansk.

The opposing armies had now assumed the positions they were to entrench and hold for more than three years. The stalemate on the German side may be accounted for by the failure to agree with the Finns on the appointment of a supreme commander in the theatre of war stretching from the Baltic Sea to the Arctic Ocean. Second, the German navy had failed to establish control over the western part of the Barents Sea, so that throughout the war the flank of the German army was exposed to attack from the sea at any point along the Arctic coast. Third, the farther the Germans had advanced towards the Murmansk railway, the more attenuated their lines of communication became, while the Soviet commanders were able to use the railway to concentrate their troops and supplies.

As a result of the stalemate, the areas behind the German front lines assumed the appearance of well-organized depots nestling snugly in an Arctic 'wonderland'. Ammunition dumps, supply centres, canteens, bakeries, charcoal kilns, hospitals, and rest camps were established, and in some parts of the front the soldiers found it possible to supplement their rations—already on the highest scale provided by the Wehrmacht, but lacking in fresh meat and vegetables—by hunting, fishing, pig-rearing, and vegetable-growing. Amateur horticulturalists discovered that, when glass was not available for the greenhouses, parchment paper dipped in cod-liver oil served as a useful substitute. Horse or reindeer dung for manure was plentiful.

Troops lying in the firing line generally received a midday meal of thick meat and vegetable soup. Those lying farther back had a more varied diet, calculated to delight the Teutonic taste, such as beans and bacon, or pork and sauerkraut, or rice soup with beef, or meat rolls, jacket potatoes, and red cabbage. In the evening there was a cold supper consisting of half a loaf of bread with butter or dripping, and canned meat or fish and cheese. A little tea or coffee was issued daily to each man. In addition there was a ration of five cigarettes a day and quite often a packet of tobacco and a roll of fruit drops. A tot of alcohol was issued three times a week, and a bar of chocolate on Sundays. Vitamin tablets and cod-liver oil completed the diet. There were occasional surprises. When an elk was unlucky enough to graze in a minefield, venison was available for the troops in the neighbourhood.

For the greater part of the year—seven months or more—the ground was frozen and snow-covered. Skis had to be used, and the Germans made every effort to encourage their

Right *The international frontier between Finland and the USSR in 1941: the German objective on this front was to capture Murmansk and thus seize the principal terminal for the Arctic convoys sailing from Britain, but the Russian port was never taken. The Germans were finally stabbed in the back by their ally, the Finns, and the former obliged to withdraw to northern Norway.*

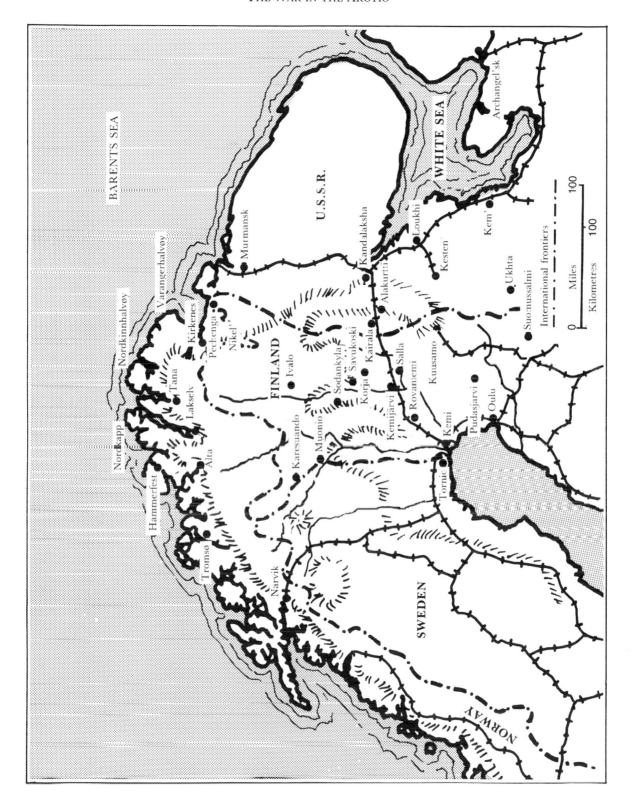

Finnish troops build an igloo on the Arctic front.

troops in their use. As a rule the Gebirgsjäger needed no instruction for, as we have already seen, they were largely recruited from the Alpine areas of Bavaria and Austria. The lowlanders from Brandenberg, Hessen, and Thüringen were not so fortunately placed, but soon learnt how to move and fight on skis. The skis used were of the best Norwegian laminated type, with Kandahar bindings. According to German reports the Soviet troops, at least during the early part of the war, had only one pair of primitive skis to every fourth or fifth man, and in winter generally came stamping forward to the attack wearing high boots, consequently sinking knee-deep at every step.

Special Arctic winter clothing was issued to the Germans. The outfit consisted of a Balaclava helmet, a cap, jacket, waistcoat, and pair of trousers, all fur-lined, two or three pairs of woollen socks, and woollen mitts strengthened with leather. Troops in the firing line wore special mitts that left the trigger-finger free. Sentries had fur-lined greatcoats and boots. White camouflage overalls were worn when snow lay on the ground and members of reconnaissance

patrols received white anoraks in addition to the rest of the winter outfit. Every November, when this clothing was issued, there was lively bargaining for various articles of uniform—larger sizes of tunic, trousers, and boots were in great demand because the normal sizes could hardly be worn with so much additional under-clothing.

For troops off-duty, numerous courses of instruction were given in a wide variety of subjects ranging from handicrafts to woodsmanship. Entertainment was provided by theatrical performances, films, concerts, various competitions, political discussions, and by two radio stations—'Lapplandsender' at Rovaniemi and 'Eismeersender' at Kirkenes. Even a newspaper, called *Lappland-Kurier*, was published. Amongst the competitions, ski-sports meetings were very popular both cross-country and downhill. Dietl was himself a champion skier and the Finnish forces included several skiers who had taken part in the Winter Olympics of 1936. The 'Lappland-Soldaten' were introduced to the joys of the Finnish sauna bath—emerging from the steam huts, after a brisk rubbing-down with bunches of leaves and twigs, before plunging into a snow hole filled with icy water. Home leave was permitted, but a leave of three weeks' duration (because of the journeys involved) generally entailed an absence of two months from the front line.

In January 1942, after von Falkenhorst had returned to Norway, Dietl was promoted to the rank of Generaloberst and given command of Mountain Corps XIX and XXXVI. Between 24 April and 23 May the Russians launched an offensive against Kesten but were beaten back after severe fighting. During the summer the various units were regrouped. In July 1942 Mountain Corps XVIII, consisting of the 6th SS and the 7th Mountain Divisions, was formed under the command of General der Gebirgstruppe Böhme and relieved the Finnish division holding Kesten. The 163rd Infantry replaced the 6th SS Mountain Division in Mountain Corps XXXVI, which was hence-

These motorcycle, half-track combinations were specialized items of equipment specially designed for the Gebirgsjäger and widely used in Lapland and the Caucasus.

forth commanded by General der Infanterie Weisenberger. The three German corps were now styled the 20th Mountain Army, under Dietl's command. Mountain Corps XIX, commanded by General der Gebirgstruppe Schörner, was now to consist of the 2nd and 6th (replacing the 3rd) Mountain Divisions, the 210th Infantry Division, Division Group 'Petsamo' (later to become Division Group van der Hoop), and naval units at Kirkenes.

Proposals for a further attempt to reach the Murmansk railway were frequently made by Dietl after 1941, but the Finns insisted that the Germans should first capture Leningrad. After the fall of Sebastopol in July 1942 preparations were accordingly made to transfer heavy siege artillery to the north, but the critical German position during and after the battle for Stalingrad upset those arrangements. There were no major events in Arctic Europe on land in 1943; at sea the Allied supply routes to Russian ports remained open. Early in 1944, however, Soviet reinforcements in large numbers appeared opposite the German positions. This development caused grave concern to the

Germans, because the Finns had determined to withdraw the division that had been holding Ukhta. The 7th Mountain Division had to fill the gap, and the 139th Mountain Brigade, veterans of Narvik, was therefore detached from Mountain Corps XIX and sent 560 miles (900 km) southwards on skis to reinforce Mountain Corps XVIII, where it henceforth formed part of Division Group 'K', commanded by Generalmajor Kräutler.

In June 1944, Generaloberst Eduard Dietl was killed in an air accident in the Alps, and Hitler chose Generaloberst Lothar Rendulic to assume command of the 20th Mountain Army in Finnish Lapland. Rendulic was no stranger to cold weather, having commanded the 52nd Infantry Division on the retreat from Moscow during the hard winter of 1941-2. The temperature in Russia dropped as low as −51°F (−46°C) and the Germans were still wearing light summer uniform. Frost-bite caused a much greater proportion of casualties among the soldiers than wounds received in action. No equipment for winter warfare was available, and even low-temperature lubricating oils for rifles,

Finnish skiers confer in a forest clearing in Finland during the Arctic campaign. The reindeer, at home in the Arctic wastes, was an ideal form of transport in the region.

guns, and mechanical transport were lacking. Rendulic had also seen service in the bitter, irregular warfare against Tito's Partisans in Yugoslavia, and had the duty of disarming Italian troops in Dalmatia, Montenegro, and Albania after Italy surrendered to the Allies in September 1943.

Hitler personally briefed Rendulic, emphasizing the great importance of his new command in the far north of Europe and warning him that an Allied landing might take place at any time in northern Norway upon the rear of the 20th Mountain Army. He also stressed the importance of the mine at Nickel', the only remaining source of nickel for the German armaments industry. Finally he warned Rendulic that Finland might suddenly drop out of

the war, and of steadily-increasing Soviet pressure in southern Finland. Hitler never once mentioned the main, original reason for the presence of German troops in Arctic Europe— the capture of Murmansk and the cutting off of the main Allied supply route to the USSR.

When Generaloberst Rendulic arrived at the German headquarters at Rovaniemi on 29 June 1944, the 20th Mountain Army consisted of seven first-class divisions and other formations, numbering more than 200,000 men in all. It lay on Soviet soil in two groups separated by a belt of trackless swamps some 160 miles (255 km) wide and between 93 miles (150 km) and 124 miles (200 km) deep. The southern group, consisting of Mountain Corps XVIII (now commanded by General der Infanterie

Hochbaum) and Mountain Corps XXXVI (commanded by General der Gebirgstruppe Vogel), lay with its right wing adjoining the Finnish positions south of Ukhta and its left resting upon the swamps north of Alakurtti. The northern group, consisting of Mountain Corps XIX (commanded by General der Artillerie Ferdinand Jodl) lay with its right wing along the Litsa River as far as the edge of the swamps. The centre lay across the neck of Poloustrov-Ribachy. The left wing occupied various points along the coast of Finnmark as far west as Tanafjorden. German forces west of that fjord were under the orders of the German Commander-in-Chief in Norway, von Falkenhorst. There were no German troops between the right flank of Mountain Corps XIX on the Litsa and the left flank of Mountain Corps XXXVI north of Alakurtti, this area being patrolled and adequately protected by a single battalion of Finnish frontier guards.

Rendulic paid an early visit to the positions of Mountain Corps XXXVI—more than 250 miles (400 km) east of Rovaniemi. He describes his visit to two of the divisions there in the following words:

In the early morning of the following day [1 July 1944] I went to the troops at the front, first to the Brandenburg 163rd Infantry Division. For a time the road could be used, then came narrow uneven paths, which had been laid over the rock surface at the cost of much labour. Corduroy tracks had been built over swampy ground. The frost was endless. The positions themselves lay in the forest. Despite the difficulties presented by the ground they were well laid out. For their appearance the huts used for living quarters offered protection from the worst winter weather. In this sector all was quiet. The men looked fine and morale was high. The main interest of all with whom I spoke was leave and cigarettes.

A supply path led northwards to the left wing of the corps, the Brandenburg 169th Infantry Division. This division and its neighbouring one were the only units in the army which did not consist of mountain troops. They had complete mountain equipment, however, and were in no way inferior in capability to the mountain troops. The left wing stretched far into the great swamps of central Lapland which begin here. In this sector there was some skirmishing in progress as the Russians were in the process of building a track round our flank. The positions lay like strong-points on small, flat hills which rise like islands out of the swamps. They were reached by footpaths, often nearly knee-deep in water. There was very little cover. The troops complained of the continuous daylight, which made movement and supply under the nose of the opponent uncommonly difficult...

What was required of the troops in these conditions in terms of courage, skill and stamina hardly allows comparison with any other front. To all other difficulties of life was added in summer in the swampy regions of Lapland an incredible plague of biting insects.

Mountain Corps XVIII, the southernmost of the three German corps, lay in a swampy forested area 93 miles (150 km) east of Kuusamo, which itself lies 186 miles (300 km) southeast of Rovaniemi. It now comprised the

German mountain troops rescue a comrade suffering from frost-bite somewhere in Lapland.

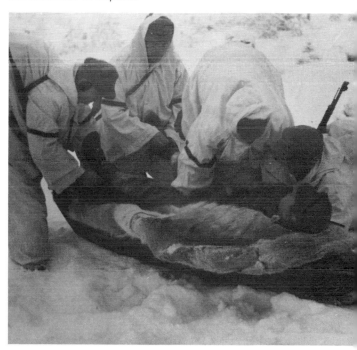

6th SS and the 7th Mountain Divisions and Division Group 'K'. The position here was exceptionally exposed because of a narrow defile in its rear at Kuusamo, where the road from Rovaniemi crosses—within a few miles—three very wide rivers. Earlier in the war the Organization 'Todt' had thrown wooden bridges over these obstacles. The bridges were specially protected from the pressure of ice during the spring break-up by a device that enabled the centre position to be swung open before the pressure of the ice became critical. The bulk of the supplies were brought up by road from the railway at Rovaniemi or at Salla. In the autumn of 1943 a field railway, capable of carrying 400 tons a day, had been built from Kuusamo to link it with the main railway at Hyrynsalmi, some 125 miles (200 km) to the southwest. In the summer of 1944, however, long lengths of the track subsided as the ground thawed, and the foundations had to be relaid.

German Jäger patrol a wind-swept sector of the Lapland coast in the depths of winter.

The headquarters of Mountain Corps XIX lay near Pechenga, north of Rovaniemi. The troops in this corps now comprised the 2nd and 6th Mountain Divisions, the 210th Infantry Division, and Division Group van der Hoop. The last-named division group lay upon a steep rock ridge, 650 ft (200 m) high, which overlooked the Soviet positions on Poluostrov Ribachiy. The viewpoint was not very good though, because of the prevalence of mist and fog. The southern side of the ridge, which was sheltered from Soviet artillery, was honeycombed with snug German dug-outs hewn out of the solid rock. The positions of the 2nd and 6th Mountain Divisions lay along the Litsa. The extreme right wing of the 2nd Mountain Division, near the source of the river, was secured by a few isolated companies manning strong-points on hills rising out of the swamps. The left flank of the corps, along the coast between Pechenga and Kirkenes, the entrance to Varangeren, and the shores of Varangerhalvøya and Nordkinnhalvøya was defended by a number of garrisons provided by the 210th Infantry Division and by batteries of artillery. Some of those batteries were inaccessible by land and could only be supplied by sea in good weather. One of the soldiers noted in his diary that the sun had been sighted in the area only seven times in the whole of 1943.

In contrast to the two southern corps, which were supplied by way of the ports of Oulu, Kemi, and Tornio on the Gulf of Bothnia, Mountain Corps XIX was maintained by monthly convoys that sailed north along the coast of Norway, rounded by North Cape, and unloaded their cargo at Kirkenes. Soviet aircraft were active upon this front and Kirkenes was usually bombed every time a convoy arrived. A squadron of some thirty German fighter aircraft was therefore stationed nearby throughout the war to protect the town and harbour. Unlike the southern route into Finland, which was blocked by ice in the Baltic Sea every winter until late in the spring, the northern route remained open all the year round. For

German mountain troops parade with their full snow apparel and skis in Finland.

their return voyage along the Norwegian coast from Kirkenes, the ships were loaded with nickel. The mine at Nickel' itself was defended by a large concentration of anti-aircraft guns, and the hydro-electric power station at Jäniskoski, which supplied current for the mine, was protected by a bomb-proof concrete cap.

The Germans had foreseen in 1943—as had the Russians—that the sudden collapse of Finnish resistance would mean a considerable depth of exposure to the German right flank. No German troops were available to form yet another front facing south and, short of capitulation, there was no alternative but to abandon the positions between Alakurtti and Ukhta and retire northwards. By holding Rovaniemi until the last possible moment the Germans hoped to extricate the two southern corps and reform them farther north between the Swedish frontier and the swamps, in new positions

that would protect the southern approaches to Nickel' and the roads running westwards into Norway. It had been foreseen that Soviet and possibly Finnish pressure might force the Germans to abandon northern Finland altogether and to retreat into Norway. Plans were accordingly made to meet either situation whenever it arose. On 2 September the Finns announced that diplomatic relations with Germany would be broken off at midnight the following day, and that all German troops would be required to evacuate the country within fourteen days. Quite apart from the fact that Rendulic's orders from the Führer did not permit him to meet this requirement, it was physically impossible for the 20th Mountain Army to leave Finland within the stipulated period. The bulk of the 200,000 German troops consisted of infantry and those at Ukhta on the right wing would have to march some 650 miles (1,045 km) on foot to reach the Norwegian frontier. Even if they were not pursued by the Russians they would inevitably take two months to cover the distance. Fourteen days was barely time enough for Rendulic to prepare the defence of his flank while the two southern corps began their withdrawal towards the north.

On 8 September definite orders were received by Rendulic from Hitler to retreat to a position in which he could continue to cover Nikel' and the roads into Norway. This movement was given the code-name Operation 'Birke'. Newly-formed motorized reserve units were at once sent to bar the southern approaches of Oulu, Pudasjärvi, and Kuusamo at river crossings, causeways, and defiles. On 9 September Finland ceased hostilities against the USSR. The Finnish Government ordered the entire civilian population—some 170,500 in all—to evacuate northern Finland and to head for the south. This was accomplished with the assistance of southward-bound German transport columns. At the same time Soviet patrol activity increased and stronger forces concentrated opposite the two southern corps. German prospects looked bleak. The retreat was likely to extend far into the Arctic winter—which usually begins in these latitudes in October—and the Finns were almost certain to take up arms against their former allies. The nights were already beginning to be cold, with hoar frost. The first snow had also begun to fall in the north.

The retreat continued in good order throughout September. By that time the Red Army had penetrated Finland only in the direction of Salla but on 28 September the Finnish General Siilasvuo concentrated an armoured division, four infantry divisions, and one infantry brigade in the vicinity of Oulu. Finnish troops suddenly attacked units of 'Kampfgruppe West', which was retiring from Oulu towards Kemi and Pudasjärvi. The 7th Mountain Division moved up in support and Pudasjärvi was held, but along the coast the Germans were forced back towards Kemi and Tornio.

Between 1 and 6 October a Finnish division led by Major General Pajari landed by sea near Tornio. Division Group 'K' at once counterattacked, with the aid of 'Kampfgruppe West' and the Motorized Ski-Brigade 'Finnland'. After 48 hours of heavy fighting in which the Finns held their ground, the effort to dislodge them was abandoned. On 4 October Generaloberst Rendulic received orders from Hitler to evacuate northern Finland and to continue his retreat into Norway.

The story of the war in the Arctic now entered a new phase. It began with the Red Army's entry into northern Norway on 25 October. The last German hold in polar regions—Arctic Norway, a territory the size of Scotland and half of England put together—began to be thrown off. On 26 October, Moscow radio broadcast an 'Order of the Day' from Marshal Stalin to General Meretskov, saying that the troops of the Karelian front had crossed the Norwegian frontier and had entered Kirkenes on 25 October. The Red Army had made its way right across northern Finland and outflanking moves brought Soviet troops into Kirkenes, the biggest German military base in the whole of the Arctic, with its port facilities, airfields, huge military dumps, and iron works, etc.

Kirkenes and neighbouring towns had been subjected to Russian bombing prior to the invasion—there were 900 alerts altogether—but only fourteen fatal casualties were caused. When the people realized that eastern Finnmark was about to become a battleground, they sought refuge from the battle and the Germans (whom they knew would try to evacuate them) in the iron mines at Bjornevatn and in the nearby woods. The Russians descended on Kirkenes so suddenly that the Germans did not have the time to round up the civilian population. They were only able to evacuate those who fell into their hands easily, such as prisoner-of-war slave workers, packing them into any sort of seacraft or road transport that happened to be available, and fleeing westwards, away from

Gebirgsjäger mounted in a light vehicle tow a 3.7 cm Pak 35/36 L/45 anti-tank gun on patrol in Lapland.

the advancing Soviet troops. Only German rearguards were left behind to destroy everything they could, in accordance with the 'scorched earth' policy the Germans applied with ruthless efficiency all the way through northern Norway.

Of the 23,000 Norwegian inhabitants of eastern Finnmark, about 20,000 had evaded Nazi deportation. When the victorious Soviet troops arrived, the Norwegians flocked out of the mines, cellars, and woods to greet them as liberators. Although they had lost everything they possessed—their homes and, in many cases, as the Germans had seized their fishing boats, their livelihoods—the Norwegians did all they could to assist the Russians. Fishermen guided them over the fjords and rivers in order to speed up the rout of the enemy, and what boats had escaped German looting or destruction were placed at the Russians' disposal. The actual fighting on this front proceeded very rapidly, and once the Germans were defeated they withdrew as quickly as they could. Only three or four civilians were hurt in the battle area. But as the Germans pulled out they destroyed not only human dwelling-places but all bridges and other means of communication. In this Arctic region, where there was but one road crossing some of the most desolate country in Europe, such action necessarily slowed up the Russian pursuit.

Meanwhile, Norwegian troops, who had been training for this day for years in Britain, were on their way to the Arctic front, transported by the British Navy. With them was a military mission whose task it was to take control of civil administration and other matters in liberated Norwegian territory. By the time this force reached Norway hundreds of Norwegian volunteers were waiting to join forces with them. In fact, two days after the Russians entered Kirkenes no less than 1,500 Norwegians, freed of the occupation, had volunteered for military service. At precisely 10:00 on 10 November 1944, the first soldiers of the Norwegian army crossed into Norwegian territory after journeying from Petsamo in Finland. Torchlights illuminated the frontier stone as they filed silently past it, and their thoughts went back to the time when they had escaped

Above *In the latter stages of the war, the Finns broke their alliance with Nazi Germany and engaged in a short war to expel the Germans from their homeland. Here Finnish troops ferry their equipment across the Simojoki River before confronting the Germans in the Battle of Kemi, 1-8 August 1944.*

Below *Finnish bicycle-equipped infantrymen cross a river in Lapland during their campaign against the Germans in 1944-45.*

from Norway, landed in Britain, and begun their training for the task ahead. To the northwest the polar darkness was relieved by the red glow of fire—a tremendous coal dump near Kirkenes that the Germans had fired before they retreated was still burning.

Soon afterwards the Norwegians reached Kirkenes, the first liberated Norwegian town. A scene of devastation and destruction met their eyes. Only 28 houses remained standing. The quays had been wrecked, the plant and installations of the iron mines had been destroyed, and half-sunken ships could be seen in the harbour. The majority of the civilian population were living at Bjornevatn, a mining community that had escaped large-scale German demolition, and it was here that the Norwegian army personnel and their northern countrymen had their first reunion. A great meeting was held—the first gathering of free Norwegians in Norway for four and a half years. All available habitation had already been placed by the Russians at the disposal of the civilian population, and now (under the leadership of Norwegian troops) these people began the task of rebuilding what the Germans had destroyed.

Other forces advanced westwards in the wake of the retreating German army, to find everywhere the same trail of devastation and destruction. In addition, they found that practically the whole of the civilian population had been deported by the Germans and only a few stragglers were discovered. As the Germans had put a safe distance between themselves and the Russians, they had effected with complete ruthlessness the forced evacuation of the population.

Those who resisted the order were shot. In small boats, dangerously overcrowded, and along the single Arctic highway leading southwards to Tromso and then on to Narvik and Trondheim, thousands of men, women, and children were deported. They were allowed to take only the barest necessities with them. Before they left they were compelled to watch their homes, which had cost so much effort to build in this hard land of the north, go up in smoke and flames. The deportation caused untold suffering and many—including young children—died during the forced marches or in the overcrowded fishing boats.

Whilst Norwegian rule was re-established in Finnmark, the German forces, which included the Finnish-Lapland army (the 20th Mountain Army), were harassed by the British navy and air force as they attempted to escape by sea down the 1,000-mile (1,600-km) long Norwegian coastline with as much material as they could. Their losses were considerable. Other troops straggled along the single northern road for weeks. In cold that sometimes reached $-2°F$ ($-17°C$) and in swirling snowstorms, they trekked hundreds of miles in lorries, cars, horse-drawn transport, and on foot—and always driving civilians along with them, partly for propaganda purposes to show how the Norwegians were fleeing from the Bolsheviks. Behind them they left an unending trail of destruction. The campaign in northern Norway with its vast distances and poor lines of communication came to an end in the harsh winter conditions that typified war in the Arctic regions.

CHAPTER 14
THE RUSSIAN FRONT

The first records of the use of skis in the modern Russian army go back to the end of the nineteenth century. The province of Finland in those days provided the Imperial Russian army's best skiers, but as time progressed Russian regiments sometimes included *Okhotniki* or 'Hunters' who were reconnaissance troops equipped with skis. Thus, as early as 1891, a ski patrol of the 20th Russian Infantry Division, stationed in Kazan, performed a remarkable march of 450 miles (725 km) in ten days under very unfavourable weather conditions—frosts reaching sub-zero temperatures and frequent blizzards. Another record exists of a ski trek over a similar distance in 1913. In the winter manoeuvres of the Petersburg garrison in 1892-3 tactical actions were 'fought' with skiers, which proved their superiority over troops less well-equipped for snow conditions. On 23 December a group of three officers and 64 men were sent by the Ismailov Guard Regiment of the 1st Guards Division (Petersburg)

to Kholmogory, near Archangel, for ski training with the local hunting command. After six weeks they set out on the return journey on skis and covered a distance of about 800 miles (1,285 km) in 20 days, including three days of rest.

As we have already seen, ski patrols were used by both sides on the Italo-Austrian mountain front in the First World War. In the Carpathians, German and Austrian skiers—using white camouflage covers—severely harassed the ski-less Russian troops. Russian ski troops, so far as the present writer has been able to ascertain, did not take active part in the fighting for two reasons: the best skiers in the Russian Imperial army were Finns and they had been exempted from front-line duties; and Russian hunter commands had not been trained for mountain work and could not be advantageously employed in the Carpathians, where some heavy fighting took place. However, Rus-

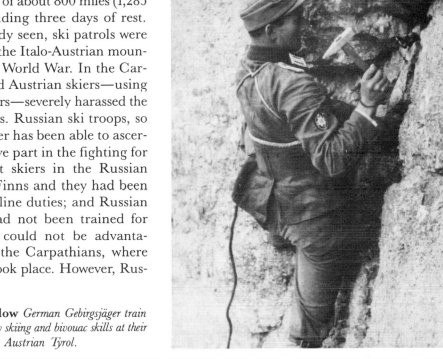

Opposite, right and below *German Gebirgsjäger train in rock-climbing, cross-country skiing and bivouac skills at their home training ground in the Austrian Tyrol.*

sian skiers were certainly occasionally used for special duties, medical service in particular.

In the Second World War, apart from auxiliary duties, skiers of the Red Army were generally employed in two main capacities: first as guerrilla detachments (the ski commandos), equipped with automatic rifles, machine-guns, and trench mortars mounted on ski-sledges and operating independently in larger or smaller groups in the enemy rear often with the support of airborne troops (although it is not clear whether or not Soviet parachutists were also equipped with skis); and second as forerunners of an offensive with the object of striking sudden blows at the nerve centres of the enemy defences, its headquarters and lines of communications in order to disorganize its resistance before the main onslaught was launched. Ski commandos were also entrusted with the task of preventing the arrival of reinforcements and cutting off the defeated enemy's retreat. Ski patrols, infiltrating through the German lines and gradually increasing in concentration, played a vital part in surrounding the opposing strong-points and also served as a screen to protect the flanks of the main force.

Another interesting feature of Russian ski-fighting tactics was the use of ski formations in combination with cavalry, particularly by Marshal Timoshenko—a practice also adopted by the Swedish army. Ski or sledge runners were used for transport of artillery. Armoured sledges were often used as 'winter tanks' in considerable numbers and apparently not without success. White camouflage was employed on a large scale as well as by ski troops and by other formations whenever conditions required. In fighting, the Germans also used skiers for patrolling, auxiliary duties, and direct offensive operations, but nowhere do they seem to have been very numerous or gained much success. At first sight this may appear surprising, knowing that Germany and Austria had always paid so much attention to ski training in their respective armies. Operation 'Barbarossa', however, gave a low priority to Alpine troops, the Germans

fully expecting to be parading in Moscow in their summer uniforms before the winter months set in.

Several instances will serve to illustrate the Soviet ski troops' tactics. In the fighting near Moscow in November 1941, where the snow had fallen rather earlier than expected, the Germans (who by then held Kalinin) were planning to envelop the Soviet capital, the northern arm of their pincers being based on that town. As a preparatory move, a German column was dispatched from Mednoye, a village about 20 miles (30 km) to the east of Kalinin, to capture the small town of Torzhok, 40 miles (65 km) northeast of Kalinin. A Soviet ski battalion under Captain Chaikovsky received orders to cut off this enemy column by a flank manoeuvre from the main forces advancing from Mednoye. The success of the operation depended on speed.

The Russian ski force covered a great distance in difficult forest country (dotted with half-frozen marshes), dislodged the enemy from several villages, and placed itself astride the road from Mednoye to Torzhok. Thus covered, another Russian force approached and attacked Mednoye from an unexpected direction. In effect, the Germans had to change their plans and to recall the units previously detailed for the capture of Torzhok. These, however, found their way back cut off by Captain Chaikovsky's ski battalion. The northern arm of the German pincers was broken, and some time later the Germans were forced out of Kalinin itself.

The same Russian source gives the following story of the capture of the strategic village of Maklaky—some 40 miles (65 km) north-northeast of Briansk and 12 miles (19 km) inside the German lines—by Russian skiers during the fighting of February 1942.

> Seven skiers started out in a terrible blizzard and stealthily approached Maklaky. Two of them, leaving their skis behind, made contact with the local inhabitants and learned that the village was garrisoned by 70 to 80 Germans with two officers.
> Sergeant Ukolov, who was in charge of

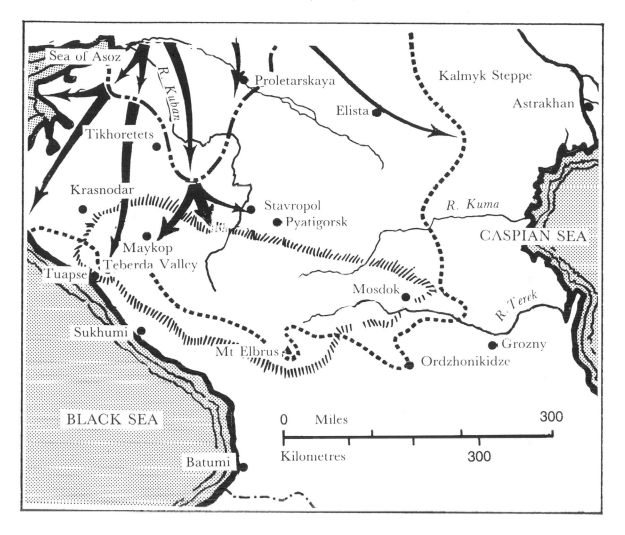

The Caucasus Front: The German XXXXIX Mountain Corps was well equipped to fight over the precipitous terrain of the wild Caucasus mountains, but the elite mountain 'hunters' from the Tyrol and Bavaria made little progress through the passes, defiles and valleys of the Caucasus against their Russian counterparts, who had known the rugged terrain since boyhood and were proficient at living off the land.

this group, made a detailed plan of the village, carefully noting all the houses occupied by the Germans and all houses with brick foundations, which the Nazis usually convert into blockhouses.

The same night a ski detachment under Captain Grigoriev, with two heavy machine-guns and four mortars mounted on sledges, approached Maklaky and silently entered the village. The Red Army men had overpowered the German sentries at the church, captured the artillery gun and occupied the school

before the Germans sounded the alarm.

By then it was too late. Using hand grenades, rifles and bayonets with deadly effect, Grigoriev's men captured house after house. Mortar fire accounted for the crews of two German artillery guns before they could fire one round each.

The next task was to prevent any German escaping to warn the Nazi command of the capture of Maklaky. Dashing across the fields, a group of Red Army men reached the opposite end of the village and cut off the retreat of the fleeing Nazis. When morning came Maklaky was cleared of the enemy. The Germans lost 72 soldiers and two officers killed or wounded; four were taken prisoner.

Grigoriev and his men held the village for three days against the troops of the 260th German Infantry Division commanded by General von Giels until they were relieved by other Soviet troops. The success of this ski unit had greatly contributed to the Russian victory over the German 216th Division and vital gains on this sector of the front.

Another example comes from the fighting of January 1942, in the Valdai Hills, where the Red Army won some of its most spectacular victories. Russian ski troops played a major part in the investment and capture of Peno, one of the German pivotal strongholds in the Valdai region. While the Red infantry with artillery

support attacked Peno from the east, ski troops infiltrated through the German lines both north and south of the town—and threw out protective screens on the flanks of the Soviet advance. The Germans sought to outflank the Russians, but their counter-attack was beaten back by the ski screen. Meanwhile the main force entered Peno, driving the remnants of the garrison westwards. The Germans tried to retreat in the direction of Soblago (the only road they thought free) but they found it cut by the Red ski detachments. In the ensuing fighting most of the Germans were annihilated and what remained took to the forests. The effect of these operations was a wedge 25 miles (40 km) deep driven into the German positions, which in conjunction with other similar advances led to the ultimate crumbling of the whole defence zone.

Russian ski troops also distinguished themselves in the battles on the Leningrad sector. On one occasion a ski detachment, equipped

German Waffen-SS troops dressed for the Russian winter.

A German ski scout on night patrol somewhere in North Russia cautiously surveys his surroundings.

with automatic rifles, machine-guns, and trench mortars on ski-sledges, made its way by night into the village of Verkhovina, which was the headquarters of the German 269th Infantry Division. The attack was a complete surprise. The sentries and staff officers were killed. Two guns, twenty-four motor vehicles, several machine-guns, and numerous automatic rifles were among the rich booty taken. An interesting detail of the marching tactics is given in the following extract from the *Soviet War News:* 'Skiers familiar with the locality usually moved at the head of the advancing Red Army men. They were followed by infantry who tramped down the snow and sappers who cleared the road of trees and covered the marshes with logs and branches. In this way the road was prepared for guns and ammunition transport'.

One of the Red Army skiers' major performances was their infiltration into White Russia during February 1942. They are said to have reached as far as the Latvian border, making contact with the local guerrilla bands, disrupting and harassing German communications, carrying out sabotage work, and attacking isolated German posts. Activities of this kind were carried out by Soviet skiers in the German rear on all sectors of the front, causing great concern to the German High Command. It appears certain that the Russians owed their winter successes largely to the training and efficiency of their ski troops and their better general preparation than the Germans for a war on snow. It is interesting to note that one observer of the western Allies noted that 'General Dietl's Alpine troops operating on the Murmansk front have proved, in fact, a spectacular failure, and German winter tactics in Eastern Karelia have earned them the derision of the Finns'.

The Russians had learned much from their brief campaign against Finland (1939-40), partly adopting and partly developing their opponents' tactics. They had turned guerrilla warfare into a fine art and developed it on a scale hitherto unknown in the history of military ski transport. Co-operation between skiers and paratroopers was a new development, while the use of ski commandos or forerunners of an armoured offensive had never before been tried out with equal success, except on one occasion by the Germans in the Norwegian Campaign of 1940 (though in this case the action was more an outflanking manoeuvre than a commando operation in the new, Second World War sense of the word). Russian ski troops certainly proved their worth in the three, hard winters of the 1941-5 war in Russia.

When Germany attacked Russia late in June 1941, three German Army groups (North, Centre, and South) struck across the frontier. One of the main objectives of the first offensives was to destroy the great mass of the Red Army in southern Russia, and this was to be carried out west of the Dnieper River by Army Group South, aided by elements from the southern wing of Army Group Centre. Von Rundstedt's Army Group South disposed three armies: Seventeenth under Stülpnagel, with 13 divisions; the Sixth commanded by Reichenau, having six divisions; and the Eleventh, under Schobert, seven divisions strong. Attached to this army group was Panzer Group 1, under Kleist—a combination of armoured and motorized divisions that was intended as the cutting edge of Army Group South's sword.

The unit concerned at this point is XXXXIX Gebirgs Corps of Stülpnagel's Seventeenth Army, and the period of action is just a few weeks from 20 July to 13 August. This Gebirgs Corps had two mountain divisions, 1st and 4th, on its establishment, together with one or more infantry divisions. During this particular operation the 97th Light, the 125th Infantry, and the 259th Infantry Divisions all served. The 1st Gebirgs Division had been formed in Garmisch Partenkirchen around the nucleus of a Gebirgs Brigade and the regiments were located in Bavaria when mobilization was ordered on 26 August 1939. Before the 1st Gebirgs Division had joined Army Group South in Russia, its units had fought in southern Poland during the autumn of 1939, in the campaign in France in 1940, and, when the armistice was signed, was trained for the amphibious operation 'Sealion' — the proposed invasion of Great Britain. When 'Sealion' was cancelled, units of the division were then posted to Besançon for a proposed assault upon Gibraltar. The 4th Gebirgs Division began to take shape on 23 October 1940 and first saw service in Yugoslavia before being sent to the Eastern Front.

The action that successfully encircled Red Army units at Uman was fought by the XXXXIX Gebirgs Corps serving in the role of light infantry. It was fought in arid desert land and so does not fall within the scope of the present book. However, this mountain corps had its first opportunity to fight in the high mountains, for which it had been trained, in the Caucasus during the German summer offensive of 1942. Hitler's Directive No. 45 laid down the guidelines for the new offensive. Army Group 'A' (List) was to drive into the Caucasus and Army Group 'B' (von Bock) towards Stalingrad and the Volga. The first result of the successful execution of those tasks, as Hitler saw it, would be the paralysis of the Soviet war effort through the seizure of its principal oilfields. Army Group 'A' was to occupy 'the entire eastern coastline of the Black Sea . . . while a force composed chiefly of mobile and fast-moving units (Panzer Group 1) will capture the area of Grozny. . . . Thereafter the Baku area will be occupied by a thrust along the Caspian coast'. The second result of the summer offensive would be the encirclement by Army Group 'B' of the enemy forces that had crossed the Don and their destruction. This was to be followed by the pursuit of, and final elimination of, the Russian left wing somewhere in the Stalingrad sector and along the line of the Volga River.

The Red Army included 18 mountain rifle divisions, each numbering approximately 17,000 men. Those rifle divisions (which contained their own artillery regiments) were enumerated as follows: Nos. 9, 20, 28, 58, 63, 75, 76, 77, 83, 96, 100, 138, 173, 192, 194, 242, 302, and 318. The Russian mountain troops were not specially trained or equipped for the mountain role. Units varied in strength and were often hastily raised. The equipment was simple but practical. All was centred on mobility, and fighting with a variety of personal weapons. A low degree of priority was given to special clothing, rations, and tent equipment. Even pack animals were in short supply. 'Ivan' was, however, noted as being stubborn in defence, tenacious in the attack, and had a remarkable ability to live off the land.

As an example, a rifle-brigade on the Maruchskoy Pass had two rifle regiments with three battalions each—an independent machine-pistol company, a platoon of heavy mortars (four), and a company of engineers.

Right *German engineers demonstrate mine-laying and detection techniques during the campaign in Russia.*

The Caucasus mountains provided a formidable barrier to German hopes of linking by means of this northern route with the Afrika Korps in Egypt. The German mountain troops, however, even with their superior training and equipment, were no match for the ragged Caucasian warriors, whose natural habitat was the mountains, and whose way of life was living off the land.

The total strength was about 2,000 men with 400 machine-pistols, 20 light and 6 heavy machine-guns, 10 light machine-guns, 25 medium and 8 heavy mortars, as well as 120 AT rifles. The rifle battalion of about 230 men had one rifle company (about 70 men) with rifles, including some automatics, 4 machine-guns, and 2 light mortars. A machine-pistol company numbered about 50 men with 24 AT rifles. A mortar platoon of about 30 men had 4 medium mortars. Mountain artillery guns were scarce, and the Russians were also short of mountain-trained gunners and observers. Some use was made of a 7.62-cm field gun, which could be stripped down and carried. There was also the mountain gun 38, which had a bi-partite shield and a rigid carriage. Artillery was largely replaced by a great number of mortars. Whenever the weather permitted, the Russians used their aircraft to attack German positions on passes and in valleys, troops on the move, and supply columns.

Unlike the Russians (who wore no special uniform) the German Gebirgsjäger dressed in a uniform that distinguished them from the other arms of the Wehrmacht. It consisted of a field-service jacket with the edelweiss badge on the right sleeve, wide-cut trousers, weighty Alpine boots, and short puttees—the latter mostly not worn. Characteristic of all German mountain soldiers was the mountain cap with the edelweiss on the left side.

Bayonets, anti-gas respirators, and steel helmets were considered too heavy to carry in action. Assault kit was carried in a rucksack, which contained a ground sheet, blanket, wind cheater, another shirt, spare pants and socks, Balaclava caps, waist belt, gloves, mess tin and cutlery, one kilo of bread, one large can of meat, and one tin of lard. On his belt he also carried a water bottle, musette bag, and entrenching tool.

The rations had to last for two days. Resupply was with the aid of pack animals. In the musette bag was an iron ration, mainly chocolate. In the blouse pockets were two field dressings, a clasp knife, cigarettes, pen and ink, and service and pay book. The weapons carried by the Jäger were usually the Rifle 98 K, two cartridge pouches (each with 50 rounds), two grenades, and sometimes an ammunition box with 300 rounds. Platoon and section commanders as well as runners had to carry binoculars, message bags, or signal pistols. The items in the rucksack weighed approximately 120 lbs

(22 kg) but the Gebirgsjäger were known to carry loads of as much as 165 lbs (75 kg). Sharpshooters using telescopic sights were widely used in the mountains.

A standard Jäger battalion had a strength of 877 officers and men who were organized into three companies—a machine-gun, an anti-tank, and a heavy-weapons company. Each Jäger company had a strength of 147 men and was equipped with 12 light machine-guns and 3 light and 2 8-cm mortars, as well as one anti-tank rifle. The machine-gun company, with a strength of 208 men, had 12 heavy machine-guns and 4 12-cm mortars, while the heavy weapons company with 201 men was equipped with 4 light machine-guns and 2 7.5-cm infantry howitzers. The anti-tank company had 4 guns and 2 rifles. Three Gebirgsjäger battalions and a headquarters group made up a regiment, which had a strength of 3,064 all ranks. Regimental headquarters was composed of a signals platoon and a heavy mountain-howitzer battery.

A Gebirgs division was made up from two Jäger regiments and an artillery regiment together with the usual support units. This formation had a strength of 13,056 officers and men. Included within the establishment were 2,330 men of the artillery regiment equipped with 24 guns of 7.5-cm calibre and 12 10.5-cm howitzers. A signals battalion, a semi-motorized reconnaissance battalion, a motorized anti-tank gun battalion, and a battalion of semi-motorized engineers were the principal ancillary units and the train (which completed the divisional establishment) included pack animals organized usually at battalion level but which, under difficult terrain conditions, could be formed so as to supply individual companies. Most Gebirgs divisions had a Hochgebirgs (high mountain) battalion of five companies and a support company with a platoon of engineers, one of signals and one of light howitzers.

The distribution of weapons amongst the units was as follows: 117 heavy machine-guns, 172 light machine-guns, 12 3.7-cm anti-tank guns, 36 anti-tank rifles, 27 5-cm mortars and 18 8-cm mortars, and 6 7.5-cm howitzers. At divisional level the anti-tank gun establishment included 25 weapons of 5-cm calibre.

Each division had 447 motorcycles, 858 lorries of various sizes, 714 horse-drawn carts, and 3,506 horses of mules. These were organized into trains each made up of 200 beasts. During the campaign in Russia and particularly in the periods of mud and snow the number of horse-drawn vehicles was increased by the acquisition of *panje* carts—light, wooden vehicles drawn by Russian breeds of horses that were better able to withstand the bitter winter conditions than the usual European breeds. Jäger regiments were allocated an Alpine scale of equipment, which included special rock-climbing equipment. Thus medical teams were issued with stretchers on which the wounded could be lowered down vertical rock faces, and the mountain artillery pieces could be broken down into mule loads and transported on pack animals. The engineer battalion was equipped with power saws and drills. The signals detachments also had equipment that could be adapted for pack transport.

Specialist equipment for German mountain troops included a pack radio-set operating off batteries. The radio team consisted of three men—one carried the set, one the batteries, and the other was the actual signaller. Dogs were frequently employed to carry messages and were also used to carry ammunition belts, food, and medical packs. St Bernards were used in mountain-rescue medical teams. The medical teams had to be proficient in dealing with snow blindness, fractures, frost-bite, rope burns, and other injuries peculiar to mountaineering. To help them evacuate the sick and wounded, certain techniques using climbing ropes were employed. These were only used, however, in the most difficult terrain. Standard Alpine evacuation of the wounded did, nevertheless, include a ski stretcher that could be broken down for man porterage, and a unicycle stretcher, the design of which included folding legs so that is could be used (in an emergency) as an operating table. This piece of equipment could also be broken to be portered in loads.

The German mountain troops used standard German personal weapons and machine-guns such as the Rifle 98 K, the Machine-Pistol 40, and the Machine-Guns 34 and 42. When the latter machine-gun was introduced it greatly increased the firepower of units in action. The principal guns and howitzers in use were the 7.5-cm Mountain Gun 15, 7.5-cm Light Mountain Gun 18, the 7.5-cm Mountain Gun 28, the 7.5-cm Mountain Infantry Gun 36, the 10-cm Mountain Howitzer 16, the 10-cm Mountain Mortar 16, the 10.5-cm Mountain Howitzer 40 (also known as Gerat 77), and the Mountain Howitzer 42. Certain other mountain guns were in service with the German army, having been acquired from the French, Italians, Czechs, and Russians.

In the mountains, the artillery detachments marched with the riflemen. Each detachment comprised a battery of four guns. The most widely-used mountain gun was the 36 version, which first went into use with the German army during the period 1940-1. This relatively light gun—without a shield and with a flat trajectory and vertical-fire capability-—could be transported broken down on a four-wheel cart drawn by two mules or packed on to mules. A battery was staffed by about 75 men and served by 68 mules, and it took 8 mules to transport one dismantled gun. Normally there were four guns in a battery. Five mules carried 40 rounds of ammunition and another two were loaded with cable-rolls, telephone stores, and wireless boxes. The Mountain Howitzer 42 first saw action in the Caucasus. It was of excellent construction. In the firing position, the lower carriage could be removed and the gun operated on a large pivot-mounting.

A mountain engineer battalion (which was partly motorized) consisted of the staff, signal platoon, two companies of men operating on foot, one motorized company, and one light-service train. Loads were carried in carts or as mule-packs. The motorized company was equipped with cross-country tractors. Each engineer was equipped with standard infantry weapons and the tools of his trade for building roads and bridges, etc. A signals unit was half motorized, half drawn by horses. The telephone and the wireless company had four platoons. There were also signal platoons in the rifle regiments and battalions. The atmospheric conditions in the Caucasus mountains made signalling by both radio and wireless telegraphy difficult. Equally, laying a telephone line was hazardous, involving treks over narrow paths, steep rocks, snow and ice-fields.

The Gebirgsjäger would never have been able to operate without their mules. A mule is a cross-breeding between a donkey stallion and a horse mare. A patient beast dark brown in colour, the mule's long ears stand up when there is trouble ahead and lie back in storm and rain. Mules are not as obstinate as many people think but they can be so if badly treated. The Gebirgsjäger tied a red ribbon around the tails of those that kicked. Every mule had its saddle-blanket with a harness on top and finally the dosser. About 225 lb (102 kg) could be loaded upon that dosser. The mules were fed with hay and oats. If fodder was unobtainable, the mules devoured the straw on the roofs of peasants' houses, leaves from shrubs, or the bark of trees. No journey seemed impossible for the mules— through valleys and over hills and dizzy heights, past rock precipices, and through torrents carrying weapons, ammunition, food supplies, dismantled guns, engineer and signal-equipment, and sometimes wounded or injured men.

The opening moves of the 1942 summer offensive found the XXXXIX Gebirgs Corps holding the line of the Mius River, positions its divisions had held since the Russian winter offensive. In July the Corps was ordered to prepare for an operation that would spearhead the eastern drive. By 26 July all was ready and the units, back in the front line, had crossed the Don at Rostov and made good progress

Above *Gebirgsjäger occupy a lofty vantage point overlooking the meeting place of deep-cut valleys in the snow-covered Caucasus mountains.*

Below *A mountain gun pounds a Russian position across a narrow valley. Note the Jäger on the left with the range-finding equipment and the detachment commander on the far left observing the fall of shot.*

against the delaying actions of Russian rear-guards. Accustomed to marching long distances, the Gebirgsjäger made their way in scorching heat through the waterless Kuban steppe-land. No trees cast welcome shadows. The marching report of one of the rifle battalions included the statement that 'During 25 days with one day of fighting and three days of rest, the battalion marched 580 kilometres'. As the march drew to its end, the men saw on the horizon the Caucasian heights, growing taller and taller and the advance parties went ahead to reconnoitre the entrances of the first mountain valleys.

The German soldiers found the mountain air cool and refreshing as compared with the oven heat of the Kuban steppe. Few mountain people were to be seen and those who were had semi-oriental features. They lived a primitive life in their wild and uncultured habitat, which had remained undeveloped for centuries. The men from the Bavarian and Austrian mountains found no Alpine resorts and colourful villages of the kind they were used to seeing at home. On the other hand, the natives were accomplished mountaineers and skilled horsemen, and they lived in clean habitations. The summer hours were short and often shrouded in mist, which made navigation on foot difficult and rather dangerous when attempting to cross a tree trunk spanning a narrow ravine. At night on the open mountain tops, the stars gave some light, but the valleys were pitch black. The first snows began to fall on 3 September and thick snow and ice soon covered the battle areas. The cold was so intense in the winter months that a sentry could freeze to death; to fall in the snow from fatigue would induce a repose from which the unfortunate sleeper might never recover.

The German army commenced the battle for the Caucasus, which formed part of the Soviet Southern front, launching General Field Marshal List's Army Group 'A' against five understrength Red armies—the Germans enjoyed the numerical superiority in men. The North Caucasian front stretched from the

mouth of the Don along the eastern shore of the Sea of Azov, the Kerch Strait, and along the Black Sea coast to Lazarevskaya. The Soviet troops were under orders to defend the eastern shores of the Sea of Azov and the Taman peninsula, and to prevent the Germans from crossing the Kerch Strait. The Black Sea fleet and the Azov flotilla were to support the ground forces and prevent German amphibious landing operations. The Soviet Transcaucasian front defended the Black Sea coast from Lazarevskaya to Batumi and further along the Soviet-Turkish border. Part of the front's forces were stationed in northern Iran where, in accordance with an agreement between the USSR and Iran, they covered the Iranian-Turkish border.

In late August the Soviet 46th Army of the Transcaucasian front clashed with the Germans in the passes of the main Caucasus range. The German force included the XXXXIX Gebirgs Corps (the 1st and 4th Mountain Divisions) and the 97th and 101st Light Infantry Divisions), whose troops had also received mountain-warfare training. The XXXXIX Corps was commanded by General Konrad, the 1st (Edelweiss) Division by Lieutenant General Lanz and the 4th Division by Major General Egelzeer. Army Group 'A' also had two Romanian mountain divisions in reserve, and a 'Special Corps' followed in the wake of the Gebirgsjäger in the hope of joining General Rommel's forces operating in Egypt.

The German troops moved from the Kuban towards the Khotyu-Tau and Nakhar Passes, along the valley of the Teberda towards the Klukhori and Dombay-Ulgen Passes, along the valleys of the Marukha and Bolshoi Zelenchuk Rivers towards the Marukha and Naur Passes, and along the Bolshaya Laba Valley towards the Sancharo and Beashkha Passes. As the Edelweiss Division advanced along the valley of the Teberda River, the Germans found the Klukhori Pass defended by a battalion of Red troops. One company was stationed at the head of the pass and on two of its southern slopes. A second battalion was deployed south of the pass in the area of Gvandra, Ajara, and Klydj, and a third battalion was at Sukhumi. With the help of reserves, which took some time to negotiate the mountainous and wooded terrain, the Russians halted the Germans but could not dislodge them from the pass. One day a group of German sub-machine-gunners was wiped out to a man by Russian mountain troops. In early September the Russians forced the Germans back to the head of the pass but the battle ended in stalemate, the opposing forces occupying dominant heights.

At this time the Germans approached the twin-crowned Mt Elbrus, whose two peaks rise to 18,476 ft (5,635 m) and 18,357 ft (5,598 m). Mt Elbrus is the highest mountain in the central Caucasus and was already known to mountaineers as a tremendous challenge. One of the German élite 'high' companies advanced eastwards over Utshkulan and upwards over the Ulla Kam valley in order to occupy the Elbrus area and to protect the left flank of the 49th Corps. A company led by Captain Groth passed through the Chotju Tau Pass and commenced the ascent of Elbrus to the mountain climbers lodges at 'Krugozov' and the 'Shelter of the Eleven'. Two Gebirgsjäger companies succeeded in capturing the two lodges and raised the Nazi flag on both peaks, a feat that was much publicized by the German propaganda machine in Berlin. Five months later, Soviet engineers scaled Mt Elbrus from its southern slope and replaced the German flag with their own 'hammer and sickle'.

The unsuccessful offensives in the Elbrus and Klukhori direction forced the Germans to mount operations in the Marukha direction. Fighting began there on 2 September when the Russian 810th Regiment held the Germans in a fierce engagement. On 5 September a regiment of the German 1st Mountain Division struck out from the Aksaut and Marukha valleys and the Uzhum range at two Russian regiments. After several actions the Germans took the Marukha Pass, which they held—in spite of determined counter-attacks—until January

An excellent shot of a half-track German motorcycle as it ploughs through the snow in the Caucasus mountains.

1943. Fighting in the Sancharo area began on 25 August. It converged in the valley of the Bolshaya Laba where units of the 4th Mountain Division fought a company of the 808th Regiment and a composite NKVD detachment. The Germans captured the Sancharo Pass and advanced southwards unopposed.

The battles for the mountain passes were numerous. Capturing a pass usually gave the Germans a good view of the green shores and the deep blue of the Black Sea. Wintering in the harsh atmosphere of the Caucasus mountains, within sight of sun-lit valleys and summer bathing resorts, filled the Germans with despair. The German tactics, which precluded the use of mechanized columns, were to penetrate on foot deep into the mountains. There the advance parties seized dominant heights and attempted to hold them until the arrival of the main forces. Tanks were brought up whenever possible and used as artillery, firing from static positions. Soviet tactics, on the other hand, also began with the use of small infantry groups with support from the sappers, who removed obstacles and assisted with movement in every way possible. The rains and mist affected both sides equally, but the Red Air Force was especially helpful, airlifting ammunition and food supplies and evacuating the wounded.

The Russians were greatly assisted by the partisans of the Kuban, Stavropol, Kabardino-Balkaria, North Ossetia, and Checheno-Ingushetia. The guerrilla fighters cut supply lines in the Kuban steppe-land and the Caucasus foothills, and raided deep into the mountains. Reconnaissance was often provided by the partisans, so that the regular forces could move in and deal with the Germans. On one occasion two women partisans (acting as scouts) cap-

tured two German scouts, who had a map in their possession that revealed that mountain units were moving to the passes. Two days later, two large partisan groups of the 1st Mountain Division arrived in the Marukha gorge. The Germans had always been confident of success in capturing the passes in the Caucasus but the partisan ambushes began to make the Germans doubtful of succeeding in crossing the great range of mountains.

In addition to ambushes, the partisans set up road-blocks, planted mines, and struck swiftly at the German mountain troops picking their way along precariously-sited paths. Before the winter had seriously set in, the troops of the Transcaucasian front had moved in and blocked the passes. The Germans failed to break into Georgia through Karachayevo-Cherkessia. Moreover, the XXXXIX Gebirgsjäger Corps

A German mountain trooper takes a break during a climb up a mountain track. He obviously feels safely out-of-range of Russian snipers.

was subjected to a two-pronged Soviet assault by regular troops, while the partisans struck at their flanks and rear from their mountain hideouts. Army Group 'A' reported to the German High Command that they had within a matter of weeks lost about 5,000 officers and men and hundreds of motor vehicles. Large forces would have to be maintained to garrison each gorge and to guard the roads and paths. The report also underlined the fact that the Caucasus ranges could not be crossed unless the partisans were defeated.

Thus as early as 11 September 1942, the XXXXIX Gebirgsjäger Corps was ordered to withdraw all its units to the main ridge line and to prepare to dig in for the winter. The order to push to the coast was suspended. Beginning on 12 September, about half of the two mountain divisions marched off in the direction of Maikop, where the Corps headquarters was set up. The Gebirgsjäger in the 'front line' now consisted of a combat group of six rifle battalions and five artillery batteries. This force occupied a line some 93 miles (150 km) long from the Elbrus to the Malaja Laba valley. The defenders of this line were at once subjected to attacks by Soviet troops operating in vastly-superior numbers. The Germans fought extremely stubbornly. The Russians attempted outflanking movements to take the Germans from the rear, but the line held.

On 27 September a spectacular action took place when a company of Russian soldiers, attacking one of the Elbrus lodges, was detected in early twilight. The fight on the icefields beyond the lodge fared badly for the Russians, who were cut off and forced to surrender. During another Russian attack in September, the Soviets attempted to break through in the Malaja Laba valley. All the attacks supported by the Red Air Force were repelled. The partisans had gained a lot of ground in the mountains, setting up their bases in the woodlands. Guerrillas were a constant threat to the rear of the Gebirgsjäger line. One of the Russian parachute forces' roles was to lead the partisans,

and so many parties of Russian parachutists were dropped into the Caucasus mountains to assist in this objective. On 5 October the last German attack in the Caucasus sector failed with heavy losses.

Without doubt the failure of the German mountain troops in the Caucasus was the difficulty of supply. Excessive strains were put on men and animals and the Luftwaffe seemed unable to help with bringing in supplies or evacuating the wounded. The Fieselar-Storch light aircraft that was especially requested for reconnoitring and lifting out wounded soldiers, did not put in a single appearance. The 4th Mountain Division did manage to build up four supply lines with twenty 'depot' points. The longest line (the S-Line), went through the Bolshaya Laba valley and over the high-mountain Achiboch Pass. Pack-mules and bearers took five days to complete the journey of 310 miles (500 km) along paths reaching an altitude of 8,202 ft (2,500 m).

In the mountain wilderness there were at first only mule tracks and barely-discernible footpaths. Bridges were erected over torrents, swamps were cleared, slopes dug away, and rocks blasted. On the S-Line alone arose 237 blockhouses, 123 dug-outs, and 20 ammunition bunkers. The frequent and heavy rainfalls turned the valley roads into quagmires. On one day alone (30 August) the mountain valleys were filled overnight with mud, bridges and footpaths were washed away, and for days traffic came totally to a standstill. The Soviet airmen—enjoying air supremacy over the Luftwaffe pilots—also played their part in harassing the enemy and supplying the partisans.

On return to their bases, the supply trains were re-loaded and after three or four days the pack-mules were on their way again to the forward lines. The losses in animals increased as the days went by. They often died for lack of fodder, from plunging into ravines, or from Russian gunfire or bombs. At the end of September, one single column lost 93 mules during a march in a blizzard that lasted 30 hours.

A Spähtruppführer *observes the lie of the land in the Caucasus theatre of operations.*

Day after day, German soldiers, Russian prisoners of war, and locally-recruited Karatshaians climbed over the mountain paths with heavy loads. Their shoes were torn to pieces. At first they were scorched in the glowing heat, then drenched by downpours, and later frozen with their lack of sufficient winter clothing. These columns were decimated by falls, frostbite, and deadly exhaustion.

The care of the wounded of the 1st and 4th Mountain Divisions was in the hands of about 11 doctors and 184 men. Motorized field hospitals were located in the main valleys and where possible billeted in solid houses capable of taking up to about 200 men. Dressing-stations were established close to the front lines. A wounded man was likely to have an uncomfort-able passage back to the rear lines. Four men were needed to lift a casualty on a stretcher. As a result of falling and sliding, the bearers often collapsed with exhaustion. Sometimes the wounded had to be lowered on ropes over glaciers and from rock precipices. During the first five weeks of combat nearly one thousand soldiers of the 49th Gebirgsjäger Corps were brought down from the mountains to the field hospitals.

The units of the 1st and 4th Mountain Divisions that had been pulled out of the line and stationed in the West Caucasus made attempts through the Russian lines in the direction of Tuapse to the Black Sea. On 17 October snow began to fall heavily and the Gebirgsjäger on both Caucasus fronts donned white camouflage suits and snowshirts. The high-mountain winter was now one of unbearable coldness, biting storms, deep snow drifts, and avalanches. The temperatures dropped deeper and deeper and the snow grew deeper and deeper. Telephone communication was interrupted and wireless connections were jammed. The German positions on the main ridge in the Caucasus were held, but re-supply rapidly became non-existent—the mules could not make their way in the deep snow.

With the turn of the new year (1942-3) and the German catastrophe at Stalingrad, the German High Command gave the order for the withdrawal of its forces in the High Caucasus. Commencing on 4 January 1943 the combat groups disengaged themselves from the passes and out of the valleys in order to retreat to the lower course of the Kuban River. The German offensive into the Caucasus mountains had not succeeded, but the counter-offensive of the Soviets had failed as well. The great adventure in the Caucasus had ended. The campaign was mountain warfare at its most rugged and it was unique to the Second World War. There were no great set battles, no clash of tanks, no mass attacks. It was a war of small units, fought out under frightful conditions and at incredible altitudes. The rich oilfields of Baku remained intact and, after Stalingrad, the tide had turned on Germany's fortunes of war.

CHAPTER 15

THE COLLAPSE OF GREECE AND YUGOSLAVIA

After the fall of France in June 1940, Hitler started to make plans to march eastwards to demonstrate that the Slavs were an inferior people. Although Operation 'Barbarossa' (the invasion of Russia) did not take place for another year, the Axis powers commenced their Balkan Campaign on 28 October 1940, when Italian forces stationed in Albania struck southeastwards into Greece. In retaliation the British landed military forces on the islands of Crete and Lemnos. Shortly afterwards in December, the Germans cancelled a plan—Operation 'Felix'—that was to employ Gebirgs-jäger of the 1st Mountain Division in seizing Gibraltar. Hitler's reaction to the seizure of Lemnos was one of concern, as the island gave Britain a stepping-stone back into continental Europe and an advanced airbase from where it could bomb the Ploesti oilfields in Romania. Hitler decided, however, to leave the attack on Greece to the Italians.

The Italian invasion of Greece—launched from Albania on 28 October—was mounted by an army of nine divisions (about 162,000 men) under the command of General Sebastiano Visconti-Prasca (shortly replaced by General Ubaldo Soddu). Greek General Alexander Papagos, whose army numbered 150,000 men, was disposed in a highly-organized defensive zone through part of the difficult mountainous border area. General Visconti-Prasca opened the attack with his nine Italian divisions (eight organized and one 'scratch' division, the Littoral Group). The Italian objective was the

'occupation' of Epirus, that is, the area between the Pindus and the Arta River and the sea. The Epirus area is like a big triangular pocket formed by the Pindus, the River Arta, the sea, and the Albanian frontier, and was at that time traversed by one single road: Borgo Tellini (now named Kakavia)-Perati-Kalpaki-Yanlna-Philippias (northwest of Arta). Since Greek troops could only enter and leave the area at two points (from the east by the Metsovon Pass—coming from Thessaly and Macedonia—and from the south through Arta and Missolonghi—coming from Sicily and Athens), Visconti-Prasca proposed to seize these two points and thus close the pocket.

The eastern arm of the pincer movement was to be provided by the 3rd Julia Alpine Division, which was to occupy the Metsovon Pass, and the western arm by the mobile forces of the Littoral Group (two cavalry regiments and one regiment of grenadiers), whose objective was the town and harbour of Preveza. The main body of Visconti-Prasca's troops, consisting of the Sienna, Ferrara, and Centauro Infantry Divisions, was to advance frontally towards the Kalamas and attack the Greek line of resistance at the key point of Kalpaki and then advance in the direction of Yanina. The plan left the whole Macedonian sector to the Parma Infantry Division. The Arezzo and Venizia Divisions were assigned to guard the Yugoslav frontier, and another Infantry Division was in reserve. About 87,000 Italians (with some Albanians) were in the forefront of the attack on Greece, and it was the Julia Division that was regarded as the crack formation.

In Epirus the Greeks had deployed their 8th Infantry Division, reinforced by a brigade of infantry and artillery. They had three reinforced battalions between Mts Smolikas and Grammos (Pindus zone), and between Mt Grammos and Lake Prespa they had the 9th Division and the 4th Brigade. Seven battalions of infantry were in the second line. Estimates of the strengths of opposing forces appear to conflict, but by 15 January 1941 there were probably 13 Greek divisions and 25 Italian divisions in this war theatre. (Greek divisions were, however, much larger in strength than their Italian counterparts.) The Greeks do not appear to have employed a specialist mountain division but they were hardy fighters roused by nationalist emotions, not entirely shared by

many of the veteran Italian soldiers, who were more disposed towards punching the noses of their young Blackshirt comrades-at-arms than those belonging to their Greek adversaries.

The Greek operational plan, dated 16 September 1940 (the date demonstrates how foreseeable the Italian moves were), was extremely simple. Papagos organized his defences on two lines: Line A, the closest to the frontier, followed the Kalamas River, Elea (Kalpaki), Mt Gamela, Mt Smolikas, Mt Stavros, Mt Psoriaka, Mt Flatsata, Mt Varba, and Laimos. Line B followed the Arachthos River (already referred to under its Italian name Arta), Metsovon, Mt Orliakas, the Venetikos River, the curve of the river Aliakhmon, the Portas Pass, the Hadovas Corridor, Mt Vermion, and Kaimaktsalan. The Greek forces' task in Epirus was to ensure—at all costs—the zone's lines of communication,

A German PAK anti-tank gun takes up its position in the Bulgarian mountains just before the Axis invasion of Greece and Yugoslavia in April 1941.

Gebirgsjäger ford a narrow river during the advance into Greece in April 1941. The Greek campaign resulted in a decisive victory for the German forces.

which were essential for the influx of reinforcements. In western Macedonia the Greek objectives were to protect the defensive positions of Line A, and if possible gain new positions in Albanian territory to be used for launching operations against the plateau of Koritsa, after the concentration of the necessary forces.

For the first three days of the campaign, the Italians' real enemy was the weather. According to the Greeks, Italian troops crossed the frontier at 05:00 (on 28 September). The Italians had to advance through a morass of mud while the Greeks had only to remain where they were and wait. The Italian columns moved forward under the driving rain. Boots sank in the mud, puttees were soon wrapped in a thick, yellow crust, and horses and mules kicked up showers of slush at every step. There was a great silence in the valleys, only broken now and again by a burst of fire. Sometimes a brief skirmish took place, but the thin network of Greek frontier posts was evidently withdrawing without resistance. The heavy rains had turned the rivers into torrents and the storms had caused the Regia Aeronautica to decline air

cover for the operation.

On the Pindus, at the junction point of the proposed Italian line of advance in Epirus and the defensive deployment in western Macedonia, the Julia Division was on the move. Troubles had occurred in the crack Alpine division earlier in the year, when Mussolini in June ordered the purging of men of Slavonic origin from the ranks of the Italian army. It appears also that the Alpini officers did not agree with Mussolini's proposed reorganization of the army, and to cap it all Alpini soldiers (while in transit towards ports of embarkation) had shouted anti-war slogans and come to blows with Fascist militiamen. The results of this discontent were stiff orders, enquiries, reports, charges, and officers put under arrest.

In spite of these troubles, the Julia was a tough division, lacking in enthusiasm but with no trace of a lack of discipline or of fighting spirit. The main units of the division, (whose home station was Udine and who were commanded by General Mario Girotti) were the 8th Alpine Regiment, 9th Alpine Regiment, and the 3rd Alpine Artillery Regiment. The division had with it five days' hard rations and four days' fodder for the mules, and in front of it was the Smolikas, one of the most towering mountains of the Pindus chain, rising to 8,640 ft (2,635 m). Two columns were to make their way round either flank of the massif and to advance to Metsovon. The first, in the north, was the tactical group commanded by Colonel Dapino. It consisted of the 8th Alpini and the Conegliano Artillery Group, with Albanian detachments in support. The second, to the southwest, consisted of the 9th Alpini, commanded by Colonel Tavoni and the Udine Artillery Group, as well as some Albanian detachments.

The 9th Alpini had to make its way along a bad road transformed into a river of mud,

and the 8th had to force its way down forest tracks. As elsewhere when the Italian division advanced, the Greeks appeared only fleetingly, and their activities were confined to putting space between themselves and the advancing columns. There were five columns of Alpini, spread out like the fingers of a hand. They consisted, from north to south, of the Tolmezzo, Gemona, Gividale, Vincenza, and Aquila (the battalion prefixes were the names of their commanders). Most of the advancing Italian divisions ran into trouble attempting to cross the swollen Ratamas River, and the Julia had difficulties crossing the Sarandaporos. The 8th Alpini experienced more difficult terrain than the 9th, the former trailing her sister regiment. Supply lines were lengthening. Albanian scouts

German mountain troops encounter opposition in the Balkan theatre in 1941.

reported a growing number of Greek units in the area.

The Julia Division, which had spread out in the advance and was gradually approaching Samarina and Konitsa, started closing ranks again. The Alpini had by now realized they were faced with anything but a picnic. However, in closing up the division a gap had been left in its rear. Dapino and Tavoni continued moving cautiously forward. The Alpini of the Aquila Battalion made the acquaintance of the Vojussa River, which was flooded and tumultuous too, at the point where the Julia Division sector joined that of the Ferrara Division. There was tension in the air that ill accorded with the hope of a lightning seizure of Metsovon. The commanders realized that the strength of a division was weakened when its lines were simultaneously engaged in a pincer movement taking in a huge mountain, gaining a great deal of ground, and in guarding its flanks and rear lines of communications. From the Grammos moun-

The invasion of Greece: After throwing back the Italian invader, the Greek army, later joined by the British and Commonwealth Expeditionary Force, were no match for Hitler's Wehrmacht, which invaded Greece across mountainous terrain from three directions.

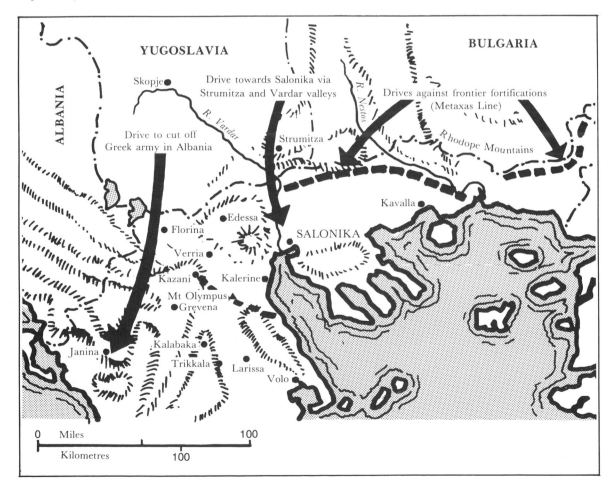

tains to the sea, the Regia Aeronautica was eliminated by the weather, and the divisional artillery, which according to Visconti-Prasca was in the van, could not keep up with even the slow march of the infantry, on whom the whole weight of the operation fell.

The Greeks, worried by the relatively deep wedge that the Julia Division was driving in their territory, began taking counter-measures. It would be a grave blow to them if the Epirus sector were isolated and communications with the Macedonian sector were cut off. As the hours passed and the columns approached the first Greek defence line, resistance became lively, the Alpini losing five officers and 30 men. The fighting was, however, still in the skirmishing stage. Italian communiqués announced that 'our troops have continued their advance', but the soldiers were drenched to the skin, the puttees round their legs weighed pounds, and in the case of the Alpini in the freezing temperatures of 4,500 ft (1,400 m) or more, they gripped their legs as in a vice. Sunny Athens seemed a long way off.

By 4 November the whole front had turned on its axis, pushed northwest by the Greeks advancing from western Macedonia and southeast by the Italians in Epirus. The Italians were on the Kalamas in Greek territory, while the Greeks were on the Devoli in Albanian territory. The Julia Division, the pivot of the whole line, had moved too. However, it had become almost detached from the two arms of the lever and was in an extremely dangerous position. Orders sent to his battalions by General Girotti from his divisional headquarters did not always reach them. The Julia Division was isolated. It could only count on the rations and ammunition that the troops had with them, and there was no way of supplying them except by air. Greek mountain cavalry, mounted on small agile horses, carried out the most damaging raids on the Alpini. But Girotti hesitated to give the order to retreat, which would indicate that the division had failed in its tasks.

Help was sent to the Julia Division in the

form of a company of Bersaglieri motorcyclists, tanks, and artillery belonging to the Centauro Division, and on 6 November the Alpini were ordered to withdraw to Konitsa and gather its remaining forces there. On 7 November, the Julia Division began fighting their way through the Greek lines. Heavy rain began to fall again. At the high altitudes it turned into sleet. The tough Alpini from the Veneto and the Abruzzi, the mountaineers from the Carnia and the Val Natisone had grown long beards and their deep-set eyes reflected fatigue. Their grey-green uni-

Two Gebirgsjäger with a Bulgarian soldier in the Strume in the spring of 1941.

forms were covered with a thick crust of mud, their boots weighed a ton, and their thick, black, helmet feathers were frayed. The Vicenza Battalion occupied the Cristobasile saddle to cover the division's retreat. Ten day after the beginning of the campaign, Italian groups were held up on the Kalamas and in a critical position on the Pindus and in western Macedonia.

On 6 November the Italian General Staff decided to organize the troops in Albania into four army corps. The Julia and Bari Divisions on the Pindus were allocated to the Ninth Army, which was to remain on the defensive throughout the winter. The Greeks, however, would not permit a lull in the fighting. The Greek general offensive opened at dawn on 14 November. On the northern front the Greek forces attacked all along the line from Mt Grammos to Lake Prespa in the direction of Morova-Ivan, covering the Koritsa junction from the east. For over a year earlier, the Italians had strengthened this naturally-strong position with field works, and at some points even semi-permanent works. The offensive was launched by three front-line infantry divisions under the orders of III Army Corps, that is, the 9th and 10th Divisions operating against the southern sector of the position in the direction of the Darja ridge, and the 15th Division operating against the northern sector in the direction of Ivan-Tsangoni. The Greeks made spectacular progress amongst the mountains, seizing heights and occupying valleys one after the other. By 21 November, the Greeks had completed the occupation of the Morova mountain range. Greek intelligence now noted the 2nd Tridentina Alpine Division's presence in the theatre. The main units of this division, which was commanded by General Luigi Reverberi, were the 5th and 6th Alpine Infantry Regiments and the 2nd Alpine Artillery Regiment. The home stations of units of the Tridentina Division were Merano, Milan, Verona, and Bergamo.

Winter had now fully set in. Mt Ivan was concealed in a cloud and wrapped with snow. The Morava was thick with mud. The Alba-

nian mountains do not rise to a great height but in winter a freezing north wind causes the thermometer to plunge many degrees below freezing. Koritsa, the Greeks' ultimate objective, lay down in the plains beyond the mountains, and the Greek soldiers fought all the more fiercely because they believed that this part of Albania belonged to Greece. Koritsa was already being bombarded by Greek artillery when more Alpini troops disembarked from Junkers transport aircraft at the airfield. Italian wounded were in turn being evacuated by the hundreds. The Taro Division and the Vestone and Verona Battalions of the 6th Alpini were rushed to the front, but the Greeks threw two more divisions into the line and still had a distinct superiority in strength. Koritsa was gloomily abandoned by the Italians on 21 November and they retreated to a new line hinging on Mt Cytetit.

According to Greek aerial reconnaissance reports, one column of retreating Italians was more than 12 miles (19 km) long. On the night of 17 December the withdrawal in the Erseke area, which opened the valley of the Ossum to the Greeks and exposed the left flank of the whole Italian Eleventh Army, added drama to an already serious situation for the Italians. The Julia Division, which had not been allowed a moment's respite, had to be thrown into the sector the Bari Division was no longer able to hold, and to preserve the Perati bridgehead. The retreat was now general, the whole of the line from the Yugoslav frontier to the sea being on the move. The weather got colder and colder and the Italians feared disaster. The 8th Alpini Regiment of the Julia Division had lost 80 per cent of its effectiveness.

Having secured the Koritsa high ground, Greek forces further south continued their advance in the area between Mt Ostravitsa and the River Aoas. After hard fighting in the Aoas valley (where the Italians were using tanks), the Greeks pushed on into the mountainous district of Frasheri where they encountered units of the 5th Pusteria Alpine Division and of the

37th Modena Infantry Division. By 8 December the Greeks had taken the heights known as Mt Mali Krasoves, Koprenska, and Mali Potomit and, although now attacked more effectively by the Italian Air Force, they were prepared to plunge deeper into the rugged Albanian mountain terrain. In Rome, as Mussolini cheerfully noted the prospect of snow for

Below right *The mule, although traditionally an obstinate animal, was a good servant in Greece, transporting supplies over rough mountain terrain.*

Below *The Greeks had a great reputation for mountain fighting, but whereas they had trounced the Italians, they were virtually powerless in the path of Hitler's new war machine. Here a Greek machine-gunner and a rifleman man a mountainside defensive position.*

Christmas, frost-bite was wreaking havoc with his army in Albania. Sleeping in the open at the highest altitudes and without proper winter clothing, huddling in undrained trenches amid the mud and snow, with no climbing boots or change of warm clothing, and often without medical services, the Italians were suffering severe casualties. By the end of December the victims numbered thousands and eventually a total of nearly 13,000 was reached.

The dreaded 'dry gangrene', or 'white death', spread insidiously. Its onset was painless. Legs swelled above the ankle, all feeling disappeared from the foot, and the flesh changed colour, turned purple and then blackish. There was then the agonizing journey to overcrowded field hospitals. The men often had

to be carried bodily by their comrades because of the lack of stretchers. They were then loaded onto lorries that caused agony at every jolt on the appalling roads to Valona or Durazzo or Tirana, where they awaited transport to Apulia. There was no Christmas truce. On Christmas Day the Greeks in fact launched a furious assault in the Ossum valley, and the Feltre and Cadore battalions of the Pusteria Division gave way.

On 29 December General Soddu went to Rome for further instructions, and he never returned to Albania. On 30 December, Marshal Ugo Cavallero assumed command of the Italian troops in Albania, in addition to his post as Chief of the General Staff. Mussolini ordered two more divisions to be sent to Albania. The New Year opened with little movement taking place on the front, and what there was was to the advantage of the Greeks. General Papagos could afford to ring the changes. He replaced the Greek 17th Division (which had fought admirably in the Pogradec sector but had suffered heavy losses) with the 13th Division, and replacements were made in other units that had taken casualties. Cavallero cautiously prepared two plans, one for an advance and the other for the contingency of another defeat. The latter provided for the setting up of two operational sectors, one to defend Valona and the other to defend northern Albania. Six divisions would occupy the Valona redoubt and thirteen the Tirana redoubt. The Eleventh Army would be deployed around Valona and the Ninth would defend northern Albania.

The Greeks again seized the initiative. In the Klisura sector, where the road towards Berati lay through the Desnizza valley between the Trebescines and the Mali Qarishta, the Greek infantry was once more faced with the Julia Division, of whom more miracles could not be expected. Girotti had been promoted to full general in recognition of the valour of the Alpini, but the division had not been restored to full strength. The Greek offensive, which was launched on 30 December, was aimed between

Tepelini and the sea. By 10 January the Greeks had succeeded in occupying the Garonin-Podgorani line and the Klisura junction. Here the Greeks found the Julia Division, the 5th Pusteria Alpine Division (which consisted of the 7th and 11th Alpine Regiments and 5th Alpine Artillery Regiment plus support troops), the 47th Bari Infantry Division, and the 6th Cuneo Infantry Division. Prisoners taken during the offensive also revealed the presence of the 22nd Infantry Division of Alpine-Chasseurs, which was otherwise known as the 22nd Cacciatori Delle Alpi Division (Infantry) and which, with its support troops, consisted of the 51st Alpi Infantry Regiment, the 52nd Alpi Infantry Regiment, and the 1st Cacciatori Delle Alpi Artillery Regiment.

The Italians were routed at Klisura and, in spite of a desperate entreaty from Rome to stand their ground, the Julia Division gave way completely. But the capture of Klisura was the last Greek success of any importance. News was now received in Rome that the Germans, impatient with the Italians, were about to send a mountain division to Albania. For Operation 'Cyclamen', Hitler's headquarters first examined the possibility of employing an army corps, including the 1st Mountain Division and armoured forces. A few days later, following conversations at Salzburg between Mussolini and the Führer, the size of the proposed expeditionary force was reduced to a single mountain division. The project was then dropped.

Mussolini arrived in Albania on 2 March 1941. On 9 March he visited an observation post at a height of about 2,500 ft (750 m) and surveyed a panorama of mountains and precipitous ridges. Below him lay the stark valley of the Desnizza, which reminded the Duce of the Carso—the rocky plateau northwest of Trieste and the scene of so many fierce battles between the Italians and the Austrians in the First World War. Visibility on the day was excellent. Cavallero pointed out the snow-capped ridges of the Trebescines and the Scindelli; the Desnizza valley, which in summer would be dried up but still covered in green; and the Vojussa River, beyond Klisura, the waters of which were glittering. But the Duce had not occupied this vantage point to merely see the landscape. Suddenly the Italian artillery opened up along the entire front and Italian aircraft flashed through the sky.

The Italian troops began advancing slowly from three start lines in the IV, VIII, and XXV Corps' sectors. The only success of any importance was gained in the IV Corps sector. Here the 11th Alpini Regiment of the Pusteria Division assaulted and took Male Spadarit. The position seized by the 11th Alpini was furiously counter-attacked by the Greeks, who forced the Alpini to withdraw. Mussolini was less than pleased with the results of the day's fighting and after two days stalemate had set in. Mussolini

raged, but had to agree with his commanders that no positive results had been obtained—apart from suffering substantial losses and a further lowering of the troops' morale. Mussolini accordingly gave orders on 16 March to break off the offensive.

The bulk of the Greek army was now fully engaged in operations in the Albanian theatre. The continued dispatch of heavy reinforcements for the Italian army in Albania, which in total included six Alpine divisions allocated to the theatre during the campaign, compelled the Greek High Command to withdraw forces constantly from the Bulgarian frontier. Thus Greece did not have enough troops in eastern and western Macedonia to defend Greece at what now appeared to be an imminent threat of a German invasion. The Greek High Com-

Although British and Commonwealth troops arrived from the Middle East to assist the Greeks, the roads to the south were soon filled with German traffic in scenes such as this. An overwhelming German victory was imminent.

mand, however, decided for what must seem irrational reasons that the threat of a German invasion was a minor matter as compared with continued opportunities for thrashing the Italians in Albania. On 22 February 1941 a conference was held at the Greek Royal Palace at Tatoi. It was attended, amongst others, by His Majesty King George II, the British Foreign Secretary, Anthony Eden, the Chief of the Imperial General Staff, General Sir John Dill, and the Commander-in-Chief of the British and Imperial Forces in the Middle East, General Sir Archibald Wavell. The outcome of the conference was that Mr Eden announced that a British expeditionary force would land in Greece as soon as the Germans marched into Bulgaria.

Eden confidently predicted at Tatoi—and Winston Churchill was of the same opinion—that Germany would neither attack Turkey nor Yugoslavia. Furious that the Yugoslavs did not appear as friendly as he had at first supposed, Hitler (who had already decided to invade Greece) issued his Directive No. 25 of 27 March 1941, in which he specified plans to attack both Greece and Yugoslavia. British and Imperial troops were by this time already in Greece. The force consisted of the 6th Australian Division, 2nd New Zealand Division, the 1st Tank Brigade of the 2nd British Armoured Division, and ancillary support units. As soon as they were landed (mainly at the Piraeus) these forces were posted to central Macedonia. The British Armoured Brigade was directed towards the lower Axios in order to take delaying action between the Axios and Vermion; and the 2nd New Zealand Division set out for the area of Ekateria, and south of it, for the defence of the passes near the coast and in the Olympus area. The 6th Australian Division set out for the area of Servia and the valley of central Aliakmon.

The German forces assembled to invade Greece and Yugoslavia were the Second Army (Weichs) and the Twelfth Army (List). Gebirgsjäger were to serve with both of these armies, fighting in the mountains and as a corps for the first time in the history of the Gebirgsjäger arm

of service. For the 4th, 5th, and 6th Gebirgs Divisions the Balkan campaign was to be their baptism of fire, and for the 5th it was another first. It was the first time that any force had attempted to attack such strong fortifications as those the Greeks had built in the wilderness of mountains along her northeastern border. The Germans launched their attack on Greece at 05:15 on the morning of 6 April. At this time the XVIII Gebirgs Corps (5th and 6th Gebirgs Divisions) was positioned in the mountains on the Greek-Bulgarian border. The German invasion developed along the whole of the borderline.

In the campaign to defeat Greece, the valley of the Struma River and the mountains rising out of it were to be of vital importance to the plans of both sides. The XVIII Gebirgs Corps was to cross the mountains and valley, advancing southwards under orders of the Twelfth Army to pierce the Metaxas Line, the Greek system of fortifications. Ringel's 5th Gebirgs Division was placed in the van of the attack. (General of Mountain Troops Julius Ringel, an Austrian, who was shortly to receive acclaim leading his troops in Crete, was probably the most popular Gebirgs troop commander of the war.) The 5th was to smash the Metaxas Line and to seize the Rupel Pass through which the remainder of the Twelfth Army would then move.

By midnight on 5 April the assault units of the 5th Division were in position and at first light the Jäger moved forward to begin a series of engagements that were to last for four days. Their first task was to drive through the Greek outpost line occupying field fortifications strung out along the rocky heights. The night was bitterly cold but no fires were allowed and smoking was forbidden. Supported by artillery fire and dive-bombers, the attackers rushed towards the pill-boxes—but the Greek defensive fire from their artillery and machine-guns was effective, and the Gebirgsjäger made little progress on the first day. The bright sunshine of that first day was replaced on the second by freezing rain and visibility was cut to a few yards. Down in the mist-shrouded valleys there was a cacophony of sound as the guns roared and shells burst on the mountain sides. Once inside the bunkers, Germans and Greeks fought hand to hand. German flame-throwers turned the interiors of defensive positions into blazing infernos.

The Metaxas Line (which was built after the style of the Maginot Line in France), as thoroughly constructed as it was, defended only eastern Macedonia against the Greeks' traditional enemy—the Bulgarians. If it was outflanked to the west, the Greeks had little in the way of fortifications to prevent a drive on Athens. However, western Macedonia is equally mountainous. The roads that pierce the mountains along the entire Greek frontier do so by steep gradients that offer every opportunity for defence. Along the coast the country is flatter but, here too, the defenders had the advantage of observation posts in the mountains. Although the Greeks had never intended, in the event of an invasion, to hold the Metaxas Line at all costs, the Greeks fought resolutely and would not abandon their bunkers.

The Germans, in fact—breaking through the mountains to the west—outflanked the Metaxas Line advancing on Monastir. Consequently, the Greek High Command ordered a general withdrawal to another mountain chain along the Aliakhmon River extending from the Albanian border eastwards to Mt Olympus, which overlooks the Aegean Sea. Here the 6th Australian Division moved up into the Kleidi area and the British Armoured Brigade moved forward to the river line in the vicinity of Axios. The 2nd New Zealand Division was centred around Katerini. The objectives of these forces was to block the mountain passes, but the German infantry edged forwards yard by yard to clear these routes for their motorized columns.

Meanwhile, patrols from the 5th Gebirgs Division slipped through the Greek lines and penetrated into the Jiamutsitsa valley to reach the bridge at Lutra, which spanned the Struma River. The Metaxas Line was formally surren-

German troops arrive on the outskirts of Zagreb during the invasion of Yugoslavia in April 1941.

dered to the Germans by the general commanding the Greek Macedonian army, but some of the units fought on as guerrillas. In the first four days the German mountain troops had lost only seven officers and 153 other ranks. The 18th Gebirgs Corps, leading the Twelfth Army through the Rupel Pass, now met the British for the first time and in violent action drove off their rearguards from Mt Olympus. The mountain was climbed in a blizzard and the Third

Reich's war flag was flown at its peak. By 19 April the 5th Division had broken the British defences and had captured Larissa. The Gebirgsjäger then pursued the British in retreat across the Plain of Thessaly pushing further southwards daily.

In Yugoslavia, the 4th Gebirgs Division, which had been taken off the strength of the Twelfth Army, was attached to Kleist's Panzer group heading for the Yugoslav capital, Belgrade. The Gebirgsjäger on this front struck westwards from the Bulgarian-Yugoslav border towards the city. Their immediate objective was to capture the high ground on both sides of the Sofia-Belgrade road. The Jäger regiments set out, climbed the almost-trackless mountains, and battled their way against gale-force winds and blizzards to keep pace with the advance of the Panzer group. Belgrade fell on 12 April and Yugoslav resistance began to fail. The German Second Army drove the virtually-defeated Yugoslav units southwards. The 4th Gebirgs Division remained in Belgrade for occupation

duties. However, the war was by no means over in Yugoslavia. For the rest of the war the Germans were to be engaged in a colossal struggle in the mountains to subdue the partisan armies of Mihailovic and Tito.

The sudden and total collapse of Yugoslavia allowed the whole might of the German war machine to be turned upon Greece and any hopes that the Royal Army and its allies might have had of fighting a successful defensive battle were destroyed. The end was inevitable, and when the Allied armies in central Greece surrendered to the Germans on 21 April, plans were immediately made to evacuate British, Australian, New Zealand, and as many Greek units as possible. The Royal Navy now commenced an epic operation to take off the escapees from ports in the Gulf of Corinth, mainly to the island of Crete. The Gebirgsjäger had little time to celebrate their victory in Athens for ahead of them lay a spell of even harder fighting in the arid, comfortless, Cretan mountains.

Italian troops attack a Yugoslav position during the combined Axis drive into Yugoslavia in April 1941.

CHAPTER 16
THE FALL OF CRETE

Crete lies about 62 miles (100 km) from the southernmost point of the Greek mainland and is a mountainous island approximately 161 miles (260 km) long and between 12 miles (20 km) and 31 miles (50 km) wide. Four principal mountain ranges divide Crete and, although the involvement of the Gebirgsjäger in the campaign on the island was not exactly an exercise in mountain warfare, two of the ranges are relevant to the present book. These are the White Mountains towards the western end of the island, which rise to a height of nearly 9,000 ft (2,750 m). The mountains on Crete are eroded, barren, and steep and in certain areas are considered to be impassable. The southern side of the island is characterized by the mountains' abrupt descent into the sea and the absence of any large harbours. There are only a few fishing ports on the southern shore. The northern shore of Crete is also rocky and has cliffs. Here there are small areas of beach behind which lies a fertile strip of intensively-cultivated land. After the fall of Greece, the German High Command considered several possible targets, including the islands of Malta, Rhodes, and Crete. Their option was for an assault upon Malta, but the fact that the choice fell upon Crete resulted from the vision of Luftwaffe General Kurt Student, the commander of the German airborne forces, which had already seen action in Norway, Belgium, and Holland.

Student persuaded Hitler that, as the Royal Navy was all-powerful, an amphibious

landing on Crete would be dangerous. Directive No. 28, dated 25 April 1941, authorized Operation 'Mercury', the airborne invasion of the island, as a springboard for similar airborne operations against Rhodes and Egypt. The forces for the operation were to be found in Student's 11th Air Corps, which numbered the battle-tested 7th Parachute Division (later to be renumbered the 1st) and the 22nd Air Landing Division. Both would be needed: the one to seize the principal airfields on the island and the other to be air-landed in Ju 52s in order to expand the perimeters the German paratroopers (Fallschirmjäger) would have gained and from which bridgeheads set out to conquer the island. In the event the 2nd Air Landing Division was not available and Ringel's 5th Gebirgs Division was chosen in its place to fight in Crete.

For the defenders of Crete there were four vital sectors. These were Maléme aerodrome, west of Canea; Suda Bay, at the eastern foot of Akrotiri peninsula; Retimo landing-ground, about 6 miles (10 km inland); Herakleon town and aerodrome, separated from each other by about two miles (3 km). These sectors were all on the north coast. Suda Bay lay about 15 miles (24 km) east of Maléme, Retimo 45 miles (72 km) east of Suda Bay, Herakleon 25 miles (40 km) east of Retimo. Road communications, except between Maléme and Suda Bay, were poor, and it was clear that Retimo and Herakleon must be manned as self-contained fortress areas. This was also true, but less rigidly, of

General Kurt Student — the 'father' of German airborne forces — is seen (standing with his elbow touching the low wall) talking to his troops during the German invasion of Crete.

Malème and Suda Bay.

Intelligence had warned of the likelihood of a German airborne attack upon Crete and General Sir Bernard Freyberg, VC, a New Zealander, was prompt to deploy his forces to cover the most probable targets. Freyberg was in command of a British and Imperial force of about 27,000 men and about 12,000 Greeks. British troops numbered 13,000, New Zealanders 7,100, and Australians 6,500. Freyberg so disposed this force that, in the fighting, Malème was defended by New Zealand, Australian, Greek, and British troops; Suda Bay by British, Australian, Greek, and New Zealand troops; Retimo by Australian, Greek and Brit-

ish troops, and Herakleon by British, Greek, and Australian troops. (In each of the above-mentioned instances, the countries represented are given in the order of their numerical strength in each particular sector.)

One of the tragedies of Crete from the Allied point of view was that the danger it stood in was realized too late. Wing-Commander Beamish, the senior Air Force commander, was not sent to Crete until 17 April, little more than a month before the invaders came. The Greek evacuation was then at hand. Beamish had no opportunity in the time at his disposal to prepare inland aerodromes. A site was, in fact, surveyed on Massara Plain and plans were made for levelling a landing-strip there. This would have been ready for operations about 28 May. But by then Crete was lost and the evacuation had begun. There were at least three places in the mountains (high plains surrounded by rugged peaks) that could have been used as sites for airfields. Aircraft could have operated from any of these points with better chances of survival when they were at rest. They could have been protected from bombs and cannon shells in pens dug into the walls of these great upland plains. But when the danger to Crete was at last apprehended it was too late to lay down runways on these admirable natural sites.

The preparatory German air attacks were so effective that when the air invasion began on 20 May 1941, the only British aircraft left standing on Crete were seven Gladiator biplanes. The rest had been shot down or destroyed on the ground. When Freyberg's men rolled themselves in blankets and greatcoats to sleep on the ground on 19 May, the night was cool, soft, and pleasant. Enemy aircraft stormed above the island from time to time, bombing Suda Bay and the vicinity of the aerodromes. But the raids were no heavier than they had been on any night for a week past. In fact, they were rather less severe because the moon was waning and would not rise to light the island until the early hours of the morning. However, that night across the Aegean, less than 200 miles

General Julius Ringel, commander of the 5th Mountain Division, inspects his men in Crete. Ringel, an Austrian and veteran, like many of his men, of the Norwegian campaign in 1940, was a popular general much respected by his mountain troops.

(325 km) away, the German Fallschirmjäger were emplaning to invade Crete.

Just after first light on 20 May the sky over the coastal littoral of Crete was filled with parachutes, mostly white, but there were also many-coloured canopies denoting that they supported supplies. The Junkers Ju 52 and the DFS-230 gliders aimed for three main points— Canea, Malème, and the village of Galatos, southeast of Malème. Possession of Canea would enable them to attack the defenders of Suda Bay and break communication between the garrison there and the force at Malème. The village of Galatos and the vicinity of the Malème aerodrome were essential objectives as starting points for an attack on the airfield.

Most of the paratroopers jumped at heights from 200 to 500 ft (60 to 150 m). They fired their machine-pistols and hurled hand grenades as they floated down. They were only a few seconds between aircraft and ground, but in those few seconds they were easy targets for anyone who could aim a rifle and press the trigger. The design of the German RZ parachute was such that the men hung 'doggy' fashion, suspended from the parachute rigging lines by ropes attached to the centre of their backs, and many who survived the bullets were badly injured on hitting the ground. Oberleutnant Ernst Kleinlein records that it was 04:00 when he spotted, through a window of his Ju 52, a small, narrow beach, the first ridges in the foreground and behind the second terrace, the white rocky peaks of the mountains of Crete. He also

saw 'hundreds of planes . . . in the cobalt-blue vapour between sky and water, droning forwards like an army of scaled dragons'. At about 04:15 he approached the door with his squad of men and one by one they dived like swimmers from the high board. Kleinlein estimates that he was only four and a half seconds in the air before landing uncomfortably in a bomb crater.

The gliders slid to earth simultaneously with the paratroop landings at the three initial focal points of attack. Some were shot up in the air, some as they grounded. A few capsized on the rough surface and broke the necks of the men they carried. But a good proportion of the gliders, notably of those that crash-landed on the beaches and in the dry bed of the Tavronitis River, west of Malème, completed their task of settling down and unloading their men. Each DFS-230 glider carried twelve men, armed with automatic rifles, carbines, light and heavy machine-guns, hand grenades, and mortars. These men were ready to fight the moment they sprang out of their aircraft on to the ground.

Not until the evening of 20 May was the

Above, opposite and below *The German 5th Mountain Division, after air-landing in Junkers Ju 52 transport planes at Malème airfield on the northwestern tip of the island, spearheaded the German advance along the northern coastal littoral. The Allied defenders of Crete commanded by New Zealand General Sir Bernard Freyberg VC packed the coastal road leading to Herakleon but the Gebirgsjäger took a line of march in the foothills of the White Mountains, thus bypassing the defences. This series of photographs illustrates the mountain troops' progress to the northeastern corner of the island.*

11th Air Corps in a position to assess the results of the day's operations, building up their picture from the mass of radio messages that had come in from the parachute and glider troops fighting on the ground. These messages showed that only in the western part of the island, at Malème, did the Germans have any sort of hold, and even this ground was dominated by the still-uncaptured Point 107. During the day, Cretan mountain people (unaware that Berlin Radio had pronounced Crete an 'Island of Doom'), observing the German landing with bewilderment, came streaming down into the coastal plain to fight the invaders. Every able-bodied man, many women, even small boys, left their flocks, crops, and cottages. They were furious not so much at the invasion itself as at the manner of it. The King of the Hellenes and his entourage, on their journey to safety across the White Mountains, saw many Cretans hurrying the other way towards the fight. A few of them had antique rifles. Most fought with long-bladed knives, wooden staves, and iron bars. Some, especially women, used strangling cords in the fashion of Indian thugs.

General Ringel, commander of the 5th Gebirgs Division, had been warned in the operational order of the part his formation was to play in the battle for Crete. Ringel's division was to supply the backup force to the paratroop offensive, and was to take over the battle and bring the operation to a speedy and successful conclusion. Ringel was advised that there were insufficient aircraft to carry out both the initial assault and the rapid build-up that were essential to capture the island. Part of his division, Ringel was told, would have to travel to Crete by boat. In the event the Gebirgsjägers' seaborne invasion of Crete failed with heavy loss of life. All attempts to reach the island were repulsed by the Royal Navy. It was now decided by the Germans that a way must be found of airlifting the division and consequently, on 22 May, the German mountain troops assembled at Tanagra airfield in Greece and climbed aboard Ju 52s, the interiors of which had been rapidly re-fitted to seat infantry passengers and their equipment.

The aircraft flew at almost wave-top height towards the island, and on crossing the coast those Jäger near the windows and looking towards the small jumble of white-washed houses that was Malème could see the airstrip ahead of them. Wave upon wave of Jus went into land, lumbering along the runway passing wrecks, some of them still burning, of planes that had crashed. The jagged metal fuselages stood piled along the sides of the runway like tombstones. The first company of mountain men went into action manning the Malème perimeter around the airstrip and soon found themselves fighting New Zealanders, cheek-by-jowl. During 22 May, Ringel assumed command of all forces in the Malème area and was charged with the task of establishing contact with the German forces isolated in the central sector, of capturing Canea and Suda Bay, and of clearing British forces from the western part of the island.

Ringel formed three battle groups: the pioneer battalion was ordered to hold Malème, which would soon be in the rear of the division's advance; a second group comprising Colonel Ramcke's Fallschirmjäger was to strike northwards to the sea and to protect the airfield along the coast road and extending eastwards. The third group, commanded by Colonel Utz, had the task of advancing eastwards with part of its forces while a second part marched into the mountains and, in a wide, sweeping movement, turned the flank of 5th New Zealand Brigade's positions along the coastal road. This manoeuvre proved successful and greatly surprised the British Command, which did not expect an attack to come out of the mountains. The heat on Crete during the day was stifling and at night gave way to bitter cold. The Gebirgsjäger were dressed in thick uniforms. Throughout the day the German mountain troops climbed heights and descended into valleys, as they moved across the trackless terrain, but by nightfall the outflanking movement had caused the New Zealanders to withdraw and Malème was no longer in range of their artillery.

During 23 May the movement eastwards made steady progress, but a temporary halt was called on 24 May to consolidate in the Platanias area. The 100th Gebirgsjäger Regiment particularly distinguished itself in the mountain trek. The intention now was to undertake assaults against new objectives. One group would advance along the coast road and attack Galatas, the key to Canea. While this group was moving forward a second group, Krakau Force, was to undertake another long outflanking trek through the mountains. Krakau Force had as its objectives the Canea-Retimo road in the area east of Suda where it could cut the British escape route. The key to success of the whole operation was the capture of Galatas, which lay a few miles inland dominating the two roads Agia Marina-Canea and Alikianu-Canea. Just as Galatas covered Canea so did that city, the island's capital, cover Suda Bay, the retention of which was essential for the defenders if they were to remain on the island.

Two Jäger battalions, the 2nd Battalion/-100th Regiment, on the left, was to attack Galatas frontally itself while the 100th Regiment's 1st Battalion, on the right, was to capture the high ground north of the village. The highest point in the area was known to the New Zealand troops as Ruin Hill and their adversaries as Castle Hill. The battle was confused and bitter. The advance was contested by marksmen and Bren gunners, who opened up at point-blank range. But Galatas was not taken that easily and at last light the New Zealanders counter-attacked with two light tanks leading the advance. The battle died away that day (25 May) after twelve hours of fierce fighting, man to man, but the following day Jäger patrols probing forwards found that Galatas had been evacuated by the New Zealanders.

While the men of 100th Regiment were fighting the battle for Galatas, other Gebirgsjäger of 85th Regiment had begun their march (much hampered by Stukas dive-bombing their own troops) to turn the flank of the New Zealand defences based upon Canea and Suda Bay. The after-combat report of Gebirgsjäger Regiment 85, by its commander, Colonel

Krakau, describes how on 26 May he was ordered to attack eastwards across the mountains south of Canea and to drive on Retimo to liberate the 'hard-pressed paratroops'. To enable the regiment to carry out its given task three battalions were assembled. After strenuous physical efforts the 3rd Battalion, moving via Alikianu, reached the heights southwest of Varypetron against only weak Allied resistance. Meanwhile, the 1st Battalion attacking the heights immediately southeast of Pirgos the previous evening made the difficult climb to break resistance on Point 542. The 2nd Battalion/85th, which was also fighting across steep, broken, and trackless mountain terrain, shortly overcame the defenders just south of Canea.

At dawn on 28 May, the regiment's eastward attack was continued. The 2nd Battalion, fighting on the regimental right flank, took the Stylos heights and succeeded in over-running the vital escape routes. During the day the Gebirgsjäger destroyed two British medium tanks. Krakau finally reported that:

> As a result of the regiment's outflanking manoeuvre through difficult and steep mountain terrain South of Canea, by the determined breaking of any enemy resistance, by the drive into the rear of and against the British roads of retreat, the strong enemy position of Suda Bay was finally smashed. The advance guard which the division sent out to pursue the beaten enemy was able to move forward along these roads. The regiment had taken a decisive part in smashing the enemy's strong positions in the Suda Bay area.

On 29 May the Gebirgsjäger elements were joining in the pursuit eastwards to Retimo.

The Germans trekking in the mountains found the terrain both forbidding and hostile. The Gebirgsjäger, in spite of their training, were ill-clad in their woollen uniforms in the searing heat of day and their rucksacks lay heavily on their backs. There were no paths in the mountains, not even animal tracks, and the point group had to cut trails for the rest of the men both uphill and downhill. The march discipline had to be very strict. There were no wells for the Germans to fill up their water bottles and they had to make do with a few tepid mouthfuls a day. A German Gebirgsjäger officer made the following interesting comment:

> We were lucky that the English were not mountain men for just to cross the White Mountains was terrible enough. To have fought across them would have been impossible. In the mountains the defender has the advantage and a handful of determined English and a few machine-guns could have held us off for days. As it was we saw nobody and nothing except for a few birds.

Back on the sector facing Canea, the Gebirgsjäger battalions were drawn up waiting only for the intelligence that 85th Regiment had reached Stylos. That news came on 27 May. Now they moved forward through olive-grove country, stopping not infrequently to engage hill positions. At this time the Germans held only about one-sixth of Cretan territory but Ringel was right in assuming that steady pressure would cause his adversaries to continue their retreat along the coastal route. On 27 May the men of the 85th Regiment came down out of the high mountains and descended upon Stylos village on the road to Vrases and Sfakia. These men were in time to help hold a British counter-attack, the Gebirgsjäger quickly re-assembling their mountain guns after dismantling them for their journey downhill. The German troops in Crete were making effective use of motorcycles in rounding up enemy prisoners and the Germans broke through against concentrated resistance using motorcycle companies, pioneer detachments, anti-tank battalions, and mountain artillery and reconnaissance battalions.

On 29 May the advance on Retimo increased in momentum with both Gebirgsjäger and Fallschirmjäger counting the hours until final victory. Again the Germans used the high ground effectively, aiming artillery fire from the heights on roads leading to Retimo. Rearguard actions supported by armour were mounted effectively by the British forces but the Germans had the upper hand. On the morning of 1 April resistance had been broken and at 09:00 the British began surrendering, leaving the Gebirgsjäger to occupy Komitades, Cora Sfakia, and Lutra. The war diary of 5th Gebirgs Division recorded that in the afternoon the last British resistance was silenced in the mountains north of Sfakia by units of the division after very heavy fighting.

The campaign in Crete was over after a twelve day battle. The Royal Navy again mounted a massive evacuation of the Allied troops although 20 per cent of Crete's defenders were abandoned to the Germans and spent the rest of the war in prisoner-of-war camps. It is likely that in German eyes the Gebirgsjäger came out of the Cretan campaign with more firmly-established laurels than the Fallschirmjäger. Adolf Hitler was so genuinely shocked by the losses amongst Student's airborne troops that Crete was deemed a pyrrhic victory and a full-scale airborne assault was never again attempted by the Germans during the war. Ringel in his report on the battle remarked that his mountain men had fought in conditions of terrible heat against an extremely tough and capable enemy backed by 'native partisans'. The Jäger had carried all their equipment, particularly the heavy weapons, on their backs and for great distances through the mountains.

Italian Army Order of Battle of Mountain and Alpine Divisions 1941-43

Mountain divisions differed from Alpini divisions, and were divisions especially adapted for operations in mountainous countries where full use could not be made of horse-drawn artillery and motor transport. The only difference in the organization of a mountain division as compared with an ordinary infantry division was the artillery regiment. All guns could be transported in horse-drawn wagon loads or on pack animals.

Alpini were essentially mountain divisions with personnel drawn from Alpine regions. Alpine regiments were self-contained with detachments of artillery, engineers, and auxiliary services permanently attached. This made the regiment self-supporting and capable of independent action for a considerable period. Decentralization was further extended to Alpine battalions and companies that were detached from their parent units were regrouped with artillery units into *raggruppamenti*.

XXIV Corps HQ Udine
Formed in May from elements of the Alpine Corps

22nd Cacciatori Della Alpi Division (Infantry)
History: In Yugoslavia

26th Assietta Division (Mountain Infantry)
History: Moved to Sicily from Turin at the end of 1941

36th Forli Division (Mountain Infantry)
History: In Greece

1st Taurinense Division (Alpine)
History: In Yugoslavia

3rd Julia Division (Alpine)
History: Largely destroyed in Russia in the winter of 1942-3

2nd Tridentina Division (Alpine)
History: Largely destroyed in Russia in winter of 1942-3

4th Cuneense Division (Alpine)
History: Largely destroyed in Russia in winter of 1942-3

5th Pusteria Division (Alpine)
History: In France

6th Alpi Graie Division (Alpine)
History: In France

German Army Order of Battle of Mountain Formations 1939-45

1st Gebirgs Division
History: In Poland, France, Russia, and Balkans

2nd Gebirgs Division
History: In Poland, Norway, Lapland, Denmark, and Germany

3rd Gebirgs Division
History: In Poland, Norway, Finland, Russia, Hungary, Czechoslovakia, and upper Silesia

4th Gebirgs Division
History: In Yugoslavia and Russia

5th Gebirgs Division
History: In Greece, Crete, Russia, and Italy

6th Gebirgs Division
History: In France, Poland, Finland, Russia, and Norway

7th Gebirgs Division
History: In Lapland and Norway

8th Gebirgs Division
History: In Italy

9th Gebirgs Division
History: Two separate divisions were known as the '9th'. The 'Nord' served in Norway and the 'Ost' in the eastern theatre

XV Gebirgs Corps
History: In Balkans

XIX Gebirgs Corps
History: In Norway and Lapland

XXI Gebirgs Corps
History: In Balkans

XXII Gebirgs Corps
History: In Greece and Hungary

XXXVI Gebirgs Corps
History: In Poland and Norway

XXXXIX Gebirgs Corps
History: In France, Yugoslavia, Czechoslovakia, and Russia

LI Gebirgs Corps
History: In Russia and Italy

20th Gebirgs Army
History: In Finland and Norway

No.1 Hochgebirgsjäger Battalion
History: Training establishment

No.2 Hochgebirgsjäger Battalion
History: Situated in Austria

No.3 Hochgebirgsjäger Battalion
History: Served in Italy

No.4 Hochgebirgsjäger Battalion
History: Served in Yugoslavia and Italy

6th SS Gebirgs Division 'Nord'
History: In Finland, Norway, and Belgium

7th SS Freiwilligen Gebirgs Division 'Prinz Eugen'
History: In Italy and Yugoslavia

13th SS Waffen Grenadier Division of the SS 'Handschar' Croatian No.1
History: In France, Yugoslavia, and Hungary

21st Waffen Grenadier Division of the SS 'Skanderbeg' Albanian No.1
History: In Albania and Aegean theatre

23rd Waffen Gebirgs Division of the SS 'Kama' Croatian No.2
History: Raised in Hungary in 1944 but shortly disbanded

24th Waffen Gebirgs (Karstjäger) Division of the SS
History: In Italy

Gebirgs Division of the SS 'Andreas Hofer'
History: Raised in Tirol but shortly disbanded

V Gebirgs Corps
History: In the Balkans and Russia

IX Waffen Gebirgs Corps of the SS (Croatian)
History: Included 'Handschar' and 'Kama' Divisions

Waffen Gebirgs Brigade of the SS 'Tartar' No.1
History: In Russia

CHAPTER 17
TITO AND THE PARTISANS

The German and Italian invasion of Yugoslavia, which commenced on 6 April 1941 with a heavy Luftwaffe attack on Belgrade and the main Yugoslav airfields, met with swift success, but the Slav nation was never brought to heel and the country was never completely occupied by the Axis forces. Within a week the Germans had claimed control of the greater part of the country and organized Yugoslav resistance had collapsed. The victors were swift to carve up Yugoslavia, which had existed as a nation only since 1919, if only on paper. Germany and Italy divided Slovenia between them. Italy took part of Dalmatia on its own behalf and the Kosovo district, and western Macedonia on behalf of Albania, setting up a protectorate over Montenegro. Bulgaria annexed most of Macedonia. Hungary took over the western half of Vojvodina (Backa) and some small districts on the Croatian border. The Croatian pro-German leader, Ante Pavelic, who was to lead the *Ustasi* puppet movement, was presented by his patrons with the control of an Independent State of Croatia. This included all Bosnia but not all Dalmatia. In reality, however, German troops occupied the eastern part of the state and Italian troops the coast and its hinterland. The rump of Serbia was placed under German military occupation and was allowed, from August 1941, to have a puppet government of its own under General Milan Nedic. The eastern half of Vojvodina (Banat) had a separate German military administration, in which members of the local German minority played the chief part.

Armed resistance to the occupation began in Bosnia, and there the Croatian Fascists began a massacre of Serbs, which was rarely surpassed for savagery in the annals of the Second World War. The surviving Serbs took to the hills and forests to defend themselves. In Serbia itself a force led by the regular-army Colonel Dragoljub (Draza) Mihailovic fought the Germans in the early summer of 1941. After Hitler attacked the USSR in June, the Yugoslav Communists, who had already made military preparations, took to the field in Serbia and Montenegro. By September a large part of both these regions was liberated by these two forces, which at first helped each other but then came to blows. In late 1941 Germans were successful in driving all resistance forces out of Serbia and massacred thousands of people in reprisal. The Communists, led by a Croat, Josip Broz (alias Tito), took to the mountains.

In the following three years the Communist forces grew, while the forces of Mihailovic lost ground. One reason was that Mihailovic came to depend on the support of various Serbian armed units in Italian-occupied territory that fought under Italian command against the Communist 'Partisans', and thus came to be widely regarded as a 'collaborator' with the occupying powers. Another was that the Partisans attracted thousands to their ranks by their slogan of the unity of all Yugoslav nations against the invaders and the traitors. This slogan provided the only alternative to the fratricidal massacres, first of Serbs by Pavelic's

Above *Women partisans advance across rock-strewn terrain under fire.*

Below *A boat packed with partisans crosses one of the many lakes in the mountainous region of Montenegro.*

Croatian Fascists, and then of Croats and Muslims by Serbian nationalist *cetnici* (Chetniks) owing allegiance to Mihailovic. In their mountain fastnesses, Tito built not only a huge Partisan army but a crude civil administration. By the summer of 1944 most of the mountainous part of Yugoslavia was in Partisan hands.

The mountain zones of western Yugoslavia vary from the tourist splendour of the Karavanke and the Julian Alps (both attenuated but lofty extensions of the Alpine ranges proper to the north), to the barren series of dry-limestone plateaux stretching from the Italian border to that of Albania in the south. The Alpine zone has naturally-strong affinities with parts of Austria and Italy, although communications with these countries are not particularly easy and only the River Drava breaks through the high mountain rim to afford a narrow passage into central Europe. In the Julian Alps,

Triglav, 9,393 ft (2,864 m), is the highest peak in Yugoslavia.

The plateaux chain ranging in altitude from about 1,000 to 5,000 feet (300 to 1,500 m) form the Kras (Karst), which has considerable significance for the whole economy and political geography of Yugoslavia, displaying the most distinctive landscape in the country. The Kras, which is embraced by parts of Croatia, Bosnia, Hercegovina, and Montenegro, presents an insuperable economic problem to the Yugoslav state since it renders sterile a very large area as well as sealing off the interior of the country from easy communication with the Mediterranean coast. The *polja* afford the only sites for agriculture and settlement. Only one large river, the Neretva, crosses the Kras and it is deeply entrenched. By virtue of its barren nature, the Kras has functioned as an important frontier. This was no less so in the Second World War

Below and opposite *German mountain troops in Yugoslavia lead their faithful pack-horses through a snowstorm (below) and along a difficult mountainside path where one slip means a shattering death in the ravine thousands of feet below (opposite).*

when the mountains of Montenegro, in particular, were the home of Tito's Partisan forces.

By the end of September 1941, Mihailovic had succeeded in establishing radio connection with the Yugoslav Government in exile in London, where at that time there was no knowledge of the patriotic Communist resistance movement. Tito made many attempts in 1941 to merge his forces with the Chetniks, on condition that the latter would help fight the common enemy, but Mihailovic's royalists took on an increasingly passive, pro-Axis stance, and Tito gave up all hope of mutual collaboration after the first German offensive in November 1941, which evicted the Partisans from Serbia. Mihailovic saw his Chetniks as units of the Yugoslav army and considered himself the representative of the former kingdom. His aim in general was to preserve its Serbian and royalist traditions.

The 'long march' or retreat by the Communists began at the small Serbian town of Uzice, which the Partisans had captured complete with its armaments factory and in which area Tito had established his headquarters. The Partisan forces formed four brigades, which were well disciplined but poorly clothed and armed. Tito formed his 1st Proletarian Brigade out of Serbian units and two Montenegrin battalions on 21 December, Stalin's birthday—no coincidence, but Tito was never to receive the military assistance from the Russians that he felt he deserved. Tito warned his brigade commanders to avoid fortified places on the withdrawal through the mountains, but the Partisans met nevertheless *en route* with sharp clashes with the Germans, Italians, and Chetniks. The Germans employed a whole army corps in pursuit of the Partisans and Italian Alpini troops found their skis useful for advance scouting.

Milovan Djilas, one of Tito's ablest commanders, described one encounter with the enemy on the march as follows:

> The march up the mountain proceeded
> without trouble: we had local Partisans to act

as guides, the cold subsided after noon, and we felt confident. At dusk we emerged from the pine forest according to plan, and made our way above a valley with hamlets. We knew there were Chetniks in the village of Kosatica, which was on our way, but we hoped they would not dare attack us. Indeed, our long column passed by undisturbed— all except our rearguard; the staff and the Second Uzice Battalion. The Chetniks fired on the staff, which, bunched together, was moving along at a rather leisurely pace. The firing of about thirty rifles from a crag to the left surprised us and we threw ourselves flat on the trail. A bullet hit next to my left ear, so deafening me that for a moment I thought I had been hit in the head. Somebody shouted 'Fire!' We all fired together, then tore across the snow-covered slope as if it had been a sheet. Somebody shouted, 'Second Uzice Detachment, forward!' The battalion behind us rushed over the snow-covered waste, crying 'Hurrah, hurrah!' and swung around the crag. The Chetnik rifles suddenly fell silent. We captured no one, we suffered no losses.

Journey's end was at Foca in the Montenegrin mountains within sight of Mt Durmitor. Here Tito set up his new headquarters in the still-undamaged town, which was built at the confluence of two mountain streams, and to win the respect of the mountain people in the area who earlier in the year had suffered grievously at the hands of both the Ustasi and the Chetniks. On one occasion the Chetniks had slaughtered groups of Muslim inhabitants whom they had tied together on the bridge over the Drina and thrown into the water. When the Partisans came to Foca, the mountain people, who were emaciated and in rags, came to life again and worked hard with the soldiers to rehabilitate the community. Tito now designated his 'Partisan Detachments' his 'Volunteer Army', and he set out to win over and encourage the peasant masses in Montenegro and eastern Bosnia to defend their villages against the enemy. Some of the Chetnik units had remained on good terms with the Partisans, but the former became increasingly hostile in 1942 and Tito's forces stood alone in their mountain base. After

another German offensive—this time directed at Foca which the Partisans were able to resist—Tito coined another new name for his men: 'National Liberation Army and Partisan Detachments'.

Marshall Tito was badly in need of material assistance from the Allies engaged in the war with the Axis powers. As a dedicated Communist he naturally looked to Moscow. The son of a Croat peasant, he had fought in the First World War in the ranks of the Imperial Austro-Hungarian army. He had been posted to the Russian front, where he was wounded and taken prisoner by the armies of the Tsar. Thus in 1917, at the time of the Bolshevik Revolution, he had found himself in Russia. All prisoners of war were set free and he himself volunteered for the newly-formed Red Army. He served in it throughout the Civil War. It was his first taste of the new ideas. He returned to his own country a convinced Communist.

In 1942 Tito is said to have radioed over 300 signals to Moscow, requesting help, but the Russians were strangely unco-operative. In February, Tito signalled 'Send us munitions, automatic weapons, boots and equipment for men. Send by air and parachute to us at Zabljak below Mount Durmitor in Montenegro. Snow has fallen here and airfields unsuitable for landing unless aircraft are fitted with runners. Anything you can send will be of great morale and material importance'. A party was sent to Durmitor to make sure that the dropping zone was prepared and that nothing would go wrong at their end of the operation. They prepared a reception area in the snow and built a hut for protection against blizzards. Then they waited night after night for the arrival of the Soviet planes, which never came. They waited for a month, during which time Tito continued to receive political direction over the radio from Moscow but no acknowledgement of his military needs.

Since Russia had failed to provide aid, Tito had to look elsewhere. The British Special Operations Executive (SOE) had sent an agent,

A party of Partisans make their way through a valley in their search for a camp in the mountains.

Captain 'Bill' Hudson to Mihailovic, but after the rift with the Chetnik leader, Tito had lost touch with the British officer. In 1942 the British made a number of attempts to send small missions into Yugoslavia to find out what had happened to Hudson and to report on the resistance situation. The first British officer to make successful contact with Tito at Foca was Major Terence Atherton, who carried gold coins to help fund the Partisans. After touring the battle area, Atherton lost his life, almost certainly at the hands of the Chetniks, who made off with his gold. Tito was dismayed. He had lost his first real chance of maintaining contact with SOE.

Partisan units were engaged in constant action along the length of the western mountains of Yugoslavia throughout 1942, the fighting being intensified in April when the Germans launched their third offensive. Tito's forces, still inadequately armed and weakened by the rigours of the previous winter, were in no condition to hold off a major assault. By May it was clear that the Partisans could not hold their positions in eastern Bosnia and Montenegro. Tito and his commanders decided to move the main guerrilla forces 200 miles (320 km) to northwestern Bosnia, a region nominally under Italian occupation. The great march continued for 115 days, covering in the mountainous terrain little more than a mile a day before it reached the comparative safety of liberated territory near the town of Bilhac on the frontier of Croatia and Bosnia, where for two months Tito established his base.

In the bitter fighting that ensued, the Partisans worst problem was care and treatment of the wounded. The barren mountains did not provide ideal sites for military hospitals. Surgery was of the most primitive kind and amputation, sometimes by hacksaw and razor, became the accepted method of treatment for wounded limbs. The problem of large numbers of wounded was eventually partially solved in 1943-4 when, after Allied recognition, military supplies began arriving in Yugoslavia and British and American planes flew out nearly 12,000 Partisans to be treated in hospitals in Italy. At the same time Tito received Allied medical aid—both supplies and trained personnel. But

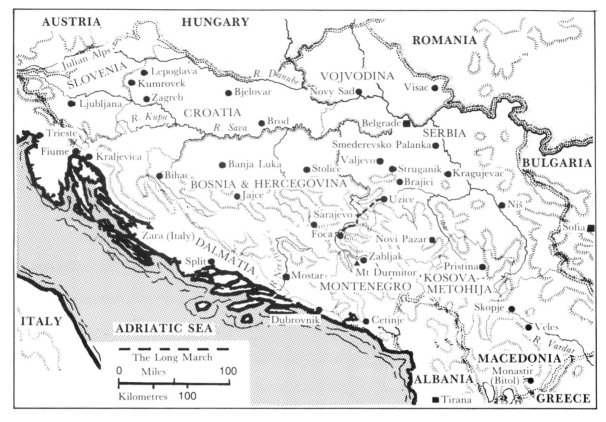

The mountain fighters: Yugoslavia, a nation newly created after the First World War, was the scene of a bitter civil war between pro-German factions, principally in Croatia with their Royalist supporters, and Marshal Tito's Communist guerrillas. The Germans, in spite of many well-equipped offensives, never succeeded in conquering Tito's mountain strongholds in western Yugoslavia.

by the time this happened, the major German offensives against the Partisans had already taken place.

Tito had started the year of 1942 with about 80,000 fighting men. By the end of that year he had some 150,000 organized into 28 brigades. Their fighting capacity was soon to be put to the most severe test. In November 1942, Hitler made the decision to crush the Partisan forces before the winter was out. Operation 'Weiss' (the fourth offensive in Yugoslav terminology) was to deploy 37 divisions (18 Italian, 7 German, 5 Bulgarian, and 7 Croatian) plus 11 independent brigades, six regiments, and 120 battalions, as well as the

assistance of some 20,000 Chetniks. They outnumbered Tito's Partisans by more than six to one. Tito planned to pre-empt German attacks by striking first from all parts of the liberated territory in Croatia. But the German-directed offensive succeeded in pushing the main Partisan forces eastwards towards the River Neretva.

The Partisans temporarily confused the Germans and Italians by destroying the bridges over the Neretva but making a crossing nevertheless, by breaking through the enemy circle at a weak point held by the Italians and Chetniks, and by pressing on into the mountains beyond. Tito's main army fought its way into the area where Bosnia, Hercegovina, and Montenegro meet, but the Partisans hardly had time to pause before the 'fifth offensive' (Operation 'Schwarz') was launched by the Axis forces. In this battle the Partisans numbered about 19,000 men, organized in four divisions and several brigades. The opposing forces numbered about 117,000. Again, the German aim was to encircle the Partisans, who found themselves enclosed in an area between the Rivers Tara and Piva and the formidable Durmitor range of mountains in Montenegro.

This time the Partisan forces found an escape route at the end of a narrow gorge on the River Sutjecka in Bosnia, which was held to allow the main Partisan forces to pass through. On 28 May, the first British mission arrived only to join Tito in the hasty retreat down the Sutjecka gorge and across the river into the Zelengora mountains. The crossing of the Sutjecka was more hazardous than the earlier crossing of the Neretva. The greater part of the sick and wounded were killed, and the losses of fighting men were as high as 30 per cent. Yet again, however, the Germans failed in their main objective, for the bulk of the Partisan forces, together with their leader, escaped.

The arrival of the British mission led by Captain William Stuart (who was killed in a bombing attack in the Sutjecka gorge) and then by his assistant Captain W.F. Deakin, was the turning point for Tito. As a result of the mission's favourable report on the Partisans' fighting qualities, a more high-ranking British mission led by Brigadier Fitzroy Maclean, who reported directly to Winston Churchill, was sent

Units of the Yugoslav Liberation Army enter Zagreb in triumph on 8 May 1945.

to Tito in September 1943. As a result, the Allies were fully informed of the Partisans intentions and requirements, and the RAF and USAAF based at Bari, Italy, maintained a regular flow of airborne supplies to the resistance in Yugoslavia.

In spite of these developments the war was not yet won, and there were considerable areas of Yugoslavia the Partisans could not control. By this time the Italians had negotiated an armistice with the Allies and their troops had left Yugoslavia, but the Germans were still present in strength in the whole area, and still capable of mounting heavy offensives. They pushed the Partisans out of territory in northwest and central Bosnia in 1944 and Jajce had to be evacuated. As the year progressed and Tito's forces had grown to three army groups, numbering 600,000 men and women, the Yugoslav leader's thoughts turned to the victorious Red Army sweeping into the country. Tito need not have worried. Stalin, whom Tito met secretly in September 1944, had other trails to blaze.

In May 1944 the German Luftwaffe launched a daring attack using gliders on Tito's headquarters, which at that time was centred in the Bosnian mountains at Drvar. The Germans landed airborne soldiers in gliders on operations in mountainous terrain on several occasions during the war, the theory being that thermal currents might make parachute descents dangerous. With the code-name *Rössel-sprung* 'knight's move', the operation was carefully planned to be carried out on Tito's birthday. The German troopers were instructed to capture Tito alive if possible. Although on 25 May Tito was surrounded in the hut he used as his headquarters, he cut a hole in the floor (which adjoined a rocky cliff above the town) and escaped by sliding down a rope to the riverbed below. He fled into the nearby forests and was later air-lifted to the Allied forces headquarters in Bari. He now agreed to make his headquarters on the island of Vis, where he had the added protection of Allied ground, air, and sea forces.

The Partisan armies still had a great deal of heavy fighting to do as the Germans retreated from the Balkans. But the most important military task for Tito in the closing stages of the war related to Istria and Trieste, which he was determined to regain for Yugoslavia. In March and April 1945 his crack Fourth Army, by this time motorized and well-armed, raced from points in northern Dalmatia towards Trieste. Local Partisan forces were already in possession of most of Istria, and on 30 April Tito's units entered Trieste itself, two days ahead of the main Allied troops. By the time the war ended, Tito's four Proletarian Brigades, which had been thrown out of Serbia and made the 'long march' into the mountains, had grown to an army of 800,000 men and women, organized in four army groups stationed in all regions of the country and around its frontiers.

CHAPTER 18
THE ITALIAN CAMPAIGN

The Gustav Line

Towards the conclusion of the North African Campaign in mid-1943, Hitler had expected an Allied landing in the Balkans, but at a top-level conference in Washington, DC, at the time the US General Dwight D. Eisenhower was ordered to plan such operations in exploitation of the conquest of Sicily as would be best calculated to eliminate Italy from the war. The decision to invade Sicily, after the completion of the Tunisian campaign, had been taken at the Casablanca conference in January 1943. Sicily was chosen because its capture would help to clear the Mediterranean for Allied shipping and provide a suitable springboard for the Italian Campaign. The battle for Sicily, launched on the night of 9 July 1943 with airborne and amphibious assaults, came to a conclusion on 19 August when Marshal Badoglio, the Italian Premier and Commander-in-Chief, established contact with General Eisenhower with a view to negotiating an armistice between Italy and the Allies.

When the Italian unconditional surrender was signed at Cassibile in Sicily on 3 September and announced on 8 September, the Allied commanders were confident that the Italian mainland would be in Allied hands in a matter of weeks. The Germans, however, who were then concentrated mainly in northern Italy, were swift to react to the invasion on 3 September, and they were to contest every yard of ground as they fell back along the Italian peninsula until the final days of the war. It was to

be a campaign in which mountains and rivers were to form seemingly impenetrable barriers and in which, with the onset of heavy rains and snows in winter, military operations inevitably ground to a halt. The Abruzzi mountain chain, forming the 'backbone' of Italy, was to be the battleground of mountain troopers seeing action in their natural habitat for the first time—the 'Devil's Brigade' and the 10th US Mountain Division being amongst them.

The initial landing was made in the 'toe' of Italy at 04:30 on 3 September by the Canadian 1st and the British 5th Divisions, meeting negligible resistance. Inland demolitions in the mountains and easily-defensible country slowed down the forward troops' rate of advance. On 9 September, as the Italian fleet was steaming out to surrender, the British 1st Airborne Division landed from sea transport and occupied Taranto. Early on 9 September, the US Fifth Army (preceded by a parachute assault) landed at two points in the Gulf of Salerno. The northern force, sailing from Sicily and North Africa and consisting of the British X Corps, assaulted with the 46th and 56th Divisions; the southern force (also from North Africa and consisting of the US VI Corps) assaulted with the 36th Division followed by the 45th. US Rangers landed to seize the defiles, through the mountains leading to Naples, and British commandos to capture Salerno. Although the Italians had capitulated they were still divided in their loyalties and in fact a state of civil war, sometimes called the 'War of Liberation', developed in the homeland.

In the chaos that followed the surrender, the Germans performed one spectacular feat when they rescued Benito Mussolini from his place of confinement in the Hotel Albergo-Rifugio on the Gran Sasso plateau northeast of Rome. His whereabouts was discovered by SS *Obersturmbannführer* Otto Skorzeny, who discarded his first idea to use parachutists for the mission because of the thermal currents in the mountains. The operational plan was first approved and then controlled from his post at the Practica di Mare airfield near Rome, by Kurt Student, the Luftwaffe general who raised the German airborne troops and who was the architect of their victory in Crete in 1941.

Whilst on 8 September 1943, *Major* Mor's parachute battalion captured the lower end of the funicular below the mountain lair to prevent the Italians sending troops to reinforce

their guards at the hotel, eight of Skorzeny's twelve DFS-230 gliders landed at the same time in the car park alongside the building. Skorzeny's mixed force of paratroopers and 'Waffen' SS Special Forces—including the reluctant Italian General Soleti—successfully located the Duce, who was flown with Skorzeny in Student's personal Fieseler Storch to the Practica di Mare airfield. The former Italian leader was then flown in a Heinkel III to Vienna and then taken by train to meet Hitler in Munich. The Duce, white-faced and somewhat shaken, was delivered safely to the Führer. Skorzeny received the accolade of supreme approval from the Nazi leaders, this admiration for many years after the war being shared by his former enemies.

By 20 September the US Fifth Army was advancing up the west coast and the British Eighth Army up the east coast. New divisions

US Army trucks are caught by flood water from the Volturno River, Piedmont, Italy, 5 December 1943.

Skorzeny's men rush into action from one of the gliders which landed successfully near the hotel, to rescue Mussolini.

arrived to join the Allied forces, but concurrently the Germans hastily reinforced their own defences. On the night of 12-13 October, the Fifth Army crossed the River Volturno after hard fighting, and the Germans withdrew to their 'Winter Line', known as the Gustav Line, destroying every bridge and culvert *en route*. This line, which the Germans had been preparing since the Allies first landed, ran athwart the peninsula through the mountains and hills generally following the courses of the Rivers Sangro and Liri (Garigliano) and defensively it was very strong. The Fifth Army found the latter river an even stiffer obstacle than the Volturno, and costly attacks to cross the lower reaches began on 6 November. On 28 November, the Eighth Army launched an attack to cross the Sangro, and after repeated attacks it achieved its object. Nevertheless, it proved impossible to reach the Pescara-Rome highway, thereby turning the defences of Rome. By now,

however, winter had really set in, and heavy rains and snows limited offensive operations.

The clock is now turned back to the dark days in Britain of 1940, when the only thoughts of offensive action by British forces were centred through the Office of Chief of Combined Operations, headed by Commodore the Lord Louis Mountbatten. Amongst many memoranda submitted to Mountbatten urging immediate attention was one from a bespectacled, rather grizzled, civilian intellectual named Geoffrey Nathaniel Pyke. Pyke, an Englishman of Dutch-Jewish descent, immodestly advocating his appointment as 'Civilian Director of Programmes of Combined Operations', went on to explain that as 70 per cent of Europe lay under snow for approximately five months of the year, a small group of 'winter fighters', who had intelligently selected their targets, could be reasonably expected to attract and tie down the efforts of an infinitely larger enemy force—and, he added, probably beat them, because the time and choice of the engagement would be under the control of the attackers.

Norway, in Pyke's opinion, would be the ideal locale for this offensive action. Where France, Belgium, or Holland might be difficult because of the openness of terrain, Norway (with its long dark nights, its mountains, and its sparse population) would be most difficult for the Germans to defend. Pyke went on to explain that if a force of well-trained and desperate men were to be parachuted into the country and provided with machines that could travel fast *over*, and not *through*, the snow, they could destroy bridges, tunnels, trains, tracks, hydro-electric stations, and other targets of opportunity in quick succession. The remainder of Pyke's memorandum was devoted to a discussion of the development of the proposed snow machine. Thus, in the sketchiest detail, was born the concept of the tracked snow 'weasel' vehicle.

'Project Plough' was promptly pushed on one side and it was not until 11 April 1942 that Winston Churchill was apprised of the plan— an invasion of Norway. The Premier was duly impressed but, smarting perhaps from the mental wounds of the Allied disaster in Norway in 1940, he suggested that this might be a plan of campaign the Americans may care to consider. Pyke was promptly flown to America where he met with General George Marshall's deputy chief of staff, Lieutenant General Joseph T. McNarney, and other high-ranking staff officers. No doubt the sidewalks of those vast boulevards in Washington had seen stranger sights than Geoffrey Pyke, but the well-groomed lions of the War Department were certain that this strange eccentric must have some powerful friends to have found his way into their august presence. 'Project Plough' was approved in principle, but a bunch of cut-throats was first needed to carry out the plan. This led to the appointment of a young American Army officer, Lieutenant Colonel Robert T. Frederick, to recruit the fighting men for this daring assault on Norway.

Colonel Frederick, an officer of great charisma and with the good looks of a Hollywood star of the 1930s, was frankly not all that keen on Pyke's scheme, but relished the opportunity of raising the toughest unit in the American army. Frederick, who was born in San Francisco, had applied unsuccessfully to join the California National Guard at thirteen years of age. At the age of sixteen he had, however, been successful in gaining a commission in the Cavalry Reserve. At the same age he obtained a place (with the help of a senator) at Annapolis, but when the youth turned up for enrolment a year late, the US Navy suggested he aimed less ambitiously and tried West Point, at which academy he found a place a year later. The fortunes of 'Project Plough' fluctuated and with it Pyke's, but Frederick went about his task of raising a unit of dare-devils with great vigour.

Churchill and Mountbatten were very keen that the British Empire had a hand in the manning of the force and Frederick found himself in Canada where he was pleasantly surprised to find that the Canadian army was officially willing to extend quick co-operation to the project. The Canadians also offered the resources to help develop the snow vehicle. Back in the USA, Frederick set about selecting officers and canvassing the American army for volunteers. Like most appeals to join 'Special Forces' and other volunteer units, the 'Devil's Brigade' was viewed with suspicion by unit commanders, who were reluctant to see their best men go to such a maverick outfit. The American army made a compromise with Frederick. He could have all the volunteers he wanted from the stockades—murderers, felons, and criminals of all descriptions, who were considered of no use as American fighting men.

Frederick set up his training camp at Fort Harrison, Helena, in the Montana mountains, where the inmates who made it from the stockades formed what, to all intents and purposes, was the atmosphere of a penal colony. Then the Canadians arrived. They bore the hat badges and flashes of famous Canadian regiments. The Queen's Own Cameron Highlanders of Winnipeg, for example, wore the large Scottish tam. The Canadians, well-trained and smartly turned out, were frankly incredulous at what they found at Harrison. The Americans were vagabonds, ill-inclined to take orders and totally lacking in military demeanour. Whatever was in store for the 'Devil's Brigade', the North American cousins from Canada had ill-assorted comrades-at-arms. The story of how the two elements fused together is the making of the toughest, and most effective, fighting force of the Second World War.

The First Special Service Force, as the unit was formally called, commenced parachute training in August 1942 making their jumps from C-47s assigned to the force. By December the troopers had begun the most rigorous training schedule ever undertaken by an American army unit. The entire programme was based on attaining and maintaining peak physical fitness and the strictest obedience. The differences between Canadian and American drill commands were an initial problem. When the Americans questioned swinging their arms high in the British tradition, they were told it would help them with ski training. Parachuting was considered an easy exercise as compared with basic drill, as well as handling arms and explosives. The standard US army three-month parachute course was boiled down to six days at Fort Harrison. First descents were made after only ten minutes of ground training. Colonel Frederick, the instructor, was anxious to get on with other things.

Mountain climbing and ski training presented another opportunity to turn the First Special Service into superbly-trained soldiers. Men from the flatlands, who were not used to mountain walks, regarded their skis as 'torture boards'. Twelve Norwegians, who had escaped from their homeland, were assigned to ski training that commenced with cross-country running and legging it with ski poles—but no skis —up a hill near Helena called 'Muscle Moun-

tain'. When the snow fell heavily, arrangements were made with one of the railways to establish a camp made up of boxcars that were normally used for work crews. Their camp was located at a place called Blossburg on the Continental Divide. At the end of six weeks, all men in the Special Service Force were able to go on a 30-mile (48 km) cross-country ski trip in one day, carrying a loaded rucksack and a rifle. This in itself was quite a feat as there were over 300 men in the force who had never seen snow before, a number of whom came from Texas and other southern states. After this phase of training, the troopers carried out several overnight exercises using the Weasels (which had been transformed from Geoffrey Pyke's drawing board to reality) and their skis when the men had learned how to look after themselves in sub-zero temperatures without shelter or the use of a fire.

Men who failed to make the grade were ruthlessly weeded out. Now even the worst of the original malcontents and social misfits dreaded the 'RTU'...'Return to Unit'. As in most volunteer units, a strong bond of mutual respect grew up between the officers and the enlisted men. No detrimental cracks about the force were acceptable to all ranks, and new recruits soon wanted more than anything else to be accepted by the Devil's Brigade. Although Colonel Frederick kept a close eye on training, he spent much of his time in Washington where he carefully considered plans for the Force's employment in action. Norway as an operational theatre had not been completely ruled out, but other assignments were considered such as a raid on the Ploesti oilfields in Romania. Frederick shortly left for London to consult with Mountbatten and other members of the British military establishment and to make further contact with General Eisenhower who was now based in the UK. A plan was also discussed to send the force to the Caucasus Mountains but Frederick declined the scheme, believing his forcemen could do nothing the Russian mountain fighters were not able to do themselves.

General Eisenhower wanted the First Special Service Force for Operation 'Husky', the invasion of Sicily, but their first operational mission was to be nearer home in the Aleutians. In late May 1943, the men who thought they were going to Europe found themselves steaming westwards across continental North America in railroad trains, and once on the Pacific coast they were embarked in ships destined for Kiska, which with Attu, were the two Japanese-held islands that were to be attacked in the Aleutians. An amphibious force, which included the Devil's Brigade as spearhead, went into action on 15 August but, in a stunning anticlimax to months of preparation, they found that the Japanese had departed before they had arrived. At the Quebec conference, which was taking place at the time, the Allied leaders were embarrassed that these élite troopers had been employed on such a pointless exercise, and the First Special Service Force was ordered to the Mediterranean theatre without further delay.

The Force arrived in Naples harbour in mid-November 1943 destined for the 'Winter (Gustav) Line', where the Germans had established fortifications in a chain of hills that barred the Fifth Army's advance on Rome. One key to cracking this line was represented by a formidable mountain mass with twin peaks named Monte la Difensa and Monte la Rometanea. No matter how ferocious a force General Mark Clark's Fifth Army hurled against these peaks, the attacks had only been repulsed, resulting in heavy Allied casualties. The area was held by a crack Panzer Grenadier Division, with the Herman Goering Parachute Division in reserve. When the Devil's Brigade arrived in the 'Winter Line', the Fifth Army had fallen back to lick its wounds. Frederick's force was assigned to the 36th Division (as the 'forlorn hopers') who would seize the two peaks, commanding one side of a pass while British troops were given a cluster of lesser peaks to attack on the other side, so to allow the main Allied force

to stream through and descend into the plain beyond.

Colonel Frederick chose 2 December as D-Day. Monte la Difensa was the closest and toughest task. Rising to 3,000 ft (900 m), Difensa loomed over the surrounding terrain and the challenge was in every way equal to the training that the special-force troopers had received in the USA. A menacing bastion, its summit was generally cloaked in clouds or swirling snowstorms. Above its 1,000-ft (300-m) tree line, there was nothing but bare crags. The only feasible approach to the summit was a trail leading up the south side. On the north side of the mountain stood a 200-ft (60-m) cliff. Above the cliff was a series of six ledges averaging 30 ft (9 m) in height. The Germans had comparatively little firepower on this flank because it seemed obvious that even a handful of men would have difficulty in scaling their way up. It would appear impossible for a full-sized attacking force to come up this way. Elsewhere in the mountain area the German defences were too well dug in among the sheer cliffs and crevices in the granite to be affected by shells and bombs.

The 1st Regiment deployed to the base of a hill and waited in their reserve position. The 2nd Regiment began the stealthy climb up Difensa, their objective being a point about half way to the crest where they would wait, under the cover of darkness, to begin the attack. The 3rd Regiment, split in half, sent one battalion to the base of the hill to remain in readiness to back up the second. The Allied guns, booming away to cover the attack, were answered by the enemy, who seemed to have all the German guns in Italy at their disposal. It seemed that the whole of Monte la Difensa was on fire. By the dawn of 3 December, all the forward units had reached their assigned positions and burrowed their way into concealment.

The 2nd Regiment reached the base of the Difensa crown by 22:30 on 3 December. Some of the men were sent to string ropes on the more difficult part of the ascent—the troopers would

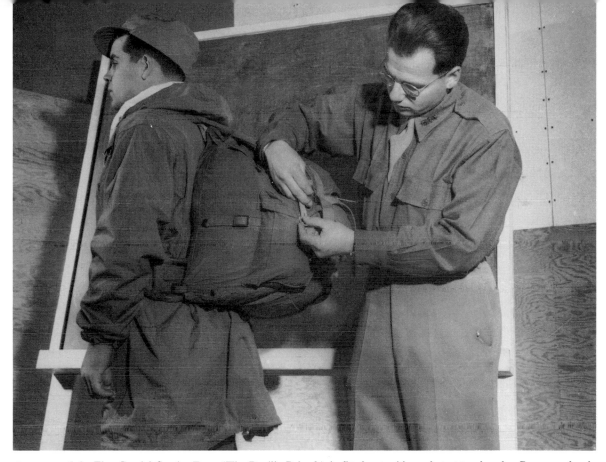

A trooper of the First Special Service Force (The Devil's Brigade) is fitted out with combat apparel and a Bergen rucksack. This elite commando unit, which was raised in the mountains of Montana and composed of Americans and Canadians, was arguably the toughest fighting force operating in the Second World War.

not have been able to make the night assault without them. The cliff face of Difensa extended upwards at a pitch of 60 or 70 degrees beginning at 2,000-ft (600-m) and extending for another 1,000 ft (300 m). The 600 men of the 2nd Regiment climbed silently. There were no signs that the Germans entrenched above were aware of their approach. By midnight, most of the men had reached concealment among the rocky ledges. The lead company of the assault force, scarcely daring to breathe, lay well within range of the German positions. Moving upwards again, the troopers groped for crevices with frozen hands while stretching their muscles to aching point to keep them from sliding backwards. Like so many snakes, the sections crawled over the cliff face and, singly, slithered over the rim.

The advance group was finally joined by Frederick and his staff, inching their way within earshot of the enemy. When all elements of the force were in position, the Colonel gave the signal for another stealthy advance. The troopers edged forward in the darkness, their blackened faces and dirt-stained uniforms making them almost completely invisible. Hundreds of the best German troops lay unsuspecting in underground emplacements, supported by others in foxholes. But a rockfall gave the American and Canadian soldiers away. Flares went up in the night sky illuminating the climbers. All hell was let loose. The Germans aimed fire from their strong-points. The special-force troopers dived for what cover they could find, some of the less fortunate riflemen sliding into the ravines. At one point a German led a small group from an emplacement with a white flag in his hands. An American stepped forward to collar the man only to be killed by one of the group aiming shots at his head. The Americans swiftly responded by killing the group. The special-force troopers never took prisoners again.

At dawn on 4 December, the fog parted momentarily. It revealed the Germans swarming away from the crest of Difensa, down the slope and across the connecting ridge to the force's second target, Monte Rometanea. But this sudden-found visibility proved a curse for the 2nd Regiment. The German artillery pinpointed their positions and casualties were heavy. The force dug in as best they could in the pill-boxes and between the rocks for the rest of the day while awaiting ammunition supplies to be sent up from the caves below where they were stored. One pack outfit supplied a battalion that was fighting on a bald, rocky ridge nearly 4,000 ft (1,200 m) high. That battalion lost a third of their men in action. All the supplies had to go up on the backs of the mules and men. Mules took them the first third of the way. Men took them the remainder, because the trails were too steep even for the mules.

Next morning Frederick received the welcome news that the British had taken their objective and were now in position to help consolidate the advantage they had realized by

Confrontation in Italy: The Gustav, or 'Winter', Line proved to be a major stumbling block to Allied progress in the Italian campaign during the winter of 1944-45. The dominating feature of the Gustav Line was the German fortified position based on the monastery, which had stood for hundreds of years at the top of Monte Cassino, and which was not only the bastion of the defensive line, which stretched from coast-to-coast across the breadth of the Italian peninsula, but which was also of vital strategic importance over-looking Route 6, the only highway through the mountains leading directly to Rome.

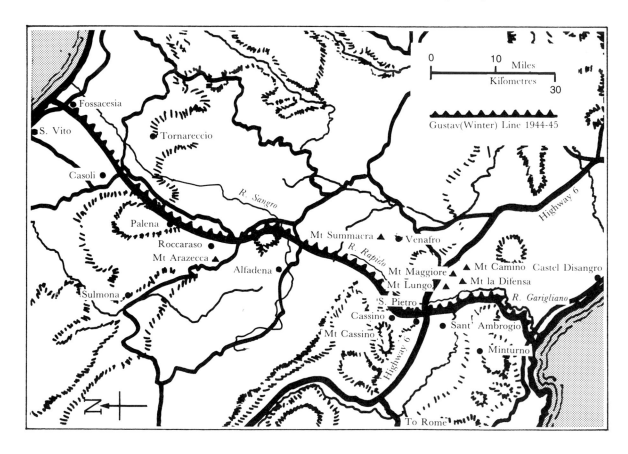

taking one side of the gap. The next morning the assault was to be made on Rometanea. The climb was achieved by the 1st Regiment, but the pounding it received during that day forced Frederick to postpone the attack for another day. Dense fog now set in which turned to shifting mist when the forcemen effectively used their grenades and knives, gradually clearing the southern slopes of the mountains. Rometanea was taken on the sixth day. The Devil's Brigade lost 532 killed, wounded or injured, one-third of the total fighting echelon of the First Special Service Force.

The Allied offensive in Italy was re-opened in the first week in January 1944. The British secured a bridgehead over the Garigliano at Minturno but were held there, while the Fifth Army (on 20-21 January) unsuccessfully attempted to force the Rapido River. Meanwhile, east of Cassino, the French corps, which included the 4th Moroccan Mountain Division, made considerable gains There were two major battles in the first five months of 1944—Anzio and Cassino. Some 50,000 Allied troops were pinned down for four months in the salient after the amphibious landing at Anzio before the breakout to Rome, and Monte Cassino was an equally formidable stumbling block in the path of the Allied armies.

Monte Cassino

Difensa was not the final obstacle to be surmounted before the Allied columns could break through the Liri valley to Rome. The entrance to the 6-mile (10-km) gap in the mountains is dominated by a rocky promontory crowned by Monte Cassino. The lowest knoll in the area is 1,000 ft (300m) high and the highest ground—the massif of Monte Caira, the summit of which is covered in snow almost all year round—rises to about 5,500 ft (1,700 m). South of Cassino, near Monte Trocchio, the Via Casilina leaves the mountains and enters the Rapido valley. After running dead straight for 3 miles (5 km), it makes a sharp turn to the south and

goes around Monte Cassino in the direction of the Liri valley. At the summit of Monte Cassino lay an abbey that, although having been savaged and rebuilt several times, dates back to AD 524. In that year St Benedict had erected the first properly-organized monastery in Italy on the site of a temple to Apollo. The abbey became the home for a Benedictine community.

On 17 January 1944 American troops of the Fifth Army captured Monte Trocchio while forward troops reached the River Rapido. The 168th Regiment of the 36th US Division entered the mountains operating at first on the slopes between Monte Caira and Monte Cassino. The 133rd Regiment's task was to gain the heights that dominated the road from Caira to Cassino, and the 135th Regiment's job was to capture the town of Cassino that lay in a valley below the monastery. The first bid to conquer the Cassino bastion was very nearly a success, but the veteran German paratroopers holding it refused to give up. The first Battle of Cassino petered out in a blinding snowstorm and the Allied sector was taken over by the New Zealand II Corps, which included the British 78th Division and the 4th Indian Division, whose corps commander was General Sir Bernard Freyberg. Their attack (scheduled for 16 February) was to be preceded by the most controversial act of the Italian campaign. General Freyberg had demanded the bombing of the Cassino monastery.

The New Zealand plan, reduced to its simplest terms, was that the 4th Indian Division would attack through the mountains, take Monte Cassino, descend into the valley, and after cutting Highway 6, attack Cassino town from the west. While the Indians were thus occupied, the New Zealand Division would make their effort from the east. Leaflets were dropped from Allied aircraft in the vicinity of the abbey warning Italian civilians that the venerable building would be shelled and bombed. Indeed, it was reported on 15 February that the abbey had been destroyed. By reducing the building to rubble, the Allies had

A British Bren-gunner in action amongst the debris of Monte Cassino caused by severe Allied bombing of the mountain strong-hold. The four-month campaign to capture the heights of Monte Cassino commenced on 17 January 1944 with an assault by units of the US Fifth Army and ended 17-18 May when the Polish Corps captured the monastery and the German defenders evacuated the position, which had for so long dominated the main line of advance to Rome from the south.

unwittingly provided the Germans with ideal defensive positions amongst the stones. The Indian Division, which included Gurkhas, Punjabis, Rajputs, Mahrattas, and Sikhs were ideally suited to fighting in lofty terrain but they made little progress up the mountain. The New Zealanders fared no better in the plain. At the end of the second Battle of Cassino (19 February), the Allies had scored success only in that General Freyberg's thrust had relieved some of the German pressure on the Anzio bridgehead.

There was a pause for re-organization and the third phase commenced on 20 February with a massive aerial bombardment. The New Zealanders were still resolved to advance from the south, join hands with the Indians, and thus encircle Monte Cassino. Whilst the New Zealand Corps was to make the main effort

again, a French and a British Corps were to assist in maintaining pressure on the Cassino defenders, and to be ready to burst into the Liri valley. The 4th Moroccan Mountain Division had joined the French Expeditionary Corps, which was north of Cassino. The British were opposite S. Giorgio on the left flank. The weather changed for the worse on 24 February and the frustrated attackers had to endure three weeks of relentless rain, which gave the Germans ample opportunity to work on their defences. A battalion of the 104th Panzer Grenadier Regiment was in the Liri valley. Up in the north, facing the French, was the 5th Gebirgs Division, and responsible for Monte Cassino itself was the veteran 1st Parachute Division. The 3rd Regiment held the town of Cassino, the 4th Regiment manned the heights north and west of the town, and the 1st Regiment was positioned on the slopes south of Monte Caira. The ruined monastery and Castle Hill were defended by the 1st Battalion of the 3rd Regiment.

The battle for Cassino pursued its grim course. Flying Fortresses, Liberators and Mitchells supported by fighters and fighter bombers pounded and strafed the area unmercilessly and artillery took over where the aircraft left off. The New Zealanders battled their way into the town and the Indians fought their way up the slopes. The 5th Indian Brigade, also involved in the

The defence of Monte Cassino was assigned to veteran German paratroopers of the 1st Parachute Division. The Fallschirmjäger withstood three major offensives against Cassino as well as air bombardment on an unprecedented scale before they evacuated the monastery area when their situation became untenable during the final stages of the Polish assault in mid-May.

assault on the town, struck out towards the monastery. In spite of heavy casualties (many unfortunately inflicted by Allied artillery), one company of Gurkhas over-ran Point 435 and finished up less than 500 yd (450 m) from their objective. The fighting was a matter of thrust and counter-thrust. The paratroopers were overwhelmingly outnumbered but they were difficult to uproot. The Germans were the acknowledged victors of the third Battle of Cassino. The Allies had to rethink their tactics but one thing was certain—the 'Winter Line' had to be smashed at the one point where it was obviously least vulnerable: at Cassino.

The next Allied move was to switch the British Eighth Army, less its V Corps, from the Adriatic to the Cassino front. The American Fifth Army, including the French Expeditionary Corps, became responsible for the area between the Eighth Army's left flank and the Tyrrhenian Sea. Plans for a fourth offensive against Monte Cassino were already in motion when the third battle ground to a halt on 25 March. On the night of 11-12 May, the mountains reverberated to the thunder of 1,600 guns, and the Allies then began advancing on a 30-mile (50-km) front. The most spectacular progress was made by General Dody's 2nd Moroccan Infantry, storming Mt Faito, and this success was followed by the capture of three other heights—Girofano, Cerasola, and Feuci. No better soldiers could have been found for war in the mountains than the Moroccans and Goums. Fearless fighters, skilful climbers, accustomed to long night marches across vast distances, they could not have been given a more suitable assignment. On that night of 11 May, after the artillery bombardment had ended, they had surged forward with alacrity, heading for Monte Faito and Monte Girofano. Nothing could stop them, not even the German 71st Division. Field Marshal Kesselring, the ruthless Commander-in-Chief of the German army in Italy, commented 'If the tactics of the English and Americans always remain conventional and if they rarely exploit local successes,

Paratroopers man a mortar-post during one of the many assaults on the heights of Monte Cassino.

the French on the other hand, and particularly the Moroccans, fight with great *panache* and exploit each success in detail by concentration of all forces on a weak point'.

The 4th Moroccan Mountain Division, which also distinguished itself in the battle for the Gustav Line, was drawn from the Atlas and Rift regions. The division consisted of a reconnaissance regiment (scout and light armoured cars), three infantry regiments, an artillery and an anti-aircraft group, a medical battalion, a transport company, and a mule train. General Henri Martin was its first commander and the division was reviewed by General de Gaulle at Terni, Algeria, on 21 August 1943. The following month the division took part in the recapture of Corsica. In February 1944 the Moroccans went into the line in Italy in the Abruzzi mountains southwest of Cassino and they saw their fiercest actions at Monte Feuci

and Monte Cescheto, the Crisano col, the Fammera gap, and Monte Aurunci. The division entered Rome on 6 June. The Moroccans went on to serve with General de Lattre de Tassigny's French First Army spending the winter of 1944-5 in the Alps and in the Vosges mountains. After crossing into Germany, the 4th Moroccan Mountain Division fought German guerrillas in the Austrian mountains.

The Polish II Corps, commanded by General Wladyslaw Anders, consisting of the 5th Kresowa Division and the 3rd Carpathian Division, now appeared on the scene. The corps faced Monte Cassino with the British X Corps on the right and XIII Corps on the left. The Polish troops occupied the sector extending from Monte Castellone in the north to Hill 174 in the south. Castle Hill remained the responsibility of the British XIII Corps. In the late afternoon of 11 May, the Polish Corps artillery ceased firing and the two divisions assembled at their start line. The two main lines of attack would be one towards the monastery itself and the other towards S. Angelo and Phantom Ridge. General Duch was to lead the 3rd Carpathian Division in the assault on the monastery and General Sulik with his 5th Kresowa Division was given the S. Agnelo-Phantom Ridge assignment. After a further bombardment the Polish corps attacked in the early hours of the following morning.

The first attack made no tactical gains and the Polish commanders had to think again. 'H' hour for the second attack would be 04:00 on the morning of 16 May. The Kresowa Division would start its assault on Phantom Ridge, while the Carpathian Division would tackle Massa Albaneta. The Polish troops were straining at the bit. Their beloved country had been occupied by the Germans for over three years and the Poles were eager to come to grips with the enemy. The Poles once more leapt to the attack and by the evening of 17 May: Phantom Ridge, Colle S. Agnelo, and Hill 593 had been taken and were securely held. Massa Albaneta, although not yet completely under Polish control at that time, had been fully neutralized and tanks that had reached to within a couple of hundred yards were held up only by mines.

While the Polish corps offensive was going on, substantial progress had been achieved by the British XIII Corps and the Canadian I Corps down in the Liri valley. There could be no doubt about it. A deep crack was in the making in the German defence system that for so many months had effectively barred the way to Rome. The isolation of the monastery indicated that the enemy would very likely retreat from the ruined building in the course of the coming night. On the night of 17-18 May the Germans made their decision. The 1st Parachute Division disengaged the bulk of its force on the Gustav Line and withdrew to the so-called Hitler Line. This last ditch before Rome was based on the following features: Monte Caira, Pizzo Corno, Hill 555, Piedemonte, Aquino,

American troops lead a mule train through mountain terrain in central Italy, December 1943.

and Pontecorvo. The Polish corps did not take long to clear Monte Cassino of the enemy.

Rome and beyond

Whilst the campaign to take Cassino was taking place, in January the 3rd Regiment of the First Special Service Force was engaged in attacking another target that was delaying the Fifth Army. This was Monte Majo, the key to the country north and south of it, and it was needed as the manoeuvre pivot for the attack on Cassino. It was the third of the mountains guarding the road to Rome—named 2,500 years ago as the Via Casilina but now known more prosaically as Highway 6. Colonel Walker commanding the 3rd Regiment developed his attack in two stages. The first was to take the high ground between his assembly area and the peak, and the second was to take the mountain itself. This intervening high ground consisted of a series of lower peaks, capable of testing the skills and endurance of the most experienced mountain climbers. The wind blew bitterly cold, and the thick snow made movement conspicuous so that infiltration had to be done by night.

Once again the force successfully used surprise as an element of their attack. Employing lessons learned from Difensa, one detachment climbed a cliff so steep that they were able to get within a few yards of Monte Majo before the German defenders became aware of their danger. Using grenades, the forcemen cleaned up four machine-gun posts and had consolidated their position well before dawn, less than five hours since the beginning of the ascent. By the dawn of 7 January, the Majo peak was firmly in the hands of the force. Despite an almost unbroken wave of German counterattacks, the 3rd Regiment held its ground. One reason for the victory was the fact that the force-

men were able to seize and use weapons and ammunition from the strongly-entrenched German positions. Everywhere the counterattacking Germans were met with their own captured guns.

General Mark Clark believed that the honour of taking Rome should fall to the Americans, so Colonel Frederick and his men were directed to advance through the mule trails of Rocca Massina and advance on the town of Artena, situated in the Alban Hills at the very gateway to Rome. By 25 May, the force, which had been employed in the Anzio bridgehead, had taken Monte Arrestina. Two days later it took Rocca Massina. In the meantime, the US 1st Armoured and 3rd Infantry Divisions had punched a wide hole in the German line, and other elements of the Fifth Army were pouring through. At the little town of Artena (a stop on Highway 6 heading into Rome) the force paused briefly to regroup and re-equip. The

Men of the 10th US Mountain Division, newly formed at Camp Hale, set out on a ski training session in the Colorado mountains. The men were subjected to some harsh training in the severest mountain conditions but they survived to make a distinguished contribution to the Allied campaign in northern Italy.

next objective between Artena and Rome on Highway 6 was the town of Valmontone. The First Special Service Force entered Rome in the van of the Fifth Army on 4 June but was shortly phased out of the Italian Campaign. Its next destination was the French Riviera: Operation 'Anvil', the Allied invasion of southern France, a far cry from Fort Harrison, Helena, and the mountains of Montana.

The war in Italy was far from over. The Allied Fifteenth Army Group made no great progress along the peninsula in the summer of 1944 and the Germans were able to fall back on another 'winter line'—the Gothic Line running from Pisa on the west coast to Rimini on the east coast. In the autumn, several breaches of the Gothic Line were sealed by the Germans and the main effort shifted to Washington where the Allied High Command, now pre-occupied with progress in northwest Europe, had to decide what to do next in Italy. Early in January the Allies advanced the line to the south

bank of the River Senio and, by their overall action, managed to pin down the German Tenth and Fourteenth Armies. Throughout the winter, the Allied air forces continued their attacks on the German lines of communication through the Alps, including oil and rail targets in Austria and southern Germany.

During mid-November 1944, things had suddenly begun to happen in the USA at Camp Swift in Texas, an unlikely home for the 10th US Mountain Division. The division was in transit at this centre on the Texan plains after spending nearly three years training as mountain infantry, first at Fort Lewis in Washington State and then, after serving on the Kiska venture, the 'mountaineers' arrived at Fort Hale, near Denver, Colorado. At Camp Swift, the 86th Mountain Infantry Regiment received orders to pack all of its gear and supplies. To the men's relief they were allowed to take their skis, ski poles, ski boots, and other winter equipment. After a four-day train journey the regi-

Mountain troopers of the 10th Division are seen on parade at Camp Hale.

ment boarded the SS *Argentina* at Norfolk, Virginia, bound for Naples. Early in the New Year the 86th's sister regiments—the 85th and 87th—boarded the USS *West Point* from Camp Patrick Henry, Virginia, bound for the same destination.

The Army had been interested in forming mountain warfare units since the 'Winter War' of 1939-40 between the Finns and Russians. The 87th Regiment had actually been activated at Fort Lewis on 8 December 1941, one day after the Japanese attack on Pearl Harbor. The Fort Lewis camp was situated close to the icy peak of the 14,408-ft (4,394-m) Mt Rainier. Over the gate hung a sign reading 'Through These Portals Pass the Most Beautiful Mules in the World'. Experienced skiers from Vermont, New Hampshire, Maine, and Massachusetts arrived, but as the 87th expanded the regiment comprised a mixed bag of volunteers. In addition to famous skiers and well-known expedition climbers, the 87th now also bristled with cavalrymen from New Mexico, artillery men from California, Montana prospectors, Idaho Park Rangers, and so on.

With so many volunteers, the unit would soon be reaching division strength. After a long search, construction began on an army camp some 180 miles (290 km) from Denver, Colorado. In April 1942 workmen started an amazing job of levelling and grading and building. Camp Hale's elevation of 9,300 ft (2,800 m) was high; so was the price of building the barracks ($28 million). Per square foot, this was one of the most expensive army posts in existence. By November the days at Fort Lewis were over. The men of the 87th and the now-formed 86th moved to their new Rocky Mountain home at Camp Hale. In July the 10th Mountain Division was officially formed.

The 10th was designated a 'light' division and equipped with 75-mm howitzer artillery instead of the bigger 105s. The 75-mm guns could be stripped down and packed on mules but this artillery weapon, handled by a four-man team, became better known in the Second

World War and after as anti-tank weapons handled by airborne troops. Detachments of the 10th ranged far and wide in search of experience. One bunch flew to the Atlas Mountains in North Africa. Throughout much of the war, instructors from the 10th trained British climbers to cross river gorges by means of a rope. Another detachment taught Polish paratroopers to ski in Italy. Other men from the division spent several months in the British Columbia icefields. Here they developed and tested various over-the-snow vehicles, including the 'weasel' that ran on tracks like a tank. For fun, the men had themselves towed behind the weasels on skis.

After the Kiska interlude, the 10th was back at Fort Hale. In summer it rained every afternoon, drenching the men. The autumn mud was as terrible as it had been on Kiska. In the winter, as the soldiers trudged up through the snows to 12,000-ft (3,600-m) elevations, temperatures could fall to $-4°F$ ($-20°C$). The dry air was not good for the lungs. One night, to 'create humidity', a private flung pails of water on the barrack floors. When the heaters went off at night-time everything froze. The signallers slept with their radio batteries against their bodies to keep them in working order. Mountain troopers slept on one blanket and covered themselves with another. Sheets were frowned upon. The 10th had no time for softies.

Route marches were made in the snow covering 15 miles (24 km) with heavy packs of 80 lbs (36 kg) or more, which on slopes tended to pull the marchers backwards. The army skis were often so stiff they sank in the snow. Each time a novice lifted a leg in the snow, muscles hurt. Each downhill turn would be accompanied by pain until a man was proficient in skiing. Climbing a steep slope was hard on

Opposite *This set of stills from an American war-time documentary film demonstrates the strenuous training undertaken by the 10th Mountain Division from their base at Camp Hale in the Colorado Mountains.*

Engineers of the 10th Division lift one of their first casualties in the Italian campaign by means of an overhead tramway system on his way to a field hospital.

A 10th Mountain Division mule train moves forward in the Monte Nuova area in the US Fifth Army zone of operations in northern Italy.

the arms as well, but the arms—with the help of ski poles—were vital to preventing the trooper from sliding backwards. Rock training was even more difficult than ski instruction. On the first days recruits were forced to balance on wet logs and to step on to huge boulders. Bound by ropes, they had to climb an almost perpendicular granite rock several hundred feet high. To toughen the men, NCOs occasionally forbade gloves, even in cold temperatures. Frozen hands would have been a formidable handicap, though, when performing the rappel. In this exercise, the roped climber descends a perpendicular cliff at a 90-degree angle, paying out the rope as he goes down, sometimes for hundreds of feet. A 'Tyrolean Traverse' was perhaps the most-feared manoeuvre for the recruits—it meant crossing high above a river gorge suspended from a rope. The slightest doubts could mean a swift death.

Day-to-day life in the Colorado mountains bristled with adventure. What other division tested snow vehicles and rescue toboggans, or learned to snow-shoe? Who but the 10th troopers were introduced to avalanche dangers and avalanche rescues? A famous Arctic explorer taught them how to build igloos and other snow caves, and the men actually slept in these snow houses. One member, a Norwegian, who had lived in the Arctic, showed his fellow troopers how they could keep their hands protected from freezing—he greased the palms with raw-bacon strips before long marches. The 'mountaineers' also learned the use of steel spikes under their boots. These 'crampons' gripped ice walls on nearby ice cliffs. The artillerymen were used to shoot down snow overhangs, called 'cornices'. When a snow slope was too dangerous, the troopers sometimes tossed hand grenades. The explosion caused the snow masses to cascade downhill without injuring anyone.

On one training course before Easter 1944, the troops ran into a blizzard, a week out of camp. Soon the snow was so deep that some of the special vehicles stuck. Food supplies dwindled. Instead of turning back, all but the sick continued by the orders of Major General Lloyd Jones, the commander. After several more days, the sky cleared and the snow became so bright that sunglasses came out of the packs. Anyone who forgot to protect his eyes risked snow blindness. At last the men reached the base of Ptarmigan Peak. It meant another hardy zigzag climb. Everyone itched with sweat. Fatigue began to mark even the toughest faces. Beards grew. The tempo slowed down. On Easter Sunday the weather warmed up a bit. Then, by a quirk of nature, a wet heavy snow began. It melted on the men, so their clothing was soaked with water. When the mercury dropped, the men's clothing turned to ice. The new snowfall was so deep that supply vehicles could not reach the snowbound mountain troopers in the back country. Thus ended another training session. When the troopers finally returned back to Camp Hale, army doctors counted 100 cases of frost-bite. The theory was that anyone who survived the course would survive anything.

Shortly before leaving for Italy, Brigadier General George P. Hays took over the command of the 10th Mountain Division and amongst his many popular decisions was the choice of the divisional nick name 'Mountaineers'. War-torn Italy offered new scenes for the 'Mountaineers', who were shocked by the poverty they found in the country. The 86th was first to see action. The regiment received its baptism of fire near Cutigliano and Orsigna on 8 January. The 'mountaineers' found comfortable quarters in the Apennine hills where they were often billeted with Italian families. In late January the 85th was scattered over the hillsides near Pisa and the 87th in their positions at Camaiore, Villa Colli, and Valpromaro had aimed their first 75-mm howitzer shells at the enemy. The 'mountaineers' were dressed for the chilly nights in their long parkas, with sweaters and heavy underwear. They wore GI gloves, but on patrol left their helmets behind—there was no use in letting a helmet scrape a tree branch, that would give the show away. His weapon was the M-1 rifle.

By early February 1945, the Allies had decided to use the 10th Mountain Division to breach Kesselring's Gothic Line. Every hill between Bologna and a point 24 miles (39 km) north of Florence was still in German hands. Germans sat on strategically-crucial peaks, on Monte Serrasiccia, on Pizzo di Campiano, on Monte Belvedere, Monte Gorgolesco, Monte della Torraccia, and on dozens of others. The Germans had had plenty of time to dig in deeply, to build more fortresses for themselves, even to use concrete and steel. The Germans were safe in their bunkers and their pill-boxes. Some 25 divisions strong, they were well supplied with machine-guns and artillery. Kesselring had every reason to believe that he could hold the Gothic Line. After five months, the Allies had not made a dent in the defensive systems. Would General Hays' 'mountaineers' succeed where other units had failed?

Where would the blow fall? For Hays and his superior, Lieutenant General Lucian K. Truscott, Fifth Army Commander, the choice soon narrowed down to two objectives. One was 3,876-ft (1,182-m) Monte Belvedere, which sits like a long, gently-sloping pear above the little villages of Vidiciatico and Quericiola. It would be a long way to the summit of Monte Belvedere, the paths being defended by German grenadier units, but the slope was not steep. General Truscott definitely wanted to start with Monte Belvedere. General Hays, on the other hand, favoured another mountain altogether. This was Pizzo di Campiano, with its rocky, perpendicular Riva ridge. 'Riva is far tougher,' Hays said. 'The Germans would never believe that anyone can scale it.' Moreover, asserted the mountain general, Riva was the key to Monte Belvedere. Finally, Hays persuaded his superior that Riva ridge would protect the flanks of other 10th Mountain units which would scale Belvedere a day later.

Riva ridge was successfully taken by the 86th Regiment and General Hays issued a simple field order for the night of 19 February 1945: 'The Tenth Mountain Division will attack . . . to seize, occupy, organize and defend Mt Belvedere, and prepare for action in the northeast'. Monte Belvedere controlled several highways leading north. If the high ground was taken, Allied troops would over-run the rich plains of the Po River and the cities of Bologna, Milan, Verona, and Venice would be in their grasp. The slopes to Belvedere were heavily mined and at the top the Germans had dug

deep ditches, which concealed mortar and machine-gun positions. Howitzer artillery was positioned to lob shells at convoys moving through the valleys. Monte Belvedere had seen action before the 10th Mountain Division arrived on the scene and the 'mountaineers' would glean invaluable information on the terrain and German dispositions from the Italian partisans operating in the area.

Before they set out, the troopers had a last warm meal. On the mountain no fires could be made. The night climb had to be made silently: no one was to speak or smoke. No trooper was to fire his rifle until the officers gave the signal. Artillery would be used only at the last moment. At 23:00 on 19 November the attack

10th mountain troopers under bombardment during training.

was set in motion. The troops moved in small groups through the villages and began to move uphill. As they climbed, the night turned colder. The ground was hard and frozen, and little could be seen. No moon shone. Now and then, a trooper would suddenly fall into a hole. The mountain had been bombarded heavily during the previous month and there were many craters. In one valley, the Americans sent up a smoke screen, just in case the Germans switched on their searchlights. For units of the 85th Regiment, everything went according to plan. The troopers scrambled up yard by yard, undiscovered by the defenders. The 1st Battalion of the 87th was not that lucky. A few minutes after midnight, one of the companies drew fire from a pill-box. German burp guns—submachine-guns—and 88-mm self-propelled artillery suddenly roared through the night. This drew artillery fire from American positions in the valleys.

From Riva ridge, which had now been in American hands for 24 hours, the mountain troopers of the 86th observed the weird flashes and heard the pounding of guns all over Belvedere and the surrounding mountains. Before dawn, the 85th Regiment received unexpected help from Royal Air Force Spitfires. They were shortly joined in the sky by several P-47 Mustangs of the US Army Air Force. One after another the planes swooped down as smoothly as birds of prey to strafe German positions. Before the sun had come up, the 3rd Battalion, 87th, moving up from another direction, was not far behind. Counter-attacks were expected

and tanks of the division were moved upwards to hold the mountain. All along the front the Fifth Army was battling for the mountain tops. The Germans tried some familiar tricks, such as feigning surrender, but the American reaction was swift and decisive. General Hays minced no words: 'Mount Belvedere and the occupied ground will be held at all costs'.

In early March, the 10th Mountain troopers were put to their biggest daylight test. The Germans had to be chased from the remaining ground held by them in the Apennines. The first two objectives were the 3,330-ft (1,010-m) Monte Terminale and the equally tall Monte della Vedetta. German artillery and mortars did not stop the two 'mountaineer' regiments involved in the assault. Both mountains were seized within hours. The 86th next struck for Iola, a hamlet on a hill just beyond Monte Terminale. Here some of Kesselring's desperadoes had barricaded themselves in the farm buildings. Now the 10th were faced with men who would fight from house to house, wall to wall, until they had no ammunition left or lay wounded or dead. While the battle went on at Iola, American tanks clanked their way uphill. From the crests they sent high-explosive shells into the German positions. But by now the 10th Mountain Division, although its entry into the line was still recent, was really finding its combat feet. As one NCO wrote in his diary, 'You take one ridge and there's another one just like it staring you in the face. Maybe someday we'll run out of ridges'.

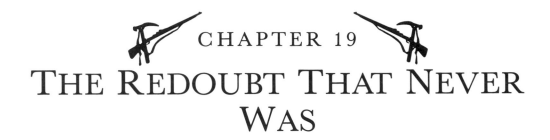

CHAPTER 19
THE REDOUBT THAT NEVER WAS

By April 1945, the general collapse of Germany had started. The Allied armies were running over western Europe, and the Russians were driving forward into eastern Germany. On 9 April the Fifteenth Army Group opened its offensive to break into the Po valley. The Eighth Army, on the east, opened the attack across difficult swamp country intersected by many small rivers and had captured Imola in the Po valley by 15 April. On 14 April the Fifth Army attacked and, after a week of heavy fighting, captured Bologna, advancing northward to the Po, over which bridgeheads were established southwest of Mantua on 23 April. Bridgeheads were also established on the Eighth Army's front, and the German forces in the centre were faced with complete envelopment. Both Allied armies now raced northward towards the foothills of the Italian Alps; the Fifth Army entered Verona on 26 April and Milan three days later.

Just northwest of Verona's bastions, the 87th reached a small town named Bussolengo, where the 'mountaineers' were too late to stop a German, manning an '88' on a rooftop, massacring a crowd of Italians in the street celebrating the Allied advance. The 85th, moving north from Villafrance to the lakes, was faced by a German suicide attack that was repulsed by machine-gun fire. The day the Italian partisans executed Mussolini (28 April), the 10th Mountain Division pushed deeper into the Italian lake country, meeting their final challenges on Lake Garda. This lake, surrounded by mountains

with a narrow strip for a highway which curves and zigzags, now leading up, now down. The road frequently disappears into tunnels. The encircling hills are not high but the elevations are full of shoulders and buttes. The Germans planned to make a stand at the northern end of the lake, the Alps forming the background to the proposed battlefield. One reason for the stand was to allow as many Germans as possible to retreat through the Brenner Mountain Pass.

When the 87th reached Garda they seized part of the highway but found bridges demolished and tunnels choked with rubble. The 'mountaineers' were then involved in a spectacular landing across the lake using amphibious vehicles ('ducks'), ably assisted by British artillerymen who had loaded their guns on to sailboats, which they used as platforms to bombard the German-held northern shore. The 'ducks' hit the shore in a hail of machine-gun and sniper fire from Gebirgstruppen sniping from the high ground. As the Americans edged around Lake Garda, they frequently encountered the tunnels that had been blocked by the German engineers. Heavy fighting occurred around the village of Spiazzo; the German troopers counter-attacking furiously from the high ground east of the town. During the night of 29 April, Colonel William Darby, of Task Force Darby fame, led a group of the 85th in another amphibious assault across the lake. The 'ducks' headed directly for a town named Gargnano. Here the troopers made a spectacular landing on Mussolini's lakeside property. The former dictator's castle retreat consisted of 37 rooms where Colonel Darby and his raiders found many important documents. The building was crammed with statues, paintings, and relics. By that time the Duce was already dead.

The Allied commanders had for some time been expecting a last-ditch stand by the Germans in an area that comprised the mountainous zones of Bavaria, Austria, and northern Italy. The area was approximately 240 miles (385 km) from west to east and 80 miles (130 km) from north to south. The alleged centre of fanatical resistance carried such titles as 'the Southern Redoubt', the *Alpenfestung* ('Alpine fortress'), 'the Bavarian Redoubt', or 'the Inner Fortress', but the Allies knew the proposed defensive zone as 'the National Redoubt'. The

'Redoubt' undoubtedly shaped Allied tactical thinking during the closing weeks of the war in Europe. Indeed the Americans, in particular, became obsessed by it.

For the GIs of the Seventh Army, pushing south from Munich toward Innsbruck and aiming for the Brenner Pass, or for the US Seventh Army, farther east, driving down on Linz, the spring-like weather made life tolerable but not so for the 88th US Division, crunching northwards in the winter-like conditions in the Dolomite Alps from Italy. Their object, too, was the Brenner Pass. The GIs had heard tales of this Alpine fortress. They knew only too well, from their own bitter experiences in struggling up and down the Apennine range to the south, what a formidable task may lie ahead of them. Peace, however, was only a few days away and the National Redoubt was even

The end of the war is near at hand. A German mountain trooper philosophically surveys the Alpine scenery.

Two German paratroopers act as sentinels in the half light of a winter evening in the mountains of northern Italy.

then almost forgotten history, but it is interesting to look at its concept—a figment in the imagination of the German High Command.

The idea for the National Redoubt began in Switzerland. In the late summer of 1940, after defeating France, the Germans considered the possibility of invading that country. The Swiss were extremely uneasy over finding themselves surrounded by the victorious European Axis powers, and a gigantic project to build a fortification system was put under way in 1940, and which took two years to construct. When completed, the fortress complex included three major forts: Sargans in the east, Gotthard to the south, and St Maurice in the west. The Swiss referred to their defence system as a *national reduit* and felt that its value lay in its deterrent power since, if the nation were attacked, the inner region of the country, it hoped, would be unmolested, while the redoubt took its toll of the Axis armies. In September

Below *German paratroopers form a defensive patrol in a wooded area of northern Italy.*

1943, the German army began to explore the general idea of using defensive Alpine fortifications, beginning at Bregenz on the Liechtenstein border and extending eastward toward Klagenfurt, following the Italian-Yugoslav frontier, then swinging northward along the Hungarian border. The southern section of the projected fortification line in the Dolomite and Carnic Alps would make use of the old Austrian mountain strongholds built before the First World War, and which formed the scene of heavy fighting in 1915-18.

On 22 April General Eisenhower sent the Third Army (Patton) and Seventh Army (Patch) into the eastern and western halves respectively of the Alpine fortress. Once the Redoubt fell, according to Eisenhower, the German garrisons holding out in Denmark, Norway, and Holland would probably fall. As the Americans drove into the National Redoubt, they were more

of Germans fleeing from the Russians, Berchtesgaden was captured on 5 May by troops of the French 2nd Armoured Division attached to XXI Corps. When the Frenchmen ascended the fabled 'Eagle's Nest', it was empty. Also, with the capture of Landeck, Innsbruck, Salzburg, Berchtesgaden, and the Brenner Pass, the Redoubt area was increasingly blanketed by American and French troops. The celebrated SS General Otto Skorzeny, whose feats as an extraordinary commando had made him one of Hitler's favourites, wandered in the area near Alt Aussée carrying vague orders to raise a group of Alpine defenders for partisan work, but found the highly touted defence system and its hidden supply caches to be non-existent.

Left *A group of 3rd Squadron British Special Air Service (SAS) troops arrived in Italy in late 1944 to serve with the partisans in the mountains in the north-east of the country. These SAS troopers with a stripped down Vickers machine-gun were photographed near the village of Castino.*

Below *German troops guide a pack-horse to a lone outpost in northern Italy in the spring of 1945.*

hampered by the logistics of supplying their motorized columns than German resistance. However, the 2nd SS Mountain Division gave a good account of itself against the 45th US Infantry Division. The myth of *Alpenfestung* was fast dissolving in the minds of the advancing American troops and it has been argued that had Eisenhower been less insistent on taking the Redoubt, the Red Army would have been less successful in over-running the 'Alpine and Danubian Districts'—the name given by the Nazis to a huge chunk of the former Austro-Hungarian Empire.

Austrian partisans helped the Seventh Army to reach the Brenner Pass, where it met with the Fifth Army, while the Third Army struck into Czechoslovakia. Although the Seventh and Third Armies effectively blocked their paths, *Alpenfestung* now figured as the destination or sanctuary for tens of thousands

Finally, Lieutenant General Hermann Foertsch, Commander of the German First Army representing his Army Group 'G', told the Americans that the Germans had food for only six days to feed the Alpine army numbering anything from 250,000 to 350,000 men. Between 3 and 5 May the bulk of the Redoubt's German incumbents surrendered unconditionally to American General Devers.

The *Alpenfestung* (its name a mockery) yielded a rich crop of German wartime leaders, as prisoners. The Seventh Army captured Field Marshals von Rundstedt, List, von Leeb, and Kesselring. Fallen Nazi political personalities also abounded in the area. Among them were Robert Ley, the former Labour minister; Julius Streicher, editor of the anti-Semitic newspaper, *Der Stürmer*; and Ernst Kaltenbrunner, the former No. 2 in the hated SS. A huge man, standing over 6 ft (2 m) tall, and having a scarred face, the cool Alpine breeze did not prevent Kaltenbrunner from sweating profusely under interrogation. Upon questioning, Kaltenbrunner talked mystically of setting up a headquarters at Alt Aussée and establishing radio contact with anti-Bolshevik underground groups all over Austria and Germany.

The dream of the National Redoubt might have become a reality had the Germans done something seriously about it early in the war, but with their armies occupying the coastline of Europe from within the Arctic Circle to the Spanish frontier with France, and advancing to the gates of Moscow, Stalingrad, and into the Caucasus mountains, the German eagle might be forgiven for neglecting its own eyrie in Bavaria and Austria. The German war leaders were so convinced of the inevitable clash between the western and eastern Allies that they actually believed the Redoubt could be utilized to drive between them a wedge that would be to Germany's advantage. But the mountains and valleys of the Alpine regions had borne witness to humanity's courage and madness in two world wars. Spring was turning to summer and tourists would soon be flocking to the resorts again. Silent, supreme, the mountains with their mantles of eternal snows would preserve their judgement of humanity's conduct until the end of time.

THE POST-WAR ERA

CHAPTER 20

IN MOUNTAIN LAIRS 1945-88

Greece

Since the Second World War, apart from major conflicts in Korea and Vietnam, war has largely been a matter of quenching brush fires. Britain's vast empire has virtually disappeared over the last 40 years, and the British army in particular has been heavily engaged for at least half this period in the often troublesome task of severing imperial connections. The insurgent or guerrilla fighter of modern times is no longer the ragged warrior armed with sticks and stones. The post-war Communist rebel has often been strongly motivated politically, well-educated, and soundly trained in the military sense. The guerrilla, however, also enjoys the age-old advantages of operating from small bases in remote areas and the mountain lair is as good a location as any to remain concealed from view. Modern insurgents have their roots in the Second World War and it was the Communists who in fact played such a large part in the resistance movements that were formed to harass the Axis powers. Since 1945, the USSR swiftly spread the Communist doctrine and looked for potential leaders who could be trained to wage rebellion in the emergent nations.

In Greece, several rival guerrilla factions fought the Germans and Italians and in the latter part of the Second World War a state of civil war existed in the country. Following the announcement of the formation of a 'provisional democratic government of Greece' on 24 December 1947 under Markos Vafiades, the Communist rebels attempted to set up a permanent base by launching a vigorous attack on the town of Konitsa in Epirus province close to the mountainous Albanian frontier. The attack succeeded but Greek Government forces retook the town on New Year's Day. The Greek army was strengthened in numbers and lavished with $15 million from the USA to improve its arms and equipment. As a result, large-scale offensive operations were carried out against rebel forces concentrated in the Roumali region of central Greece, the Mt Olympus area, and the Grammos massif on the Greco-Albanian frontier, the last operation commencing in the middle of June and continuing until the end of August. The rebel forces were finally liquidated in 1949 after being driven from their last remaining strongholds in the Mt Vitsi and Mt Grammos areas.

Korea

Communist forces first struck in strength when, on 25 June 1950, North Korean forces crossed the 38th parallel into South Korea. Thus commenced a three-year war (1950-3). Korea is a mountainous country, and only about one fifth of the total area consists of lowlands that are suitable for farming. A great mass of mountains occupies almost the whole of north central Korea. It is dominated by the country's highest peak, Mt Paektu, which reaches 9,000 ft (3,000 m) above sea-level. A chain of mountains called the Taeback Range extends from this mass along the east coast down into the

southeast corner of the peninsula, almost to Pusan. Just below the 38th parallel a major spur, the Soback Range, runs off toward the southwest. Although the Korean War is largely remembered for its stalemate, and the fighting for isolated hill positions in the latter half of the conflict, the fighting moved to North Korea in October 1950 when Republic of Korea (ROK) and UN forces crossed the 38th parallel and advanced to the Yalu River on the Manchurian border. The North Korean capital, Pyongyang, was captured by a combined airborne landing and overland advance on 20 October, and the Yalu was shortly reached by the ROK 6th Division.

Between 16 and 26 October, the US X Corps was embarked at Inchon, and the corps was moved around to the east coast to Wonsan. General Douglas MacArthur, who was in overall command of the ROK and UN troops, intended to advance up the entire front of the peninsula, X Corps on the east coast, the Eighth Army on the west. Since the rugged, desolate, central massif precluded mutual support, these forces would act independently with the com-

bined objective of enveloping all the North Korean forces south of the Manchurian border. The Eighth Army began its advance on 24 November only to be struck a massive blow by 180,000 Chinese troops the following day. (China had already given due warning that it would enter the war if North Korea was invaded.) The invaders on the west were overwhelmed and fell back to the 38th parallel. In the eastern zone, an additional 120,000 Chinese troops advanced on both sides of the Chosin reservoir, isolating three divisions. MacArthur ordered evacuation of the entire force, since the Communist drive, directed on the ports Hungnam and Wonsan, threatened its piecemeal destruction. Navy transports were rushed to both ports. Defensive perimeters were established. US marines featured strongly in the fighting— the 1st US Marine Division leading the breakout from the Chosin reservoir area. Despite continued Communist attacks on the perimeters of both ports, evacuation by air and sea went smoothly and by 15 December 105,000 ROK and US troops were lifted out by the US Navy, together with 98,000 civilian refugees.

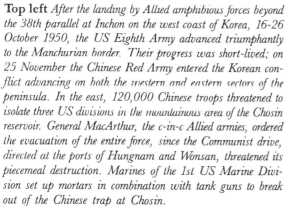

Top left *After the landing by Allied amphibious forces beyond the 38th parallel at Inchon on the west coast of Korea, 16-26 October 1950, the US Eighth Army advanced triumphantly to the Manchurian border. Their progress was short-lived; on 25 November the Chinese Red Army entered the Korean conflict advancing on both the western and eastern sectors of the peninsula. In the east, 120,000 Chinese troops threatened to isolate three US divisions in the mountainous area of the Chosin reservoir. General MacArthur, the c-in-c Allied armies, ordered the evacuation of the entire force, since the Communist drive, directed at the ports of Hungnam and Wonsan, threatened its piecemeal destruction. Marines of the 1st US Marine Division set up mortars in combination with tank guns to break out of the Chinese trap at Chosin.*

Above *Marines load up with everything that will help them breakout of the Chinese encirclement.*

Top right *These Marines of the 5th and 7th Regiments fought for five days and nights in below-zero winds and on icy roads and paths before breaking through the Chinese hordes on the southern tip of the reservoir and making their way along trails to the sea.*

Right *Marines of the US 1st Marine Division retreat along the ice-covered mountain pass, gathering refugees on the way. In spite of relentless Chinese attacks, the Marines managed to bring out their wounded and all their equipment as a fighting force for sea evacuation.*

Kenya

The Mau Mau rebellion of 1952-6 had its origins in a dispute over land ownership in the sparsely-populated White Highlands, which had been farmed by British settlers since before the First World War, and which the Africans claimed was still tribal territory. The Highlands of Kenya form an area of some 17,000 sq. miles (44,000 km^2) with the Aberdare mountain range to the northwest of the capital, Nairobi, and Mt Kenya to the northeast of the city. The highest point in the Aberdares is 13,104 ft (3,997 m) and the summit of Mt Kenya is 17,058 ft (5,202 m). A wave of massacres of white Europeans by the Mau Mau tribe led to the arrival in Kenya of British troop reinforcements to help round up the terrorists. As the effectiveness of military measures increased, many Mau Mau withdrew into the Aberdare mountains, adding to the difficulties of maintaining contact with an enemy well able to conceal itself. Aerial bombing at the end of the year also caused some shift of Mau Mau from the forests towards Mt Kenya. The Aberdares and Mt Kenya were classified as prohibited areas. The prohibited areas included a strip one-mile wide along the eastern edge of the Aberdares and a similar strip on the south and east sides of Mt Kenya. These strips were controlled by police and army patrols and camps. Within the prohibited areas the security forces were able to operate on a war footing. Troops were allowed to open fire on sight.

There were only 12,000 guerrillas in early 1953, and they received no support from outside Kenya. Very few were armed with proper firearms and none had any military or revolutionary training abroad. The Aberdare range is over 60 miles (95 km) long. Up to about 9,000 ft (3,000 m) the bamboo gives way to moorland covered in jungle grass interspersed with streams and rivers. It is not surprising that working in an almost impenetrable forest at a considerable altitude presented serious problems to the British troops. Moreover, the Mau Mau in their mountain lairs organized

excellent lines of supply for food, money, recruits, information, and medical supplies, stretching across the Kikuyu tribal lands and even into Nairobi. The British troops had not been trained to operate in this kind of terrain and were pitted against an enemy who, whatever its limitations, possessed an acute sense of smell, hearing, and stealth.

During 1953, British battalions were involved in many clashes in the Aberdares. The Lancashire Fusiliers, the Devons, and the Black Watch all saw service in the mountains, and in September, 49 Brigade consisting of only two battalions, namely the Northumberland Fusiliers and Royal Inniskilling Fusiliers, arrived as reinforcements in the country and were deployed to the lower slopes of Mt Kenya, where the Meru and Embu tribes were succumbing to Mau Mau intimidation. Meanwhile, the King's African Rifles (KAR) battalions were generally kept in Kikuyuland or in the white settled areas. However, they also supported British troops in the Mt Kenya area. The Mau Mau had to be hunted not only in the mountains but also the lowlands and even in Nairobi. More British troops arrived in 1954 replacing units that had seen some hard campaigning. The New Year brought a greater emphasis on offensive operations in the forest areas. Continual sweeps, patrolling, and ambushing (although they did not result in great numbers of enemy casualties) kept the Mau Mau on the move. By 1955 over 8,000 Mau Mau had been killed, nearly 1,000 captured, and 22,500 placed in detention. The number of terrorists still active in the forests was now estimated to be approximately 5,000 with about 800 firearms among them.

Operations 'Gimlet', 'Dante', and 'Beatrice' took place during July and August 1955 in the Aberdares and Mt Kenya areas. The 49 Brigade was supported during Operation 'Dante' by Harvard and Lincoln bombers and 3.7-in shells from the guns of 156 Anti-Aircraft Battery. Neither the heavy bombers nor guns killed many terrorists but they did succeed in unsettling them and keeping them on the move. Operation 'Beatrice' was the last large-scale operation mounted during the Kenya Emergency. The emergency was not officially declared at an end until January 1960. Almost its sole function in the latter years was to keep suspects in detention. The security forces lost 590 killed and 1,500 loyal Africans also lost their lives. At least 11,500 Mau Mau were killed during the struggle. The Mau Mau were motivated by extreme fanaticism and were capable of the most appalling atrocities committed in the name of 'freedom' upon African and European Kenyans alike.

Cyprus

British security forces were to learn the techniques of counter-insurgency during the civil war and terrorism that took place in the Mediterranean island of Cyprus during the troubled years of 1954-9. Cyprus was ceded to Britain in 1878 by Turkey. It remained a colony of little importance, even during the Second World War, until the British evacuation of Egypt made it the obvious choice for the site of Middle East Headquarters in June 1954. It was exactly at this juncture that the movement for union with Greece (or *Enosis*) under the leadership of Archbishop Makarios, patriarch of the Orthodox Church in Cyprus, was beginning to gain momentum. Makarios led 419,000 Greek-speaking Cypriots who shared the island with 105,000 Turks. There was little love lost between the two communities. Not surprisingly, the Turkish population and their sponsors on mainland Turkey were not going to agree to any form of *Enosis*.

The British commenced the build-up of their military forces in Cyprus, hitherto a holiday paradise for British troops on leave from the Middle East. In December, serious rioting in Nicosia and Limassol ended when British soldiers shot two rioters. Meanwhile, the self-styled General George Grivas, a retired Greek army colonel, was busy setting up an army of

guerrillas in the mountains of Cyprus. The movement was named EOKA (*Ethniki Organosis Kypriou Agonistou*). The campaign can be said to have started on 1 April 1955 when a series of bombs exploded in different parts of the island. Leaflets, signed 'The Leader Dighensis' (after a legendary Byzantine warrior) proclaimed that with God's help and the support of all the forces of Hellenism the struggle to throw off the British yoke had begun.

The island of Cyprus may be divided, from north to south, into four distinct physiographic regions. The Kyrenia mountain region, running for 50 miles (80 km) along the northern coast, and the Karpas peninsula, which is a narrow limestone range, no higher than 3,000 ft (900 m). The Troodos massif occupies about half of Cyprus, including Mt Olympus (Olimbus), the country's highest peak at more than 6,400 ft (1,950 m). It is separated from the Kyrenian range by the 80-mile (130 km) long and 15- to 30-mile (25- to 50-km) wide Mesaoria, the fertile heartland of the island. The southeastern portion of the island is composed of a high plateau that emerges into the country's fertile coastal plains. On 19 June 1955 EOKA opened its second major offensive with attacks on police stations in Kyrenia. A few days later, a mountain guerrilla group led by Renos Kyriakides attacked the police station in Amiandos, a small village in the Troodos mountains, and killed the sergeant in charge. Bombs were thrown in bars and in army houses all over the island. Rioting in Nicosia followed on 2 August.

On 25 September Field Marshal Sir John Harding handed over his job as Chief of the Imperial General Staff and was appointed Governor of Cyprus. He arrived on the island on 3 October followed by a heavy influx of British troops. These men were spread throughout the island with headquarters in Nicosia, Xeros, Paphos, Limassol, Famagusta, Kyrenia, and Larnaca. Harding announced a £38 million development plan but it was too late to appeal to the good will of the Greek population, and on 26 November the Governor proclaimed a

State of Emergency. The death penalty was extended to offences other than murder, including the discharge of firearms or the placing of explosives with intent to cause injury or kill. Life imprisonment was the penalty for the possession of firearms or explosives, and provision was made in the Emergency Regulations for collective punishment, for the whipping of youths under eighteen, for deportation, and for censorship.

Meanwhile in the Troodos range, where the pine-covered mountains rise on average to over 5,000 ft (1,500 m), the Commandos, the Royal Scots, and the Gordon Highlanders combed the high terrain and hillsides for the EOKA squads that operated from the villages, monasteries, and caves in the area. Grivas himself had been hiding in a cave overlooking the village of Spilia. On 11 December a combined force of Commandos and Gordon Highlanders mounted a cordon and search operation in the area. Fortunately for Grivas his guards spotted the arrival of the British troops. Cypriot sniper fire caused the British troops to take evasive action and Grivas himself escaped through thick woods. On 15 December 1955, a terrorist group led by one Markos Drakos ambushed a jeep in the Troodos mountains killing the driver. Harding realized that he needed still more troops to comb the mountains for terrorists. In January 1956 the 1st and 3rd Battalions of the Parachute Regiment were flown out from Aldershot to hutted camps in Nicosia, where they formed the Island Reserve. The 1st Battalion, the Royal Warwickshire Regiment, also arrived a few weeks later.

The British persisted with their stern and often brutal measures to control the Greek civilian population in the towns and villages. Schools were closed and the British were portrayed as persecutors of Cypriot schoolchildren, who were powerless to influence the situation. EOKA stepped up its bombing campaign and a decision was made by the British Government that in order to resist *Enosis* Archbishop Makarios would have to be deported. On 9

March he was arrested in Nicosia and put on an aeroplane destined for the Seychelle Islands. By mid-May the British army had built up its strength to fifteen fighting units with the arrival of the Royal Horse Guards and the 1st Battalion of the King's Own Yorkshire Light Infantry. It was now possible to revert to the offensive. A big operation was planned in the Troodos mountains with the aim of flushing out for good the guerrilla groups in hiding there and, if possible, eliminating Grivas himself.

Two thousand troops took part in the operation, mostly parachute troops, marine commandos and Gordon Highlanders. They were aided by tracker dogs, helicopters, and Auster spotter aircraft. In a series of cordon operations covering 400 sq. miles (7,000 km^2) seventeen leading guerrillas and large quantities of weapons were captured. The most important result of the Troodos operation was that thousands of documents exposing EOKA's plans and the identities of its members were found, and the mountain squads were consequently broken up and no longer able to operate with impunity as they had done for so long. Grivas himself narrowly escaped capture in the early afternoon of 11 June when he and his five companions stopped in a wooded valley in the southern half of the Troodos range above Limassol to fill their water bottles and rest in the shade. The Cypriots were surprised by a patrol from the 3rd Battalion of the Parachute Regiment, with a tracker dog appearing in the bed of a stream. The six guerrillas disappeared through the trees followed by a hail of fire, leaving behind many of their belongings including Grivas's binoculars and spectacles.

The collapse of the mountain squads was not followed by a parallel decline in violence in the rest of the island. To complicate matters further, President Nasser of Egypt seized the Suez Canal at the end of July, necessitating the withdrawal of the 1st and 3rd Battalions of the Parachute Regiment and 3 Commando Brigade to take part in the Suez landings, but these troops returned to the fray in Cyprus after re-grouping following the unsuccessful campaign in Egypt in December. In early October a search operation code-named 'Sparrowhawk' was carried out in the Kyrenia mountains covering about 200 sq. miles (400 km^2). During the search the security forces found isolated caches of arms and captured six guerrillas, which included Pliotis Christofi, a leading commander with £5,000 on his head. A few days later, Evaghoras Pallikarides, another eminent guerrilla, was captured in the Paphos forest, with two donkeys loaded with a Bren gun and other equipment.

EOKA continued its campaign of terror in 1957 with conspicuous success and it was said that they learned many of their guerrilla techniques from the methods of the British Special Air Service Regiment (SAS), with which the Royal Greek Sacred Squadron had served in the campaign in the Western Desert in the Second World War. One SAS speciality was to blow up German and Italian aircraft on the ground on airfields behind the lines, a practice that was repeated with some thoroughness by EOKA on RAF airfields in Cyprus. The British Government decided to try a more conciliatory tone. Archbishop Makarios was released from the Seychelles and returned in triumph to Athens. Field Marshal Harding was replaced by a colonial servant of liberal tendencies, Sir Hugh Foot. However, the British army reached its peak strength in mid-June with the arrival of 16th Parachute Brigade from Britain followed closely by the 1st Guards Brigade, some minor units, and the Headquarters of the 3rd Infantry Division.

In 1958 the UN made strenuous efforts to solve the Cyprus issue. The degree of accord reached at the UN between the Greek, Turkish, and British representatives led to the Zurich Agreement of February 1959, providing for one state in Cyprus with a Greek President and a Turkish Vice-President. On 1 March Archbishop Makarios was permitted to return to Cyprus. On 9 March, Grivas—who had not liked the agreement—reluctantly ordered a

ceasefire. On 17 March the guerrilla leader was flown unobtrusively to Athens where he was given a hero's welcome. As a rebel commander, Grivas was remarkably successful. He tied down 40,000 British troops and killed 99 of them. He avoided capture in a small island for years on end. But in a wider sense the most Grivas achieved was to bring British colonial rule to an end a little sooner than it might otherwise have done. On 16 August 1960 the Republic of Cyprus came into being after 82 years of British rule. Today Britain maintains two sovereign base areas in Cyprus, at Dhekalia and Akrotiri, both on the south coast of the island and in all covering some 99 sq. miles (256 km^2). In addition, some installations were designated 'retained sites', including the radar station on Mt Troodos, still manned by British army or RAF crews.

Middle East: Israel, Syria, Lebanon

Nowhere has the possession of key heights been more important than the 7,992 sq. miles (20,700 km^2) of the Israeli-occupied territory in Syria's Golan Heights. In the 'Six-Day War' that broke out between Israel and Egypt from 5 to 10 June 1967, the opposing forces faced each other on the southern Sinai front, but Israel had also to face opposition from Jordan, Iraq, and Syria to the north. Between 5 and 8 June, the Golan Heights were held by six Syrian brigades with six more in reserve east of Kuneitra. Artillery fire was exchanged between the rival forces, but a UN ceasefire initiative was violated by both sides and Major General David Elazar of the Israeli Northern Command was ordered to launch a major offensive with all available units. He consequently concentrated his forces for an initial advance through the Dan-Banyas area on the northern Golan plateau, and along the foothills of the 9,232-ft (2,816-m) Mt Hermon, the highest point in Syria's mountain zone. By nightfall the Israelis had fought their way through the first line of Syrian defences guarding the approaches to the northern Golan, and three brigades were poised to break out on to the plateau early the following morning. Meanwhile, other units were forcing their way up the escarpment north of the Sea of Galilee.

The Israelis pushed through the crumbling Syrian defences on the northern Golan early in the morning, then pressed ahead across the plateau to converge on Kuneitra from the north, west, and southwest. In the meantime, Israeli troops re-deployed from the Jordan front had driven northeastward up the Yarmut valley to occupy the southern Golan and to threaten Kuneitra from the south. By dark Kuneitra was surrounded and captured by an armoured unit. The fighting was at an end. The brief three-front campaign had demonstrated the combat effectiveness of the Israeli forces over their more numerous foes. Syria lost the Golan Heights, which became 'Israeli Administered Territory', a key factor in Israel's northern defence strategy with its observation posts overlooking Lebanon, Syria, and Jordan.

In the 'October War' (Yom Kippur War or the War of Ramadan) of 6-24 October 1973, the fighting began simultaneously with a massive Egyptian air strike against Israeli artillery and command positions on the Bar Lev Line fortifications along the Suez Canal on the Sinai front, and a Syrian air strike of equal proportions against Israeli positions and installations on the Golan Heights. The Israelis were taken by surprise on both fronts. Syrian commandos, in a ground-helicopter attack, captured the fortified Israeli observation post on Mt Hermon, overlooking the Golan plateau and the Damascus plain. In spite of the mountainous terrain, tanks in great numbers were deployed by both sides. North of Kuneitra the Syrian 7th Infantry Division was repulsed by the Israeli 7th Armoured Brigade, most of the Syrian tanks being destroyed. On the other hand, the Syrian 5th Mechanized Division broke through the defences of the Israeli 188th Armoured Brigade. In two days of fighting the Israeli force was virtually destroyed. Spearheads of the 5th Mechanized Division, reinforced by the 1st

Tank Division, halted near the western escarpment of the Golan, partly because of the need to re-supply and partly because the Israeli defence was stiffening.

On 8-9 October, Israeli units counterattacked followed by a full-scale counteroffensive with three divisions, in general north of the Kuneitra-Damascus road. At this stage a number of Israeli units were airlifted to the Sinai front but an assault by the Iraqi 3rd Armoured Division, on the south side of the Israeli salient, was ambushed and repulsed. More Arab counter-attacks mounted by Jordanians and Iraqis were also repelled (16 October). The lines stabilized on the Damascus plain. On 22 October the Israelis retook Mt Hermon after two earlier attempts had failed. In the final effort, just before the ceasefire became effective, heli-borne Israeli paratroopers seized the original Syrian observation post, higher up than that of the Israelis' and the 'Golani' Infantry Brigade finally took the lost Israeli position. Save for some fighting continuing briefly on Mt Hermon, an uneasy lull came over the front. The Yom Kippur War ended with another Israeli victory over their Arab neighbours on 24 October 1973. In 1974 Syria initiated a protracted artillery and small-arms duel along the entire ceasefire line between Kuneitra and Damascus, and UN observers were sent to the Golan Heights. In 1974 Israel finally gave up all of the territory captured from Syria in October 1973, plus two small strips taken in 1967, including the town of Kuneitra. Military forces were to be limited in zones on either side of the new ceasefire line, and a narrow buffer zone was to be patrolled by units of the UNEF.

Both Syria and Lebanon have been hotbeds of intrigue and dissent since the Second World War. In this period eleven *coups d'état* have taken place in Syria. The Jebel Druze uprising (1953-4) was suppressed by the Syrian army after extensive fighting. Between 19 and 23 September 1970, Syrian troops assisted by Palestinian commandos, fought a short, undeclared war with Jordan. In 1976 Syria moved some

20,000 troops into the Lebanon, first to assist the Christian militia of that country and then later shifting its support to the Moslem factors. The Syrians were deployed in Beirut and south of the Damascus-Beirut highway, along the western slopes of Mt Hermon and in the Bekaa valley. Syrian forces remained for five years in the Lebanon.

The civil war that flared up in the Lebanon in 1975 has scarcely abated in the late 1980s. The establishment of the Palestine Liberation Organization (PLO) in Lebanon exacerbated tensions between various Moslem and Christian factions. Full-scale civil war broke out (13 April 1975). The PLO, whose objective was the destruction of Israel, used Lebanon as a staging area from which to conduct raids into Israel and to use long-range artillery and rockets to shell Israeli territory. In 1982 the Israelis were moved to launching a major offensive into Lebanon to destroy the PLO forces who were largely grouped in the southern part of the country. Israeli task forces were deployed on the left, along the coastal route into Tyre, securing bridgeheads over the Litani River and taking the Arnoun Heights. On the right, one of the task forces advanced up the Bekaa valley, at which stage the Syrians joined in the fighting in support of the PLO. The mission of the Israeli Bekaa Forces Group (BFG), about two divisions in strength, was to gain control of the Bekaa valley and the flanking mountains, the western slopes of the Anti-Lebanon mountains and Mt Hermon on the east, and the Lebanon mountains on the west. The BFG would then cut the Beirut-Damascus Highway. (The Mt Lebanon range extends almost the entire length of Lebanon, a distance of about 150 miles—240 km—with northern outliers stretching into Syria. Average heights are 7,000 ft—2,100 m—and some of the peaks are snow-capped.)

Task Force H advanced up the Bekaa valley and through the Anti-Lebanon mountains to envelop the Syrian-PLO left flank. Task Force A continued to mop up in southern Lebanon, including Sidon and the El Hilweh refugee camp where there was considerable resistance. Task Force B advanced towards the mountain town of Kfar Matta while Task Force C, reinforced by elements of Task Force A, reached the outskirts of Khalde about 3 miles (5 km) from the Beirut international airport. Task Force D mopped up in Ain Zhalta, approached Ain Dara and came to within 2 miles (3 km) of the Beirut-Damascus highway. A ceasefire was called on 11 June. In six days of fighting, the Israelis had destroyed the military forces of the PLO in Lebanon and captured enormous quantities of equipment. They had also decisively defeated the Syrians and had artillery within range of Damascus. In spite of the ceasefire, however, Israeli units continued to pursue PLO groups surviving in the Lebanon.

Between 4 and 25 September, civil war broke out in the Chouf mountains of Lebanon. As the Israelis were completing their withdrawal, Phalangist troops and the Lebanese army began to move into the areas evacuated. The local Druze Moslem militia began immediately to attack both Phalangist and Lebanese army forces. The Druze attacked major strongholds at Aley (Alieh) 10 miles (16 km) east of Beirut and Bhamdun south of the Beirut-Damascus highway. In subsequent fighting the Druze militiamen surrounded Deir al Qamar, and attacked Suk al Gharb, which directly overlooked the President's palace. A Druze armoured assault was turned back from Suk al Gharb with the help of US naval gunfire support from offshore. The warring Lebanese factions agreed to a ceasefire arranged by a Saudi mediator.

Aden: the Radfan

The British Crown Colony of Aden and the Protectorate extended over the tribal territories had enjoyed a peaceful existence until President Abdul Nasser of Egypt (after the débâcle of the Anglo-French Suez campaign, and supported by the USSR) spearheaded the campaign against the British presence in South

Arabia. Furthermore, in the early 1960s relations with Yemen deteriorated steadily. In June of that year the National Liberation Front was formed in the Yemen to carry the revolutionary struggle into Aden. It was only a matter of time before serious violence erupted. The frontier with Yemen was closed and the Federal Government of Aden declared a State of Emergency throughout South Arabia. It was now

The campaign of subversion that commenced in 1963 in the British Crown Colony of Aden and the Protectorate was prosecuted mainly amongst the tribes of the hinterland. British and Federal Regular Army (FRA) forces were despatched to subdue the most troublesome of these tribesmen in the rugged mountain terrain of the Radfan, in actions that were reminiscent of the campaigns on the North-West Frontier of India. The soldiers of the British Raj were not equipped, however, with such modern weapons as the helicopter, and these two photographs demonstrate how useful these modern workhorses of the Army could be in landing supplies, including a 105-mm gun, on Radfan mountain-top positions. The helicopter seen in both photographs is a Westland Wessex of the Royal Air Force.

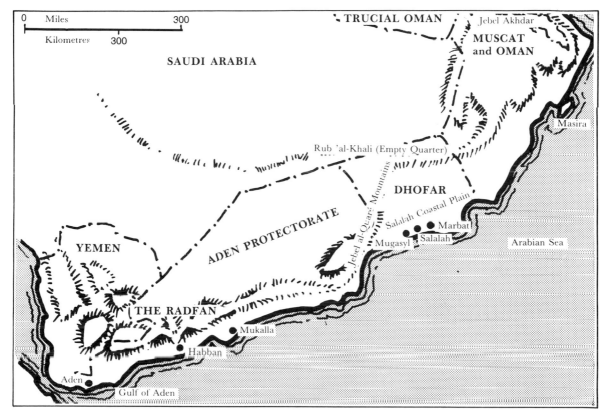

Fighting the rebels: The British army since 1945 has played a major role in the 'winding down' of the empire and containing insurgents in many lands. This map illustrates the locations of a few of the 'small wars' of the period, namely in the Aden Protectorate, the Dhofar Region, and in Muscat and Oman. The Aden conflict saw the Parachute Regiment, the Royal Marines and the SAS engaged in some tough fighting in the mountainous Radfan area, and the earlier operations in Muscat and Oman are remembered especially for the epic scaling of the Jebel Akhdar by a small SAS force, newly arrived in the country to assist the Sultan's armed forces in their fight against Communist guerrillas.

clear that an insurgency campaign was being waged against the federation.

The campaign of subversion that commenced in 1963 was mainly prosecuted among the tribes of the hinterland, in particular the tribesmen of the Radfan who were offered arms, cash, and promises by Yemeni and Egyptian agents to close the main road from Aden to the frontier town of Dhala. The tribesmen of the Radfan inhabited a land of mountains and defiles lying to the east of the Dhala road— much of which had never been visited by a white man. The 'Red Wolves of the Radfan' were natural warriors and made excellent guerrillas. They were more than glad to oblige their

Arab cousins as, in 1961, the British had curbed the tribesmen's practice of collecting 'tolls' from travellers and merchants on the Dhala road. It has been estimated that among perhaps 40,000 Radfan peoples some 7,500 in all were fighting men.

The first incursion into the Radfan was mounted by three battalions of the Federal Regular Army (FRA), formerly the Aden Protectorate Levies, supported by a troop of Centurion tanks manned by the 16th/5th Queen's Royal Lancers, a battery of 105-mm pack howitzers of the 3rd Royal Horse Artillery, and a troop of Royal Engineers. The operation to subdue the Radfan was code-named 'Nutcracker' and began on 4 January 1964. It was commanded by Brigadier J.D. Lunt who was commanding the FRA in Aden at the time. The mission to 'show the flag' was not a conspicuous success and resulted in Yemeni involvement to the extent of their MiGs and helicopters attacking frontier towns and villages. Despite 'Nutcracker', attacks on the Dhala road intensified and it was decided to launch a much bigger operation to crush the insurgency—this time involving British troops.

A task force was formed from the Aden garrison. This was commanded by Brigadier Louis Hargroves and on 26 April it consisted of Joint Force Headquarters, 45 Royal Marine Commando, 1st Battalion the East Anglian Regiment, B Company 3rd Battalion the Parachute Regiment, (from Bahrain), A Squadron SAS, J Battery Royal Horse Artillery (RHA), A Squadron 4th Royal Tank Regiment (RTR), and two FRA battalions. As air support there were two Hunter fighter squadrons, a small squadron of Shackleton bombers, four (later six) Belvedere helicopters, a Twin Pioneer Transport Squadron, and some Scout helicopters and a Beaver spotter aircraft of 653 Squadron Army Air Corps.

On 29 April the operation began when 3 Troop of 22nd SAS commanded by Captain Robin Edwards landed by helicopter in the Radfan to mark a dropping zone (DZ) for a drop by the parachute company on Cap Badge. After an all-night march 3 Troop lay up in a sangar and came under fire from forty to fifty tribesmen. The patrol called for air support that was immediately provided by Hunters of 43 and 208 Squadrons, RAF. The SAS men calculated that they and the Hunters killed twenty to thirty of the enemy during the day. As night fell, however, the Hunters could no longer provide support, and a determined attack by about ninety tribesmen was mounted on the ten SAS men. Trooper Warburton, the radio operator, was hit and died instantly. Captain Edwards led a breakout but he was killed by a burst of automatic fire. The remainder of the patrol reached

their base just after daybreak on 1 May. This patrol received much publicity when it was announced that the bodies of Edwards and Warburton had been decapitated and their heads exhibited on stakes in Taiz.

The various British units set about their operational tasks. The two companies of 45 Commando reached the summit of Cap Badge after a brilliant night move along the ridge leading to the feature from the southwest. The plan provided for B Company 3rd Parachute Battalion to approach Cap Badge via the low ground to the south of the mountain and meet up with the commandos on Cap Badge. The parachute troops lost two men in a firefight but reached the top of the mountain after 30 gruelling hours in action. The general objectives were to seize the dominating positions from which to observe and deploy against the tribesmen. During the ensuing days operations in the fertile areas continued. The Rabwa Pass was occupied and the East Anglians were introduced into the Wadi Taym. In order to maintain the pace of operations it was decided that more troops would be required. Battalion Headquarters of 3rd Parachute Battalion was therefore moved from Bahrain to join Brigadier Hargroves' force, who were later joined by the King's Own Scottish Borderers arriving from the UK.

Another mountain climb was performed by a company of 3rd Parachute Battalion when the men advanced up on to the Bakri ridge and southeast along it down the Al Dahira ridge, where the anti-tank platoon dislodged twelve guerrillas from the fortified village of Arzuqm. By 24 May, after several skirmishes, the parachute troops were in firm control of the length of the Bakri ridge. On 26 May the Wadi Dhubsan was taken by 45 Commando, some men having to descend part of the way on ropes into the wadi floor. Here the commandos encountered some thirty to fifty enemy, armed with automatic weapons as well as rifles, and a sharp battle took place until the tribesmen withdrew.

The final phase of the Radfan operation

started on 30 May. The aim was to capture the Jebel Huriyah, the highest peak. It was almost certain that the rebels would defend this feature as its possession was known to be a matter of prestige to them. The task of taking the Jebel Huriyah was given to the 1st East Anglians supported by an FRA battalion and a squadron of tanks. The climb was achieved without serious mishap but the assault force came under fire on the ridge from about fifty guerrillas, who stood their ground in spite of a pounding from Hunter aircraft and from artillery below. On 8 June the East Anglians established themselves on the peak of the Jebel Huriyah and saw the lights of Aden 50 miles (80 km) away. This effectively was the end of operations in the mountainous Radfan area but the fighting was to continue in the streets and environs of Aden for several long years.

Muscat and Oman

The British involvement in Muscat and Oman (1957-9) might have been taken from a story book by Rudyard Kipling. The imperial connection with Muscat dates back to the early days of the East India Company in the seventeenth century. By a treaty of 1852, Britain recognized the independence of the Sultan though, under subsequent agreements, he was able to call on British help in time of trouble. In 1952 troops from Saudi Arabia occupied the strategic oasis of Buraimi—part of which belonged to the Sheikh of Abu Dhabi, a Trucial State, and part to the Sultan of Muscat. The British Government responded by authorizing the formation of the Trucial Oman Scouts (TOS), a force recruited in the Trucial Oman States and lead by British officers and NCOs that was immediately employed to repel the Saudis. However, Saudi influence had also spread to the Oman, and in 1955 the Muscat and Oman Field Force was sent to occupy Nizwa, Ibri, and other main centres in Oman. At this juncture, the Beni Riyam tribe (which inhabited the villages in the Jebel Akhdar) resorted to rebellion.

The Jebel Akhdar is one of the greatest natural fortresses in the world, a sheer limestone massif 40 to 50 miles (65 to 80 km) in length, and 20 miles (30 km) wide, with peaks rising to nearly 10,000 ft (3,000 m). At ground level the mountainous terrain appears to be completely barren, but the Jebel plateau (10 miles—16 km—wide) is fertile ground where people have lived for centuries. Throughout Arabia the Jebel was believed to be impregnable, for it had never been taken by invaders. In the tenth century the Persians are reputed to have lost 9,000 men in an unsuccessful assault. The few routes that led into the Jebel were difficult to follow and easy for a defender to dominate. The three main villages on the Jebel Akhdar were Sharaijah, Saiq and Habib.

The Sultan's Armed Forces (SAF) and a new commander, Colonel David Smiley, was seconded by the Foreign Office from the British army. Smiley was certain that the only way to subdue the tribesmen was to send a force up the hard way by climbing the sheer rock of the Jebel Akhdar. As it happened the Special Air Service (SAS) had just completed a seven-year tour of duty fighting terrorists in the Malayan jungle, and D Squadron (Major John Watts) was sent in mid-November 1958 to join Smiley's force in the Oman. D Squadron was organized in four troops or patrols of about sixteen men each, and within weeks were in action against the tribesmen in the village of Tanuf at the base of the Jebel Akhdar. Later in December an SAS troop, along with 20 Life Guardsmen, managed to establish itself on top of the Jebel some 2,000 yd (1,800 m) from the principal rebel strongpoint, Aquabat al Dhafar. The ascent was all the more remarkable for the fact that the guardsmen carried up nine .5-in Browning machine-guns, removed from the turrets of their scout cars. Several attacks were mounted on the tribesmen but Smiley decided he needed another SAS squadron before the rebels would be defeated.

On 1 January, Lieutenant-Colonel Anthony Deane-Drummond, Commanding

Officer of 22nd SAS, arrived in Muscat and twelve days later A Squadron (Major John Cooper) flew in from Malaya. It was decided that on the next full moon, which was on the night of 25-6 January, a direct assault should be made on the Jebel by the shortest possible route. Due to low cloud over the Jebel the operation was postponed for 24 hours. Then at 21:00 on the evening of 26 January both A and D Squadrons of 22nd SAS, supported by the dismounted Life Guards, started the assault on the Jebel. Also involved in the operation were some tribal irregulars led by British officers. Some of these were to provide support to the SAS squadrons, but the larger part, accompanied by a platoon of the Muscat Regiment were to attempt to reach the top of the Jebel from the Awabi area to the north.

The night air was a lot colder than the SAS had been used to in Malaya. The climb commenced but about a third of the way up, a sniper's bullet hit and exploded a grenade in an SAS trooper's rucksack. He and the two men behind him were seriously wounded. Although they were evacuated by helicopter as quickly as possible, two of the three men died the next day from their wounds. Soon after this unfortunate incident the leading SAS troopers came under .5-in Browning fire but one of the men stalked the enemy gunners and killed them with a well-placed grenade. Both SAS squadrons were on top of the Jebel shortly after dawn when RAF Valettas from Bahrain dropped 30,000 lbs (13,500 kg) of equipment, ammunition, food, and water to the waiting troops. The supply drop gave the tribesmen the impression that parachutists were descending and the opposition melted away without a fight. The three main villages were entered unopposed.

The rebels lay low for some six months after being dislodged from the Jebel Akhdar, but by the summer of 1959 they were again mining the roads. The SAS left for England in March, and the last of the Life Guards in May for Aden. After the ascent of the Jebel Akhdar, Cairo Radio reported that 120,000 men had been employed in the attack and Moscow embellished the story still more, claiming that 13,000 paratroopers had been dropped. In fact, barely 1,000 troops of which only 250 were British had smashed the myth of the Jebel Akhdar's impregnability.

The Sultan's Armed Forces still patrol Muscat and Oman today from the Wadi Jizzi in the north to Masira in the south. They still maintain an uneasy peace in a country that remains vital to western interests. The threat today no longer comes from Saudi Arabia, with which the present Sultan maintains cordial relations, but from the Communist regime in the South Yemen Republic, formerly the British protectorate of Aden.

Dhofar region

The harsh regime of Sultan Sa'ib bin Taimur, the thirteenth hereditary monarch of Oman, was particularly oppressive in the Dhofar region. In 1970 there were no schools in Dhofar and only one road inland from the coastal plain. There were no hospitals, running water, or electricity. Lying between the South Yemen Republic and Oman on the Arabian Sea, the region's northern boundary has never been defined, but generally included in the territory is the Wadi Mugshin, located about 150 miles (250 km) inland. To the northeast of Dhofar is a large desert of stony plains and sand dunes that contribute to the region's isolation from northern Oman. The Salalah coastal plain—about 40 miles (65 km) long and ranging from 1 to 6 miles (1.5 to 10 km) wide and facing the Arabian Sea—is considered one of the most beautiful in Arabia. About 10 miles (16 km) inland the rugged Jebel al-Qarā mountains rise to heights of between 3,000 and 4,000 feet (900 and 1,200 m). Further north the Jebel al-Qarā give way to a pebbly desert, beyond which lies the Rub'al-Khali (the Empty Quarter) of Saudi Arabia.

In 1965 the mountain tribesmen of Dhofar rose in revolt against the Sultan. Across the border in the Eastern Aden Protectorate and further west in Aden and the Radfan, the British had been engaged in a bitter struggle with Arab Nationalists since 1963. It was inevitable that the struggle should spread. At first the rebellion was little more than a nuisance: the Dhofari tribesmen engaged in a sporadic campaign of mine-laying and ambush. However, the situation changed when the British left neighbouring Aden in 1967. The new Communist Government in what was now the People's Democratic Republic of Yemen (PDRY) provided a secure sanctuary and source of supply for the rebels. Moreover, the Dhofari tribesmen's ethnic links were with the people of South Yemen. Many Dhofaris were trained in the PDRY and then returned to their homeland armed with Soviet weaponry to win over others. The mountains of Dhofar provided an ideal situation for a guerrilla uprising. The monsoon brings low cloud and rain to the Jebel between June and September. However, because of the scorching sun for the rest of the year, the luxurious growth of grass resulting from the monsoon only lasts for a further two to four months. The lower slopes of the hills are precipitous making access to the Jebel from the plain difficult in the extreme. Caves and gullies abound. This belt of tropical vegetation and limestone caves varies between 1 and 10 miles (1.5 and 16 km) in depth.

In 1970 an SAS advisory team was sent to Dhofar and the SAS presence was shortly built up to squadron strength. The SAF was reinforced by troops from Jordan and Iran but it was the SAS that made most impact in the war against the guerrillas. The most audacious attack in the war (which lasted until 1976) by the Dhofar Liberation Front (DLF) was on the small garrison at Marbat, which lies only a mile or so from the Jebel. Some 65 men were stationed in the compound with a ten-man SAS advisory team on strength. On 18 July 1972, about 250 tribesmen rushed the garrison. Heavily outgunned the defenders did have a 25-pounder gun, which was not all that useful for

close-quarter fighting. After breaching the wire defences, the guerrillas began inflicting casualties but the tide began to turn when the attackers were subjected to air attack. The arrival of the SAS reinforcements was perhaps the greatest stroke of luck of all. G Squadron had already been scheduled to fly to Marbat before the attack, so coincidentally they were equipped for the fight. After a fight lasting a few hours, the guerrillas fled, after sustaining thirty fatal casualties. The hero of the day was Captain Michael Kealy, the SAS advisory team's commander, who received the Distinguished Service Order (DSO) for his bravery.

In March 1974 a line of mines and barbed wire known as the 'Hornbeam Line' was built inland for 48 miles (53 km) from the coast and some 60 miles (90 km) from the border with South Yemen, an outstanding feat of engineering by Royal Engineers and some Jordanian engineers working for an entire year under the protection of an Omani battalion. The effect of the line was to restrict supplies from reaching the guerrillas in the central and eastern areas of Dhofar. Operations were then accelerated in the Jebel north and northeast of Salalah so that by May 1975 the rebels had been pushed back to a narrow strip adjacent to the South Yemen border. Although up to four companies of PDRY regulars had been operating inside Dhofar in support of the rebels up to mid-1974, their enthusiasm for fighting other people's battles had by October 1975 been exhausted.

In April 1972 an SAF battalion captured the Sarfait air base after a daring heli-borne operation. The base was situated on a tactically-important mountain-top only 5 miles (8 km) from the border. Although the SAF unit held the mountain they were in fact unable to dominate the supply route in dead ground below. They were not strong enough to break out and could not be reinforced because the Sultan's Air Force had only 12 helicopters and it was all they could do to re-supply the troops already on the position. Even water had to be ferried in. Withdrawal would have been a blow to the prestige of the SAF, so the men stayed put for three-and-a-half years until their breakout in October 1975 finally won the war.

The Dhofar war was a unique victory for the forces of counter-insurgency. The Dhofar Brigade, which was formed to assist the Sultan's Armed Forces, consisted of the Imperial Iranian Task Force; 5 battalions (2 Omani, 2 Baluch with about 12 British officers each, plus 3 independent companies); 3 engineer squadrons; an SAS squadron; and 24 Saladin armoured cars, with artillery and signals support. The SAF was officered half by British officers on secondment from the British army and half by contract officers, mostly British but some from other Commonwealth countries. The contribution by the Royal Engineers was vitally important but that of the SAS and their 'hearts and minds' campaign winning over the people of Dhofar was perhaps the most vital of all. It is surprising how few people know about the part played by British soldiers in securing peace and prosperity for this strategically important Arab state.

Cuban guerrillas

The purest and most efficient form of guerilla warfare inspired by Marxism was the revolution in Cuba, 1958-9. Having gained its independence from the USA in 1902, it is said that Cuba never had an honest president, and Fulgencio Batista (who reclaimed his presidential throne after a military coup against the reigning incumbent in 1952) was no exception. Batista was in turn overthrown in the revolution of 1959, by the young Communist lawyer, Fidel Castro. On 26 July 1953, Castro had led a desperate and unsuccessful attack on the Santiago army barracks, intending to begin the overthrow of Batista. The rebel was sent to prison for his pains. After being released by amnesty in 1955 he went to Mexico and began organizing an invading force of Cuban exiles. On 2 December 1956, Castro landed with 81 revolutionaries on the southern shore of Oriente province, 600 miles (950 km) from Havana. They were met by overwhelming Batista forces and only a dozen escaped capture or slaughter.

Castro's purpose in landing in Oriente was to reach the sanctuary of the Sierra Maestra mountains, which present the most rugged relief of Cuba, and which stretch a distance of 150 miles (240 km) from Cape Cruz to Guantanamo. The range rises steeply and majestically to heights of more than 6,578 ft (2,006 m); the southern slopes are almost uninhabited, but the northern slopes are less rugged, and the valleys are used for growing coffee. Fidel Castro was amongst the survivors and, along with his brother Raul and Ernesto 'Che' Guevara (an Argentine doctor), they made their way into the Sierra Maestra, finding their lairs in areas of sheer cliffs and impenetrable hills overgrown with vines and forest. Castro got word of his survival to a small underground of supporters, and in time weapons and food began to reach him from Cuba and from abroad.

As a prudent guerrilla in the mountains, Castro did not set up a permanent base. As he told an American journalist in 1959, 'We have no encampment except for the night. No one ever knows where we are or where we are going. The physical exertion is good and we train by marching and fighting'. Long, straggling lines of men were to be seen walking over trails cut into the gullies of the Sierra Maestra, at the height of day the sun beating down on the rocky peaks. In appearance Castro's army was the essence of a rabble in arms. They wore blue jeans, work-shirts, khaki pants, cheap green trousers, Truman shirts, and Eisenhower jackets. Most were in semi-military dress if only for a forage cap, but no two were uniformed alike except that somewhere on each man was the '26th of July' emblem, so-named after the abortive July 1953 attack.

Their weapons were corroding cowplunkers, .22 target rifles, ancient double-barrel shotguns, Garands, Springfields, 1892 Spanish Mausers, and a few .30-calibre machine-guns. They wore sidearms—cheap, mail-order nickel-plated revolvers beginning to rust, and some business-like automatics. On their backs they carried heavy packs—mostly produce sacks stuffed with a few clothes, and supplies of ammunition. And their waists were girdled with bayonets, hunting knives, and frayed ammunition belts to which they tied two or three homemade hand grenades or Molotov cocktails made of beer bottles and cloth wicks. Castro's men did not have a single field radio, semaphore, walkie-talkie, field phone, or anything resembling a modern communications device. All communication was by runner. Furthermore, Castro had no field company, no typewriter, no office.

Concealment was no problem on the jungled slopes of the Sierra Maestra. The rebels could even afford to be careless about the matter, so remote were their training grounds to topple the Batista Government. At the end of a march the encampment was often established in the most informal manner, each person hanging their hammock where they pleased and guards were posted with apparent carelessness. The guerrillas were off before daybreak the following day and marched for at least two hours from the bivouac location before eating breakfast, which may have consisted of dried shredded codfish, or bananas, or boiled yucca root, or racoon, or boa constrictor. About midday a can of condensed milk would be passed round and each person would take a swig, or eat a slice of a bar of sweetened guava candy. At night there may be rice, chickpeas, or malanga root (the black bread of Fidel's revolutionaries) with some meat, all cooked in ten-gallon buckets. The mountaineers of the Sierra Maestra were made of iron. They would walk all day up and down the hills in the rain, ford streams, clamber over boulders, and then run for their lives if they had to do so.

Castro's ramshackle war machine belied the intellectual strength of its commanders. Che Guevara, the son of an Argentinian architect, shortly after receiving his medical degree enlisted in the cause of the oppressed of Latin America. He fought in Guatemala, served with distinction under Castro in Cuba, and died in Bolivia in 1967 at the age of 39. His *Guerrilla Warfare* handbook was aimed principally at training the 'soldiers of liberation', dedicated to freeing and educating townspeople in the Communist cause. The Sierra Maestra provided the depot and springboard for the guerrilla attacks on the populated areas in the lowlands. The guerrillas, however, had to be prepared to face attacks in the mountains. The number of people in a guerrilla band did not ideally exceed ten to fifteen. A force of this size could hide anywhere and at the same time help each other in putting up a powerful resistance to the enemy. Four or five would perhaps be too small a number, but when the number exceeded ten the possibility that the enemy would discover them in their camp or on the march was much greater. Also, the velocity of the guerrilla band on the march was equal to the velocity of its slowest member.

The life of guerrilla fighters carrying their houses on their backs was the long hike. On the wooded slopes of the mountains, they might be under constant harassment by the enemy. The guerrilla band moved during the daylight hours, without eating, in order to change its position. When night arrived, camp was set up in a clearing near a water supply according to a routine, each group assembling in order to eat together. At dusk the fires were lit with whatever materials were to hand. When sleeping in hammocks, a waterproof nylon sheet served as cover against the rain. The guerrilla's rucksack, weapon, and ammunition was placed ready to hand beneath the hammock. Whilst asleep boots were never removed. The mountains were cold at night time and a blanket was indispensable. Thus, the guerrilla fighter would live for days without approaching any inhabited place, avoiding all contact that had not previously been arranged, staying in the wildest zones, knowing hunger, at times thirst, cold, and heat—sweating during the continuous marches and letting the sweat dry on the body without the possibility of any regular cleanliness.

To care for the rifle, special greases were necessary, and these had to be carefully administered—sewing-machine oil was very good if there was no special oil available. Also needed were cloths that would serve for cleaning the arms frequently and a rod for cleaning the gun inside. The ammunition belt could be of the commercial type or homemade, according to the circumstances, but it had to be so made that not a single bullet was lost. Ammunition was the basis of the fight, without which everything else would be in vain: it had to be cared for like gold. In self-care a canteen or bottle of water was essential.

Among medicines, those of general use were carried, for example: penicillin or some other type of antibiotic, preferably the types taken orally, carefully closed; medicines for lowering fever, such as aspirin; and others adapted to treating the endemic diseases of the area. There may have been tablets against malaria, sulphur for diarrhoea, and medicines against parasites of all types.

When trekking across mountains the golden rule is to wind your way to the top to cross each summit and not to be tempted to descend through the lines of contours to find an easy route across a valley bed. Bivouac positions were chosen on ground as high as possible, dominating a wide area by day and difficult to approach by night. If the plan was to stay for several days, it was worth while to construct defences that would permit a sustained fire in case of an attack. These defences could be obliterated when the guerrilla band moved on, or they could be left if circumstances no longer made it necessary to hide the guerrillas' path. If permanent camps were to be established, the defences were improved constantly. The only heavy arm effective in the mountains was the mortar. As protection against mortar shells, shelter roofs were reinforced with materials from the region, such as wood, and rocks, etc.

Che Guevara's rules for guerrilla conduct and fighting efficiency were many and though seemingly complex were simple in essence. They covered the general principles of guerrilla warfare, the guerrilla band, and the organization of the guerrilla front. The *modus operandi* was strongly motivated by the promotion of the Communist cause and the defeat of President Batista's Government in Cuba. Fidel Castro's successful guerrilla campaign mounted from the Sierra Maestra mountains of Oriente province gained increasing popular support and in October 1958, encouraged both by his military success and his effective propaganda, he moved his revolutionaries out of the mountains. On 1 January 1959, Batista fled the country and Castro's forces seized Havana seven days later. Fidel Castro was proclaimed President of Cuba and he set in motion the organization of a Communist state.

The Long March

Guevara's little handbook was roundly based on a similar work written in the 1930s by the great Chinese Communist leader, Mao Tse Tung. On 16 October 1934, Mao led about 100,000 Chinese Communist men and women on one of the most extraordinary marches in human history. Abandoning their base (as large as Belgium) in the south-central province of Kiangsi, they burst through the stranglehold of their enemy, Chiang Kai-shek's Nationalist or Kuomintang forces, and began a trek on foot that was to last for a whole year and take them 6,000 circuitous miles (10,000 km) to the other end of China. The Long March led the Communists through eleven provinces, over raging rivers and snow-capped mountain ranges, through swamps and forests. They had to fight against Nationalist armies as well as the troops of provincial warlords, local bandits, and hostile tribesmen. As Mao's men disappeared from view in the impenetrable interior of western China, abutting on Tibet, many observers assumed that Chiang Kai-shek had won his civil war and that Communism was decisively beaten in China—but the Communists sought

In 1934, the Communist leader, Mao Tse Tung, led an army of guerrillas, 100,000 strong, on a 6,000-mile (10,000 km) trek across China to evade Chiang Kai-shek's Nationalist forces and to set up a base in the safety of the mountains. 'The Long March', which took a whole year, was the supreme test of human endurance unparalleled in the history of warfare.

a sanctuary for their forces' organization for the struggle for power that was to take place in the coming years.

The worst obstacle the Long Marchers had to face on their journey to Shensi province (in the shadow of the Great Wall of northern China) was the Great Snow Mountain range, which separated, at a latter stage of the march, Mao's army from the Communist Fourth Front Army under Chang Kuo-tao and Hsu Hsiang-chien less than 100 miles (160 km) away in northeastern Szechuan. But it took seven weeks before the union could be accomplished. Seven distinct ranges of high mountain had to be negotiated, of which the Great Snow Mountain—Chianchinshan—was only the first. Paotung Kang Mountain, the Chung Lai range, the Dream Pen Mountain and the Big Drum Mountain also lay ahead.

There was a preliminary scuffle with Tibetan warriors before the ascent of the Great Snow Mountain began. The Red Army had given ten days' preparation for surmounting the glaciers and snow. Every person had to carry enough food and fuel to last ten days, and go as warmly clothed as possible. They were never to march for more than six or seven hours a day. They had to be ready to build shelters and to use white camouflage when necessary. Rivers would have to be crossed with captured boats, or else the men and women would have to be prepared to build their own of wood or leather. The officers inspected their people closely, looking at their shoes, lifting packs to test the weight, and inquiring into their health. Medical units were told to march in the rear and care for the old, the exhausted, and the sick who fell behind.

Chianchinshan was blanketed in eternal snow and its chasms were deep and silent. No paths existed for the Long Marchers who, the higher they climbed, the more they were greeted by heavy fog, wind, and rain. Men and animals staggered and fell into chasms and disappeared forever.

259

As the columns descended into the valleys they found no sign of habitation. The troops advanced like dragons spiralling upwards, the summit of the Great Snow Mountain glittering above them. Those who were fortunate to travel astride mules found their situation precarious at the higher altitudes and preferred to dismount and hang on to the animals' tails, as they climbed. Not all the hazards were geographical and natural phenomena: the Long Marchers were harried by hostile tribesmen and Nationalist aircraft that bombed and machine-gunned the columns.

The Red Army ascended to 16,000 ft (4,900 m) on the Great Snow Mountain, and from the crest its soldiers could gaze through the rarefied air, over a sea of snow peaks in far-off Tibet. It was June, but many of the poorly-clad, thin-blooded southerners in the ranks, unused to high altitudes, died of exposure. Once across the seven high mountain ranges, and junction with the Fourth Front Army, Mao's forces descended into 'The Grass Lands', a vast and trackless swamp stretching for hundreds of miles over the high Chinese-Tibetan borderland.

On emerging from 'The Grass Lands', the depleted Red Army encountered one final bottleneck through which it had to pass before it could spill into the soft provinces of northern China, one last trap on which Chiang Kai-shek could possibly count to destroy his most obstinate enemy. This was the only pass leading across the Min mountains between the headwaters of the Min and the Pailung Rivers. At the Latzu Pass—Latzukou—the only passable road led between vertical cliffs along which the Nationalists had constructed bunkers and trenches and installed guns. The only entrance to the narrow defile was a single, plank bridge over the waist-high river that ran through it. The Communists outflanked the Kuomintang division guarding the pass by climbing the sheer cliffs in the surrounding area.

After the Latzu Pass, the Long Marchers crossed through the Lungshi basin and the Liupan mountains, the crossing of which (though not without difficulty) was nothing compared to the Great Snow Mountain range. Towards the end of October 1935 Mao's army approached the town of Wuchichen on the upper reaches of the Lo River, inside the Red-occupied northern Shensi province. The epic trek across China was over. Mt Liupan, where the Communists had encountered opposition for the last time, had been the last battleground. Mao Tse Tung himself commemorated the battle in which Mt Liupan was captured with a poem, which included the following lines.

> If we do not reach
> the Great Wall we are not true men.

However, the Long Marchers did reach the Great Wall, although it would take fourteen years and a world war before Mao seized power in China.

CHAPTER 21
THE HIGHLANDS OF VIETNAM

The Central Highlands of Vietnam were inhabited by some 300 primitive, nomadic tribes known collectively as the Montagnards (Mountain People), a name given to these diminutive, fleet-footed, hardy peoples by the French during their tenure of their southeast Asian empire, which effectively commenced towards the end of the last century. The Montagnards, principally the Rhade and Jarai tribes, loyally served their French masters in the First Indo-China War (1946–54), and their devotion to the 'round-eyed' white man continued in the ensuing years with the American involvement in the Vietnam conflict. The origins of the Montagnards in Vietnam dated back over the centuries, and these warriors hated the Vietnamese inhabitants of the lowlands, of both North and South, whom the 'Yards'—to use their American nickname—regarded as alien intruders in their homeland.

A Special Forces advisor (left) gives a last minute briefing to his Montagnard strike force. The Montagnards, or 'mountain people', so-called by the French colonials in Indo China, were descended from nomadic tribesmen who had roamed the Highlands for centuries. The US Special Forces, the 'Green Berets', settled many communities of Montagnards in Highland villages, which were fortified and from which groups were mobilized to go further afield to combat the Viet Cong guerrillas.

The lowland peoples of North and South Vietnam, the former of Chinese and the latter of Melanesian ethnic stock, had also lived in the country for many centuries, and regarded the Montagnards as 'moi'—'savages', the mountain tribes having, however, a just claim to being a displaced, nomadic horde. In the 'inter-war' years from 1954 to 1965, the Montagnards constantly harassed South Vietnamese government officials, including the army and police, which resulted in their primitive cross-bows and spears being impounded. The Montagnards roamed the mountains and hills, clearing the bush with their machetes to grow crops and build temporary homes. After a year or two the group would move on to seek fresh pastures. The Montagnards raised large families, in which the mother was the dominant factor. Religious beliefs were animistic and their priest and medical practitioner was the local witch doctor.

Several years before the 1965 arrival of American combat forces in South Vietnam, the US Special Forces in the pre-conflict, 'advisory years' developed the concept of settling the Montagnards in permanent villages where the Green Beret A-teams organized thriving communities based on soundly-cultivated farm plots and rice paddies, medical centres, and instruction on essential trade skills. The Special Forces' political-cum-military motives were the establishment of fortified villages that, armed with militiamen drawn from male youths and very old men of the community, would defend against Viet Cong attack. The 'Civilian Irregular Defense Group' (CIDG), as the programme was called, was quickly developed to send fighting patrols recruited from young and middle-aged, able-bodied men into the jungle. The CIDG scheme proved to be a great success. The Green Berets relied mainly on the Rhade tribe to form their defended communities, and many heroic actions took place in these mountain lairs, both before and during the Vietnam War against the Viet Cong guerrillas and even the North Vietnam army regulars. As the war got underway, the military side of the CIDG programme took on a new importance with the forming of the Mobile Strike 'Mike' Forces, which were parachute-trained and capable of being dropped or air-landed in helicopters on instant notice into the middle of a battle taking place anywhere in the South Vietnam corps zones.

The Vietnam War saw the introduction of the new era of airmobility, made possible by the advances in the late 1950s in helicopter technology. The US army created for Vietnam its own airmobile division, tested it in the USA, and concluded that, in terms of ground tactics, airmobility was here to stay. On 28 July 1965,

A Montagnard strike force supervised by US Special Forces personnel files past a typical Highland dwelling place.

A Montagnard strike force patrols a jungle path.

nearly 20,000 men of the 1st US Cavalry Division were assigned to Vietnam. The division set sail from US ports on the aircraft carrier, USS *Boxer*, three military sea transportation ships, six troop carriers, and seven cargo ships. Their cargoes included Huey and Chinook helicopters. On arrival in Vietnam, the Air Cavalry was posted to An Khe, situated between the coastal town of Qui Nhon and Pleiku on the 100-mile (160-km) eastwest stretch of road called Route 19, and this was to be the Air Cavalry's highlands base in the heart of Viet Cong territory. An Khe itself is a tiny village 2 miles (3 km) off the main highway, and here the advance party commenced clearing the surrounding countryside for what was to be the world's largest helipad—the take-off and landing platform of the new heli-borne assault troops, who were to wage war against the Viet Cong guerrillas in highland and lowland areas for eight years.

In the context of mountain warfare, the helicopter replaced not only the mule but also the *telerifica*—the Alpine cable cars of the Italian front in the First World War—and the climber's rope and tackle. Helicopter transport aircraft (slicks) could move men swiftly to mountain plateaux and passes landing them on firm ground at the highest altitudes. Some techniques of the mountain climber remained, for example, rappelling, the practice of lowering men from helicopters by the use of ropes for commando missions and medical attention in the field. The heavy-duty cargo-carrying helicopters had an important contribution to make in lifting artillery and their crews, ammunition, and other supplies, to lofty positions in the mountains where the guns were placed in temporary fire bases dominating lines of communication in the valleys below. Once the assignment had been completed the guns could be lifted at short notice to another mountain-top position, artillery fire directed from small spotter aircraft playing a big part in the war in the Central Highlands.

The workhorse of the US and South Vietnamese airmobile units was the Bell UH-1 Iroquois, a general-purpose helicopter used in the attack role as a gunship ('guns') and as a troop transport ('slick'). Both UH-1Bs and IDs had seen action in Vietnam by mid-October 1965 when the Cavalry Division fought its first major battle. The North Vietnamese Army (NVA) had

A Montagnard strike team with its 'Green Beret' NCO returns to its Civilian Irregular Defense Group (CIDG) camp. These men are Rhade tribesmen serving under the guidance of the US Special Forces in the Highlands in the Vietnam War.

begun a major operation in the Central Highlands, and there was every reason to believe its objective was to cut South Vietnam in half. The Communist regulars opened their campaign with an attack on the Pleime Special Forces Camp sited 25 miles (40 km) southwest of Pleiku. The 'Air Cav' was directed to seek out and destroy the enemy force consisting of the 32nd, 33rd, and 66th North Vietnamese Army Regiments, and this began the month-long campaign known as the Battle of Ia Drang Valley. The Ia Drang battle actually lasted 35 days and on 26 November 1965, the 1st Cavalry Division had completed its mission of pursuit and destruction in the highland territory. In those 35 days, aircraft delivered 5,080 tons of cargo from main bases into the hands of troops in the field. In addition they transported 8,216 tons into Pleiku and other field depots. Whole infantry battalions and artillery batteries were moved by air, and the Huey 'Dust-Off' helicopters registered a major success in evacuating the wounded.

If the Huey was the cavalry horse and endowed with the tradition of the US cavalry of 'old army' years, the Boeing-Vertol CH-47 Chinook was more akin to Hannibal's elephants. The most spectacular mission in Vietnam for the Chinook was the placing of artillery batteries in mountain positions that were inaccessible by any other means, and then keeping them supplied with large quantities of ammunition. A heavy 155-mm howitzer lifted by a Chinook to a dominating mountain-top position could create havoc with enemy movement in the valley below. The 1st Cavalry Division found that its Chinooks were limited to a 7,000 lb (3,200 kg) payload when operating in the mountains, but could carry an additional 1,000 lb (455 kg) when operating near the coast. During the first Battle of the Ia Drang Valley, the 1st Cavalry Division covered such a wide zone that the siting of artillery was of utmost importance. Not only was it necessary for the prior arrivals to cover the landing zones of the incoming assault forces, but it was also necessary to place the guns in such a position that they could join other artillery in co-ordinated fire plans. Not infrequently the guns' crews came face to face with the Viet Cong, assuming the impromptu role of infantrymen.

The Chinook was later teamed in 1st Cavalry Division with the greater lift capacity of the US army Sikorsky CH-54 Tarhe ('Sky Crane'), which was capable of lifting heavy, outsized loads, of recovering downed aircraft and, by the use of detachable pods, of the transportation of personnel, vehicles, and equipment. The CH-54's equipment included a 15,000-lb (6,900-kg) hoist, a sling detachment, and a load stabilizer to prevent undue sway in cargo winch operations. In addition to heavy ordnance such as the 155-mm howitzer, the Sky Crane could

transport bulldozers, road graders, and armoured vehicles. The CH-54s were widely used in Vietnam after September 1965, and both Cranes and Chinooks were featured prominently in the 60-day Cambodian mountain campaign, which commenced on 1 May 1970. Besides the 1st Cavalry's own Cranes, the 273rd Aviation Company (Heavy Helicopter) was under the operational control of the 1st Cavalry during the campaign. This company with its CH-54s lifted engineering equipment (272 bulldozers, 54 backhoes, and 41 road graders) as well as 155-mm howitzers into (and out of) the operational area. They moved bridge sections and recovered $7,315,000 worth of downed aircraft.

CHAPTER 22
WARS IN AFGHANISTAN

No one since Alexander the Great has completely conquered Afghanistan. Between 1737-8 the Persian Nadir Shah did, however, take Kandahar after a nine-months siege and attempted to occupy and pacify the disaffected Persian provinces of Balkh and Baluchistan. Nadir Shah's successor, Ahmad Shah, assumed control of the Afghan provinces of Persia, his military operations extending over much of central Asia, including nine invasions of India. On the death of Ahmad Shah, the Afghan Empire extended over eastern Persia and all the region south of the Oxus, including Baluchistan, Kashmir, the Punjab, and Sind. In the early nineteenth century, imperial Russian intrigue caused the rival British throne to order the penetration of Afghanistan, where an officer of the East India Company, Captain Eldred Potter, successfully organized the impromptu defence of Herat City against the forces of Mohammed Shah of Persia. At the turn of the nineteenth century (whilst Russian and British intriguers worked on controlling the country), the Afghan people were again harassed by their western neighbour, Persia, and by Sikh invasions from the Punjab in the east.

The First Afghan War (1839-42)—in the British context—commenced when Sir John Keane led the Army of the Indus, 21,000 strong, into Afghanistan. He occupied Kandahar, Ghazni, and captured Kabul. Dost Muhammad, the Afghan ruler, was captured and sent to India. A rising took place against the British in Kabul. This was led by Akbar Khan, son of Dost Muhammad, and resulted in the murder of the two British agents. The British/Indian garrison of 4,500 men, under the elderly Major-General William G.K. Elphinstone, was surrounded in 1842 but was permitted to leave Kabul under safe conduct with 12,000 refugees and to return to India. Elphinstone's force met with disaster in a defile on the Khyber Pass near Gandamak. After ineffectual resistance, most of the British and Indian soldiers and the refugees were massacred. A few were taken prisoner, but only a handful survived in captivity. The small British garrison at Ghazni had also been forced to surrender. Other British detachments at Kandahar and Jalalabad held out. Later in 1842 the British invaded with a punitive force commanded by Sir George Pollock, storming the Khyber Pass and relieving both Jalalabad and Kabul. A stern reprisal for the massacre followed, the citadel and central bazaar of Kabul being destroyed. The East India Company decided, however, that continued occupation of Afghanistan would be both unprofitable and dangerous, so the country was evacuated, and Dost Muhammad returned to his throne.

In 1878 the British once again invaded Afghanistan and thus the Second Afghan War (1878-80) was set in motion—ostensibly to 'defend' the country against Russian invasion. The British/Indian troops, under Sir Frederick (later Lord) Roberts, advanced from India seizing the frontier passes. A peace treaty was signed (May 1879) but the newly-installed British

Above *British troops arrive above Kandahar in Afghanistan during the Second Afghan War (1878-80).*

Below *Indian troops are in position on the Sapper & Miner Bastion, Sherpur Fort, during the Second Afghan War.*

resident in Kabul, Sir Louis Cavagnari, was murdered and this led to Roberts' field force advancing on Kabul from Kurram and Kandahar. At Charasia in October 1879, the British and imperial troops (numbering 7,500 men) defeated an Afghan army of 8,000 and then occupied Kabul. Roberts, two months later, routed a force of at least 100,000 Afghan levies in the Battle of Sherpur. In June 1880, Ayub Khan, laying claim to the throne and leading the Afghans, seized control in Herat and then marched with 25,000 men on Kandahar. During Ayub Khan's advance he met and defeated at Maiwand a small British force comprising British and Indian troops. Roberts immediately moved out of Kabul to intercept Ayub. With him were 10,000 men and a transport corps specifically organized on his own plan. He reached Kandahar in 22 days, covering 313 miles (504 km) over mountainous country. At the Battle of Kandahar on 1 September 1880, Roberts attacked at once, completely routing the Afghan army and capturing all its guns and equipment. A pro-British government was established under Abdul Rahman before the British and imperial force evacuated the country, in 1881.

In 1919 the Afghan ruler, Amir Amanullah, proclaimed a *jihad* (religious war) against Britain. Afghan levies broke across the Indian border near Landi Kotal and occupied Bagh. Immediate mobilization of British/Indian troops followed, the punitive expedition moving through the Khyber Pass to Landi Kotal and driving the invaders out of Bagh. The expedition then thrust through the pass completely and into Afghanistan to reach Dakka, while Jalalabad and Kabul received a series of aerial bombardments. Amanullah sued for an armistice and the halt in hostilities that ended the Third Afghan War lead to the Treaty of Rawalpindi (8 August). However, sporadic guerrilla activity continued along the Afghan-Indian border. A civil war broke out in Afghanistan between January and October 1929 when a bandit leader, Habibullah Ghazi,

captured Kabul, only to be defeated and executed by General Mohammed Nadir, who (aided by the British) reformed his army and restored stability in Afghanistan.

Mountains and deserts have played an important part in Afghanistan's troublesome history. The Afghan's homeland is green and pleasant—the summers are hot and dry and the winters bitterly cold, especially in the high country, and from November to mid-March snow makes travel difficult. The rains, when they come, fall from December to February. The Hindu Kush slices across the country, east to west, cresting in the Pamir mountains of the Wakhan corridor. North of the Hindu Kush are yet more mountains, fading northwards into the arid steppes of central Asia. In the west, the Iranian plateau extends to the cities of Herat and Shindand before rising to merge with the fastness of the Hindu Kush, ringing like ramparts the central Hazara Jat area—the land of the Hazaras. The south and southeast are largely desolate, rocky deserts. The north and west are mountainous, curving from the Pamirs down to the fringe of the Registan deserts. Agriculture is the primary occupation of the Afghan people, but it requires intensive irrigation to grow anything. Afghanistan is one of the world's poorest countries.

Russian imperialist designs on Afghanistan were renewed with great enthusiasm after the Bolshevik Revolution of 1917. The British left India and Pakistan—and thus the borders of Afghanistan—in 1947, and by the 1950s the country was considered to be firmly in the Soviet sphere of influence. The Government, especially the military, was penetrated by the Soviets and their sympathizers. Soviet aid poured in and the Afghan army was trained and re-equipped on Soviet lines. The monarchy was dissolved in 1973, King Mohammed Zadir being sent into exile and the Communists taking control of the Government. In December 1973, President and Prime Minister Nur Mohammed Taraki set about turning Afghanistan into a model of Stalinist Russia.

Every facet of Islamic and Afghan life was to be forced into line with Marxism-Leninism. By early 1979 there was armed resistance in 25 of Afghanistan's 28 provinces. The resistance fighters that inevitably banded themselves together called themselves *mujahideen* ('fighters for the faith') and their struggle a *jihad*. Open war followed, and an anti-Communist uprising in Herat on 21 March 1979 left 5,000 dead. By October 1979 the USSR started mobilizing its forces to aid the Afghan Government and army, and in mid-December elements of the 105th Guards Airborne Division started to fly into Kabul airport, joining Soviet Air Force units already in the country.

The *mujahideen* guerrillas set up their headquarters in Pakistan and used their mountain

Afghanistani villagers survey an unexploded 500 lb bomb dropped by a Soviet aircraft in the neighbourhood in 1986.

lairs in Afghanistan to attack the Afghan Government (DRA) and Soviet armies in the valleys and urban centres. In September the DRA, already heavily depleted by desertion, and the Soviets launched their first major offensive into the Panjsher valley, which caused the first condemnation of the Soviet invasion by the UN General Assembly, the Non-Aligned Movement, and the Organization of Islamic Nations. At this stage the Red Army placed less reliance on the Afghan Government's forces, introducing instead their own airmobile infantry. In 1982 the Soviets conducted large-scale ground sweeps, combined with air strikes and heliborne operations. The biggest offensives were Panjsher V (April-May) and Panjsher VI (September), but the Communists failed to destroy a guerrilla stronghold in a dominating position within striking range of both the Salang Pass and Bagram airfield. A series of sweeps later in the year was aimed at destroying not so much the guerrillas themselves but rather the areas that could lend support to the *mujahideen* near Kabul and other important targets. Combined guerrilla action in April, however, decimated a DRA division in Paktia province.

In 1983 and 1984 the Soviets increasingly developed their air-war strategy. Guerrilla-held urban areas in Herat and Kandahar were heavily bombed, the Panjsher ground offensives gaining momentum monthly. Heavy fighting took place around Herat and Kandahar but despite the thoroughness and efficiency of Soviet strategy and tactics, the Afghan resistance fighters fought back—now armed with modern weaponry from the USA. In 1985 the air strikes continued on a vast scale, Soviet missile launchers and artillery being used to an increasing extent to obliterate areas of resistance. The year saw the Afghan rebel fighters confronting the Soviet forces in strength rather than limiting the action to ambushes and hit-and-run tactics. Despite greatly increased Communist defences, the *mujahideen* focused their main attacks on Kabul. During 1986 the Soviets announced the withdrawal of six regiments,

Mujahideen guerrillas regroup in a ruined Afghan village in 1986.

though the USA claimed the move was merely troop rotation. Border incidents between Afghanistan and Pakistan and the possibility of Soviet military strikes into the Baluchistan area of Pakistan became a real threat, and the USA was prompted to send military aid to Pakistan's armed forces. At the end of 1986 it was estimated that three million Afghan refugees had settled in Pakistan and a further two million in Iran.

In 1986-7 some 115,000 Soviet troops were still reported to be in Afghanistan. There were conflicting reports on the military successes of both the resistance movement and the Communist forces. Western diplomats, however, reported fighting in all the major provinces, with heavy casualties on both sides. A cease-fire called for by the Soviet Government on 1 January 1987 was rejected by the guerrillas, who although they did not gain the upperhand during the year, continued to be well supplied with American weapons and equipment. The military capabilities of the *mujahideen* were greatly

increased by the deployment of ground-to-air missiles forcing the Soviets to place less reliance on air strikes. Large-scale bombing was replaced by the use of Soviet *Spetsnaz* special airborne commando forces in rapid strikes against rebel mountain bases and supply lines, particularly in the border areas.

By the middle of 1986 the strategically-important Panjsher valley, north of Kabul, had been all but given up to Soviet and Afghan Government control. The most sustained conflict centred around the cities of Herat in the west and Kandahar in the south, while in the eastern provinces major assaults against rebel strongholds and supply routes heightened tension along the nearby border with Pakistan. A subterranean guerrilla base at Zhawar was overrun and partly destroyed but it was later re-occupied by the rebels. Heavy fighting was reported particularly in Konar, Nangarha, and Ghazni provinces; fighting in the border region continued with great ferocity. The ancient city of Herat, regarded as Afghanistan's religious and cultural centre, was by now almost completely destroyed. Kabul, too, was badly hit, the guerrillas mounting assassination missions in small groups in the streets and on one occasion blowing up an ammunition depot. On 8 February 1988 the Soviet Communist Party General Secretary Mikhail Gorbachev announced that Soviet troops would start a ten-months period of withdrawal from Afghanistan commencing on 15 May. The Soviets kept their word, and by the turn of the year, communist forces had left the country.

The Soviet army at the height of the war in Afghanistan was largely composed of motor-rifle units riding in armoured personnel carriers. The use of heliborne forces gave the Soviets additional capabilities, but even these showed limitations. In both the 1982 Panjsher V and 1984 Panjsher VII offensives, battalion-sized heliborne forces were badly cut up by the rebels. The troops of the airborne regiments, the air-assault brigade, and the one battalion per motor-rifle brigade and division having

Soviet troops parade in Kabul.

received special training, were frequently used for heliborne operations. Many of the Soviet troops were young conscripts with no prior combat experience and no special training to fight in the mountains, valleys, and deserts of Afghanistan. Although the DRA armed forces included some élite units such as a mountain brigade, an airborne battalion and several commando brigades, the infantry divisions were said to be understrength and in a poor condition of training, a state of affairs apparently approved of by the Soviets in case the Government troops should turn against them.

As in the Vietnam War, ground attack aircraft could strike at the most inaccessible mountain outposts although the guerrillas—like the Viet Cong—were also to be found in the lowland areas making their bases openly in villages. Soviet strike aircraft included MiG-21s, MiG-23s, and MiG-27s but the most important single Soviet weapon used in the war was the helicopter. The *mujahideen* particularly feared the Mi-24 Hind attack helicopter, which was

assigned to close air support, bombing villages, and for patrolling and destroying whatever they found moving in any location in Afghanistan. The Hind is heavily armoured and hard to destroy. The Mi-8/Mi-17 Hip series was the standard transport helicopter and pre-dominated in Afghanistan. They carried troops and equipment for Soviet heliborne operations. They can also be heavily armed—up to six rocket pods, plus machine-guns and 30-mm grenade launchers—although the Hips are not armoured.

The Afghan resistance fighters were not so much an army as a people-at-arms. The strength of the *mujahideen*, which consisted of seven different Islamic groups, may have numbered as many as three quarters of a million warriors with ages ranging from 12-year-old boys to 80-year-old men. The guerrillas were lightly armed with weapons as ancient as Martini-Henrys taken from the British in the Second Afghan War to Second World War .303 Lee Enfields in various versions and a wide

The Soviet Mil-24 Hind attack helicopter gunship, which was used on a wide-scale to hunt out and attack the Mujahideen freedom fighters in their mountain hide-outs.

range of 7.62-mm Russian Kalashnikov assault rifles—a collection of other captured infantry weapons also being used. For fighting tanks the guerrillas relied on RPG-7 anti-tank grenade launchers and anti-tank mines. The most common anti-aircraft weapons were Soviet-designed DSLK 12.7-mm and 14.5-mm KPV heavy machine-guns. The man-portable heat-seeking SA-7 Grail surface-to-air missiles introduced in 1980 were never in plentiful supply. Most Afghan men learn to shoot when they are boys but this does not mean that the guerrillas were necessarily skilled marksmen. Formal military training among the *mujahideen* was rare but hit-and-run and ambush techniques come easily to them. The guerrillas were capable of beating the DRA in a pitched battle but fared badly against Soviet firepower. The Afghan rebels are, however, firmly of the warrior caste and their fighting spirit will have changed little since the days of Alexander the Great.

CHAPTER 23
THE INDIAN SUB-CONTINENT

The Invaders

The Indian sub-continent, or Hindustan as it once was called, may be divided into three major physiographic regions (south to north): the Deccan plateau and central highlands; the plains region (a contiguous lowland surrounding the plateau region and comprising the northwestern deserts, the Ganges Basin in the northeast, and the western and southeastern coastal plains); and the Himalayas extending from the northwest to northeast, surmounting the Indian sub-continent. The Deccan plateau and central highlands have seen ferocious battles by mountain warriors, as well as guerrilla warfare on varied scales, but it was in the mountains of the northwest that lay the paths of the foreign invaders who sought the treasure troves of India. Darius I, the Achaemenid King of Persia towards the end of the sixth century BC conquered part of northern India, extending from the Brahmaputra River on the east to the Beas River on the west, and Alexander of Macedon led his victorious army as far as the Beas in 327-325 BC. After Alexander's departure from India the great Indian warrior King Chandragupta founded an empire that embraced nearly all of northern India and probably included lands further south.

Over the centuries, many dynasties and kingdoms came and went in northern India, but no doubt the most significant factor for the later development of India took place in the Middle East. The Prophet Mohammad, who died in AD 632 had founded not only a new religion,

Islam, but had also turned the Arabs into a militant nation. By 650 they had over-run the Persian Empire, Syria, and Egypt, and had advanced as far as the Oxus River (Amu Darya). While they naturally cast long eyes on India their early attempts at conquest were not successful. By the mid-tenth century, however, the Muslim presence was being felt. The great Moghul Empire was founded in 1526 and lasted nearly 200 years (1526-1707). The dynasty was created by Babur, who counted amongst his ancestors Tamerlane and Genghis Khan. Shortly after his victory at Panipat, Babur faced the brave Rajputs led by Rana Sanga of Mewar, but he obtained another brilliant victory at the Battle of Khua (1527).

Akbar Khan was the greatest of the Mughul Emperors. During his long reign (1556-1605) he conquered Malwa, Gujarat, Gondwana, Bengal, Kashmir, Khandesh, Berar, and other provinces, and won over the Rajput states by a policy of conciliation. Akbar was not only a brilliant general but also a sound administrator and he was ahead of his time in displaying religious tolerance of the Hindus. Aurangzeb (1658-1707) was another great Moghul general and monarch, but he was ruthless in his suppression of the Hindus and the destruction of their temples and idols. After concluding a treaty with the Rajput ruler of Mewar, Aurangzeb led his army to the Deccan to consolidate Mughul supremacy there. He remained in the Deccan for nearly 26 years. During this period he finally conquered Bijapur and Golconda and advanced (1690) as far as Trichinopoly. Although under Aurangzeb the Mughul Empire reached its greatest extent, Aurangzeb failed to conquer the Marathas and this effectively ended the rule of the Mughul Emperors in India.

The period of British conquest of India (1707-1815) was marked by Anglo-French conflict in southeastern India. The British gained the upperhand when, by the Treaty of Paris, French positions in India were reduced to a few small trading posts. In 1757 the Battle of Plassey was fought with, on the one side, 2,000 sepoys

Below *The British declared war on the mountain people of Nepal in November 1814. In a two-year campaign, the Nepalese staunchly resisted the invaders but in 1816 a British Resident was installed at Katmandu. British progress in the Nepal War was seriously hampered by the mountainous nature of the Nepalese terrain. The Gurkhas, the warriors of Nepal, were tactically astute, as is demonstrated by the soundly-built, well-sited fort seen here.*

and 1,000 Europeans led by the young Robert Clive defeating, on the other side, a vast Indian army weakened by treachery. Political intrigue, skirmishes with the 'natives', and outright war in northwest India in the nineteenth century were largely caused by Russian imperial designs on India, which were in turn the cause of the First Afghan War (1838-42) and the Second Afghan War (1878-80) (dealt with in Chapter 22, 'Wars in Afghanistan') and by those troublesome mountain tribesmen—the Pathans—who harassed many a column moving through the defiles and passes of the North West Frontier.

The ill-starred First Afghan War had its biproducts in the conquest of Sind (1842-3) and of the Punjab (1845-9). The Sind, now part of Pakistan, consists of a central plain, the Kirthas range in the west, and an eastern desert belt. The province, which is bordered by the provinces of Baluchistan on the west and north, Punjab on the northeast, and the present Indian states of Rajasthan and Gujarat to the east, and the Arabian Sea to the south, was conquered successively by the Persians, Greeks, Parthians, Säsanians, Brahmins, and Arabs, the British adding to these conquests in 1842-3. The Punjab, the scene of British wrath against the Sikhs in 1845-9, became a province of British India, with 34 princely states. The name 'Punjab' ('five rivers') was derived from its position astride five great rivers (Beas, Ravi, Chenab, Sutlej, and Jhelum), which unite and, south of the Punjab, merge in an affluent of the Indus. Before partition in 1947 it was bounded on the north by Kashmir, on the east by the Himalayas, on the south by Rajputana and Sind, and on the west by Baluchistan and the North West Frontier province. The Punjab territory is now split between India and Pakistan.

The original concept of Pakistan was formed in 1933. In it 'P' stands for the Punjab, 'A' for Afghans ('Frontier province'), 'K' for Kashmir, and 'S' for Sind—the idea being to create a Muslim state independent from the Hindu Indian peoples. In the events and discussions that led to the partition of India 1947, the Muslim leader, Mohammad Ali Jinnah, demanded a state that would still be called Pakistan but that would additionally consist of Bengal. In the event Pakistan came to consist of the North West Frontier, Baluchistan, Sind, West Punjab, and East Bengal. East Punjab and later part of Kashmir opted for India, and East Bengal became known as East Pakistan, which was some 1,000 miles (1,600 km) from West Pakistan. Pakistan as it is today (Asia's seventh

Left *The Battle of Peiwar Kotal was an Indian army success at the beginning of the Second Afghan War in December 1878, the 5th Gurkha Regiment of Roberts's Kurram Valley Field Force particularly distinguishing itself after a night flanking march to out-manoeuvre and then outfight the Afghans of Sher Ali who were routed.*

Below *A party of Gurkhas in action during the Black Mountain Campaign of 1888. The rifles are Lee Metford magazine weapons, whose firepower was devastating for the day, particularly against ill-armed tribesmen.*

ft (305 m) in elevation with many ridges crossing it from northeast to southwest, is in the west. The Indus plain and the desert areas are in the east and southeast respectively. The Indian army of the British Raj spent the greater part of its life on the North West Frontier, and its most potent weapon against the fierce and unruly tribesmen in those arid, boulder-strewn, and mountainous parts was the mountain gun. In such operations both British and Indian mountain batteries played their part, but the former (which had in their ranks British gunners and Indian drivers), were fewer in number. Although mountain regiments were formed, individual batteries usually acted independently, movement along mountain paths and narrow defiles being more easily coordinated than by the larger unit. There was another reason why the battery was preferred to the regiment as individual weapons and that was that before the Second World War, Indian army units were not equipped with wireless for movement and fire control. The Indian mountain battery was accordingly self-contained and independent in nature, which was later to make the unit equally valuable in the jungles of Burma. (Mountain batteries distinguished themselves at the Battles of Kohima and Imphal.)

The Indian mountain battery consisted of four British officers (the commanding officer was a major), and three Indian officers. Senior among the NCOs were the havildar-major and the quartermaster havildar, after whom the batteries consisted of ten havildars comprising one signal havildar, four gunners numbers one, four drivers numbers one, and one clerk. Under them were more than 200 rank and file, about 30 of whom were survey specialists and signallers, 60 gun numbers, and 110 mule drivers. The rest comprised farriers, blacksmiths, saddlers, bootmakers, carpenters, cooks, trumpeters, a tailor, and sweepers. The main armament of the battery was its four 3.7-in howitzers, one of the most remarkable and most accurate artillery weapon ever invented. It was

The Chitral affair was a typical Victorian campaign. In 1892 the fort at Chitral, which is situated in the far north of Afghanistan, was besieged by the tribesman of Umra Khan of Jandol. The photograph shows a column of the 3rd Gurkha (Rifle) Regiment, which undertook the long march to relieve Chitral, at the foot of the Sowarai Pass in 1895.

largest country) is situated at the western end of the Indo-Gangetic plain, covering an area of 307,374 sq. miles (796,098 km^2). Pakistan can be divided physiographically into four regions: the great highlands, the Baluchistan Plateau, the Indus Plain, and the desert areas. The Himalayan and Trans-Himalayan mountain ranges (the Karakoram and the Pamirs), rising to an average elevation of more than 20,000 ft (6,100 m), and including some of the world's highest peaks, such as K2 (28,251 ft—8,611 m) and Nanga Parbat (26,660 ft—8,126 m), make up the great highlands that occupy the entire northern region. The Baluchistan plateau, a broken highland region about 1,000

The inside of the Chitral fort seen after the relief of 1895. Light field artillery was particularly important in frontier operations; it had frequently to be moved swiftly over extremely steep terrain.

carried in parts on the backs of eight mules, two of these parts forming the gun barrel when locked together by a junction nut, and it was an earlier gun of similar design that inspired Rudyard Kipling to write his famous ballad 'Screw-Guns'.

The following extract is from *The Jungle Book* by Rudyard Kipling.

'Her Majesty's Servants'
The big parade of all the thirty thousand men was held that afternoon, and Vixen and I had a good place close to the Viceroy and the Amir of Afghanistan, with his high, big black hat of astrakhan wool and the great diamond star in the centre. The first part of the review was all sunshine, and the regiments went by in wave upon wave of legs all moving together, and guns all in a line, till our eyes grew dizzy. Then the cavalry came up, to the beautiful cavalry canter of 'Bonnie Dundee', and Vixen cocked her ear where she sat on the dog-cart. The second squadron of the Lancers shot by, and there was the troop-horse, with his tail like spun silk, his head pulled into his breast, one ear forward and one back, setting the time for all his squadron, his legs going as smoothly as waltz-music. Then the big guns came by, and I saw Two Tails and two other elephants harnessed in line to a forty-pounder siege-gun, while twenty yoke of oxen walked behind. The seventh pair had a new yoke, and they looked rather stiff and tired. *Last came the screw-guns, and Billy the mule carried himself as though he commanded all the troops, and his harness was oiled and polished till it winked. I gave a cheer all by myself for Billy the mule, but he never looked right or left.* [my italic]

'Screw-Guns'
by Rudyard Kipling
Smokin' my pipe on the mountings, sniffin' the mornin' cool
I walks in my old brown gaiters along o' my old brown mule,

With seventy gunners be'ind me, an' never a beggar forgets
it's only the pick of the Army that handles the dear little pets — 'Tss! 'Tss!

For you all love the screw-guns—the screw-guns they all love you!
So when we call round with a few guns, o' course you will know what to do—hoo! hoo!
Jest send in your Chief an' surrender—it's worse if you fights or you runs:
You can go where you please, you can skid up the trees, but you don't get away from the guns!

They sends us along where the roads are, but mostly we goes where they ain't:
We'd climb up the side of a sign-board an' trust to the stick o' the paint:
We've chivvied the Naga an' Looshai, we've give the Afreedeeman fits,
For we fancies ourselves at two thousand, w' guns that are built in two bits—'Tss! 'Tss!

For you all love the screw-guns...

If a man doesn't work, why we drills 'im an' teaches 'im 'ow to behave;
If a beggar can't march, why, we kills 'im an' rattles 'im into 'is grave.
You've got to stand up to our business an' spring without snatchin' or fuss
D' you say that you sweat with the field-guns? By God, you must lather with us—'Tss! 'Tss!

For you all love the screw-guns ...

The eagles is screamin' around us, the river's a' moanin' below,
We're clear o' the pine an' the oak-scrub, we're out on the rocks an' the snow,
An' the wind is as thin as a whip-lash what carries away to the plains
The rattle an' stamp o' the lead-mules—the jinglety jink o' the chains—'Tss! 'Tss!

For you all love the screw-guns...

There's a wheel on the Horns o' the Mornin', an a wheel on the edge o' the Pit,
An' a drop into nothin' beneath you as straight as a beggar can spit:

With the sweat runnin' out o' your shirt-sleeves, an' the sun off the snow in your face
An 'arf o' the men on the drag-ropes to hold the old gun in 'er place—'Tss! 'Tss!

For you all love the screw-guns...

Smokin' my pipe on the mountings, sniffin' the mornin' cool,
I climbs in my old brown gaiters along o' my old brown mule.
The monkey can say what our road was— the wild-goat 'e knows where we passed.
Stand easy, you long-eared old darlin's! Out drag-ropes! With shrapnel! Hold fast—'Tss! 'Tss!

For you all love the screw-guns—the screw-guns they all love you!
So when we take tea with a few guns, o' course you will know what to do—hoo! hoo!
Just send in your Chief an' surrender—it's worse if you fights or you runs:
You may hide in the caves, they'll be only your graves, but you can't get away from the guns!

First published in *The Scots Observer* on 12 July 1890. Sung to the tune of 'The Eton Boating Song'.

The remarkable mobility of the mountain battery could not have been achieved without its mules and horses, and in spite of the exceptional gun in its possession, it was in these animals, particularly the mules, that the pride of the battery lay. Without wireless sets, the manner in which communications were established between observation post (OP) and gun position was quite spectacular. The OP party was usually fully mounted, the specialists (surveyors) carrying their artillery boards strapped to their backs, with the tripod stands for them attached vertically to their saddles in leather cases. Each mounted signaller carried two drums of telephone cable on either side of his saddle and a field telephone strapped to his back. It was thus a highly-mobile party, as capable of moving on foot as on horseback, and frequently the line from OP to gun position was laid at the gallop. Any delay in establishing line communication was overcome by heliograph, lamp, or even flag, the latter being frequently used for passing orders and messages within the battery when it was on the move. The signallers earned the highest reputation and were the life-blood of the battery.

Indian army units fighting in the mountains were not necessarily drawn from those regions but the Punjab Frontier Force might truly be said to have been drawn from mountain stock. The force saw widespread service in the days of the Raj in India from 1846 onwards and in the First World War was on active service abroad in Gallipoli, Egypt, Mesopotamia, and in Persia. The mountain batteries of the Punjab Frontier Force consisted of the following units:

1st Royal (Kohat) Mountain Battery, RA, Frontier Force
2nd (Derajat) Mountain Battery, RA, Frontier Force
3rd (Peshawar) Mountain Battery, RA, Frontier Force
4th (Hazara) Mountain Battery, RA, Frontier Force

Just as an example of one mountain battery's deployment on the Punjab frontier, the Kohat may be listed in action against the Sheranis, 1853; Bozdars, 1857; and the Kabul Khel Wazirs, 1859. The battery was also involved in the Mahsud Campaign, 1860; an affair at the Ublan Pass, with the Bizoti Orakzais, 1868; the expedition against the Jowake Afridis 1877-8; the expedition against the Zaimukhts, 1879; the Mahsud expedition, 1881; the expedition against the Khiddarzai Sheranis, 1890; and the Mahsud Expedition 1894-5

Two mountain batteries (the 7th British and 30th Indian) took part in Younghusband's expedition to Tibet in 1903-4. Lieutenant G.A. Hassel-Yates of the 7th British Mountain Battery mentions in his diary:

30 May 1904
To Jeyluk, a steep rocky path straight up the hill, a really bad pull up for mules who had to be helped up all the way with ropes, 6,000

ft rise in six miles. We are now at 9,000 ft. It is getting chilly.

2 June 1904
Started with a pull up from GNATONG to KADOOP, then over the TARKHOL LA, 14,300 ft and a drop down to 13,000 ft. The air is rare and a lot of the men have got mountain sickness, I don't feel too good myself, with a bad headache, and aches and pains all over me.

19 June 1904
To stop the advance of the Mission and its escort in March, they [the Tibetans] manned this wall with a great number of men. The ensuing fight was short and sweet, and as soon as the two guns of 7 Mountain Battery opened up the enemy fled, leaving a lot of dead.

17 July 1904
We camped in a more or less open space as best we could beneath a vast glacier—solid ice—which comes down from the great snow peak of NUI-JIN-KIN-SUNG, 23,000 ft high. A feeble snow fell all day, and the howling wind tearing down the gorge is pretty bad.

18 July 1904
Off at 7 a.m. to the top of the pass 16,000 ft. The enemy have built and are holding three lines of rock sangars, right across the valleys on the other side, one behind the other, and at about 200 yards distance, and also a number of sangars perched up on the precipitous cliffs on either side wherever one could be put; some of these must have been at about 18,000 feet.

3 August 1904
The Dalai Lama has, we hear, gone to Peking. So we are here, at Lhasa, the Forbidden City, the first military force to have done so, and, I suppose, we have made a bit of history in the doing of it.

India and Pakistan

The strife and bloodshed that occurred across India in the year before partition in 1947 intensified immediately upon independence. The decision of the Hindu Raja of Kashmir to have his state join India (October 1947) precipitated an uprising of the predominantly Muslim population, who wished to join Pakistan. Afridi and Mahsud tribesmen, who had crossed into Kashmir from Pakistan, joined in a march on Srinagar. Indian troops were flown into Kashmir to quell the uprising, and intensive fighting broke out between the air and ground forces of the Indian Government and the rebellious Muslims and their supporters from Pakistan. Sporadic clashes continued in Kashmir until Pakistani regular troops crossed the border into Kashmir and an undeclared state of war existed between India and Pakistan. A ceasefire agreed on 1 January 1949 brought about an uneasy truce along the fighting front in Kashmir, ending fourteen months of warfare.

The Himalayan frontier between India and China has been an area of dispute and conflict for over thirty years. Chinese troops in massive surprise attacks defeated frontier forces in Jammu and in the northeastern frontier region (October 1962), on fronts 1,000 miles (1,600 km) apart. The eastern drive, in particular, was spectacularly successful, and all Indian resistance north of the Brahmaputra valley was over-run. One bone of contention between the Chinese Communists and India was the region of Ladakh, which is infrequently mentioned in the world Press. Certainly very few would have credited a prediction that armed clashes and the threat of full-scale war between India and China would arise over possession of the high alkaline plain known as the Aksai Chin ('white stone' desert) where the frontiers of Tibet, Sinkiang, and Ladakh march together. The Aksai Chin is beyond doubt among the world's bleakest stretches, a land where it has been said 'no people live and no blade of grass grows'. By 21 November 1962, China had gained all the border regions they claimed, and India (reluctant to continue the fighting) settled for an informal truce along the Himalayan frontier.

Serious hostilities occurred between India and Pakistan (May-September 1965) that began with a frontier dispute in the Rann of Kutch. The Pakistanis seemed to get the better of the struggle before monsoon rains ended operations. Border clashes in Kashmir and the Punjab followed, and in August Indian troops crossed the ceasefire line into Kashmir. In retaliation Pakistan initiated a major invasion of Kashmir. Both sides undertook minor air raids against nearby Punjab cities, as well as against Karachi and New Delhi. Indian troops launched a major attack against Lahore (6 September). In large-scale armoured battles, Indian units achieved marginal success over Pakistani tanks. On balance, however, a stalemate resulted. The civil war that broke out in Pakistan in March 1971 was focused on the Pakistani army's suppression of dissidents in East Pakistan, which was proclaimed the independent state of Bangladesh on 26 March. Indian support of the Bangladesh rebels led to another major Indian-Pakistani confrontation in December 1971. A ceasefire the same month, after heavy losses on both sides, led to the recognition of Bangladesh as a new nation.

The Chinese threat to India continued after the 1962 invasion. In September 1967 Indian troops clashed again with the Chinese on the Sikkim-Tibet frontier. India and China accused each other of border violations. However, the clashes were limited to exchanges of rifle and artillery fire, and no substantial movement was made into either Tibet or the Indian protectorate of Sikkim. Chinese Communist forces had invaded Tibet in 1950 but the Dalai Lama was permitted to remain as a figurehead ruler in Lhasa. Widespread revolt against the Communists broke out into a full-scale rebellion in March 1959, but the Chinese suppressed the revolt, killing over 65,000 Tibetans. The Dalai Lama fled from Lhasa to India. The mountain retreat of Nepal (like Tibet, a seemingly inaccessible territory to the European traveller not so many years ago) was also a political cauldron post-1956. A civil war, March-December 1961, resulted in the defeat of the anti-government rebels.

Today, both India and Pakistan maintain modern armies, the former supported with arms and *matériel* by Soviet Russia and the latter, which still displays a strong pro-British stance, by the USA. Bitter rivalries of yesterday between Hindu and Muslim have not diminished, and both countries remain in a state of combat alertness. Border friction still also exists between India and neighbouring territories. Between 1975 and 1979 Indian Government troops carried out counter-insurgency operations in the northeastern region against tribal rebels seeking independence for Mizoram and Nagaland. The Nagas—who inhabit a state that is almost entirely covered with ranges of hills that are part of the Himalayan system, and that abuts the Burmese border—ended their 20-year rebellion in exchange for a general amnesty at the end of the period, but the Mizos continued their guerrilla war against India.

India-Pakistan incidents in 1981 were largely caused by Indian fears that the Pakistanis were developing nuclear capabilities. At this time Indian army units carried out suppression operations in Assam, Gujerat, Manipur, Mizo, Tripura, and Bombay. In 1982 India and China held border talks concerning disputed territories in the Ladakh region of Kashmir (which was still under Chinese control) and along the border of Bhutan under Indian control.

Military tension in Pakistan in the 1980s has largely been caused by the conflict in Afghanistan. Hundreds of thousands of Afghan refugees have now been settled in camps in Pakistan, which also provides the staging ground for the supply of military aid to the *Mujahideen*. The Afghan Air Force has now on a number of occasions attacked villages in North Gaziristan and Kurram agencies (both major staging areas for rebel-arms supply caravans situated in the North-West Frontier province). In response to those air attacks Pakistan has reportedly moved ground-to-air defence systems to the Afghan border and on 30 March 1987 two Pakistani fighter aircraft engaged and shot down an Afghan ground-attack jet flying in Pakistani air space. In July and August 1987, frontier tribes in Kurram were involved in very serious clashes, resulting in thousands of deaths, with the Afghan rebels supported by Pakistani regular units, who sought to seize their lands for the re-settlement of the refugees from across the border.

CHAPTER 24

BRITISH MOUNTAIN TROOPS

The British mountain gunner was a master of the screw-gun. He was said to be able to cover long distances of four miles in 50 minutes and take his gun anywhere an infantryman could go. The first mention of mountain artillery in the British army was in the Peninsular War. Unfortunately, as the record goes, a Royal Artillery battery lost two 'mountain guns' to the French at Castalla on the east coast of Spain on 12 and 13 April 1813. A year later, mountain guns were carried on elephants in the war against Nepal, and on camels in the Pindari Mahratta War of 1817-20. (As late as 1897, 'A' battery (Chestnut Troop) Royal Horse Artillery was equipped with 12-pounder BL guns on elephants during the Tirah Campaign.) The first 'genuine' mountain battery with mule transport and Indian gunners was formed in India in 1841 under Captain J.B. Backhouse of the Bengal Horse Artillery, and it served with distinction in the heavy fighting in Afghanistan. Half the guns were lost in the retreat from Kabul and the battery was disbanded in 1843.

The first permanent British mountain battery was 5th Battery/25th Brigade that took part in the Bhutan Campaign of 1864-5 and the Abyssinia Campaign, 1869. The development of British mountain artillery was stimulated by the Second Afghan War 1879-80, when Lord Roberts—who had served in the 3rd (Peshawar) Indian Battery—took two British mountain batteries and one Indian mountain battery (and no other artillery) on his celebrated march from Kabul to Kandahar. The mountain batteries were the admiration of all, and before the end of the century the organization of the Indian army for service beyond the frontier included three such batteries in the establishment of each division. The two British mountain batteries were increased to six in 1881, ten in 1889, and eighteen in 1920.

The British gunners of 2nd and 3rd Light Batteries, taking part in the Khaisora Campaign on the North West Frontier in 1937, were the last of their kind to be engaged in operations for light (previously designated 'pack' and before then 'mountain') batteries, which were abolished in 1938. The British mountain gunner, as known to Kipling, then disappeared from the Regular Army. The 1st, 3rd, and 7th British Mountain Artillery Regiments were raised a few years later during the Second World War, serving in Palestine, Madagascar, North Africa, Italy, Walcheren Island, and Norway, but hardly in the traditional role of mountain artillery and they were disbanded at the end of the war.

Returning to Scotland after the fall of France in June 1940, the 52nd (Lowland) Division, a Territorial formation, was allocated to an anti-invasion function in Scottish Command. Assigned to 'commando' training, in April 1942 the main body of the 52nd was, however, moved to the mountainous region of the northeastern Highlands that has its approximate centre at Aviemore in the valley of the Spey. It then became known that the Lowlanders were to go into highly-specialized training as mountaineers. These mountain men had the satisfaction of being unique in the British army. Equipped with the latest infantry weapons, from Bren gun to flame-thrower, from the PIAT (the anti-tank weapon) to the walkie-talkie, and the portable radio set that so miraculously speeded up communication in battle, the mountaineers faced the problems of the transportation of men and materials at high altitudes and on rough ground above the level of even sheep tracks. The man-drawn sledge, the pack animal, and even the stout-hearted jeep, all had their serious limitations where large-scale movements were concerned.

Meanwhile, the Americans had been working on a new type of vehicle, using specifications originally provided by the British Ministry of Supply. A prototype was built. Films of it in action were flown across the Atlantic and shown to the Lowlanders for comment. International co-operation finally produced quite a new sort of tracked vehicle—popularly known as the 'Weasel' (see Chapter 18)—with a quite remarkably high degree of efficiency in many different sorts of conditions, and in due course a party of some 70 officers and men of the 52nd crossed to the USA to witness it and to carry out experiments with it. The party from Scotland found itself at Camp Hale in Colorado. Here the visitors saw that the 'Weasel' could do all and more than had been claimed for it. They tested it in snow 14 ft (4.3 m) deep at 14,000 ft (4,300 m) above sea-level and found it worked miraculously as compared with the best of animals.

Back in the Highlands of Scotland, the 52nd received instruction in skiing, the use of the snow-shoe, making igloos and of shaping and living in holes scooped out of the mountain-top snows, and in the art of firing its percussion weapons at slow rates most carefully tabulated, so that the rates of fire possible in low-lying terrain would not burn out the guns and rifles when used in the rarefied air of cold and high altitudes. Two mountain regiments of the Royal Artillery were allocated to the division and in

1943 were issued with the American 75-mm pack howitzer, truly a mountain gun. (In the same year the 75-mm was also assigned for use by British airborne troops and carried in gliders.) Also under the command of the 52nd were a Norwegian brigade, ancillary units of the same nationality, and a host of specialists from many other countries. Indian transport units were even attached to the division in the experimental phase of its training and it made an unusual sight to see dark-faced men in khaki turbans moving along paths in the Scottish Highlands with horses and mules.

At the full tide of its training this large force occupied rather more than one-third of Scotland—roughly, the parallelogram of high country between the Great Glen and the Forth-Clyde valley. Its most intense concentrations were in the northeastern corner of this expanse, where the wild Cairngorm group of mountains, the cluster of peaks about the headwaters of the Dee, Don, Spey, and Findhorn Rivers, and the cold uplands of the Cabrach provided the nearest approach to Norwegian conditions available in Britain. Divisional Headquarters was located in a mansion house near Craigellachie. For three years the Lowlanders enjoyed the scenery tourists would have travelled thousands of miles to see. The soldiers operated over grouse moors and in deep forest. They bridged and forded rivers sacred to the anglers. The engineers even made an attempt to straighten out the bends of the Devils' Elbow. After snow fell on the high tops of the Cairngorms, the skiers and snow-shoers of the 52nd would often find themselves soaked by driving rain, while a route march on lower ground would be held up by snowdrifts. The men in training suffered indiscriminately from exhaustion through cold and nausea through the strangeness of the pemmican ration, not to mention a host of broken bones.

The following are passages taken at random from Divisional Standing Orders.

If any personnel of the Div. becomes a

casualty through frostbite, he will be placed on a charge and brought before his C.O., so that the circumstances may be thoroughly investigated ... Care of Skis: (a) Snow and ice will be removed from runners at end of day's run; (b) Skis will not be taken into warm huts or rooms; (c) When not in use skis will be kept with block and stretcher in posn ... The expression 'Rapid fire' will NOT be used by any officer or N.C.O. controlling fire ... Under settled snow conditions S.A. weapons will be left OUTSIDE the tent. They will be wrapped in tent bag or sandbag and slightly buried in the tent entrance to avoid drifting snow. If snow is falling or in a high wind, weapons will be brought INSIDE the tent AFTER primus stoves have been put out. They will be laid along the tent wall ... Smocks, white, cam, will normally be worn OVER web eqpt.

An appendix on the clothing and equipment to be carried by the mountain soldiers mentions accoutrements hardly heard of in the British army—neck squares, angola shirts, string vests, and white smocks, trousers, and rucksack-covers for camouflage against snow. The mountaineer carried lengths of whipcord and rope, snow goggles, quantities of wax and cork, footless stockings, and various sorts of pullovers, gloves, and mittens. There were eight-man tents and two-man bivouac tents to be taken along, not to mention sleeping bags, boucheron boots, skis, ski sticks, snow-shoes, spare tips for skis, and the all-important, life-saving primus stove with its precious supply of fuel. The division had even to work out a code of distinguishing marks whereby officers and NCOs wearing peaked caps or hoods could be distinguished *from behind*. This was based on a simple enough system of horizontal strips of coloured material sewn on to the headgear. The standard vehicles of the British army were never so severely tested as on those mountain passes in Scotland—nor was any body of army drivers and gunners, learning to control their monstrous trucks and their ponderous weapons on roads without a surface, on interminable sheets of ice, on bouldered slopes, and in the mud produced from a peaty soil. As for the ordinary infantrymen turned mountaineer, only the very fittest could possibly survive continuous and gruelling exercises in such conditions.

Rigorous, full-scale exercises took place in 1942 and 1943, the schemes working up from the battalion level until the complete division was functioning as one over wide areas and long distances in conditions as near the anticipated actuality as could possibly be imagined. The order came that, on exercise, there was to be no sleeping in houses. For days on end the mountaineers knew only the comfort of the hole in the snow, the hollow in the heather, or—at the very best—the shelter of the bivouac tent. There was no discrimination in favour of officers. The general himself might be found asleep in the lee of a boulder or, in special circumstances, enjoying the doubtful comforts of a jeep. The rations came out of tins and packs; all cooking had to be done over the primus stove. But the men of the 52nd (Lowland) Division were not destined to operate on active service in the mountain function. In July 1944 the division was turned into an air-portable role scheduled for the Arnhem battle in September. The landing of the Lowlanders on Dutch polderland never took place, the mountain men finally going to war in September 1944 in France. The main body landed in flood and mud on the South Beveland peninsula and Walcheren Island, Holland, the following month. The amphibious operation was a far cry from foot-slogging in snow and ice in the Scottish Highlands.

CHAPTER 25
NATO AND THE WARSAW PACT, NORTHERN AND CENTRAL FRONTS

When the first experimental atomic bomb was exploded at Alamogardo, New Mexico, on 16 July 1945, secret training immediately began in the desert areas of Utah for dropping atomic bombs on two targets in Japan. On 6 August an atom bomb was dropped on Hiroshima, killing 78,150 people, injuring 70,000 others, and destroying two-thirds of the city. Three days later, another atom bomb was exploded over the seaport and industrial city of Nagasaki. Here 40,000 people were killed, about 25,000 injured, and half of the built-up area obliterated. Thus ended the Second World War and the opening of one of the most significant crossroads in world history—the inauguration of the Nuclear Age. The USA exercised a monopoly of the atomic secret for three years until, in 1949, the USSR detonated a nuclear explosion. Mutual annihilation of the western and eastern nations in an all-out war was now guaranteed, and means were swiftly sought to cement alliances on both sides for purposes of collective defence.

On 4 April 1949, in Washington, a treaty was signed to establish (effective on 24 August) the North Atlantic Treaty Organization (NATO) by Belgium, Canada, Denmark, France, Iceland, Italy, Luxembourg, the Netherlands, Norway, Portugal, and the UK; the USA, Greece, Spain, Turkey, and West Germany joined later. France withdrew from the integrated military command of NATO in 1966, though it remained a member of the organization. Despite near-catastrophic losses of manpower, materials, and production facilities at the close of the Second World War, the USSR, on the other hand, began to rival the USA as a superpower. Soviet armies occupied all of eastern Europe, much of central Europe, northern Iran, Manchuria, and northern Korea. Moreover, while the western Allies demobilized their armies as quickly as possible after the war, Soviet military forces were maintained close to their wartime strengths. Refusing to release their hold on eastern Europe, the Warsaw Pact—formally the Warsaw Treaty of Friendship, Co-operation, and Mutual Assistance—was signed on 14 May 1955. The treaty established a mutual defence organization (Warsaw Treaty Organization), and was signed by the USSR and its satellites—Bulgaria, Czechoslovakia, East Germany, Hungary, Poland, and Romania. (Albania, an original signatory, withdrew in 1968.) Confrontation between east and west was now an ugly reality.

NATO's land forces assigned to holding the northern flank include the Anglo-Dutch 1st Amphibious Combat Group (SAOG) drawn from the British Royal Marines and the Royal Netherlands Marine Corps. These men receive instruction on how to live and operate in desolate, mountainous, and Arctic regions under the harshest conditions. The annual training cycle includes a rigorous course in the Scottish Highlands and the north of Norway. The Whiskey Company (WCOY) of the Dutch Marines, also known as the cold weather company, in addition to mountain and Arctic training also receives comprehensive parachute training.

The Northern Flank

Norway constitutes NATO's northern flank and because of its geographical position is of vital importance to the Alliance. Situated between two major Soviet maritime concentrations, one to the north and one to the south, Norway is defended by her own peace-time force of 55,000 men, many of whom are conscripts undergoing their National Service. Although Norway's armed forces can be increased to 300,000 men in the event of mobilization, she relies heavily on NATO's reinforcement capability.

At present these reinforcements consist of four brigade-sized formations: the ACE Mobile Force (AMF), a multi-national force consisting of units from various member nations, and which for the past four years has included a British contingent from the 1st Battalion, the Parachute Regiment, specially trained in Arctic warfare; a United States Marine Amphibious (MAB), consisting of specially trained and equipped troops of the US Marine Corps; the Canadian Air-Sea Transportable (CAST) Brigade Group; and Britain's 3 Commando Brigade Royal Marines. These forces are supported by a total of 16 squadrons of aircraft and a number of integral and external naval units.

3 Commando Brigade RM is a United Kingdom based formation consisting of 40 Commando RM (based in Plymouth); 42 Commando RM (based in Taunton); 45 Commando Group (which includes a Base Company and the Mountain & Arctic Warfare Cadre, all of which are located at Arbroath, Scotland); a Commando Logistic Regiment; 3 Commando Brigade Air Squadron RM; 29 Commando Regiment, Royal Artillery; 59 Independent Commando Squadron, Royal Engineers; and 3 Commando Brigade Headquarters and Signal Squadron RM. Most of the brigade is based in the Plymouth area but the entire formation spends three months of the year deployed in Norway for Arctic warfare training and a series of small and large scale exercises.

Top left *A Norwegian armoured recovery vehicle built on a Leopard chassis deploys from a tank landing craft.*

Middle left *A West German Leopard I main battle tank in Norwegian army service. Note the snow camouflage net.*

Left *An amphibious assault tracked vehicle (LVTP-7) of the United States Marine Corps goes ashore on an exercise on the Northern Flank.*

Above *Over-snow, tracked military vehicles are used to inspect the Alaska oil pipe-line, which connects the Alaska oil-wells with refineries in the United States and which is of enormous strategic and economic importance to US interests.*

Right *CH-46 Sea Knight helicopters with combat-equipped Marines aboard prepare to launch from the USS* Belleau Wood *for a rehearsal landing at the Naval Air Station, Adak, Alaska, as part of a US Third Fleet exercise in 1987.*

Below *A Marine Corps CH-53E Super Sea Stallion helicopter brings second wave assault troops ashore at Shemya Air Force Base, Alaska, during the same six-day exercise in 1987. About 2,000 Marines, 12,000 sailors, 115 aircraft and 14 ships, including the aircraft carrier USS* Carl Vinson *and the amphibious carrier USS* Belleau Wood, *participated in the exercise.*

Under NATO this company is fully integrated in 45 Commando Royal Marines. The 1st Amphibious Combat Group can be deployed by NATO for amphibious operations on the northern and southern flanks of the western European coastline. The Dutch combat group is fully integrated in 3 Commando Brigade Royal Marines.

The training programme starts in Scotland with one-day marches without heavy packs to familiarize the Marines with the terrain and climate. The final part of the course consists of an exhausting four-day march, which includes all aspects of mountain-warfare training. River crossings are made (with or without

Left *US Marines from 11th Marine Amphibious Unit move out across the snow at Shemya Air Force Base during the same exercise in 1987.*

Below *A Norwegian pack-horse company with sledges is landed from the LCT KNM* Borgsund *during the NATO exercise 'Atlas Express' in Norway, February 1976.*

Above *The Swedish armed forces operate outside the structure of the armies of the NATO alliance. The Swedes, whose skills in the Arctic snows date back to the skiers of earliest times, maintain a small but efficient army equipped with the latest weapons. This full-track, over-snow armoured vehicle is equipped with a 90-mm anti-tank gun.*

Right *An Austrian Jäger climbs a glacier face. Note that the Austrians, like the Gebirgsjäger, wear the Edelweiss insignia.*

lines) and lines are used to practise techniques of rock-climbing and rappelling with or without heavy equipment. Extensive practice is taken in individual and team shooting-skills, with a wide range of weapons. One of the heaviest weapons employed is the 'Dragon' anti-tank weapon system, which can eliminate targets at a distance of approximately 1,100 yd (1,000 m). Towards the end of the course a short exercise is held, which may include the deployment of amphibious ships and helicopters. (Since the Vietnam war, helicopters have added a new

Finland maintains another non-aligned army, totally trained to fight in Arctic conditions. Here a party of Finnish soldiers undergo winter training. Note the signaller in the foreground.

dimension to mountain combat and have frequently demonstrated their ability not only to lift troops and supplies over vast distances but also to land them at high altitudes in the mountains.)

In Norway, the unit trains near the Norwegian village of Mo-I-Rana situated 50 miles (80 km) south of the Arctic Circle. Skiing skills are taught and practised during the first three weeks of the annual Arctic warfare training. The men live in tents and igloos, the latter taking four hours to build. Amphibious exercises are handled by the Royal Netherlands Navy, manned by personnel of the RNLMC, the home base of this force being the Joost Dourlein

Barracks on the island of Texel off the Dutch coast. Parachute drops are made by the Marines, who are also air-landed from helicopters at unknown places and often in bad weather, which requires advanced map-reading skills when the men are on the ground. When the Marines are operating without supply facilities, helicopters fly in fuel and ammunition with *pulks* (sledges) to support the heavy loads. Yomping with heavy packs will involve weights of anywhere from 75 to 110 lb (35-50kg).

Since the Second World War, rocketry, on land, sea, and in the air, has emerged as the major element of artillery. Its projectiles, capable of carrying either nuclear or high-explosive

The Central Front

The German 1st Mountain Division (1 GebDiv) of the Bundeswehr belongs to the same direct lineage of German mountain troops dating back to the First World War. The divisional headquarters is situated at Garmisch-Partenkirchen in southern Germany and its brigades are located in the mountains in the area between Sonthofen, München, Freyung and Bad Reichenhall.

Its establishment of 18,000 men consists of one mountain infantry, one mechanized infantry and one armoured brigade. The divisional equipment includes the traditional pack animals, mountaineering and skiing gear as well as such modern weapons systems as, for example, the main battle tank Leopard 2, the self-propelled armoured defence gun system Gepard, the missile-equipped tank destroyer Jaguar, and the field howitzer 70.

In addition to training on modern weapons, the men of the Mountain Infantry Brigade are trained to conduct military operations at high altitudes, both in summer and winter. Gebirgsjäger especially suited to Alpine climbing are allocated to the high mountain platoons of the mountain infantry brigade. These Alpine specialists are frequently used for tourist rescue missions, which confirms the high standards of performance that must be attained. The 'Edelweiss' (lion's foot) is the insignia of the division which is worn as the cap badge and on the jacket.

This page and overleaf *This selection of photographs of the Gebirgsjäger training in the mountains of southern Germany demonstrates their basic skills. The German mountain men play a key role in the defence of NATO's Central Front and in retaliatory offensive measures in the event of Soviet aggression.*

Above and right *The Italian Alpini also play their part in defending NATO's Central Front. The present-day Alpini make worthy descendants of their forebears who fought with such distinction in the First World War against their Austrian adversaries above the perpetual snow-line in the Alpine frontier regions of Italy and Austria.*

warheads, have ranged from the giant intercontinental missile (ICBM), with practically worldwide range, to the one-man 'bazooka' type of the foot soldier. In the nuclear context, the prospect of mountain warfare seems most unlikely but in conventional war, German and Austrian mountain troops—the Federal Republic of Germany has one mountain corps, consisting of four mountain brigades and Austria has two mountain corps, each of two brigades—have a positive role to play thrusting across the mountains and valleys of eastern Europe. Both the German and Austrian mountain men inherit the impressive fighting traditions of their forefathers—the Gebirgsjäger. Currently stationed in Bavaria, in fact, the

modern mountain men bear a direct lineage to the mountain units that fought on the Alpine frontier of Austro-Hungary and Italy in the First World War and those who, in the Second World War, took part in the Norwegian, Balkan, Cretan and Caucasus Campaigns in the USSR.

The Red Army's 1,991,000 regulars do not number specialist mountain troops amongst their ranks. The largest body of combat soldiers form 142 motor rifle divisions and 51 tank divisions. Airborne divisions (officially listed as seven) are thought in total to be at least eleven or twelve. No doubt the feats of Ivan, the ragged warrior of the Caucasus mountains of the Second World War, can, however, be performed by any number of the Red Army's front-line troops, which include ten helicopter-borne, air-assault brigades and the special forces (*Spetsnaz*), which number sixteen brigades and three regiments. *Spetsnaz*, it is rumoured, can perform any military task, at the double. The eastern European satellite armies are also well supplied with air-assault troops and paratroopers, and it is only Romania that supports mountain troops—three mountain brigades. It is assumed that the border guards found in all the Communist forces will be familiar with mountain terrain.

We are the pilgrims, master we shall go
Always a little further; it may be
Beyond that last blue mountain
    barred with snow
Across that angry or that glimmering sea,
While on a throne or guarded in a cave
There lives a prophet, who can understand
Why men were born; but surely we are
brave,
Who make the Golden Journey to
Samarkand.

James Elroy Flecker

MOUNTAIN TROOPS CURRENTLY EMPLOYED BY WORLD ARMIES

Afghanistan:	3 mountain battalions	Italy:	1 Alpine corps
Argentine:	3 mountain infantry brigades	Morocco:	1 mountain battalion
Austria:	2 mountain corps	Romania:	3 mountain brigades
France:	1 Alpine division	Spain:	2 mountain divisions
W. Germany:	1 mountain corps	Switzerland:	1 mountain corps
India:	7 mountain divisions	Yugoslavia:	3 mountain brigades

BIBLIOGRAPHY

Anzulovic, James Venceslav (ed.), *The Russian Record of the Winter War, 1939-40*, University Microfilms International, Ann Arbor, Michigan, 1981.

Auchinleck, (Sir) Claude John Eyre, 'Report on Operations in Northern Norway', 13 May-8 June, *London Gazette Supplement*, HMSO, London, 10 July 1947.

Auty, Phyllis, *Tito*, Ballantine Books, New York, 1972.

Avec La 4ième Division Marocaine de Montagne, compiled by officers of the division, Mulhouse-Domach, 1945.

Béthouart, Marie Emile, 'Les Bataillons de Chasseurs en Norvège, Avril-Juin 1940, *Révue Historique de L'Armée*, 1re Année, no.2, Paris, 1945.

Blyth, J.D.M., 'The War in Arctic Europe'. *The Polar Record*, Vol.7, no.49, London, 1945.

Caracciolo, Mario, *Italy in the World War*, Edizioni Roma, Rome, 1936.

Casewit, Curtis W., *Mountain Troopers! The Story of the Tenth Mountain Division*, Thomas Y. Crowell Co., New York, 1972

Cervi, Mario, *The Hollow Legions: Mussolini's Blunder in Greece, 1940-41*, Chatto & Windus, London, 1972.

Connell, Charles, *Monte Cassino (The Historic Battle)*, Elek Books, London, 1963.

Dewar, Michael, *Brush Fire Wars*, Robert Hale, London, 1984.

Djilas, Milovan, *Wartime*, Harcourt Brace Jovanovich, New York and London, 1977.

Edmonds, (Brigadier-General, Sir) James E., *History of the Great War—Military Operations Italy 1915-1919*, HMSO, London, 1919

Edwards, Roger, *German Airborne Troops*, Macdonald & Jane's, London, 1974.

Falls, Cyril, *History of the Great War—Military Operations Macedonia: From the Outbreak of War to the Spring of 1917*, HMSO, London, 1933.

Falls, Cyril, *History of the Great War—Military Operations Macedonia: From the Spring of 1917 to the End of the War*, HMSO, London, 1935.

Firsoff, V.A., *Ski Track on the Battlefield*, Lindsay Drummond, London, 1942.

Gario, Gino, *Italy 1914-1918*, Norris, London, 1937.

Grechko, (Marshal) André, *Battle for the Caucasus*, Progress Publishers, Moscow, 1975.

Guevara, Che, *Guerrilla Warfare*, Penguin Books, London, 1986.

Isby, David, *Russia's War in Afghanistan*, Osprey, London, 1986.

Lucas, James, *Alpine Elite—German Mountain Troops of World War Two*, Jane's, London, 1980.

Maclean, Fitzroy, *Eastern Approaches*, Jonathon Cape, London, 1949.

Madej, W. Victor (ed.), *Italian Order of Battle 1939-1943*, Allentown, Pennsylvania, 1982.

Midans, Carl, and Midans, Shelley, *The Violent Place—A Report on Wars in the Postwar World*, Atheneum, New York, 1968.

Norway Information Office, *Arctic War. Norway's Role on the Northern Front*, HMSO, London, 1945.

Palmer, Alan, *Macedonian Campaign—The Gardeners of Salonika*, André Deutsch, London, 1965.

Papagos, (General) Alexander, *The Battle of Greece, 1940-41*, Hellenic Publishing Co., Athens, 1949.

Powell, E. Alexander, *With the Italians and Allies in the West*, Heinemann, London, 1917.

Ravol, Joseph-Fortune, *La Guerre en Montagne au XXe Siècle*, Éditions Lavauselle, Paris, 1936.

'The Arctic Front', *The Norseman*, Vol.II, no.6, 1943.

The Midnight Sun (British service newspaper), published by the British Contingent of the North-Western Expeditionary Force, Harstadt, Norway, 1940.

Touring Club of Italy (various authors), *The War in Italy*, Turin, 1919.

Trevelyan, G.M., *Scenes from Italy's War*, T.C. & E.C. Jack, London and Edinburgh, 1919.

Upton, Anthony, F., *Finland 1939-40*, Davis-Poynter, London, 1974.

Villeri, Luigi, *The War on the Italian Front*, Cobden-Sanderson, London, 1932.

Walton, (Colonel) George and Adleman, Robert H., *The Devil's Brigade*, Chilton Books, Philadelphia, New York, 1948.

Wilson, Dick, *The Long March 1935—The Epic of Chinese Communism's Survival*, History Book Club, London, 1971.

INDEX

Index of military formations (Brigade designations and above)

First World War

Austro-Hungarian and German units
Borovič Army Group, 64
Third Army, 51
Fifth Army, 54, 63, 77
Sixth Army, 81, 86
Seventh Army, 78
Tenth Army, 64
Eleventh Army, 51; (German), 98
Fourteenth Army (German), 64
VII Corps, 81, 86
VIII Corps, 81
Bavarian Alpen Korps, 66
Austrian Edelweiss Alpine Division, 82
12th Division (German), 69
26th Schützen Division, 85
42nd Division (German), 85
50th Division, 69
58th Division, 43

British units
XI Corps, 95
XIV Corps, 77
10th Division, 90
22nd Division, 94
26th Division, 94
60th Division, 94
79th Brigade, 94

French units
Armee d'Orient, 89
XII Corps, 77
16th Division, 94
17th Division, 97
24th Division, 86

Serbian and Greek units
First Army (Serbian), 95
Second Army (Serbian), 94
Cretan Division (Greek), 96

Italian units
First Army, 50, 51, 69, 74, 78, 82
Second Army, 23, 42, 43, 48, 51, 53, 54, 63, 64, 65, 66, 69, 77
Third Army, 28, 42, 43, 51, 53, 54, 60, 63, 69, 70, 74, 77, 81, 82
Fourth Army, 28, 42, 43, 51, 53, 54, 60, 63, 69, 70, 74, 77, 81, 82, 86
Fifth Army, 53, 63, 78
Sixth Army, 77, 86
Seventh Army, 77 82
Eighth Army, 77, 84
Tenth Army (Italian and British), 82
Twelfth Army (Italian and French), 82, 86

I Corps, 82
III Corps, 43
IV Corps, 66, 68, 69
VI Corps, 53, 66, 78, 82
VII Corps, 54, 78, 82, 85
IX Corps, 86
XI Corps, 54
XIII Corps, 54, 78
XVIII Corps, 78, 79
XX Corps, 66, 75
XXX Corps, 82, 83
2nd Assault Division, 87
8th Division, 43
14th Division, 87
18th Division, 78, 82
20th Division, 78, 86
33rd Division, 80
43rd Division, 68
46th Division, 68
47th Division, 82
48th Division, 78, 81, 87
50th Division, 81, 82
57th Division, 86
70th Division, 86
Abruzzi Brigade, 81
Barletta Brigade, 81
Bari Brigade, 82, 83
Basilicata Brigade, 82
(3rd) Bersaglieri Brigade, 75
Bisagno, Brigade, 85
Como Brigade, 78
Forli Brigade, 83
Lecce Brigade, 86
Murge Brigade, 86
Novara Brigade, 75
Palermo Brigade, 81
Ravenna Brigade, 78
Sassari Brigade, 85

Second World War

The Allies
Allied Fifteenth Army Group, 227, 234

British and Commonwealth units
British Eighth Army, 214, 234
British X Corps, 213
Canadian I Corps, 235
British 1st Division, 213
  2nd Armoured Division, 192
  5th Division, 213
  46th Division, 110
  56th Division, 213
Australian 6th Division, 192, 193
New Zealand 2nd Division, 192, 193
British 15th Brigade, 192
New Zealand 5th Brigade, 192

French and colonial units
French First Army, 224
French XIV Corps, 129
  X Corps, 129, 133
Moroccan 4th Mountain Division, 222, 224
French Demi-Brigade (Chasseurs-Alpins), 117, 125

Norwegian units
6th 'Polar' Division, 114, 115, 116, 122, 124
6th Brigade, 127

Polish units
II Corps, 224
3rd Carpathian Division, 125
Kresowa Division, 125
Highland Brigade (Carpathian Chasseurs), 118

Soviet units
9th, 20th, 28th, 58th, 63rd, 75th, 76th, 83rd, 96th, 100th, 138th, 173rd, 192nd, 194th, 242nd, 302nd, 318th Mountain Rifle Divisions, 170

United States units
US Third Army, 236
  Fifth Army, 213, 214, 215, 218
  Seventh Army, 235, 236
US XI Corps, 213
US 10th Mountain Division, 226-33
  36th Division, 213, 221
  45th Division, 213
US 1st Special Service Brigade (the 'Devils' Brigade), 217-22

The Axis powers
German units
Army Group A, 170, 176, 179
Army Group B, 170
Second Army, 194
Twelfth Army, 192
Seventeenth Army, 192
Twentieth Mountain Army, 155, 156, 159, 163
XI Air Corps, 199
V Mountain Corps, 203
XV Mountain Corps, 203
XVIII Mountain Corps, 154, 156, 157, 192
XIX Mountain Corps, 151, 154, 157, 158, 203
XXXXIX Mountains Corps, *167*, 170, 174, 176, 203
LI Mountain Corps, 203

Italian units

Since the Second World War